Labours old and new

Manchester University Press

Critical Labour Movement Studies

Series editors
John Callaghan
Steven Fielding
Steve Ludlam

Already published in the series

Jenny Andersson
*Between growth and security: Swedish social democracy from
a strong society to a third way*

John Callaghan, Steven Fielding and Steve Ludlam (eds)
*Interpreting the Labour Party: approaches to Labour politics
and history*

Andrew Gamble, Steve Ludlam, Andrew Taylor and Stephen Wood (eds)
*Labour, the state, social movements and the challenge of
neo-liberal globalisation*

Dianne Hayter
Fightback! Labour's traditional right in the 1970s and 1980s

Jonas Hinnfors
*Reinterpreting social democracy: a history of stability in the
British Labour Party and Swedish Social Democratic Party*

Ben Jackson
*Equality and the British Left: a study in progressive political
thought, 1900–64*

Leighton James
*The politics of identity and civil society in Britain and Germany:
miners in the Ruhr and South Wales 1890–1926*

Declan McHugh
*Labour in the city: the development of the Labour Party in
Manchester, 1918–31*

Jeremy Nuttall
*Psychological socialism: the Labour Party and qualities of mind
and character, 1931 to the present*

Lucy Robinson
*Gay men and the left in post-war Britain: how the personal
got political*

Labours old and new

The parliamentary right of the
British Labour Party 1970–79 and
the roots of New Labour

Stephen Meredith

Manchester University Press
Manchester and New York
distributed exclusively in the USA by Palgrave

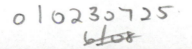

The right of Stephen Meredith to be identified as the author of this work
has been asserted by him in accordance with the Copyright, Designs and
Patents Act 1988.

Published by Manchester University Press
Oxford Road, Manchester M13 9NR, UK
and Room 400, 175 Fifth Avenue, New York, NY 10010, USA
www.manchesteruniversitypress.co.uk

Distributed exclusively in the USA by
Palgrave, 175 Fifth Avenue, New York,
NY 10010, USA

Distributed exclusively in Canada by
UBC Press, University of British Columbia, 2029 West Mall,
Vancouver, BC, Canada V6T 1Z2

British Library Cataloguing-in-Publication Data
A catalogue record for this book is available from the British Library

Library of Congress Cataloging-in-Publication Data applied for

ISBN   978 0 7190 7322 9 *hardback*

First published 2008

17 16 15 14 13 12 11 10 09 08   10 9 8 7 6 5 4 3 2 1

Typeset
by Florence Production Ltd, Stoodleigh, Devon
Printed in Great Britain
by Cromwell Press, Trowbridge, Wiltshire

To my mother for her strength and to my father for his industry.
To them both for their love and support.

Contents

Series editors' foreword   *page* ix
Acknowledgements   xi

1 Introduction   1

2 The parliamentary Labour right: views and perspectives   25

3 Parliamentary Labour right factionalism and organisational
  fragmentation in the 1970s   42

4 A prelude to secession? The parliamentary Labour right
  and Europe   71

5 *In Place of Strife*? The parliamentary Labour right and the
  'trade union question'   103

6 The 'frontiers of social democracy': public expenditure,
  redistribution and divisions of social democratic political
  economy   137

7 The parliamentary Labour right, Labour Party revisionism(s)
  and the roots of New Labour   159

8 Conclusion   173

Bibliography   185
Index   203

Series editors' foreword

The start of the twenty-first century is, superficially, an inauspicious time to study labour movements. Political parties once associated with the working class have seemingly embraced capitalism. The trade unions with which these parties were once linked have suffered near-fatal reverses. The industrial proletariat looks both divided and in rapid decline. The development of multi-level governance, prompted by 'globalisation' has, furthermore, apparently destroyed the institutional context for advancing the labour 'interest'. Many consequently now look on terms such as the 'working class', 'socialism' and 'the labour movement' as politically and historically redundant.

The purpose of this series is to give a platform to those students of labour movements who challenge, or develop, established ways of thinking and so demonstrate the continued vitality of the subject and the work of those interested in it. For, despite appearances, many social democratic parties remain important competitors for national office and proffer distinctive programmes. Unions still impede the free flow of 'market forces'. If workers are a more diverse body and have exchanged blue collars for white, insecurity remains an everyday problem. The new institutional and global context is, moreover, as much of an opportunity as a threat. Yet, it cannot be doubted that, compared with the immediate post-1945 period, at the beginning of the new millennium, what many still refer to as the 'labour movement' is much less influential. Whether this should be considered a time of retreat or reconfiguration is unclear – and a question the series aims to clarify.

The series will not only give a voice to studies of particular national bodies but will also promote comparative works that contrast experiences across time and geography. This entails taking due account of the political, economic and cultural settings in which labour movements have operated. In particular, this involves taking the past seriously as a way of understanding the present as well as utilising sympathetic approaches drawn from sociology, economics and elsewhere.

John Callaghan
Steven Fielding
Steve Ludlam

Acknowledgements

In the long gestation period of this book, I would like to heartily thank Steve Ludlam for his continued support, sometimes well beyond the call of duty. I would similarly like to thank Steven Fielding and the series editors for their enthusiasm and support for the project from the outset, and my editors at Manchester University Press for their very professional and efficient contribution to the completion of the project. A number of libraries, librarians and archivists have been unfailingly helpful in the course and cause of my research. Particularly, I would like to thank those at the Labour History Archive and Study Centre in Manchester, the British Library of Political and Economic Science, the National Library of Scotland in Edinburgh and the University of Liverpool. I would also like to express my gratitude to many of the key participants in the events and developments described here who kindly agreed to subject themselves to yet another request for an interview.

Most of all I would like to thank my parents. Their belief in the value of education and desire that I was able to benefit in ways that they never could are typical characteristics of the culture from which they come. Without their long and continued support and encouragement this book would never have seen the light of day. To Tina and Jack for the future, but it is to my parents that this book is dedicated with my love and thanks.

1

Introduction

So much public attention has been riveted upon the dilemmas of the Labour Left by journalists and scholars that the layman may be forgiven for believing that the Left-wing represents more than a minor faction of the Party as a whole. At certain periods the Left has played a crucial role in Labour's development, but normally the Party is governed and controlled by the Right. To understand the contemporary Labour Party one must first understand its Right-wing.[1]

The Labour Right in the 1970s and early 1980s was too fragmented, and politically and intellectually ill-equipped to take the Party on a revisionist course.[2]

The Labour right: Labours old and new

A welcome recent study of the variety of Labour Party political thought since 1945 has identified five broad core positions and strands of ideas. These include the 'Old Left', the 'New Left', the 'Centre', the 'Old Right' and the 'New Right' or 'New Labour'. As the collection suggests, the precise 'timing of the transition from "Old Right" to "New Right" – the creation of New Labour – is hard to pinpoint', but undoubtedly a Labour right contribution, predominantly in its parliamentary manifestation, has been critical to the post-war ideological and political experience and development of the Labour Party.[3] Among many diverse attempts to explain the ideological and political configuration of the contemporary Labour Party, the problems of such an exercise notwithstanding, some commentators present the New Labour leadership in direct descent to Labour's historic post-war revisionist social democratic tradition. Some further point to the influence of what has been termed 'neo-revisionist' attempts to respond to the crisis of Keynesian revisionist social democracy and the break-down of the post-war British political (social democratic) settlement in the 1970s.[4] This study is concerned with the 'Old' Labour right at a critical juncture of British and Labour Party politics and attempts to understand, at least in part, the complex transition from 'Old Right' to 'New Right' or 'New Labour'. It attempts to locate at least some of the roots of the latter in the complexity and divisions of the former in the 1970s. Particularly, the analysis addresses the short-term and long-term implications of the emerging

ideological, organisational and policy tensions, divisions and eventual fragmentation of the parliamentary Labour right and Labour Party revisionism in the late
1960s and 1970s, a period in which the particular economic and political
configuration represented a fundamental challenge to the prevailing norms of both
British government and British social democracy.[5]

The study adopts a methodology that attempts to disaggregate conventional
interpretations of a monolithic and homogeneous Labour right or revisionist
leadership tendency. Alternatively, it suggests that the Labour right has been a
heterogeneous, complex coalition of traditions and political tendencies, divided
over a range of key policy themes and even the relative priority of fundamental
concepts in social democratic thought and practice. It argues that substantive
ideological and policy differences were previously concealed within the loose
cohesive framework of Keynesian revisionist social democracy. As this framework
unravelled in the problematic economic and political context of the 1970s, it was
the inability of this complex body to unite in the face of adverse events and
developments that is a neglected factor in explanations of the trajectory of the
Labour Party and British social democracy: in explanations of Labour's subsequent
shift leftwards, the longer and more complex evolution of the Social Democratic
Party (SDP) and the extent to which 'New' Labour is a legatee of at least certain
elements of the disparate and discordant Labour right of the 1970s. In doing
so, it contributes to the understanding of a key moment in the development
and transition of social democracy and the making of the contemporary British
Labour Party.

The influential but neglected parliamentary Labour right

Royden Harrison has written of the relative paucity of studies of the parliamentary
Labour Party (PLP) and Labour Party factions in general.[6] Moreover, in spite of
its significant position and role in Labour's post-war development, the Labour
right, perhaps because of its traditional position close to the parliamentary
leadership and less explicit dissenting or factional behaviour, has received
comparatively less attention than the Labour left. There is a substantial body of
literature devoted explicitly to the various traditions, ideas, groups, dissent and
frequent conflict of the Labour left. Studies of the Labour right are limited to those
of intra-party left–right conflict, in which it has been presented as a largely
homogeneous unit loyal to the parliamentary leadership,[7] and particular studies
of the so-called Gaitskellite revisionist tradition[8] and its relative contribution to,
first, the SDP[9] and, more recently, to the emergence of New Labour.[10]

Perhaps before going further, the study should briefly consider two (of the few)
related works that directly address the decline and subsequent recovery of the
Labour right either side of the intra-party developments that surrounded the
formation of the SDP in 1981. Dianne Hayter, in this series, has recently written
of the attempts of the 'traditional right' in the wake of the defections to the SDP
to reclaim a more moderate organisation and course for the Labour Party.[11] In
doing so, she argues that after the SDP split 'Labour's "traditional right" exhibited

... different characteristics from those of its predecessor elements'. The post-Limehouse Labour right determined to review the nature of its response and to put policy differences aside to work and organise assiduously in conjunction with sympathetic trade union leaders to resist the advance of the left inside the party. She relates the story of how 'Labour's traditional right, weakened and tested by defections to the ... SDP in 1981 ... set about its objective of reclaiming the Labour Party to make it electable'.[12] The present study offers a 'prequel' to Hayter's story. It surveys the implications of the complex character, tensions and fragmentation of the pre-1981 parliamentary Labour right that contributed to the need for the strategic re-evaluation and organisational effort of the 'traditional right' of Hayter's study. Hayter concerns herself with the specifically 'anti-left groups' of 'moderate trade unionists and parliamentarians' of the 'traditional right' after 1981. This study concerns itself with the reasons why a diminished Labour right arrived in this situation. It addresses the inherent tensions and divisions of a more broadly constituted, diverse and fractious 'pre-split' Labour right involved with a broader range of issues and concerns.[13] Hayter's study emphasises the need to explain the inability of the Labour right to unite in the intra-party and wider context of the 1970s and why it was politically and organisationally ill-equipped to stem the flow of the party's subsequent shift leftwards.

Giles Radice, writing on the period immediately prior to that of Hayter's study, also identifies the emerging intellectual, organisational and leadership vacuum of the parliamentary Labour right in the intra-party and wider context of the 1970s. He attributes the tensions and lack of cohesion of the parliamentary Labour right largely to the personal ambitions and antipathy between three of the major figures of post-war Labour revisionism: Anthony Crosland, Roy Jenkins and Denis Healey (who can broadly be said to have embodied the dimensions of the emerging divisions of Labour Party revisionism and the parliamentary Labour right in the 1970s).[14] While undoubtedly true that they were influential and ambitious politicians, often in competition for major government and Labour Party offices, this study attempts to address the diversity, tensions and conflict of Labour Party revisionism and the parliamentary Labour right in wider intellectual, ideological and policy terms. It suggests that the fracture and shortcomings of the Labour right in the 1970s had deeper, more complex roots than mere personal ambitions and antagonisms.

Much other recent scholarship on the Labour Party has focused on analyses of the nature of its recent transformation, particularly the origins, character and (likely) trajectory of New Labour. Labour's 'modernisation' through the 1980s and the subsequent emergence of New Labour have prompted a variety of explanations as to the influences and nature of this process: as a capitulation to Thatcherite-style capitalism;[15] as a return to, or the culmination of, an earlier revisionist tradition and approach in the Labour Party;[16] or as something qualitatively new, a 'post-Thatcherite', modernised social democracy, 'ideologically' underpinned by the Third Way.[17] Some recent attempts to 'historicise' New Labour have pointed to its revisionist social democratic antecedents (among other 'progressive' influences).[18] This has included looking for New Labour's roots not just in the

relatively homogeneous Gaitskellite revisionism of the 1950s, but also in the
emergent 'neo-revisionist' social democratic response to social democratic
problems and dilemmas of the 1970s, so much so that the evolution of New Labour
has been a 'staged transformation' that began in the 1970s. The developments of
the 1970s are very important to understanding New Labour, at least as important
perhaps as Thatcherism in the 1980s.[19] In this sense, the emergence of New Labour
represents neither a simple capitulation to, or accommodation of, neo-liberalism
and a largely Thatcherite agenda, nor a largely new, 'post-Thatcherite', modernised
or Third Way social democracy, nor even the culmination of a constant, uniform
revisionist tradition in the Labour Party. Rather, it could be interpreted (at least
in part) as concomitant with certain themes and ideas that emerged in the
complexity and divisions of the 'old' parliamentary Labour right in the 1970s,
which were temporarily diverted through the formation of the SDP.

The focus of this study, then, is the Labour right at the parliamentary level in
the 1970s, drawing upon other organs of the party structure in the constituencies,
trade unions and National Executive Committee (NEC) and earlier periods such
as the 1950s and 1960–64 as wider context and historical background, and as far
as they illustrate ideas, traditions, strategies, policies or groups on the parliamentary
Labour right. Of course, in a number of controversial and divisive key policy
contexts, such as Common Market membership and industrial relations and trade
union reform, it is difficult to understand the debates of the 1970s without
reference to the 1960s.[20] The parliamentary Labour right is an obviously important
(and neglected) subject of analysis. It has embodied the principles and politics of
the emergent (revisionist) social democratic politics of the Labour Party and
Labour Governments of the post-war period, and provided the core membership
of Labour's post-war 'dominant coalition' and 'governing elite'. The remainder
of the chapter sets out the wider context and core methodology of the study. It
takes the form of a rationalisation and discussion of central themes and issues of
the selected periodisation and case studies. The former includes consideration
of the general economic and political context of the 1970s. It also addresses the
relevance of the study to related wider themes and debates: the apparent break-
down of the post-war British political (social democratic) 'consensus' and the
broader crisis of European social democracy. The case studies consist of an analysis
of the character (and limitations) of parliamentary Labour right group and
factional activity in the 1970s, the European dimension of intra-party divisions,
attitudes to industrial relations policy and trade union reform, and public
expenditure debates and problems of social democratic political economy in the
context of emerging tensions of Labour Party revisionism over the balance and
priority of underlying philosophical concepts of social democratic thought
and practice.

Context and case studies

The fat years and the lean ones are, of course, interconnected . . . Lines of cleavage
may develop, along with ambitions and hopes, points of possible conflict, and areas

of disagreement. The good times will thus produce their own challenges over new ways of organizing society, new values, and rising aspirations. And they create fault lines that may emerge in the next downturn. But more obviously, it is the crisis years that put systems under stress. Hard times expose strengths and weaknesses to scrutiny, allowing observers to see relationships that are often blurred in prosperous periods, when good times slake the propensity to contest and challenge. The lean years are times when old relationships crumble and new ones have to be constructed.[21]

The 1970s have been represented as a decade of political, economic and social upheavals.[22] Particularly, developments of the 1970s revealed the failings of, and acted as a turning point in, the post-war political economy.[23] A conventional view of the period is that the Labour Governments of 1964–70 and 1974–79 'represented the failure of social democracy to cope with economic difficulties', and that it witnessed the 'formal abandonment' of the traditional tools (and some goals) of social democratic political economy. The economic response of the latter government particularly was to prefigure a new concern with British economic decline and emphasis on monetarist themes such as the control of inflation and limits to public expenditure, although others, of course, have questioned the extent to which the government ushered in a shift to the monetarist orthodoxy and economic liberalism of the 1980s.[24]

Assessments of the relative performance of the 1974–79 Labour Government from different political perspectives have generally been harsh, with only recent revisionist attempts at a re-evaluation in light of adverse economic, social and political circumstances.[25] Whatever the normative judgements of these years, particularly of the performance of the 1974–79 Labour Government, the period represents one of transition in the 'intellectual direction' of 'post-war economic policy-making' and 'in attitudes to the expectations and effectiveness of government stimulus to the economy', among other aspects of the post-war social democratic framework.[26] Debate over the conduct and priorities of economic policy characterised British politics and political parties in the 1970s. The essence of Labour's socio-economic and political statecraft was undermined by the wider crisis of social democracy and the fracture of its post-war settlement. In the context of continued economic decline and the perceived failure and increasing disaffection with its governing doctrine, it witnessed the emergence of discontents of both the 'socialist' left and 'social democratic' right and the declining authority of the parliamentary leadership. In the context of the perceived limits of a 'Croslandite' analysis and the emerging intellectual fissure of Labour revisionism in the 'search for a post-Croslandite social democracy',[27] the left was able to reassert itself both intellectually and organisationally to challenge existing power bases in the party.

By early 1977, the challenge to Labour's traditional revisionist social democracy from both without and within had reached an advanced stage. The Labour Government had encountered serious difficulties of both economic management and wider manifesto commitments, and relations with the party and NEC deteriorated significantly. Crosland's earlier optimistic predictions of economic growth had patently not materialised, the rate of inflation had reached double figures, unemployment rates had increased steadily and public economies were painfully enforced following the IMF crisis. The government had carried the nation but not its own party through the referendum on the Common Market: a broad left coalition had opposed membership, while there remained significant divisions, both substantive and tactical, within Labour's centre-right coalition. Neither had the Labour Government–TUC 'social contract' fulfilled expectations. During the first two years of its existence the trade unions had broadly cooperated with government dictates on wage demands as a means of containing inflation but, after 1976, modest wage claims were eventually abandoned and augured for a disruption of industrial relations and the deterioration of the relationship between the Labour Government and the trade unions.[28] Eventually, of course, it ended in the so-called 'Winter of Discontent', which had the effect of sealing the emerging sense of antipathy of the 'new' social democrats to the trade union movement. The latter represented looming symbols of the (failed) 'kind of social democracy we have known since the war', thereby rupturing a traditional pillar of right-wing ascendancy in the party.[29]

Wider context, themes and debates

(The end of) the post-war consensus

These developments also possess implications for our understanding of two kinds of related wider context and themes of post-war politics and recent academic debate: the notion and break-down of the so-called post-war (social democratic) 'consensus' in British politics and wider crisis of European social democracy in the 1970s. Although some commentators have questioned the extent to which post-war British politics can be defined by the notion of 'consensus',[30] it has long been part of the literature of post-war Britain. It broadly refers to a lesser or greater degree of policy convergence between the political parties that established a bi-polar 'technocratic social democratic' settlement in British politics that emerged out of the Second World War. It has been characterised not as the absence of disagreement or as the pinnacle of elite political collusion, but as 'a set of parameters bounding the set of policy options regarded . . . as administratively practicable, economically affordable and politically acceptable'. It represented broad agreement on a consultative style of government and set of parameters within which particular party policies could be defined rather than the absence of competition between the parties or an absence of distinction between them by voters.[31]

Although it is generally accepted to have broken down during the 1970s, there has also been considerable disagreement over the precise point and nature of the demise of the post-war (social democratic) consensus. Did it come with the Heath Government's apparently 'non-consensual' and confrontational testing of a free market economic policy and industrial relations and incomes policies? Or did it come with Denis Healey's 1976 budget, which contained no provision for full employment, and Callaghan's signalling of the limits of public expenditure? Or did it arrive with the election of the self-confessed anti-consensus and conviction-led Margaret Thatcher in 1979? Whatever the relative merits of these competing views, it is clear in this study that agreement on some of the key tenets of the post-war settlement had broken down on the Labour right and within Labour's erstwhile revisionist tradition in the 1970s.

Through the particular influence of Anthony Crosland, broad commitment to a form of Keynesian social democracy in pursuit of the core value of greater economic and social equality provided the unifying framework through which Labour Party revisionism and the Labour right operated in the post-war period.[32] In any assessment of the break-down of a post-war consensus, intra-party tensions and divisions of Labour Party revisionism, initially some of the keenest advocates of a settlement based around the mixed economy, Keynesian economic management, welfarism and integration of the trade unions, over central planks of economic management and trade union relations must be seen as an important dimension of what appears to be a staged and complex process from the late 1960s. The foundations of the post-war settlement did not come under attack just at the extremes of the emerging economic liberalism of the New Right or the 'new' Labour left's Alternative Economic Strategy (AES), but was also increasingly subject to question on different levels by some of those earlier architects and advocates of a post-war settlement based on Keynesian social democracy. This is demonstrated in this study in the divisions of the Labour right in key policy areas and the ideological divergence of Labour Party revisionism in the 1970s.

The crisis of European social democracy

The decline of the British post-war (social democratic) consensus and the crisis of the Labour Party and its programme was part of a wider generic crisis of social democracy in the 1970s. Social democratic parties and their ideology and programmes found themselves in 'hard times' after 1973 when the long post-war boom was followed by lower economic growth and higher inflation and unemployment. In the context of socio-economic change that impacted upon most of the advanced economies of Western Europe, socialist and social democratic parties throughout Europe were faced with a sustained challenge to their political ideology, political economy and programme, political support base and political culture. The demise of the intellectual basis of the social democratic paradigm undermined its previous ascendancy over other ideologies as social democracy generally came under increasing attack from intellectual positions of both right and left.[33]

Difficulties with the Keynesian perspective had been building up, exacerbated by the effects of the 1973 oil crisis on world trade and government budgets. The core problem of Keynesianism was its apparently intrinsic tendency to the growth of public expenditure and high levels of inflation. Keynesianism assumed that demand could be controlled rationally but, given its commitment to full employment, there was no obvious constraint on wage demands by trade unions even if they had an inflationary effect. The attempts of social democratic governments to counter this problem through agreements with the trade unions on wage restraint began to falter by the 1970s. As increasing numbers of workers enjoyed a more affluent, consumer-based existence and were also subject to higher marginal rates of taxation, it proved increasingly difficult to coax trade unions to accept incomes restraint. The imperatives of electoral competition further eroded the rational basis of Keynesian incomes policy. Governments had found it easier to stimulate demand and increase welfare benefits than to raise levels of taxation. While this was feasible in periods of sustained growth, it engendered considerable problems of economic management in periods of low growth. It was economic growth, or rather the lack of it, that was central to the unravelling and subsequent intellectual challenges to post-war social democracy.[34]

This study offers a vignette of the wider crisis of social democracy and the erosion of the post-war (social democratic) consensus in western democracies in the 1970s. It suggests that in addition to the major intellectual challenges from the wider extremes of left and right, the problems and failings of post-war British social democracy elicited an emerging critique from a divergent strand of Labour Party revisionism, which favoured a fundamental reappraisal and revision of the foundations, methodology and even purpose of the post-war social democratic framework. Claims that realistic 'neo-revisionist' attempts to engage with the challenges of the new post-Keynesian context only occurred in the Labour Party after 1983 ignore the tensions and divergence of Labour Party revisionism over key themes of social democratic political economy and ideology during the 1970s.[35] Within the Labour Party in the 1970s, goals of social democratic revisionism and modernisation were frustrated (temporarily at least) by a political culture that appeared to be much more resistant to the ideological and programmatic renewal of social democracy than some fellow European socialist and social democratic parties.

The indicative 1976 Labour leadership contest

The Labour Party leadership contest after Wilson's surprise resignation in March 1976 offers an indication of the extent of, and support for, ideological alignments within the parliamentary party at the time. The leadership election of April 1976 can be seen as a turning point for the Labour right as an opportunity to reassert itself. There had been considerable dissatisfaction with Wilson's leadership among Labour revisionists as well as among those on the left, but his tenure was largely secured because of the significant rivalries of the parliamentary Labour right and the inability to agree and support a single candidate to challenge Wilson's leadership. By April 1976, the main candidates of the Labour right, Crosland, Callaghan and Jenkins, each represented different constituencies of support on the (centre-) right of the parliamentary party, with conflicting personalities, styles and policies. The centre-right Manifesto Group of Labour MPs, for example, was unable to endorse a particular candidate because significant bodies of support existed for Callaghan and Jenkins and a smaller body of support for Crosland.[36]

Crosland, anyway, was never really a serious contender for the leadership, but his candidature perhaps represented a final breach with the 'Jenkinsites' and the fragmentation of Labour Party revisionism, a process which can be dated to 1971, if not before.[37] If he was ever to be a serious contender for party office, advisers and friends of Crosland frequently counselled some sort of rapprochement with Jenkins and his supporters, if only 'in the name of a united opposition to the Left'. This was to prove a difficult if not impossible task, given the distance that had emerged between the two camps since the European vote of October 1971.[38] Crosland's strategy for the leadership was, rather, to present himself as the unity candidate of both right and left. He sought to 'draw . . . support from those who are looking for the common ground which unites both right and left in my Party'.[39] It had been a consistent position adopted by Crosland since his (unsuccessful) attempt to win the deputy leadership of the party in April 1972 (after Jenkins' resignation from the post over the European issue). He considered it imperative that the Labour Party should 'set aside its factional warfare' and 'whatever our different views on Europe, unite on a clear and positive domestic policy' with the first aim of removing 'a reactionary and repressive Tory Government'. He claimed to be 'running . . . on a non-sectarian ticket', with the purpose of recreating 'Party unity on the basis of a radical, egalitarian socialist programme' based on 'full employment, housing, education, redistribution of wealth and an attack on social and economic privilege and inequality'.[40] It only managed to foster the impression in others (the 'Jenkinsites') that 'he had become much more of a straight party man'. For their part, the Jenkinsites had come to view Crosland with some suspicion after his apparent volte-face over Europe, and as an unreliable ally in, what they considered to be, the significant causes of the Labour right.[41] One view suggested that the

> Crosland of today rejects the fundamentalism of the right. He is the man of the centre, the democratic socialist. He has already put the Right's nose out of joint over Europe, and this may account for some of the falling off of his stock within the parliamentary party.[42]

In the circumstances, it was Callaghan (as perhaps the most likely social democratic 'consolidator') who was able to defeat the nominal parliamentary factional figureheads of right and left, Jenkins and Michael Foot (Tribune Group), along with Healey, Tony Benn and Crosland. The election of Callaghan as party leader can be interpreted as a victory for the perceived benefits of unity, pragmatism and moderation, a more comfortable candidate for those elements of the centre-right unconcerned with ideas. In the

> febrile state of the Labour Party in spring 1976, Callaghan was the natural unifying candidate, 'more so than either Foot on the left or Jenkins on the pro-market right, more personally approachable than Healey and with more weight than Crosland'.[43]

In the context of the powerful constraints of a strong left and powerful trade unions in the 1960s and 1970s, 'credible "consensus" leaders from the centre of the party, like Wilson and Callaghan', were 'better able to unite the warring party factions'.[44]

The combined first-round tally of 114 votes for Callaghan and Healey indicated a clear inability of its major representatives to cooperate and unite the Labour right around a single candidate. Crosland's core support consisted of a 'motley collection of screwballs and crackpots', including at least one Tribunite, Bruce Grocott, and the conspicuous lack of any backing from pro-European Labour MPs, signifying the lack of 'an alternative power base inside the party'. It is probable that the small number of Crosland's votes transferred to Callaghan, but perhaps the major surprise (and disappointment) for the Jenkinsites was the poor performance of the talismanic Jenkins. He scored only fifty-six votes in the first ballot, compared, for instance, to the ninety for Michael Foot. Similarly, Healey, as a ' "loner", who, unlike Callaghan or Jenkins, had not bothered to build up a network of allies in the PLP', lacked the requisite level of support to make an effective showing. The candidatures of Healey and Crosland obviously impacted upon the votes that Jenkins required to challenge Callaghan and emerge as the main candidate of the right to fight Foot in a second or third ballot. Equally 'serious for the Jenkins cause was that between fifteen and twenty pro-European MPs who would have voted for him four years before now went to Callaghan. They included . . . Hattersley . . . John Smith . . . Cledwyn Hughes, the chairman of the PLP, and Ernest Armstrong.'[45] Jenkins reflected on his relatively poor showing and, in the circumstances, he immediately decided to withdraw from the contest, 'in effect releasing my votes to Callaghan' who 'I . . . greatly preferred . . . as Prime Minister to . . . Michael Foot, the only practical alternative'. Jenkins also indicates clear differences with Callaghan, 'believing him to have been wrong on devaluation, East of Suez, immigration policy, most libertarian issues at the Home Office, trade union reform and Europe', although he was at least 'sound on the Atlantic Alliance, was no dogmatic supporter of nationalisation and had a built-in respect for the rule of law'.[46]

Jenkins' disappointing performance in the leadership election was to hasten his departure from the Labour Party to become President of the European Commission. In the aftermath of the election, Callaghan made Crosland Foreign Secretary in preference to Jenkins: the former 'was not nearly as committed . . . to Community membership and would not arouse much suspicion when he took the necessary decisions, as he must, that would link Britain with the Community'. He was much less likely to fatally divide the party than Jenkins, whose 'every action . . . would have been regarded with deep suspicion by the anti-Marketeers', and Callaghan himself was no great EEC enthusiast.[47] The leadership election also marked the end of Jenkins' bid to become party leader, the Jenkinsites were leaderless and scattered in the Labour Party and the Jenkinsite project was to find pastures new. One interested participant reflects on the issues and problems of the (centre-) right in the 1976 leadership election, an episode characterised by a clear lack of strategy among the leading (revisionist) right-wing candidates and which marked a watershed for the Labour right in the party:

> Of course, even if two out of Crosland, Healey and Jenkins had stood down, there is no guarantee that their combined vote could have been transferred to the one candidate. There were certainly many Labour MPs on the centre-right . . . who wondered why . . . the three men . . . could not get together . . . But there were others who only emphasised the differences. A number of pro-European Jenkinsites still had

not forgotten the behaviour of Crosland and Healey over Europe in 1971 and 1972, while Croslandites charged Jenkins not only of not being a real socialist but, even worse, a 'crypto-coalitionist'. Supporters of Healey claimed that Jenkins was now too divisive and Crosland not decisive enough to be elected as leader . . . In one way these divisions . . . only highlighted what a formidable candidate for the leadership . . . Callaghan was, given the divided nature of the Labour Party in the 1970s and the existence of a strong left wing . . . many observers believed that, even if only one of the three had been running against him, he would have still carried the day.[48]

Left-wing advance and emergence of an organised Labour right

An important corollary of the decline of revisionist social democracy and the disintegration of the Labour right in the 1970s was the corresponding resurgence of the (new) Labour left. While it was events and developments inside the Labour Party after the 1979 election defeat that consolidated this trend, the advance of the left in the party was a more or less continuous process through the decade.[49] The 1973 Annual Conference had abolished Labour's list of proscribed organisations, facilitating a greater degree of left-wing entryism. In 1975 the Secretary of State for Education, Reg Prentice, was deselected in his Newham North East constituency, followed a year later by Frank Tomney in Hammersmith. Dick Taverne had already been deselected by his constituency Labour party (CLP) in Lincoln, which precipitated his battle against the left to regain the seat as an independent Democratic Labour candidate.[50] The two general elections of 1974 also enabled the recruitment of MPs within Parliament by the left-wing Tribune Group and, although never a majority of the PLP, it delivered sufficient votes to elect Ian Mikardo as chairman of the PLP the same year.[51] The parliamentary profile of the Tribune Group was augmented by three further developments: first, significant left-wing Cabinet representation in the form of Foot, Benn and Albert Booth; second, highly organised and sustained expression of factional dissent in the House of Commons; third, Foot's election over Shirley Williams as deputy leader of the party in 1976.[52]

Conference also came to represent an increasingly important forum for a broad left alliance, and the general left-wing resurgence was accompanied by a growing proliferation of factional groupings of the left. Of these, perhaps the most significant was the Campaign for Labour Party Democracy (CLPD), whose *raison d'être* was to lobby for the internal constitutional change broadly favoured by the left. The demand for constitutional change within the party was threefold, and represented an attempt to 'democratise' the relationship between the different institutions of the party's federal structure and realign the intra-party balance of power: first, the mandatory reselection of Labour MPs; second, control of the Labour Party manifesto by the NEC rather than the PLP; third, an electoral college to replace the existing exclusive franchise of the PLP in the election of the party leader. By 1977, CLPD held the affiliations of over 170 party organisations, including seventy-four CLPs compared to only six in 1974.[53] At the 1977 Annual Conference, seventy-nine CLPs submitted resolutions in favour of mandatory reselection of Labour MPs. On the basis of a report of a working party of the NEC instructed by the 1976 Annual Conference, three alternatives for the election of the party leader were to be processed 'in suitable form to enable the Annual Conference in 1978 to make a decision following which a subsequent amendment to the Party Constitution would be placed before the subsequent Conference'.[54] Any such recommendation was, of course, opposed by the (natural centre-right majority of the) PLP on the grounds that the election of the party leader by Labour's elected parliamentary representatives 'is as democratic an electoral college as it is possible to achieve.[55]

There were some signs of an organised response on the centre-right of the PLP. The Manifesto Group of centre-right Labour MPs was launched in December 1974 as an organised attempt to provide support for the Labour Government and the manifesto on which it had been elected, and to counter the success of the Tribune Group in elections to the PLP Liaison Committee and other PLP subject groups.[56] It met with some success in this respect: within two years of its formation, around eighty broadly centre-right Labour MPs had been recruited, and Cledwyn Hughes had been elected to replace Mikardo as Chairman of the PLP. However, the diversity and divisions of its membership over crucial policy issues undermined the attempt to offer a sustained rejoinder to left-wing organisation and advance in the party (see Chapter 3).

The Manifesto Group also worked alongside the Campaign for Labour Victory (CLV) from its formation in February 1977. CLV shared broadly similar views with the Manifesto Group, supporting the Labour Government while upholding a broadly social democratic perspective. CLV was a primarily extra-parliamentary organ of the Labour right, and eventually became an organisational catalyst for secessionist activity. It worked at the constituency level and its aims included the regeneration of party membership and organisation. Although there were no formal connections between the two organisations, they worked together on a number of occasions, notably in the issue of a joint statement that addressed the democratic and policy-making structure and weaknesses of the party and the need to revitalise membership and participation in the party after the shock of the 1979 election defeat.[57] Otherwise, organised groups of the Labour right were largely small, peripheral and often elitist associations of limited appeal, functioning outside Westminster on the social democratic fringe. One such group, the Social Democratic Alliance (SDA), launched in 1975, provided the first signs of authentic extra-parliamentary counter-campaigning on the Labour right. Ultimately, however, it proved ideologically too narrow and politically strident to command a broader right-wing appeal, and failed to rise beyond the level of a small, hard-right faction. The social democratic 'house' journal, *Socialist Commentary*, and associated group, Friends of Socialist Commentary, had long offered an outlet for the dissemination of views and ideas. From 1978, however, declining funds and circulation led to the demise of the journal, which contributed to the social democratic intellectual malaise.[58]

The problem of Labour right group organisation and activity in the 1970s also appeared to be one of dimension. Although it embraced a number of revisionist causes, the earlier Campaign for Democratic Socialism (CDS) campaigned primarily (and with leadership approval) on one specific platform, namely, that of multilateral nuclear disarmament.[59] By contrast, the 1970s presented the parliamentary Labour right with a more comprehensive set of challenges on a much wider scale. Nor was group organisation and activity on the parliamentary Labour right now sanctioned by the party leadership, and the political realignment of major trade unions further undermined its cause. The parliamentary Labour right also lost some of the most articulate proponents of revisionist social democracy during the decade. Dick Taverne was finally defeated at the October 1974 general election. Brian Walden left Parliament for an alternative career in television. Jenkins left British politics to become President of the European Commission, taking David Marquand with him as a personal adviser. Crosland, himself, was to die from a sudden stroke in February 1977, although he had by then, according to the Jenkinsites, undergone a 'transition from revisionist *enfant terrible* to responsible Labour statesman', and the 'symbiosis between Croslandism and Labourism' represented 'a symbiosis of exhaustion'. They argued that, although the 'times cried out for a further instalment of revisionism which would do for Croslandite social democracy what *The Future of Socialism* had done for Clause Four socialism', the 'Crosland of the 1970s was too distracted by the responsibilities of office and too encumbered by the claims of party loyalty to make the attempt'.[60] The death of John Mackintosh in 1978 robbed the new wave of revisionism of, perhaps, its most promising exponent, and contributed further to the decline of *Socialist Commentary* and wider intellectual malaise of revisionist social democracy and the Labour right. Such a development was predicted to have damaging consequences for the Labour Party, which 'will succumb to a kind of ideological paralysis and cease to do anything worthwhile with the majorities it wins'.[61]

During the 1970s, Labour's post-war social democracy experienced significant challenges to its governing and institutional norms. Considerable problems in the structural political economy were accompanied by the manifestation of growing left-wing dissent and responses to the perceived failure and break-down of Labour's post-war philosophy and its association with the gradual reformism and 'pragmatic centrist' approach of Labour's centre-right 'governing elite'.[62] One of the consequences was that 'those normally labelled as the Right, who have provided most of the ideas since the late 1950s, have been so upset and thrown off balance by their recent defeats that they appear to be divided and somewhat demoralised and have managed only to fight rear-guard actions'.[63] In the circumstances, the intellectual and political fragmentation of the Labour right was part cause and part effect of the rise of the left.

Case studies

The empirical basis of the study consists of a number of case studies of key ideological and policy themes, which explore the dimensions of the complexity and divisions of the parliamentary Labour right in the 1970s. These include the crucial issue of European membership, industrial relations and trade union reform, debates over the role and levels of public expenditure and the nature and efficacy of parliamentary Labour right factional organisation in the 1970s. The selected case studies represent key themes of policy and issues of intra-party debates and divisions that do not coalesce simply on left–right lines.

Europe: the Common Market debate

British membership of the European Economic Community (EEC) (in common with the proposed devolution of powers to elected assemblies in Scotland and Wales) reflected the centrality of Westminster/parliamentary sovereignty in intra-party debates. Both issues represented a major point of dissent and division in the 1970s and led to some of the most serious rifts within both main parties during the 1974–79 Parliament.[64] It represents a central plank of post-war British foreign policy that was a recurrent feature of Labour's intra-party debates and divisions since the early 1960s.[65] In spite of some claims to the contrary, it did not conform to a simple left–right division in the party.[66] It provoked serious divisions both between and within left and right, and has been debated as a critical dimension in explanations of the trajectory of the 'social democrats' out of the party and the creation of the SDP.[67]

The European issue had been a crucial division of the parliamentary Labour right and Labour Party revisionism since the heady days of Hugh Gaitskell. The issue aroused strong passions on all corners of the Labour benches in the 1970s. Jenkins' large minority of right-wing pro-Marketeers regarded the issue as one of high principle. To ensure that the European Accession Bill was safely guided through Parliament, they were even prepared to sustain the Heath Government in office. Directly opposed to them was an equally determined minority of anti-Marketeers, mainly but not exclusively from the left. They were bitterly opposed to the buttress provided to the Heath Government from the Labour benches that enabled it not only to take Britain into the EEC but also to introduce legislation on issues such as industrial relations and housing finance. Other influential representatives of the parliamentary Labour right, including Callaghan, Crosland and Healey, displayed attitudes to the issue that were characterised by a much greater degree of pragmatism, indifference and indecision. Of these, Crosland had been most closely identified with the post-war Gaitskellite revisionist tradition, and his refusal to regard British membership as a matter of principle infuriated former close allies among the Jenkinsite pro-European grouping.[68] It was an issue that, perhaps, demonstrated the character of the respective 'labourisms' of Crosland and Jenkins. For Crosland, voting for entry into the Common Market was not worth the risk of splitting the Labour Party and maintaining the Conservatives in office. He pondered that 'some who thought of themselves as Gaitskellites had moved so far to the Right that they disappeared from view'.[69] Thus divided, the 'capacity of the right to resist the advance of the left – its ranks temporarily swelled by right-wing anti-Marketeers – was enfeebled'.[70]

As arguments over Europe raged in the party from the early 1970s, and as party policy and wider party opinion moved against them, pro-European social democrats who regarded the issue as an over-riding matter of principle found themselves both increasingly marginalised in the party and divided from Labour right and centrist colleagues who were not similarly disposed to the Common Market.[71] The pro-European social democrats had, to some extent, 'always respected the consistency of the position' of the 'small but long-standing forces of opposition to the Common Market' (of both left and right), and who continued to oppose entry. The 'real problem lay with bulk of the centre and right of the party who now saw it as politically prudent to execute a timely about-face on Europe'. Critical divisions over the European issue – either substantive or tactical – were to prove fatal to attempts to recreate a 'moderate' alliance and organisation of 'the revisionist Labour right and centrists in the Labour Party'. The compass and cohesion of the Manifesto Group of centre-right Labour MPs was constrained by the fact that its key policy statements had to avoid contentious policy issues such as Europe, which was 'a problematic omission' stemming from the fact that the committee that wrote them contained both pro-European social democrats and other Labour right-wingers opposed to the Common Market.[72]

Industrial relations and trade union reform

Issues of industrial relations and trade union reform also provoked divisions beyond the conventional dimensions and cleavages of Labour's essentially contested political culture and divided the Labour right in the 1970s.[73] Its centrality to traditions and 'structures of feeling' in the Labour movement offered a potentially divisive issue of both policy and party management. The so-called 'rules of the Labour movement' and the central role and influence of the trade unions in the Labour Party and British politics provided the context in which the underlying tensions of the Labour right on the 'trade union question' were revealed. It represented a further dimension of the increasing frustration of revisionist 'social democrats' with the Labour Party and a sub-text of their departure to the SDP. The disenchantment was partly founded on the perception of a potential conflict between trade union power and collectivism and emerging themes of individual freedom in political discourse.[74]

This feeling was particularly acute after the ignominious climb-down over *In Place of Strife* in 1969, through which Barbara Castle attempted to reform the context of industrial relations. It was an attempt to encourage the trade unions to accept measures that would restrict unofficial strike activity in exchange for the extension of union rights in the workplace. Many of the traditional 'trade union' right opposed an attempt to impose a legal framework on trade union activity and lined up with the left in opposition to the initiative. The *In Place of Strife* White Paper was subsequently withdrawn in the face of opposition from the PLP, NEC and trade unions.

Labour right divisions over *In Place of Strife* to a large extent followed a traditional distinction between the 'old' union right and 'intellectual' revisionist right,[75] but the controversy and its aftermath also revealed emerging divisions of Labour revisionists in their respective responses to the 'trade union question'. Callaghan, backed by Dick Marsh and Ray Gunter, provided the main opposition to the bill. Although his position gradually became more ambiguous because 'he no longer thought that the fight was worth the cost',[76] Jenkins initially supported the proposed legislation with the added proviso that it 'should be rushed through immediately as he did not want the consultations dragging on'.[77] Crosland considered the legislation to be ill-timed, and his response reveals at least tactical differences with Jenkins over the issue: 'Tony . . . was incredulous . . . he agreed with [Castle] on issues about 70 per cent of the time; but to contemplate a policy like this late in a Parliament was mad . . . As Chancellor, surely Roy would help persuade the Prime Minister of the folly of putting through a Bill you could not enforce'. However, 'the Chancellor was on the Cabinet Committee which had already discussed *In Place of Strife*, and Roy supported it'.[78]

According to one keen observer of the Labour alliance, 'ex-Gaitskellite revisionists' responded very differently to the emergence of a new radicalised trade unionism and 'crisis over power within the party' that coincided with, and was stimulated by, the 'broad crisis of revisionist social democracy'. For some, the 'trade union question' would provide a further point of departure in their trajectory out of the Labour Party:

> Faced with a reappraisal of means and ends the majority of ex-Gaitskellite revisionists met the new political problems with an uneasy mixture of moderation, adaption and pragmatism. The early death of ... intellectual leaders, Allan Flanders in 1974 and Tony Crosland in 1977, left Roy Jenkins as the senior ex-Gaitskellite. Flanders and Crosland had sought to preserve their socialist values and Labour's special link with the organised working class but to reorder priorities and reaffirm distinctive institutional responsibilities – and passed on this legacy. But Jenkins was much readier to shed the socialist ascription, some of the main commitments and ultimately the fundamental values and 'rules' of the Labour Movement.[79]

In the wider context of British economic decline, the 'trade union question' became a central aspect of British political discourse and debate in the 1970s. The failure of *In Place of Strife*, the rise of trade union militancy and the industrial unrest that accompanied the Heath Government's Industrial Relations Act, and the critical role of the trade unions in both the production and implementation of government economic and industrial policy and the internal politics and decision-making of the Labour Party and Labour Government, provided the context in which the emerging strand of (Jenkinsite) liberal revisionism undertook a fundamental reassessment of this relationship and wider role of the trade unions.

Distributional issues, public expenditure and divisions of social democratic political economy

Attitudes to public expenditure and distributional issues in the context of the crisis of revisionist social democracy in the 1970s similarly reveal emerging tensions of Labour Party revisionism over traditional methods and goals of social democratic political economy and the underlying concepts and principles of social democratic thought and practice. Again, the classification of political views and positions as left or right 'obscures more than it illuminates'.[80] Crosland's ideas, for example, have been caricatured as being distinctly of the right of the party, based on issues such as the nuclear deterrent (which he supported) and the Common Market (on which he was lukewarm). On the cause he considered to be the real test of political belief, equality, and in his commitment to his classic revisionist social democratic economic analysis, he would be considered to be an orthodox democratic socialist or even traditional left-wing or radical egalitarian, if it was not for his clear rejection of public ownership as a central plank of this analysis: 'if you took public spending as being the touchstone of the left, then Tony Crosland was a hard left radical and others who would regard themselves as instinctively on the left were much more conservative'.[81]

Roy Jenkins, on the other hand, after taking over as Chancellor from Callaghan after the forced devaluation of 1967, demonstrated almost 'Crippsian austerity and unyielding determination until the balance of payments moved into the black'. Admittedly, his task there 'was as simple as it was forbidding: the forced devaluation ... had come at the wrong time and in the wrong way ... what mattered was to make devaluation work'.[82] However, he was, it seems, well suited to the task: his 'near Gladstonian programme of economic stringency at the Exchequer' was familiar to his tradition of 'radical liberalism'. Its intellectual roots lay in the 'New Liberal' thinking of the Edwardian era, which 'adopted an interventionist economic role for the State, although public expenditure was to be held in check'.[83] Jenkins' apparent suitability for such a task may, in Harold Wilson's eyes, have been one reason for his elevation to the Chancellorship ahead of Crosland to staunch the economic crisis that accompanied devaluation. Signalling the 'ascendancy of Jenkins', it was a move which has been seen to have had damaging effects on the 'cohesion of the Labour right over the next eight or nine years'. Jenkins reflects that had they 'been able to work together as smoothly as did Gaitskell and Jay or Gaitskell and Gordon Walker a decade before it might have made a decisive difference to the balance of power within the Labour Party and hence the politics of the early 1980s'.[84]

The divisions of the parliamentary Labour right and Labour Party revisionism over public expenditure and social democratic political economy came to the fore in the controversy surrounding the IMF loan of 1976. The pragmatic outlook of politicians such as Callaghan and Healey included a willingness to pursue financial orthodoxy and economic stringency in the cause of confidence and party unity. For Crosland (initially at least), public expenditure for redistributive purposes remained the core instrument of his wider programme of egalitarianism and major social change.[85] During the IMF Cabinet debates, there were essentially two groups opposed to the IMF terms of substantial public spending cuts. One group consisted of those of the left and centre-left, such as Tony Benn, Michael Foot, Stan Orme and Peter Shore. The other group consisted of Crosland, Roy Hattersley, Harold Lever, Shirley Williams, David Ennals and Bill Rodgers of the right and centre-right. Of the latter, the opposition of Ennals, Rodgers and Shirley Williams was qualitatively different to that of Crosland, based primarily on the desire to protect their respective departmental budgets. Crosland believed the whole exercise to be unnecessarily deflationary. Intellectually, he remained less than convinced of the rectitude of the intended cuts in public expenditure throughout the crisis, but in the cause of the unity and survival of the Labour Government he ultimately accepted the decision of the Chancellor and Prime Minister.[86] The IMF crisis represents a seminal development in this context, not least because it aligned Crosland (and Hattersley) with the left and centre-left and set him against the majority of the Labour right. By this point, he had arrived at the conclusion that some former revisionist allies had abandoned social democracy. Labour's post-war revisionist tradition was essentially divided between Keynesian social democrats and liberals in their respective views of the role and limits of public expenditure.

Conclusion: summary of key themes and arguments

The parliamentary Labour right has been a more complex, heterogeneous and disputatious body than conventional accounts of a monolithic ruling Labour right or revisionist tendency would allow. It was divided by more than personality traits and conflicts in the pursuit of political ambition. It was fundamentally divided over key political and policy issues of the 1970s and even over the balance and priority of first philosophical concepts in social democratic thought and practice. Previously, the contours of these fissures were concealed in the loose cohesive framework of Keynesian revisionist social democracy. As this framework collapsed in the particular economic and political circumstances of the 1970s, the underlying political and philosophical complexity and tensions of the parliamentary Labour right emerged, which undermined attempts to respond to challenges to its revisionist social democratic framework.

The study utilises selected cases studies of key policy themes – European membership, industrial relations and trade union reform, social democratic political economy and public expenditure, and questions of organisation and leadership – to explore the nature and degree of separation. On the basis of the case study analysis, it is possible to broadly distinguish between different 'types' on the parliamentary Labour right in the 1970s. First, the moderate, centrist, pragmatic, 'non-intellectual' Labour right – legatees of Labour's (Morrisonian) 'consolidator' tradition – concerned in most cases with party loyalty, party unity and the preservation of the Labour alliance.[87] Second, the egalitarian revisionist Labour right, concerned to maintain traditional 'Croslandite' principles and priorities in the face of a crisis of social democratic political economy in the 1970s. They were unwilling to endorse Roy Jenkins as the new intellectual guru of Labour Party revisionism and, in their similar approach to party loyalty and party unity rather than dedication to (non-economic/egalitarian) issues of principle, emerged closer to the former group. Third, an emerging liberal revisionist strand of the Labour right, which found itself increasingly alienated, not only from the left, but within the wider party and movement over a number of related political and intellectual themes. It was the emerging divisions of the final two groupings that proved the most debilitating in terms of the unity and cohesion of the parliamentary Labour right in the 1970s, and a number of implications can be read into this analysis: it has been a neglected factor in accounts of Labour's subsequent shift leftwards, it provides a longer perspective of the roots and evolution of the SDP and, in the longer term, helps to 'historicise' 'New' Labour in divisions and developments of the 'old' Labour right and Labour Party revisionism in the 1970s. The study addresses a key moment and factors in the evolution of social democratic politics and the making of the contemporary Labour Party.

Chapter 2 addresses the conceptual basis of the study. It undertakes a broad appraisal of the philosophy, ideas, traditions and dimensions of the parliamentary Labour right. Chapter 3 considers the (limitations) of group and factional organisation and activity on the parliamentary Labour right in the 1970s. It suggests that intra-party group and factional behaviour in the PLP in the 1970s was not the preserve of the Labour left, nor was it expressed in simple oppositional-leadership/loyalist, left–right terms.[88] Its limited impact on the politics of the Labour Party reflected the diverse and disputatious nature of its core body of support. Chapters 4 to 5 are concerned with the individual case studies of key policy themes. Together they reveal dimensions of the political and ideological tensions and complexity of the parliamentary Labour right and Labour revisionism in the 1970s. Chapter 7 addresses some of the short- and longer-term implications of the analysis for understanding the subsequent trajectory of the Labour Party and British social democracy, and something of the roots of New Labour.

Notes

1 S. Haseler, *The Gaitskellites: Revisionism in the British Labour Party 1951–64*, London, Macmillan, 1969, p. ix.

2 G. Daly, 'The Campaign for Labour Victory and the Origins of the SDP', *Contemporary Record*, 7 (2), 1993, p. 282.

3 R. Plant, M. Beech and K. Hickson (eds), *The Struggle for Labour's Soul: Understanding Labour's Political Thought since 1945*, London, Routledge, 2004, pp. 1–3 and pp. 120–4; also see E. Burns, *Right Wing Labour: Its Theory & Practice*, London, Lawrence & Wishart, 1961.

4 See, for instance, S. Fielding, *The Labour Party: Continuity and Change in the Making of 'New' Labour*, Basingstoke, Palgrave, 2003; T. Jones, *Remaking the Labour Party: From Gaitskell to Blair*, London, Routledge, 1996.

5 As Eric Shaw notes, it was a period that witnessed the demise of the twin social democratic pillars of Keynesianism and corporatism and in which 'revisionist social democracy fell to pieces': E. Shaw, *The Labour Party since 1945*, Oxford, Blackwell, 1996, p. 7.

6 R. Harrison, 'Labour Party History: Approaches and Interpretations', *Labour History Review*, 56 (1), 1991, pp. 8–12.

7 See, for example, R. Rose, 'Parties, Factions and Tendencies in Britain', *Political Studies*, 12 (1), 1964, pp. 33–46.

8 Haseler, *The Gaitskellites*.

9 I. Crewe and A. King, *SDP: The Birth, Life and Death of the Social Democratic Party*, Oxford, Oxford University Press, 1995; R. Desai, *Intellectuals and Socialism: 'Social Democrats' and the Labour Party*, London, Lawrence & Wishart, 1994.

10 See S. Fielding, 'New Labour and the Past', in D. Tanner, P. Thane and N. Tiratsoo (eds), *Labour's First Century*, Cambridge, Cambridge University Press, 2000, pp. 367–92; Fielding, *The Labour Party*; Jones, *Remaking the Labour Party*; P. Larkin, 'New Labour and Old Revisionism', *Renewal*, 8 (1), 2000, pp. 42–9.

11 D. Hayter, *Fightback! Labour's Traditional Right in the 1970s and 1980s*, Manchester, Manchester University Press, 2005.

12 *Ibid.*, pp. 3–6; also see G. Jones, 'A left house built on sand', *Socialist Commentary*, November 1978.

13 Hayter claims that the 'traditional right' after 1981 concerned itself far less with key policy issues and leadership roles and focused much more narrowly on internal organisational and constitutional matters: Hayter, *Fightback!*, pp. 5–7.

14 G. Radice, *Friends & Rivals: Crosland, Jenkins and Healey*, London, Little, Brown, 2002.

15 See C. Hay, 'Labour's Thatcherite Revisionism: Playing the "Politics of Catch-Up"', *Political Studies*, 42 (4), 1994, pp. 700–7; C. Hay, *The Political Economy of New Labour: Labouring Under False Pretences?* Manchester, Manchester University Press, 1999; R. Heffernan, 'Accounting for New Labour: The Impact of Thatcherism 1979–1995', in I. Hampsher-Monk and J. Stanyer (eds), *Contemporary Political Studies*, Exeter, Political Studies Association, 1996, pp. 1280–90; R. Heffernan, *New Labour and Thatcherism: Exploring Political Change*, Basingstoke, Macmillan, 1999.

16 See Jones, *Remaking the Labour Party*; M. J. Smith, 'A Return to Revisionism? The Labour Party's Policy Review', in M. J. Smith and J. Spear (eds), *The Changing Labour Party*, London, Routledge, 1992, pp. 13–28; M. J. Smith, 'Understanding the "Politics of Catch-Up". The Modernisation of the Labour Party', *Political Studies*, 42 (4), 1994, pp. 708–15.

17 See T. Blair, *The Third Way: New Politics for the New Century*, London, Fabian Society, 1998; S. Driver and L. Martell, *New Labour: Politics After Thatcherism*, Cambridge, Polity Press, 1998; A. Giddens, *The Third Way: The Renewal of Social Democracy*, Cambridge, Polity Press, 1998.

18 Fielding, 'New Labour and the Past'; Fielding, *The Labour Party*; also see Larkin, 'New Labour and Old Revisionism'.

19 Fielding, *The Labour Party*, pp. 70–4.

20 Dick Taverne, Interview with the author, 18 January 2001.

21 P. Gourevitch, *Politics in Hard Times: Comparative Responses to International Economic Crises*, New York, Cornell University Press, 1986, pp. 9–10.

22 C. Booker, *The Seventies: Portrait of a Decade*, Harmondsworth, Penguin, 1980; P. Whitehead, *The Writing on the Wall: Britain in the Seventies*, London, Michael Joseph, 1985.

23 R. Coopey and N. Woodward (eds), *Britain in the 1970s: The Troubled Economy*, London, UCL Press, 1996; N. Tracy, *The Origins of the Social Democratic Party*, London, Croom Helm, 1983, pp. 17–24, 25–33.

24 Tracy, *The Origins of the Social Democratic Party*, p. 25; and see K. Hickson, *The IMF Crisis of 1976 and British Politics*, London, I. B. Tauris, 2005.

25 See A. Seldon and K. Hickson, 'Introduction', in A. Seldon and K. Hickson (eds), *New Labour, Old Labour: The Wilson and Callaghan Governments, 1974–79*, London, Routledge, 2004, pp. 1–2.

26 See Fielding, *The Labour Party*, pp. 70–1; M. Holmes, *The Labour Government 1974–1979: Political Aims and Economic Reality*, London, Macmillan, 1985, pp. 163, 179–82.

27 See D. Marquand, *The Progressive Dilemma: From Lloyd George to Kinnock*, London, Heinemann, 1991, pp. 170–1, 175, 177; D. Marquand, *The New Reckoning: Capitalism, States and Citizens*, Cambridge, Polity Press, 1997, pp. 11–20.

28 S. Ludlam, 'The Making of New Labour', in S. Ludlam and M. J. Smith (eds), *New Labour in Government*, Basingstoke, Macmillan, 2001, p. 13; S. Ludlam, 'New Labour

and the Unions: the End of the Contentious Alliance?', in Ludlam and Smith (eds), *New Labour in Government*, pp. 112–13.

29 D. Marquand, 'Inquest on a Movement: Labour's Defeat and its Consequences', *Encounter*, July 1979, pp. 8–18; D. Marquand, 'Why Labour cannot be saved', *Spectator*, 27 September 1980; also see P. Jenkins, 'The Crumbling of the Old Order', in W. Kennet (ed.), *The Rebirth of Britain*, London, Weidenfeld & Nicolson, 1982, pp. 41–4; R. Jenkins, 'Home Thoughts from Abroad: The 1979 Dimbleby Lecture', in Kennet (ed.), *The Rebirth of Britain*, pp. 26–7; Tracy, *The Origins of the Social Democratic Party*, pp. 40–3.

30 P. Kerr, 'The Post-War Consensus: A Woozle that Wasn't', in D. Marsh, J. Buller, C. Hay, J. Johnston, P. Kerr, S. McAnulla and M. Watson, *Post-war British Politics in Perspective*, Cambridge, Polity Press, 1999; B. Pimlott, 'The Myth of Consensus', in L. M. Smith (ed.), *The Making of Britain: Echoes of Greatness*, London, Macmillan, 1988.

31 P. Addison, *The Road to 1945: British Politics and the Second World War*, London, Jonathan Cape, 1975; P. Jenkins, 'The Crumbling of the Old Order', pp. 38–51; D. Kavanagh and P. Morris, *Consensus Politics from Attlee to Thatcher*, Oxford, Blackwell, 1989; also see K. Hickson, 'The Postwar Consensus Revisited', *Political Quarterly*, 75 (2), 2004, pp. 142–54, who defends the notion of a post-war consensus on the level of a broad convergence and continuity of policy rather than any convergence of (social democratic) ideology or values.

32 Hickson, 'The Postwar Consensus Revisited', pp. 143–6; also see N. Ellison, *Egalitarian Thought and Labour Politics: Retreating Visions*, London, Routledge, 1994.

33 See J. Callaghan, 'Social Democracy in Transition', *Parliamentary Affairs*, 56 (1), 2003, pp. 125–6, 139; also see J. Callaghan, *The Retreat of Social Democracy*, Manchester, Manchester University Press, 2000, pp. ix, 29–47, 204–8; I. Favretto, *The Long Search for a Third Way: The British Labour Party and Italian Left since 1945*, Basingstoke, Macmillan, 2003, pp. 98–100; S. Padgett and W. E. Paterson, *A History of Social Democracy in Postwar Europe*, London, Longman, 1981, pp. 149–50; W. E. Paterson and A. H. Thomas, 'Introduction', in W. E. Paterson and A. H. Thomas (eds), *The Future of Social Democracy: Problems and Prospects of Social Democratic Parties in Western Europe*, Oxford, Clarendon Press, 1986, pp. 7–13.

34 Paterson and Thomas, 'Introduction', pp. 7–9; also see R. Dahrendorf, *Life Chances: Approaches to Social and Political Theory*, London, Weidenfeld & Nicolson, 1980, pp. 106–7; R. Skidelsky, 'The Decline of Keynesian Economics', in C. Crouch (ed.), *State and Economy in Contemporary Capitalism*, London, Croom Helm, 1979, pp. 67–8.

35 See Favretto, *The Long Search for a Third Way*, pp. 104–5.

36 John Tomlinson, Interview with the author, 27 March 2001. Healey had gained the reputation (and 'paid a penalty') for being a loner: 'Note on talk with Bill Rodgers in Italy', 6 September 1973, Crosland Papers, 6/2; David Lipsey, Memorandum to Anthony Crosland, 29 March 1976, Crosland Papers, 6/3.

37 Anthony Crosland, Memorandum, n.d. 1971, Crosland Papers, 6/2; W. Rodgers, Interview with the author, 18 February 2001. Crosland reveals that 'not for 1st time, but more acutely, uncomfortable. Ambivalent relationship: CDS, Euro, Right, who now totally Jenkinsite'. He also muses to himself, 'after all, don't desperately want to be leader'; 'Note on talk with Bill Rodgers in Italy', Crosland Papers, 6/2.

38 David Lipsey, Memorandum on Panorama Profile, 4 March 1976, Crosland Papers 6/3; Lipsey, Memorandum to Anthony Crosland, 29 March 1976, both of which indicate the degree to which Crosland had become separated from, and the difficulties involved in 'winning over the disheartened "Friends of Roy"', to his cause. Lipsey's speculations

about Crosland's core support during the 1976 leadership contest revealed a small number of relatively unknown Labour back-bench MPs: David Lipsey, Letter to Peter Hardy MP, 29 April 1976; David Lipsey, 'Crosland Votes – David Lipsey's Final Guess at 8/4/76', Crosland Papers 6/3; Radice, *Friends & Rivals*, pp. 236, 238–9.

39 Anthony Crosland, Statement to the Press Association, 17 March 1976, Crosland Papers 6/3; Tomlinson, Interview with the author.

40 Anthony Crosland, Speech to the Conference of the Labour political Studies Centre, 16 April 1972; William Hamilton, 'Press Statement', 17 April 1972; Anthony Crosland, 'Statement by the Rt. Hon. Anthony Crosland MP', n.d.; Notes for Lobby, n.d., Crosland Papers, 6/2.

41 Marquand, *The Progressive Dilemma*, p. 169; Rodgers, Interview with the author. For instance, his close friend (and biographer of Hugh Gaitskell), Philip Williams, complained that he had publicly supported the official Labour Party candidate against Dick Taverne (campaigning as a Democratic Labour candidate after problems with his local constituency party largely over the EEC) in the Lincoln by-election in 1973. It was thought by some on the Labour right that a Labour victory would only justify the aggressive tactics of left-wing constituency activists towards sitting Labour MPs.

42 *New Statesman*, 19 November 1976.

43 R. Jenkins, *A Life at the Centre*, London, Macmillan, 1991, p. 434; Radice, *Friends & Rivals*, p. 234.

44 Radice, *Friends &Rivals*, p. 4; Tomlinson, Interview with the author.

45 *Ibid.*, pp. 4–5, 212, 234–40. Hattersley's reason for not supporting Jenkins' candidature was ideological, stemming from his unease with a speech made by Jenkins in Anglesey in which he claimed that the public spending level compatible with a pluralistic democracy would soon be reached. Crosland's programme of greater economic and social equality was still predicated on high levels of public expenditure for purposes of redistribution. Hattersley, as 'an intellectual disciple of Crosland, gave this as his reason for not voting for Jenkins, though he also told Crosland that he was supporting Callaghan for fear of splitting the vote and letting Foot in'.

46 Jenkins, *A Life at the Centre*, p. 436.

47 J. Callaghan, *Time and Chance*, London, William Collins, 1987, p. 399; J. Callaghan, *James Callaghan on the Common Market*, London, Labour Committee for Safeguards on the Common Market, 1971, pp. 1–4; P. Kellner and C. Hitchens, *Callaghan: The Road to Number Ten*, London, Cassell, 1976, p. 164; K. O. Morgan, *Callaghan: A Life*, Oxford, Oxford University Press, 1997, p. 180.

48 Radice, *Friends & Rivals*, pp. 239–40; Rodgers, Interview with the author.

49 D. Kogan and M. Kogan, *The Battle for the Labour Party*, London, Kogan Page, 1982, pp. 17–35; H. Berrington, 'The Labour Left in Parliament: Maintenance, Erosion and Renewal', in D. Kavanagh (ed.), *The Politics of the Labour Party*, London, Allen & Unwin, 1982, pp. 69–94.

50 See Crewe and King, *SDP*, p. 55.

51 Berrington, 'The Labour Left in Parliament', pp. 70, 83. Also, the combined first-round vote for the left-wing candidates in the 1976 leadership election, Foot and Benn, registered a respectable 127 (ninety for Foot and thirty-seven for Benn).

52 See P. Norton, *Dissension in the House of Commons 1974–1979*, Oxford, Clarendon Press, 1980, pp. 431–2, 434–7.

53 Kogan and Kogan, *The Battle for the Labour Party*, pp. 35–7, 46.

54 Labour Party Annual Conference Report (LPACR) 1977, pp. 11, 379–80; also see Kogan and Kogan, *The Battle for the Labour Party*, pp. 36–53.

55 LPACR 1977, p. 381.
56 Given that Labour's 1974 manifesto was conceived as a relatively radical left-wing document, there is some irony in the name of the group. It was coined by Jim Wellbeloved to indicate that 'when we call ourselves the Manifesto Group, we don't mean that we like the manifesto, what we mean is that the manifesto is as far as we're prepared to bloody well go': cited in Desai, *Intellectuals and Socialism*, p. 171.
57 *Reform and Democracy in the Labour Party: A Joint Statement by CLV and the Manifesto Group of MPs*, September 1979, Neville Sandelson Papers, 6/3.
58 See V. McKee, *Right-wing Factionalism in the British Labour Party 1977–87*, unpublished M.Phil. Thesis, CNAA, 1988, pp. 43–5.
59 B. Brivati and D. Wincott (eds), 'The Campaign for Democratic Socialism 1960–64', Witness Seminar, *Contemporary Record: The Journal of Contemporary British History*, 7 (2), 1993, pp. 363–4.
60 See Marquand, *The Progressive Dilemma*, pp. 170, 174–5; also see G. Radice, 'Revisionism Revisited', *Socialist Commentary*, May 1974, pp. 25–7.
61 D. Marquand, 'The Challenge to the Labour Party', *Political Quarterly*, 46, 1975, p. 398.
62 Bill Rodgers, Interview with the author: the expression of left-wing discontent was a direct consequence of the perceived inadequacies of the 1964–70 Labour Governments and was, at least partly, facilitated by the fragmentation and disorganisation of the right resulting from deep-rooted splits over the European issue.
63 J. P. Mackintosh, 'Socialism or Social Democracy? The Choice for the Labour Party', in D. Marquand (ed.), *John P. Mackintosh on Parliament and Social Democracy*, London, Longman, 1982, p. 155.
64 P. Norton, *Dissension in the House of Commons 1974–1979*, pp. 429, 438.
65 R. Broad, *Labour's European Dilemmas: From Bevin to Blair*, Basingstoke, Palgrave, 2001; H. Young, *This Blessed Plot: Britain and Europe from Churchill to Blair*, Basingstoke, Macmillan, 1998, pp. 257–305.
66 See, for example, P. Clarke, *A Question of Leadership: From Gladstone to Thatcher*, Harmondsworth, Penguin, 1992, p. 263.
67 See Crewe and King, *SDP*, pp. 106–14 and Desai, *Intellectuals and Socialism*, p.146 for relative views of its significance in this respect.
68 Marquand, *The Progressive Dilemma*, pp. 169–70, 176–8.
69 S. Crosland, *Tony Crosland*, London, Jonathan Cape, 1982, p. 222.
70 Shaw, *The Labour Party since 1945*, p. 116.
71 Desai, *Intellectuals and Socialism*, pp. 145–6; T. Nairn, 'The Left Against Europe', *New Left Review*, 75 (September–October), 1972, p. 75.
72 Desai, *Intellectuals and Socialism*, pp. 146–50, 170–2; and see Hayter, *Fightback!*, pp. 50, 51–2, 71–2.
73 Crewe and King, *SDP*, pp. 104, 106.
74 L. Minkin, *The Contentious Alliance: Trade Unions and the Labour Party*, Edinburgh, Edinburgh University Press, 1991, pp. 208–13. John P. Mackintosh, for one, was particularly critical of what he saw as the corporatist roots of Britain's crisis and aware of the need to restore the balance between equality and liberty in social democratic theory and practice: see J. P. Mackintosh, 'Britain's Malaise: Political or Economic?', in Marquand, *John P. Mackintosh*, 1982, pp. 202–20; J. P. Mackintosh, 'Liberty and Equality: Getting the Balance Right', in Marquand, *John P. Mackintosh*, pp. 182–9.
75 See J. Jupp, 'The British Social Democrats and the Crisis in the British Labour Party', *Politics*, 16 (2), 1981, pp. 253–60.
76 B. Castle, *The Castle Diaries 1964–1976*, London, Macmillan, 1990, pp. 342–3.

77 B. Castle, *Fighting All The Way*, London, Macmillan, 1994, p. 419.

78 S. Crosland, *Tony Crosland*, p. 202.

79 Minkin, *The Contentious Alliance*, pp. 208–9.

80 See S. Brittan, *Left and Right: The Bogus Dilemma*, London, Secker & Warburg, 1968; S. Brittan, 'Further Thoughts on Left and Right', in S. Brittan, *Capitalism and the Permissive Society*, London, Macmillan, 1973, pp. 354, 358–9.

81 Tomlinson, Interview with the author; also see M. Francis, 'Mr Gaitskell's Ganymede? Re-assessing Crosland's *The Future of Socialism*', *Contemporary British History*, 11 (2), 1997, pp. 61–2; G. Goodman, 'The Soul of Socialism', in G. Goodman (ed.), *The State of the Nation: The Political Legacy of Aneurin Bevan*, London, Gollancz, 1997, pp. 30–1; R. Hattersley, 'Crosland died 25 years ago: But his definition of a good society is still the best I know', *The Guardian*, 18 February 2002; A. Howard, 'It is savagely appropriate that the 25th anniversary of Crosland's death should mark the moment Labour renounces loyalty to him', *The Times*, 12 February 2002; R. Wicks, 'Revisionism in the 1950s: The Ideas of Anthony Crosland', in C. Navari (ed.), *British Politics and the Spirit of the Age*, Keele, Keele University Press, 1996, pp. 199–217.

82 Marquand, *The Progressive Dilemma*, p. 187.

83 G. Daly, *The Crisis in the Labour Party 1974–81 and the Origins of the 1981 Schism*, unpublished Ph.D. Thesis, University of London, 1992, pp. 48–9.

84 Jenkins, *A Life at the Centre*, p. 217; Radice, *Friends & Rivals*, pp. 151–3.

85 See Daly, *The Crisis in the Labour Party*, pp. 56–62. Healey regarded Crosland as a theoretical economist who paid scant attention to financial realities and practicalities.

86 See S. Crosland, *Tony Crosland*, pp. 376–82; Daly, *The Crisis in the Labour Party*, pp. 51–5; Whitehead, *The Writing on the Wall*, pp. 256–8. Crosland's resistance to the principle of spending cuts was indicative of his 'democratic socialist' philosophy of a society characterised by a high measures of egalitarian social change.

87 See V. Mckee, 'Fragmentation on the Labour Right 1975–87', *Politics*, 11 (1), 1991, pp. 25–6; V. McKee, 'Scattered Brethren: British Social Democrats', *Social Studies Review*, 6 (5), 1991, pp. 171–3.

88 See, for example, Norton, *Dissension in the House of Commons 1974–1979*; D. M. Wood and W. G. Jacoby, 'Intraparty Cleavage in the British House of Commons: Evidence from the 1974–1979 Parliament', *American Journal of Political Science*, 28 (1), 1984, pp. 203–23.

2

The parliamentary Labour right: views and perspectives

Conceptually, the Labour 'right' is not without its problems. Designation of the label 'right-wing' to individuals and groups of a left-wing party can be difficult and unsatisfactory given its often pejorative implications.[1] There has also been a tendency to homogenise complex (and often conflicting) groups of traditions and ideas into some sort of undifferentiated non-left, moderate, loyalist tendency. Richard Heffernan, for example, sums up the orthodoxy of writing Labour's history when he describes the Labour Party as 'a left–right political coalition fashioned by its labourist political culture . . . The historical division most often alluded to is that between a majority right and a minority left, most recently modernisers and traditionalists in new and old Labour.' The dominant position of the former in the PLP has ensured a 'centrist, indeed predominantly right-wing institution' and 'leadership support base'.[2] Hence, Alan Warde has been able to suggest that it has been:

> unfortunate that ideological diversity within the Party has been distilled into the hoary imagery of a left–right continuum. While serviceable enough in everyday usage, the distinction becomes a liability in precise, historical analysis. One of its failings is that it imposes non-existent continuities, by neglecting to specify the content of alternative strategies and philosophies at stake. Hence the fact that the right has been, variously, socialist, utilitarian, and liberal, with distinct and important consequences for British politics, is lost from view.[3]

This chapter addresses the dimensions of the complex ideological and political character, development and trajectory of Labour's post-war 'dominant coalition'. It surveys the broader historical and ideological terrain of the Labour right, and reviews attempts to disaggregate what many have considered to be Labour's monolithic dominant 'right-wing' or revisionist tendency. It suggests that the Labour right was a complex, heterogeneous, loose coalition of tendencies, profoundly divided over key policy themes and even basic philosophical concepts. The inability of this diverse body of opinion to unite in the party and wider economic and political context of the 1970s had important consequences for the Labour Party and British politics. First, it will consider some of the difficulties of defining the Labour 'right' in terms of the criteria used to define placement on Labour's left–right ideological spectrum. Second, it will address the theoretical basis of its ideological and political disposition, including the potential conflict of concepts of liberty and equality in social democratic philosophy. This tension emerged in debates and divisions over industrial relations and trade union reform and the limits of public expenditure in the 1970s. Third, it will address the analytical limitations of principal conceptualisations of Labour's dominant homogeneous right-wing or revisionist tendency, which neglect the underlying complexity and tensions of the parliamentary Labour right and emerging fracture of Gaitskellite revisionism. Finally, it offers a sympathetic critique of accounts and typologies that disaggregate the standardised concept of the Labour 'right' in an attempt to provide a more discriminating and fluid conception of its constituent beliefs, ideas, traditions, personal affiliations, strategies and tactical considerations. This approach will be given contextual and empirical substance in the case study chapters that follow.

'Defining' the Labour 'right'

As noted, the nebulous concept of the Labour 'right' has been difficult to define in any generally agreed and objective sense. One difficulty is that 'few in the Labour Party admit to being on its right unless they are about to jump ship'. In their ideological battles with the Tribunites in the 1950s, for instance, the Gaitskellites claimed to represent the centre of the party in their loyalty to the parliamentary leadership against the so-called democratic socialist left.[4] It is not always easy to clearly distinguish between the centre and right of the PLP. It is 'always very difficult to decide where the line is'.[5] Where do the 'large and amorphous' centre in the party, or even the 'Morrisonian consolidators', give way to the 'firm right'?[6]

In their classic study of the SDP, Ivor Crewe and Anthony King provide definitions of varying degrees of specificity. On a broad level, they define Labour's right-wing in the 1970s as 'all those . . . who did not think of themselves as left-wingers and did not belong to left-wing organisations like the Tribune Group or the Campaign for Labour Party Democracy'. According to this definition, there were 'about 150 MPs on the Labour right in 1981, comprising most of those who did not vote for Michael Foot on the first ballot in the 1980 party leadership contest'. A 'narrower definition of "right wing" might reduce the size of the right in parliament to about 120, somewhere between the number who voted for Denis Healey on the first ballot in 1980 (112) and the number who voted for him on the second (129)', although not all those who voted for Healey in 1980 might be considered committed right-wingers.[7] They also suggest that a 'different indicator produces a similar number. There remained in the 1979 parliament 118 MPs who in July 1975 had signed a letter of support for Reg Prentice when he faced de-selection by his local party in Newham North-East.'[8]

There were a number of partly overlapping right-wing groups and organisations in the PLP during the 1970s. The Manifesto Group, which organised the 'right-wing' slate for Shadow Cabinet elections, could depend on a core membership of about eighty, but this reflected a broader centre-right range of opinion in the PLP. The combined vote of 'the two indisputably right-wing candidates, Jenkins and Healey' in the first round of the 1976 party leadership contest was eighty-six,[9] but was probably not an absolute reflection of right-wing representation in the PLP as a number of those considered to be of the right supported Callaghan as the most effective anti-left unity candidate. None of these estimations appear adequate or tell us much about the constituent beliefs, ideas, traditions and strategies of the Labour 'right'. Beyond narrow personal affiliations and tactical considerations, there is a need to say more about the criteria used to define placement on Labour's left–right ideological spectrum.

The theory and ideology of the Labour right: the formative and cohesive influence of *The Future of Socialism*

A distinct literature of Labour right theory emerged in the aftermath of the 1945–51 Labour Governments in the writings of the so-called 'New Thinkers'. Broadly, it aimed at revising traditional socialist analysis on the basis that the worst excesses of pre-war capitalism had been ameliorated by the policies of the Labour Government and the socio-economic changes of the immediate post-war years had rendered capitalism manageable for social purposes.[10] Crosland's major work, *The Future of Socialism* (1956), offered by far the most sustained and articulate synthesis of post-war revisionist social democratic thought. It offered a political analysis and strategy and central revisionist framework around which broadly similar intellectual dispositions might coalesce.[11]

Crosland forcefully deconstructed traditional Marxist/socialist arguments concerning the nature of capitalism and capitalist society as it had manifested itself 'in post-war British or Scandinavian society after several years of Labour government'. The harsh, private and profit-driven character of pre-war capitalism had been dismantled and replaced by 'a qualitatively different kind of society'.[12] In light of the apparent metamorphosis of capitalism, he proposed a significant revision of traditional socialist means and ends. On the basis of changes in the economic order, he predicted continuous economic growth on a scale sufficient to produce an adequate fiscal dividend to underwrite the case for the redistributive egalitarianism at the centre of his ideological and political project. The particular economic arrangements were less important; it was the social management of economic growth that now mattered. Public ownership and nationalisation were relegated to just one means among many to achieve the goal of greater economic and social equality. The reformulation of democratic socialism emphasised consistent and stable economic growth, the expansion and equalisation of educational opportunities, and a mixed and balanced public-private industrial sector that reflected changing social trends and developments.

Crosland's work represented an attempt to recast the conceptual balance of Labour's socialism in ethical rather than economic terms. In this respect, his ideas 'came to stand for the platform of the Right within the party'. The willingness to confront directly issues of public ownership and equality 'gave an intellectual

expression to the concerns and aspirations of many on the right wing of the party'
and, in the hands of the Labour leader, Hugh Gaitskell, 'Crosland's writings
became an important weapon against the Bevanite Left' in the bitter intra-party
conflicts of the period. Crosland's concern to move 'from an economic to a social
conception of equality' and diminish traditional socialist arguments and methods,
was regarded with some distrust by many of the 'fundamentalist' left. In the intra-
party political context of the time, however, Crosland's work was (and has been)
caricatured as a right-wing Gaitskellite manifesto. Although his economic and
social analysis broke with Labour's established doctrine, Crosland's evaluation
largely 'pursued traditional socialist lines: both inequality and class feature
strongly'. His prescriptions included a strong degree of redistributive equality. His
critique of sacred means angered traditionalists 'even when his ideas were radical
in their policy implications . . . or when they expressed concerns which were shared
by the Left'.[13]

Crosland intended a thoroughgoing transformative equality that sought to
overthrow traditional patterns of status, privilege and wealth in British society.
To view him as simply 'on the right' or as a 'revisionist' conceals more than it
reveals of the fundamental ideological character of his analysis and prescriptions.
His clear egalitarian philosophy and vision of democratic socialism distinguished
him to some extent from less intuitively egalitarian revisionists, who were brought
together as much by the force of Gaitskell's charismatic personality and leadership
and the promise of Labour Government after thirteen 'wasted years' in opposition
between 1951 and 1964 as much as by a shared sense of egalitarian fundamentalism.[14] As developments of the 1970s began to undermine the economic
foundations of Crosland's egalitarian philosophy, an emerging strand of Labour's
Gaitskellite revisionist tradition was already moving away from (if they had ever
fully accepted) the elemental ideological glue of Crosland's egalitarian principles.

Tensions of equality and liberty in social democratic theory

A further implicit theme of the new revisionist thinking was some discussion of
whether the pursuit of equality was a danger to individual liberty.[15] Roy Jenkins
had written that the 'desire for greater equality has been part of the inspiration
of all socialist thinkers and of all socialist movements. The absence of this desire,
indeed, provides the most useful of all exclusive definitions of socialism. Where
there is no egalitarianism there is no socialism.' He also noted that the protection
of liberty was still necessary, 'ensuring that our new society of near equals is left
confronting a state machine in which power, both economic and political, is as
widely diffused as possible'.[16] This dilemma re-emerged much more starkly for
some Labour revisionists in the context of the 1970s as the New Right critique of
trade union collectivism and the 'electoral liabilities of various labour institutions'
came to the fore. It remained an 'unresolved problem' of social democratic theory
of reconciling an 'individual-focused and negative concept of freedom – absence
of restraint – with trade union collectivism and the culture that sustained it'
in the industrial sphere. One revisionist strand had 'always defined freedom in

positive terms as 'something that needs to be enlarged' rather than as simply the absence of restraint. Such a perspective could more readily appreciate the benefits to the individual of collective capacity in the face of the powers of the employers', but others now openly questioned whether the pursuit of equality had 'gone far enough' and whether it was time to 'reassert' the 'freedom of the individual'.[17]

For some, the fundamental difference of political principle between left and right (and between the 'Left of the Left' and the 'Right of the Left') is 'the difference in the relative priority assigned to the traditional ideals of liberty and equality': 'for the Left of the Left, equality has unequivocal priority over liberty . . . for the Right of the Left, equality has priority over liberty provided that both are constrained by the ancillary value of justice'. On the egalitarian left, 'the priority given to equality can genuinely follow from a conviction that without a restriction on the liberties of the better-off . . . the absolute as well as the relative position of the disadvantaged is bound to worsen'. On the liberal left, 'the appeal to justice can genuinely follow from a conviction that all inequalities have to be defensible to those who are disadvantaged by them and that all institutions ought therefore to be so designed and controlled that privilege is distributed as widely as is compatible with basic individual freedom'.[18] Respective intellectual perspectives of the relative balance and priority of fundamental philosophical concepts remained a problematic tension of Labour Party revisionism, and was an underlying feature of political and policy divisions of the parliamentary Labour right in the 1970s. They may also offer a further dimension to explanations of the 'considerable defector-loyalist puzzle' of the SDP. Crewe and King suggest that the answer to this puzzle lies in the nature of respective backgrounds in, and attachments to, the Labour Party. They claim that Roy Hattersley, for example, although sympathetic with the founders of the SDP on the critical issue of European membership, remained in the Labour Party in 1981 on the grounds that 'by his background and . . . path of entry into the Labour Party . . . was very much a party machine man'.[19] But what does that make someone such as Bill Rodgers? He claims to be 'someone who believes in social justice and doesn't find acceptable the social inequalities which were all around me and growing up in the 1930s this was absolutely plain . . . Because I'm basically a Labour man and I joined when I was sixteen'.[20]

Hattersley possessed a fundamental belief in the egalitarian foundations of freedom, and has never wavered from the ethical framework provided by Tony Crosland: that socialism 'is about the pursuit of equality and the protection of freedom – in the knowledge that until we are truly equal we will not be truly free' and that 'the good society is the equal society'.[21] Influenced by Tawney, Crosland and, 'to an extent', John Rawls, his position involved absolute loyalty to the idea (as 'the first political obligation') and priority 'of creating a more equal society'.[22] In contrast, a keener sense of the limits and potential dangers to liberty of egalitarian 'redistribution of material wealth' based on high levels of public expenditure is apparent in the 'exit' texts of those who founded the SDP. A common theme in this writing is that the interpretation of socialism as just equality, and equality only in terms of distribution, represents a narrow definition that underplays the 'predisposition for liberty' of 'any thinking democrat'. The relentless pursuit of equality through distribution might be used as 'justification for abandoning liberty . . . to be sure of achieving equality'. Rodgers, for example, argued in Jenkinsite terms that just as 'public *ownership* was not socialism', the Croslandite preoccupation with 'public *expenditure* is not socialism either'.[23] It represents a different approach to the nature of equality and the centrality of public expenditure to that end to that expressed in Hattersley's observation of the repercussions of the IMF crisis that '[s]ocialism is about equality and we cannot have greater equality if we cut public spending'.[24]

Rodgers and other Jenkinsites were increasingly critical of the view that (high) public spending was, by definition, virtuous. As the 'mass abundance' predicted by Crosland did not materialise, and as levels of economic growth receded, Rodgers was concerned with the lack of attention paid to value for money across the public services. He argued that increased public expenditure should be 'dependent on achieving economic growth and rising personal living standards *first*'. Perhaps owing more to Evan Durbin than Crosland, whom he considered to be 'courageous and clear-headed . . . about the meaning of freedom', he claimed that individuals desired more control of their own lives. This demanded greater attention to individual freedom, including lower personal taxation, and to certain spheres of collective activity such as greater industrial democracy in which individuals were more effectively included in decisions governing their working lives.[25] The general thrust of his argument was that the Labour Party should recognise that most individuals now placed personal consumption and individual freedoms above the pursuit of equality. It was a view that 'lacked any sense of Crosland's commitment to equality as the central feature of Labour's vision of the future'.[26]

The emerging philosophical tension of social democratic theory and practice in the 1970s is explored further in the case study chapters concerned with industrial relations and trade union reform and debates over public expenditure and redistribution. The purpose of the final sections of this chapter is to offer a critical perspective of the main analytical constructions of the Labour right, which it argues are limited by a tendency to utilise a concept of a homogeneous, cohesive and loyalist unit, or a basic distinction between the old, authoritarian trade union or labourist right and an intellectual, liberal revisionist tendency. They lack an explicit sense of the contextual complexity and divisions of the parliamentary Labour right and the emergence of a critical division of Labour Party revisionism in the 1970s.

Revisionists revise: misreading Labour Party revisionism?

Labour Party revisionism has been said to represent the 'most influential perspective concerning social democracy in the UK since the second world war' and, during the 1950s, 'became established as the basis of Labour's social democracy'.[27] The 'revisionist approach', is often represented as a homogeneous and fixed intellectual and political social democratic doctrine and strategy.[28] Revisionism is often defined simply in terms of views of a particular socialist method (nationalisation) and a broader economic perception (belief in a reformed capitalism).[29] However, the term 'is itself problematic, a short-hand for a clutch of sometimes disparate approaches'. Its analytical value depends on 'remembering the historical disjunctures and complexities of that very tradition'.[30] David Lipsey reminds us that 'revisionists revise'. Revisionism, as a relative, historically contingent and progressive disposition,

> is not a body of doctrine. It was not what ... Bernstein [or Crosland] thought. Revisionism was and is a cast of mind ... that says: here is the world, here are the most important facts about it, here are the values we bring to bear on the facts, here are our conclusions. Indeed [Crosland] was always looking to see who would be writing the new *Future of Socialism* for a changing world.[31]

Revisionism represents a historically dependent process of (re)emphasis and modernisation, as opposed to a broader ideological approach. It is a tradition only in the sense that it is a continuous reflection of specific practices: scrutiny of means, wider analysis of contemporary perspectives and policies and some radicalism in the willingness to embrace change. In the context of the Labour Party, and in broader political terms, revisionism represents not a homogeneous ideological tradition or project but, rather, a historically informed political task or process. Revisionism does not possess a set of core principles but is, rather, a practical means of accommodating change.[32] Labour Party revisionism has incorporated diverse, historically specific varieties of revisionist thought, ideas and strategies ranging, chronologically, from Bernstein, Tawney, Jay, Durbin, Crosland,[33] through to the neo-revisionism of those such as Hattersley, Radice, Bryan Gould and Austin Mitchell in the 1980s,[34] and even the rethinking of fundamentals undertaken by New Labour.[35]

Labour Party revisionism of the mid-1950s was not without its own complexities and internal differences. There were a 'complex of ideas associated with this grouping' of 'self-styled "revisionist" thinkers', ranging from 'the "ethical" revisionism of Allan Flanders' (and the Socialist Union) to 'the "sociological" current of ... Crosland', with Rita Hinden's *Socialist Commentary* offering an intellectual bridge to the different 'social democratic networks'.[36] While Gaitskellite revisionists were broadly united on what they saw as the negative aspects of Labour's doctrine, such as public ownership and economic planning, they were much less agreed on the precise meanings of equality and social justice and failed to establish 'a clear unequivocal doctrine of equality complete with strategies suitable for its realization'.

Differences over key components of social democratic strategy, including redistribution, education policy and the nature of equality, exposed a 'void in Gaitskellite egalitarianism' and contained the seeds of 'a future division within Keynesian socialism which was later to prove extremely damaging'. Some revisionist intellectuals around Gaitskell, such as Jay and Jenkins (and often Gaitskell himself), 'developed an increasingly liberal bias, stressing individual freedom, a predominantly free market economy and a broad equality of opportunity'. Crosland 'developed rather different ideas' in his goal of greater social equality rather than a more limited 'straightforward meritocratic equality of opportunity'. Although broadly supportive of the conviction that '"equality" should be regarded as the centrepiece of socialism', embryonic divisions were discernible in education policy and approach to industrial relations in the 1950s that reflected different understandings of equality and 'visions' of the egalitarian future. In the context of the 1970s, and after further differences over British membership of the Common Market and Crosland's decision to support Callaghan rather than George Brown in the leadership contest after Gaitskell's premature death setting him slightly apart, 'personal and policy disagreements, and the obvious difference of vision in which they were rooted, had developed to the point where Keynesian socialism terminally divided between a Croslandite and "Jenkinsite" or liberal Keynesian variant'.[37]

Representations of the (parliamentary) Labour right

The dimensions of the parliamentary Labour right more broadly have been represented in three main ways. First, there are those who emphasise the standard left–right dichotomy and, occasionally, a nebulous, non-aligned centre motivated by the desire 'to hold the ring and reconcile the warring factions'.[38] As noted, this distinction has often been framed in terms of divergent attitudes to the centrality of public ownership and the meaning of socialism.[39] Second, those who adopt variations of the rudimentary distinction between the intellectual, revisionist social democratic right and non-intellectual, pragmatic, old trade union right.[40] As noted, there are problems with basic schemes of analysis. They posit homogeneous, unchanging 'doctrinal' blocs or factions that cohere around fundamental ideological positions on a largely single theme or issue. They often do not account for the complexity or anomalies of such broad categories in particular historical contexts or circumstances. There is also a tendency to conflate the parliamentary Labour right with a dominant revisionist leadership tendency and lump together the non-revisionist Labour right in an ill-defined 'centre' or 'consolidator' camp. They also say little about the diversity and contradictions of 'revisionism' (or for that matter, 'fundamentalism'). Rudimentary distinctions of Labour right tendencies have been consolidated against the backdrop of the SDP split by a 'loyalist and secessionist' framework of analysis,[41] which does not fully explain the discrepancies of Labour's revisionist tradition and personnel in this process. Third, there has been some attempt, characterised by recognition of recurrent, systematic intra-party segmental competition and conflict that often transcend conventional intra-party dimensions,[42] or analysis of underlying intellectual and philosophical currents,[43] to provide a more eclectic sense of the constituent traditions and components of the parliamentary Labour right (and shades of Labour Party revisionism).

'Revisionists' and 'consolidators'
The orthodoxy (and some of the problems) of defining the Labour right has been encapsulated as follows:

[u]ntil the 1970s the term 'Right' was simply used in the labour movement to denote the established leadership of that movement and its policies . . . For over sixty years 'Right' has meant those who wish to move slowly, if at all, towards a socialist society in which the major part of the economy will be collectively owned, while 'Left' has meant those who wish to move quickly in that direction.

Otherwise, variations of a basic distinction have been made between 'the machine-union Right' and 'the Fabian intellectual Right'. Historically, they shared support for parliamentary democracy, belief in limited nationalisation and opposition to forms of revolutionary socialism and communism. The 'machine-union Right' was 'sustained throughout the 1930s, 1940s and 1950s by union leaders like Bevin, Citrine . . . and by party organisers like Morrison and Morgan Phillips'. As the 'Right' dominated the party at all crucial points, it had little need of intellectual justification. The most important intellectual influences were those of Keynes and Beveridge from outside the party. Almost the only attempt in the party to elaborate a thorough gradualist theoretical position was made by Evan Durbin (who died in 1948, having influenced Gaitskell). By the 1950s, the Labour right could broadly be identified by its support for the consolidation of the policies and achievements of the Attlee governments. However, Gaitskell's emergence as party leader in the 1950s aroused a desire to develop a clearer intellectual case for the Labour's right which, in turn, precipitated a clearer distinction between 'consolidators' and revisionists as Labour's 'two schools of moderation'. Gaitskell 'felt it necessary to redefine the party's ideology and purpose. In so doing he elaborated a specifically "Right" ideology which has served those calling themselves social-democrats ever since. Nearly all the . . . defectors are those who followed Gaitskell in this exercise between 1955 and 1963.'[44] The latter point represents a questionable assertion that fails to address the dynamics and divisions of Labour Party revisionism particularly.

Particularly, the case of British membership of the Common Market betrays the notion of a homogeneous, hegemonic revisionism from as early as the summer of 1962 after Macmillan's decision to seek entry in 1961. It reflected the range of opinion of Labour revisionists, from the outright support of those such as Jenkins, Rodgers, Marquand and Shirley Williams to the more studied or pragmatic ambivalence of Crosland and Healey, to the outright opposition of those such as Douglas Jay, Patrick Cordon Walker and Gaitskell himself.[45] It was, perhaps, 'the clearest sign' of the complexity and potential fragmentation of Labour Party revisionism and the parliamentary right. It was also a major factor in the emerging 'oppositional' status of the core Jenkinsite grouping in the party. Jenkins had already demonstrated his dissent from official Labour Party policy when he resigned from the front bench in response to the conditions which Harold Wilson had laid down in the House of Commons as essential to Labour's acceptance of EEC membership after Macmillan's bid to join in July 1961.[46] In the vote on the principle of British entry into the Common Market in October 1971, he led sixty-nine pro-EEC Labour rebels into the Conservative Government division lobby. This was followed swiftly in April 1972 by his resignation as deputy leader of the party after Wilson agreed a compromise between the pro- and anti-European factions to hold a referendum on the terms of entry agreed by the Heath

Government. During the 1975 Common Market referendum, the cross-party, pro-European platform of Jenkins and his supporters was pursued in opposition to official Labour Party and TUC, although not necessarily government, policy.[47]

'Consolidators' were, perhaps, less identifiable and cohesive as a tendency of the parliamentary Labour right than revisionists. They lacked the intellectual and theoretical foundations of revisionism and a firm organisational basis, 'but possessed enough stable characteristics to merit separate recognition'. The amorphous social democratic consolidator tendency was significant as much for the range of its personnel as its political strategy. Parliamentary representatives of this tendency at various times have included an assortment of experience and opinion on the Labour right, ranging from Callaghan, Healey, Hattersley, Eric Varley, Fred Mulley and John Golding and, more recently, the likes of Gerald Kaufman and Austin Mitchell. Even 'Crosland drifted towards this camp after tactically deserting Jenkins around 1972', and Labour right and centre-right trade union leaders 'all proved firm advocates', among whom there was solid 'hostility towards the Left, but also a will for keeping Jenkins at arms length'. Key consolidator themes included a preference for constitutionalism and antagonism towards Marxist and other doctrinaire political philosophy and a 'marked distaste' of factionalism of both left-wing and revisionist varieties. The issue of Europe had failed to rouse much enthusiasm, but on issues of defence there was more agreement between the two tendencies. In the absence of an explicit intellectual position, consolidators relied upon

> other, less sophisticated, identities. They were essentially Labour loyalists, orthodox and moderate, working class in personnel and character . . . Their primary concerns have been Labour unity, halting the Left, winning elections, and consolidating Labour in public office . . . Accordingly, though Revisionism and Consolidationism occupied much common ground, nevertheless their accents, styles and priorities differed. So too did their ultimate destinations.[48]

The basic orthodox distinction of 'revisionists' and 'consolidators' is not without its limitations. Attitudes to the Common Market issue were not an unambiguous reflection of divisions between revisionists and consolidators.[49] A number of so-called consolidators cut their ideological and political teeth as erstwhile Gaitskellite revisionists. The post-1981 split in the Labour Party is used as a post-hoc justification of a simple distinction between 'revisionists' and 'consolidators', given that a core feature of the latter was a commitment to party loyalty and unity. In so doing, Labour's post-war revisionist tradition is reduced to the small, liberal and unequivocally pro-European and increasingly marginal Jenkinsite perspective. Although his future remained to fight in a defeated and divided Labour Party in 1981, as a self-professed, unreconstructed Croslandite egalitarian, Roy Hattersley, for instance, could not be considered to be a 'consolidator' in the Morrisonian or even the Callaghanite or Healey sense. Crosland, himself, although he was perhaps to develop a more consolidatory approach as a politician and minister in the context of the intra-party debates and divisions of the 1970s, also uneasily straddles the conventional distinction of 'revisionists' and 'consolidators'.[50]

Intra-party 'social tendencies' and competition

Further attempts have been made to transcend the basic left–right scheme of Labour's intra-party divisions. Attempts to chronicle the main currents and conflicts in the development of Labour's post-war strategy have been framed in terms of competition between factions or 'social tendencies' advocating competing and often incompatible strategies or 'visions' for Labour. This perspective contends that 'intra-party conflict can best be understood in terms of competing strategies, where strategy is more than ideology and where segments, as bearers of strategy, are not reducible simply to organized groups with boundaries identifiable through the conscious appropriation of a group identity'. To 'understand the cleavages and the trajectory of the Party its members must be seen as collective bearers of social interests within a complex social system which is a severe constraint on both consciousness and action'. These intra-party 'segments' and 'strategies' are variously described as 'social reformism', 'fundamentalism' and 'technocratic-collectivism' and 'Keynesian socialist', 'qualitative' and 'technocratic'. 'Social reformism' provided the 'architecture' of the post-war consensus and consisted primarily of 'the New Thinkers', the 'Gaitskellites' or 'Revisionists' who, 'instead of reviving socialism, substituted a quite distinct tradition of political thought – New Liberalism'. Socialist 'fundamentalism' has been the antithesis of, and subordinate to, 'social reform'. 'Technocratic-collectivism' is described as largely a temporary expedient; as a product of those who frequently 'seek to procure a compromise between various segments in the Party'. It 'has been deemed either an opportunistic pragmatism, or a "centrist" tactic aimed at establishing unity'. Technocratic-collectivism lacked 'the kind of ideological coherence of Social Reformism. It was a hybrid combination of various themes, which bore some relationship to classical Fabianism, but which drew on several traditions of thought within the Labour heritage.'[51]

This perspective usefully locates Labour's conventional intra-party dimensions and groupings in wider currents and conflicts over the party's social strategy. It acknowledges the demise of 'social reformism' in the period 1970–78. It further acknowledges the fact that at different times each of the 'strategies' or 'visions' divided, 'producing an additional or alternative understanding . . . from within the original', and the bifurcation of 'Keynesian socialism' into 'liberal' and 'socialist' variants, 'the first signs of which emerged in the 1950s, though the major split occurred in the early 1970s'. However, the 'construction of pure types of strategic orientation' remains very reminiscent of standard, often undifferentiated categories of left, right and centre, or fundamentalism, revisionism and the compromise between them of centre-left technocratic 'modern socialism' or 'Wilsonism', and only partly manages to complexify what Alan Warde frustratingly describes as 'the hoary imagery of a left-right continuum' that dominates representations of Labour's ideological character.

Intellectual currents of the parliamentary Labour right

With the odd important exception, few studies have directly addressed the 'intellectual stockpot' of Labour's political thought. Histories of the Labour Party have often 'tended to ignore the political thought underlying its development' and constituent components and traditions beyond broad left–right dimensions.[52] Views of Labour as a 'non-ideological party, intent merely on gaining parliamentary power irrespective of principle' have tended to neglect 'the diversity and limitations of its political thought'.[53] Possibly, this has been a reflection of the perceived 'moderation' and 'pragmatism' of the historically dominant right-wing parliamentary leadership.

There has been some attempt to identify the different ideas, traditions and general 'intellectual milieu' that challenge 'the received opinion of the Labour Right being a homogeneous group' and 'to explain subsequent events and divisions within the Party's hegemonic group'. These intellectual traditions have been summarised as the 'radical liberalism' associated with Jenkins, with its intellectual roots in the thinking of Edwardian New Liberalism; the 'Fabianism' supposedly personified by Gaitskell; the 'democratic socialism' best represented in the work of Crosland; 'trade union economism' and 'non-intellectual gradualism' represented by the likes of Callaghan and George Brown; and the 'pragmatic radicalism' of such diverse 'centrists' as Wilson, Healey, Crossman and Shore whose 'rhetoric [was] often at variance with their practice', and who shared a 'technocratic approach to problems and a belief in statism in the sense of running the economy and social welfare provisions'.[54]

In the literature these 'groups of ideas' are often conflated in more manageable political 'chunks', although Tim Bale strikes a note of caution that the 'interaction of ideology and political actors' is far from clear. It assumes that abstract, 'rootless' and 'exogenous, pre-existing ideological preferences' are the source of political perceptions and choices, and neglects 'how the variations in those preferences' are, at least in part, created and recreated 'by variations in institutional location'. It suggests an overly instrumental link between 'the ideologies and the interests of the various components of a party', and contributes to the artificial separation of 'the world of power struggles evidenced in the nitty gritty of manoeuvres over rules, roles and regulations' on the one hand, and 'some disembodied universe we call "political thought"', as expressed in the sacred tracts and texts, on the other.[55]

Conclusion

The intention here has not been to develop an alternative model or framework. It has been to identify the principal representations of the parliamentary Labour right, and to indicate their limitations, ambiguities an inconsistencies. The examples offered are by no means exhaustive, but intended to illustrate a line of argument and enquiry rather than to systematically document each framework or narrative. Attempts to analyse the parliamentary Labour right have taken three broad forms. First, a schema based on the standard monolithic political dimensions of left and right (and a nebulous and shifting centre). Second, a rudimentary distinction between old trade union right 'pragmatists' and intellectual revisionist 'dogmatists', to borrow Drucker's terms. However, it is not always clear where or when the boundaries of the distinction apply. Like the problematic dimensions of 'left' and 'right', they may be taken to imply that such groupings possess a uniformity of outlook. A simple distinction between 'labourists' and 'revisionists' fails to reveal the complexity and divisions of the parliamentary Labour right and Labour Party revisionism as they developed and emerged in the 1970s. As one participant reflects, 'it's always more complicated than that'. The distinction approximates in only

> a very, very rough and ready kind of way . . . if you take the so-called radical revisionists . . . it's not the case that they all went over to the SDP where as the trade union right did not all go over to the SDP. How would you classify somebody like [James] Wellbeloved for example? He certainly isn't . . . at first sight one of the intellectual revisionist social democrats, but he did go over to the SDP. On the other hand, how would you classify Giles Radice who did not go over to the SDP or Philip Whitehead who did not go over to the SDP . . . so . . . there are a lot of nuances for that picture.[56]

Third, there has been a wider attempt to address the variety of Labour's political thought and underlying intellectual influences of the constituent traditions and personnel of the parliamentary Labour right, although the extent to which they can be separated from institutional and political context as a guide to perceptions and preferences is problematic.

As one set of commentators note, 'ideology and behaviour that are relatively straight forward to identify or quantify deviate most unpredictably from traditional core positions in response to political and external factors and events'. A set of perceptions and preferences developed in political life and conflict might, at best, 'only approximate to a pure orientation'. It is preferable to analyse political identities and affiliations both 'through time' and 'in time'. It is important to think relationally as well as categorically.[57] There is a need to consider the interaction between core positions and political and institutional context. The political environment of the 1970s and the selected case studies provide an apposite opportunity to explore this interaction and to consider the explanatory limitations of conventional fixed conceptions of Labour's intra-party dimensions and divisions, and the character of the parliamentary Labour right. The following chapter addresses the complexity, divisions and intra-party vulnerability of the parliamentary Labour right through the lens of its atypical and ineffective group and factional organisation and activity in the 1970s.

Notes

1 See D. Hayter, *Fightback! Labour's Traditional Right in the 1970s and 1980s*, Manchester, Manchester University Press, 2005, pp. 6–7; D. Taverne, *The Future of the Left: Lincoln and After*, London, Jonathan Cape, 1974, pp. 8–9, 13–15.

2 R. Heffernan, 'Leaders and Followers: The Politics of the Parliamentary Labour Party', in B. Brivati and R. Heffernan (eds), *The Labour Party: A Centenary History*, Basingstoke, Macmillan, 2000, p. 246.

3 A. Warde, *Consensus and Beyond: The Development of Labour Party Strategy since the Second World War*, Manchester, Manchester University Press, 1982, p. 3.

4 H. M. Drucker, 'Changes in the Labour Party Leadership', *Parliamentary Affairs*, 34 (4), 1981, pp. 369–91.

5 W. Rodgers, Interview with the author, 18 February 2001; also see T. Bale, 'Broad Churches, Big Theory and One Small Example: Cultural Theory and Intra-party Politics', in M. Thompson, G. Grendstad and P. Selle (eds), *Cultural Theory as Political Science*, London, Routledge, 1999, p. 89; M. Wickham-Jones, *Economic Strategy and the Labour Party: Politics and Policy-Making, 1970–83*, London, Macmillan, 1996, p. 31.

6 See I. Crewe and A. King, *SDP: The Birth, Life and Death of the Social Democratic Party*, Oxford, Oxford University Press, 1995, p. 534; W. H. Greenleaf, *The British Political Tradition: Volume Two The Ideological Heritage*, London, Methuen, 1993, p. 474; L. Minkin, *The Labour Party Conference: A Study in the Politics of Intra-Party Democracy*, London, Allen Lane, 1978, p. 11.

7 Crewe and King, *SDP*, pp. 105–6, 534.

8 *Ibid.*, pp. 17, 534.

9 *Ibid.*, p. 534.

10 E. Burns, *Right Wing Labour: Its Theory & Practice*, London, Lawrence & Wishart, 1961, pp. 6–9, 14, 15–16; R. H. S. Crossman (ed.), *New Fabian Essays*, London, Turnstile Press, 1952; also see C. A. R. Crosland, 'The Transition from Capitalism', in Crossman (ed.), *New Fabian Essays*, pp. 33–8.

11 R. Hattersley, *Choose Freedom: The Future for Democratic Socialism*, London, Michael Joseph, 1987, p. xix; R. Hattersley, *Who Goes Home? Scenes from a Political Life*, London, Little, Brown, 1995, pp. 173, 179; R. Hattersley, 'Crosland died 25 years ago: But his definition of a good society is still the best I know', *The Guardian*, 18 February 2002; D. Marquand, *The Progressive Dilemma: From Lloyd George to Kinnock*, London, Heinemann, 1991, pp. 166–7; D. Marquand, *The New Reckoning: Capitalism, States and Citizens*, Cambridge, Polity Press, 1997, pp. 11–12; R. Plant (1996) 'Social Democracy', in D. Marquand and A. Seldon (eds), *The Ideas that Shaped Post-war Britain*, London, Fontana, 1996, pp. 165–6; Rodgers, Interview with the author.

12 C. A. R. Crosland, *The Future of Socialism*, London, Jonathan Cape, 1956, p. 63; also see Crosland, 'The Transition from Capitalism', pp. 33–45.

13 M. Francis, 'Mr Gaitskell's Ganymede? Re-assessing Crosland's *The Future of Socialism*', *Contemporary British History*, 11 (2), 1997, pp. 50–64; A. Howard, 'It is savagely appropriate that the 25th anniversary of Crosland's death should mark the moment Labour renounces loyalty to him', *The Times*, 12 February 2002; R. Wicks, 'Revisionism in the 1950s: the Ideas of Anthony Crosland', in C. Navari (ed.), *British Politics and the Spirit of the Age*, Keele, Keele University Press, 1996, pp. 204–12.

14 L. Abse, Interview with the author, 20 June 2001; L. Abse, *Private Member*, London, Macdonald, 1973.

15 E. Dell, *A Strange Eventful History: Democratic Socialism in Britain*, London, Harper Collins, 1999, p. 229; R. Jenkins, 'Equality', in Crossman (ed.), *New Fabian Essays*.

16 Jenkins, 'Equality', pp. 69, 88–9, 90.

17 L. Minkin, *The Contentious Alliance: Trade Unions and the Labour Party*, Edinburgh, Edinburgh University Press, 1991, pp. 212–13; also see S. Fielding, *The Labour Party: Continuity and Change in the Making of 'New' Labour*, Basingstoke, Palgrave, 2003, p. 71; J. P. Mackintosh, 'Liberty and Equality: Getting the Balance Right', in D. Marquand (ed.), *John P. Mackintosh on Parliament and Social Democracy*, London, Longman, 1982, p. 189; D. Taverne, *The Future of the Left: Lincoln and After*, London, Jonathan Cape, 1974, pp. 133–4.

18 W. G. Runciman, *Where is the Right of the Left?*, London, Tawney Society, 1983, pp. 1–2, 5; also see M. Freeden, *Ideologies and Political Theory: A Conceptual Approach*, Oxford, Clarendon Press, 1996, pp. 464–9; W. H. Greenleaf, *The British Political Tradition: Volume Two: The Ideological Heritage*, London, Methuen, 1983, 452–63.

19 Crewe and King, *SDP*, pp. 104, 113–14.
20 Rodgers, Interview with the author; also see W. Rodgers, *The Politics of Change*, London, Secker & Warburg, 1982, p. vi; W. Rodgers, *Fourth Among Equals*, London, Politico's, 2000, pp. 1–22.
21 R. Hattersley, *Choose Freedom: The Future for Democratic Socialism*, London, Michael Joseph, 1987, p. xix; also see R. Hattersley, 'Why I'm no longer loyal to Labour', *The Guardian*, 26 July 1997; R. Hattersley, 'Crosland died 25 years ago: But his definition of a good society is still the best I know', *The Guardian*, 18 February 2002; R. Hattersley, 'The enemy of liberty', *The Guardian*, 31 October 2005; R. Hattersley, 'Meritocracy is no substitute for equality', *New Statesman*, 6 February 2006.
22 Hattersley, 'Why I'm no longer loyal to Labour'; R. Hattersley, 'It's no longer my party', *The Observer*, 24 June 2001; R. Hattersley, 'The importance of loyalty to an idea is not just a matter of personal conscience. It is a requirement of genuine democracy', *New Statesman*, 11 July 2005.
23 D. Owen, *Face the Future*, Oxford, Oxford University Press, 1981, pp. 6–7; Rodgers, *The Politics of Change*, 7–9.
24 R. Hattersley, *Who Goes Home? Scenes from a Political Life*, London, Little, Brown, 1995, pp. 178–9; Rodgers, *Fourth Among Equals*, pp. 291–2; Rodgers, Interview with the author. Although Rodgers himself was unhappy with the stringent IMF terms and Healey's initial response, as he believed that appropriate levels of taxation and public spending were indispensable to social justice, he adopted a more measured approach to the public expenditure dilemma. Ultimately, he felt that Crosland's proposals 'were not credible as the alternative' and the need to be 'hard headed enough to do the sums . . . to recognise that in the end we have to find a solution that the IMF found acceptable . . . you have to have balance'.
25 W. Rodgers, 'Socialism Without Abundance', *Socialist Commentary*, July/August 1977; also see Owen, *Face the Future*, p. 6; Rodgers, *The Politics of Change*, pp. 4–8.
26 N. Ellison, *Egalitarian Thought and Labour Politics: Retreating Visions*, London, Routledge, 1994, p. 200.
27 M. Wickham-Jones, *Economic Strategy and the Labour Party: Politics and Policy-Making, 1970–83*, London, Macmillan, 1996, pp. 14, 34–5.
28 See M. Beech *The Political Philosophy of New Labour*, London, I. B. Tauris, 2006, p. 43; R. Desai, *Intellectuals and Socialism: 'Social Democrats' and the Labour Party*, London, Lawrence & Wishart, 1994; H. M. Drucker, 'Changes in the Labour Party Leadership', *Parliamentary Affairs*, 34 (4), 1981, pp. 374–5, 388; also see B. Brivati, 'Revisionists', *Socialist History*, 9, 1996, pp. 109–14 for a critical perspective of this tendency.
29 See P. Dunleavy, 'The Political Parties', in P. Dunleavy, A. Gamble, I. Holiday and G. Peele (eds), *Developments in British Politics 4*, London, Macmillan, 1993, pp. 123–43; M. Maor, *Political Parties & Party Systems: Comparative Approaches & the British Experience*, London, Routledge, 1997, pp. 155–60; T. Jones, *Remaking the Labour Party: From Gaitskell to Blair*, London, Routledge, 1996, pp. vii–viii, 2, 27–8.
30 S. Brooke, 'Evan Durbin: Reassessing a Labour "Revisionist"', *Twentieth Century British History*, 7 (1), 1996, pp. 29, 52.
31 D. Lipsey, 'Revisionists Revise', in D. Leonard (ed.), *Crosland and New Labour*, Basingstoke, Macmillan, 1999, pp. 14–15; David Lipsey, Interview with the author, 17 January 2001.
32 G. Radice, 'The Case for Revisionism', *Political Quarterly*, 59 (4), 1988, pp. 406–7; also see D. Lipsey, 'Crosland's Socialism', in D. Lipsey and D. Leonard (eds), *The Socialist Agenda: Crosland's Legacy*, London, Jonathan Cape, 1981, p. 35; G. Radice, *Labour's Path to Power: The New Revisionism*, Basingstoke, Macmillan, 1989, pp. 1–15.

33 M. Beech, 'Analysing the revisionist tradition of political thought in the Labour Party: Eduard Bernstein to New Labour', paper presented to the Third Essex Graduate Conference in Political Theory, University of Essex, 17–18 May 2002.

34 Fielding, *The Labour Party*, pp. 70–3; N. Thompson, *Political Economy and the Labour Party*, London, UCL Press, 1995, pp. 251–66.

35 See Lipsey, 'Revisionists Revise', pp. 15–17.

36 See Ellison, *Egalitarian Thought and Labour Politics*, pp. 73, 84–108, 243; K. Coates, *The Social Democrats: Those Who Went and Those Who Stayed: The Forward March of Labour Halted?*, Nottingham, Spokesman, 1983, pp. 10–11; also see L. Black, '"The Bitterest Enemies of Communism": Labour Revisionists, Atlanticism and the Cold War', *Contemporary British History*, 15 (3), 2001, p. 43; Wickham-Jones, *Economic Strategy and the Labour Party*, pp. 14–15, 226.

37 Ellison, *Egalitarian Thought and Labour Politics*, pp. 73–4, 92–8, 103–4, 105–6, 107–8; also see C. A. R. Crosland, *Socialism Now and Other Essays*, London, Jonathan Cape, 1974, p. 15.

38 S. Haseler, *The Gaitskellites: Revisionism in the British Labour Party 1951–64*, London, Macmillan, 1969, pp. 9–10.

39 See, for example, S. H. Beer, *Modern British Politics: A Study of Parties and Pressure Groups*, London, Faber, 1965, pp. 219–27, 236–9; J. Brand, 'Faction as its Own Reward: Groups in the British Parliament 1945 to 1986', *Parliamentary Affairs*, 42 (3), 1989, pp. 148–64; Jones, *Remaking the Labour Party*; R. Rose, 'Parties, Factions and Tendencies in Britain', *Political Studies*, 12 (1), 1964, pp. 33–46.

40 See Desai, *Intellectuals and Socialism*, pp. 8–9; H. M. Drucker, *Doctrine and Ethos in the Labour Party*, London, Allen & Unwin, 1979; Haseler, *The Gaitskellites*, pp. ix–x, 4–10; S. Haseler, *The Death of British Democracy*, London, Elek Books, 1976; S. Haseler, *The Tragedy of Labour*, Oxford, Blackwell, 1980; J. Jupp, 'The British Social Democrats and the Crisis in the British Labour Party', *Politics*, 16 (2), 1981, p. 254; D. Marquand, 'Inquest on a Movement: Labour's Defeat and its Consequences', *Encounter*, July 1979, pp. 8–18; V. McKee, 'Fragmentation on the Labour Right 1975–87', *Politics*, 11 (1), 1991, pp. 25–8; V. McKee, 'Scattered Brethren: British Social Democrats', *Social Studies Review*, 6 (5), 1991, pp. 171–4.

41 See Jones, *Remaking the Labour Party*, pp. 111–12; Jupp, 'The British Social Democrats and the Crisis in the British Labour Party', pp. 253–6.

42 Ellison, *Egalitarian Thought and Labour Politics*; A. Warde, *Consensus and Beyond: The Development of Labour Party Strategy since the Second World War*, Manchester, Manchester University Press, 1982.

43 G. Daly, *The Crisis in the Labour Party 1974–81 and the Origins of the 1981 Schism*, unpublished Ph.D. Thesis, University of London, 1992; K. Middlemas, *Power, Competition and the State, Volume II: Threats to the Postwar Settlement: Britain 1961–74*, Basingstoke, Macmillan, 1990.

44 Jupp, 'The British Social Democrats and the Crisis in the British Labour Party', pp. 254–6; also see D. Howell, *British Social Democracy: A Study in Development and Decay*, London, Croom Helm, 1976, pp. 190–4; V. McKee, *Right-wing Factionalism in the British Labour Party 1977–87*, unpublished M.Phil. Thesis, CNAA, 1988, pp. 8–23; McKee, 'Fragmentation on the Labour Right', pp. 25–7.

45 See B. Brivati, *Hugh Gaitskell*, London, Richard Cohen, 1996, pp. 405–7, 412–13; Ellison, *Egalitarian Thought and Labour Politics*, pp. 107–8; Haseler, *The Gaitskellites*, p. 228; LPACR 1962, p. 155.

46 Brivati, *Hugh Gaitskell*, p. 404.

47 See L. J. Robbins, *The Reluctant Party: Labour and the EEC 1961–75*, Ormskirk, G. W. & A. Hesketh, 1979.

48 McKee, *Right-wing Factionalism in the British Labour Party 1977–87*, pp. 16–18; also see McKee, 'Fragmentation on the Labour Right'. Differences between the respective Labour right tendencies, centred on policy priorities, party management and campaigning tactics, and issues of contention included the apparent 'Euro-zeal, social elitism and suspect party loyalties of some revisionist social democrats'.

49 Crewe and King, *SDP*, pp. 104, 106–14.

50 See Marquand, *The Progressive Dilemma*, pp. 170, 173–4, 176–8; Radice, *Friends & Rivals*, p. 329.

51 See Ellison, *Egalitarian Thought and Labour Politics*, pp. ix–xiii, 73–4, 187–200; Warde, *Consensus and Beyond*, pp. 9–24, 43–5, 75–7; 94–5, 125–40, 211; also see T. Bale, *Sacred Cows and Common Sense: The Symbolic Statecraft and Political Culture of the British Labour Party*, Aldershot, Ashgate, 1999, pp. 4–5.

52 See Jones, *Remaking the Labour Party*, p. 2. Studies include F. Bealey (ed.), *The Social and Political Thought of the British Labour Party*, London, Weidenfeld & Nicolson, 1970; G. Foote, *The Labour Party's Political Thought: A History*, third edition, Basingstoke, Macmillan, 1997; and for a recent addition see Beech, *The Political Philosophy of New Labour*.

53 Foote, *The Labour Party's Political Thought*, p. 3.

54 See Daly, *The Crisis in the Labour Party 1974–81*, pp. 48–63.

55 Bale, *Sacred Cows and Common Sense*, pp. 23, 25; also see Drucker, *Doctrine and Ethos in the Labour Party*, pp. 46, 65–6; A. Wildavsky, 'Choosing Preferences by Constructing Institutions: A Cultural Theory of Preference Formation', *American Political Science Review*, 81 (1), 1987, pp. 4–5.

56 Marquand, Interview with the author, 16 January 2001.

57 D. Baker, A. Gamble and S. Ludlam, 'Mapping Conservative Fault Lines: Problems of Typology', in P. Dunleavy and J. Stanyer (eds), *Contemporary Political Studies: Volume One*, Belfast, Political Studies Association, 1994, pp. 280, 286; J. Bulpitt, 'The Conservative Party in Britain: a Preliminary Portrait', paper presented to the Annual Conference of the UK Political Studies Association, University of Lancaster, April 1991; Warde, *Consensus and Beyond*, pp. 21–2.

3

Parliamentary Labour right factionalism and organisational fragmentation in the 1970s

This chapter provides an analysis of group and factional organisation and activity on the parliamentary Labour right in the 1970s. In doing so, it takes issue with one-dimensional accounts of Labour's internal divisions. It also takes issue with the conventional view that it is only the Labour left that has operated at group or factional level. Increasingly from the early 1970s, factional organisation and activity became a feature of the parliamentary Labour right. The chapter evaluates the organisational character and activity of Labour right groupings in the 1970s against both general models of factional behaviour and standard representations of Labour Party factionalism. It further comments on the effectiveness of Labour right factionalism in this period, and the important implications of the particular form of factional behaviour for the unity and cohesion of the parliamentary Labour right and Labour's 'dominant coalition' and the subsequent trajectory of the Labour Party and British social democracy.

It suggests that the particular economic and political context of the 1970s, and intra-party debates and divisions over a combination of ideological and policy themes, produced a qualitatively different type and variations of parliamentary Labour right factional identity and behaviour than the limited leadership/ loyalist formations of the past. This was expressed in the form of two distinct but overlapping parliamentary groupings. First, an increasingly distinctive, 'oppositional' Jenkinsite group emerged as Labour entered opposition after 1970. As official party policy on key issues such as Europe and industrial relations shifted in seemingly contradictory directions to that of the previous Labour Government, the Jenkinsites found themselves moving away from both main-stream party opinion and centre-right colleagues. The development of a 'separatist' Jenkinsite group identity and agenda was a key factor in the gradual fragmentation of the parliamentary Labour right in the intra-party context of the 1970s. It was also an early signal of the potential (and likely) political separation of Labour's social democrats. Second, the broader Manifesto Group of centre-right Labour MPs, formed to combat the increasingly organised and influential Tribune Group within the PLP, represented more conventional formal factional organisation on the right of the PLP. Although broadly supportive of the 1974 Labour Government and aspects of the manifesto on which it was elected, as time (and policies) progressed it perceived its role to be only that of a 'critical friend' of the Labour Government. Given its broad centre-right membership, some of the deliberations (or non-deliberations) of the Manifesto Group further illustrate the inconsistencies and divergence of the parliamentary Labour right over critical policy themes.[1] The chapter addresses standard conceptual frameworks of factionalism and Labour Party factionalism, against which to undertake an evaluation of the character, progress and implications of enhanced and atypical social democratic factional activity in the 1970s in the form of the loosely organised, but ideologically and politically cohesive, Jenkinsite group and the formally organised but more disparate Manifesto Group of centre-right Labour MPs.

Factionalism and Labour Party faction

Richard Rose identified the existence of factions (and tendencies) as an integral part of the internal life of British political parties. He argued that an understanding of the internal balance of power between factions was crucial to understanding the likely policy direction of an 'electoral party'. Rose further suggested that the PLP was more prone to faction than the parliamentary Conservative Party, which has been primarily a party of political tendencies. The model of intra-party organisation and activity proposed by those such as Rose and David Hine develops a framework for the classification and analysis of intra-party divisions and group behaviour.[2] The main classifications can be summarised as factions, tendencies and single-issue groups, and the model assesses the dimensions of group behaviour in terms of both policy goals and internal cohesion. They distinguish between factions and tendencies in terms of the degree of internal cohesion and organisation.[3] Pertinent to the classification of the Jenkinsites in factional terms, it should be noted that quite 'what level of organisational cohesion and continuity a group actually has to display before it can be known as a faction is of course problematic'. Analytically, it is

> useful to distinguish between different dimensions of group conflict in a party . . . between . . . what divides groups [policy], and . . . how much groups, once divided, are organised [organisation] . . . the distinction is not always easy to identify, but it would be misleading to assume that there is a direct correlation between the intensity of policy differences between intra-party groups and the degree of organisational coherence and complexity these groups display.[4]

Standard factional models formulate a 'tendency' as a stable set of attitudes, political predispositions and, over time, a range of policies. Some central cohesion and corporate structure is often evident, but not in the same depth as that of more formal party organisations. Tendencies rarely survive over a long period without incurring objective and corporate changes and 'membership' turnover, often in response to changing events and currents within the party. 'Factions' are subject to 'more consciously organized political activity', and extol the virtues of self-awareness, discipline and stable, loyal membership. In turn, this generates some degree of ideological and corporate cohesion and a greater degree of identity and stability than tendencies.[5] This staple model of intra-party parliamentary groups possesses applicability to, and provides a theoretical point of reference for, the analysis of right-wing group identity and behaviour in the PLP.[6] Labour Party revisionism more broadly meets the criteria of a tendency, organisations such as the Campaign for Democratic Socialism (CDS), the Manifesto Group and even Labour Solidarity in the early 1980s possessed clear factional attributes, while the Jenkinsites trod a more fluid line between that of faction and tendency.[7] The Jenkinsite group of the emerging liberal strand of Labour Party revisionism in the 1970s represented more than the limited concerns of a single-issue group based on its primary pro-European identity. Preoccupation with the European issue conceals the extent to which the Jenkinsites exhibited a strong sense of ideological, if not formal organisational, cohesion across a range of critical issues such as industrial relations and trade union reform and public expenditure issues.[8]

Rose's seminal study further established the conventional wisdom of the dimensions of factional organisation and competition in the PLP on relatively stable left–right lines, while the remainder of 'non-aligned partisans' provided a resource to be mobilised by the two broad factions Moreover, while the 'Labour left' faction has been 'notoriously schismatic' and left factions have persisted 'from generation to generation', the Labour right has been represented only intermittently by a 'moderate' faction operating in defence or support of the parliamentary leadership.[9] During the period of Labour Government of 1974–79, it has been suggested that a 'Labour left' was more identifiable than a 'Labour right'. Surprisingly, during this highly divisive period of Labour politics, it was found that the Labour right faction was 'submerged within the larger body of "non-aligned" supporters of the party leadership': a separate 'moderate faction' could not confidently be identified, an observation explained by the fact that 'because Labour was in power and moderate official party policies were prevailing, it was more likely that the left wing would seek to display separate factional identity than would the party moderates'.[10] The findings are methodologically dependent on the analysis of a selection of House of Commons divisions in the 1974–79 Parliament, and fail to account for the wider complex associations and activity of the parliamentary Labour right away from the division lobbies in this period.

Cleavage based on a simple left–right, oppositional-leadership/loyalist dimension has limited application to the intra-party dynamics of the PLP in the 1970s.[11] Although the 1974–79 Labour Government was inevitably one 'in which some of those who were active on the Labour Right were also members of the administration . . . it is wrong to equate the organized Labour Right which was emerging during these years with the Labour Party Establishment – the leadership and its acolytes in the Party organisation': while 'the newly organised Labour Right defended the Labour government from its Left-wing critics on the NEC and at conference, some groups on the Labour Right were hostile to the Party Establishment or to the policies of the Labour government. The Party leadership kept the organized Right at arms length.'[12] An examination of two 'organised' groupings of the parliamentary Labour right in the 1970s, the Jenkinsites and the Manifesto

Group, reveals that right-wing group organisation and activity was far from concealed within the confines of the 'non-aligned', centrist orthodoxy of the PLP, or merely the product of an uncritical vehicle of the parliamentary leadership. Rather, it reveals the group and factional mentality and character, and the complex, and ultimately fragmentary nature, of the parliamentary Labour right within the intra-party and wider political context of the 1970s. The perception of the relative lack of formal group behaviour of the parliamentary Labour right probably reflects its relative strength in the PLP, needing to resort to organised faction only when it perceived the moderate, centre-right orthodoxy of the parliamentary party to be under threat; but the general absence of right-wing factionalism in the PLP does not indicate that the Labour right has not featured recognisably distinct sections and traditions within it.[13] It has been suggested that Labour's 'social democrats' 'had a more advanced form of factional organization in the 1970s than scholars have generally recognized'. The intensification and relative departure of explicitly social democratic factionalism in the 1970s was provoked by a number of 'economic and social trends [which] played a major role in undermining social democracy's formerly dominant position in the Labour Party. Economic crisis and the rise of the post-industrial economic sectors and classes formed the context for both a new kind of Labour Left and a new model of social democracy.'[14] It is the purpose of the remainder of the article to examine the nature and implications of this expanded and 'deviant' factional behaviour of the Labour right in the 1970s.

Organising against the left and beyond: the emergence of Labour right factionalism in the 1970s

The growing influence of the Labour left in the party after the 1970 election defeat, partly in response to the perceived failures of the Wilson administrations in which influential figures of the party right were seen as culpable, and critical policy divisions, precipitated the development of identifiable groupings of the parliamentary Labour right in the 1970s both to counter the progress of the left and to pursue specific policy agendas. Intra-party machinations over the seminal (and deeply divisive) issue of Europe, particularly the evasive, highly pragmatic and apparently inconsistent approach of the party leader, Harold Wilson, to the issue, was to have a profoundly disillusioning effect for the positively pro-European Labour right. In the deliberations of a series of party conferences in 1971 and 1972, the wider party's hostility to the Common Market was made apparent. Entry to the Common Market, at least 'on the terms negotiated' by the Conservative Government, was opposed by a large number of trade unions, the majority of the Labour left and among elements of Labour's centre-right coalition. Ultimately, Wilson's primary desire to 'not sacrifice our Party's basic unity' saw him follow the tide of party opinion and move more clearly in the direction of the anti-Market position of the Labour left and the wider Labour movement.[15]

The European divisions and direction of the party in this period clearly played a principal role in precipitating the emergence of a distinct pro-European Jenkinsite tendency of the parliamentary Labour right. For Wilson, concerned to maintain the appearance of party unity as a priority of leadership, the emergence of a conspicuous Jenkinsite grouping on the Labour right raised the spectre of the Gaitskellite CDS. He complained of the Jenkinsites that 'a party within a party is no less so because it meets outside the House in more socially agreeable surroundings', which was interpreted as a snipe at 'pro-Market gatherings at St Ermin's Hotel, the Reform Club and in Harold Lever's palatial flat in Eaton Square'.[16] However, the emerging Jenkinsite group was different to the previous Gaitskellite revisionist vehicle in the sense that its particular ideological and policy preferences and trajectory would differentiate it from both the mainstream of party opinion and erstwhile revisionist centre-right colleagues, and take it out of reach of the reins of power in the parliamentary leadership. Further divisions over industrial relations and trade union reform and political economy and public expenditure issues would further harden the core ideological and factional cohesion and the 'oppositional' and potentially separatist 'party within a party' status of the Jenkinsites. Jenkins described his eventual departure to Brussels as President of the European Commission in 1976, in the wake of his disappointing performance in the 1976 Labour leadership election, as 'something quite new for me and in which I believed much more strongly than the economic policy of Mr. Healey, the trade union policy of Mr. Foot or even the foreign policy of Mr. Callaghan'.[17]

The leftwards shift of the party was further reflected in the publication of *Labour's Programme 1973*, which advocated radical proposals of nationalisation, economic planning and wealth redistribution,[18] and the subsequent formation of the left-wing CLPD in 1973 to promote internal constitutional reforms designed to favour the wider organs of the party structure.[19] These developments, together with the perception of the onset of aggressive industrial action and the challenge to the rule of law, provoked consternation among Labour's increasingly identifiable faction of 'social democrats'. It represented a snapshot of the general dissatisfaction of this group with the circumstances and trajectory of the Labour Party. If the roots of the SDP were to be found in the European divisions of 1971 particularly, the general mood and direction of the party thereafter added substantially to the maturity of an alternative vehicle of social democracy.[20] John Mackintosh warned against the dangers of a 'populist socialist' appeal to sectional and class-based politics and spoke of the need for a 'renewed emphasis on parliamentary democracy' in the national interest:

> [i]f these objectives are not successfully pursued . . . the Labour Party . . . will become merely the puppet party of those powerful union leaders whose first interest is not socialism or social justice but simply the well-being of the particular groups of wage earners whom they represent. Then the Party will not only suffer further electoral defeats but it will deserve them.[21]

Roy Jenkins further spoke of the need for the Labour Party to shed its class-based, sectional image and appeal.[22] Others expressed concern over the ability of an increasingly disparate Labour right to return the party to a path of moderation necessary to appeal to a dealigned electorate: Brian Walden believed that 'the Right was clapped out and ideologically incoherent'. In the circumstances, the 'Right did not know what to do'.[23]

The narrow election victory of October 1974 served only to conceal trends that indicated the decline of Labour's electoral support, and prefigured the general rise of the Labour left and a growing trade union militancy that included a shift to the left among a number of trade unions.[24] The difficulties and conflicts of the Labour Party were to be compounded rather than moderated by its experience of office. It was in the context of left-wing and trade union pressures on the economic and industrial policies of the Labour Government, and the success of left-wing organisation and activity in the PLP, that the Labour right decided to organise more formally in the form of the Manifesto Group. Ryan suggests that one consequence of the challenge to Labour's pursuit of the moderate policies of traditional social democracy was the notable, if insufficient, reappearance of dormant social democratic factionalism: the 'Labour Right was both better organized than is often assumed and less organized than it needed to be to retain control of the party. In retrospect ... the Labour Right contained factional organizations from 1974 onwards, and ... social democracy developed into a pre-party faction and, later, a party.' Adapting the terms of Rose's analysis, he notes that the social democratic Labour right moved from the position of 'dominant tendency' (in 'the period of the 1964–1970 Wilson Government'), to that of 'declining tendency' (following 'Labour's loss of the 1970 election'), to that of 'embattled' and 'pre-party' faction (following 'Labour's return to power in 1974 ... in order to protect their position in the party against the rising Labour Left'), and eventually to that of political party. The combination of economic and social trends, and a range of divisive 'policy issues and disputes over organizational matters propelled factional development', and the 'very appearance of a social democratic party' requires us to take the notions of tendency and faction seriously. It is useful to refine traditional models of factionalism to take account of 'such phases of factional development as the pre-factional tendency and the pre-party faction',[25] and it may be possible to detect these stages of factional and party development in a study of the Jenkinsite grouping and Manifesto Group of the parliamentary right in the 1970s (although this is not to necessarily suggest a clear linear process of development between the Jenkinsites, Manifesto Group and SDP).

Parliamentary Labour right factionalism in the 1970s: the Jenkinsites

An important strand of Labour right opinion and personnel coalesced around the influential figure of Roy Jenkins in the years of opposition after 1970, occasioned by the contentious and divisive issue of Europe. Bill Rodgers has noted the emergence of the core of an active, like-minded group in this period out of former loosely aligned and associated supporters of Gaitskell's political leadership and Crosland's revisionist social democratic ideas:

By the end of the 60s . . . those who might have been Gaitskellites and Croslandites were Jenkinsites . . . I don't think that within that group there was any core until the 70s . . . that was the core of people who were now Jenkinsites who had voted for Europe . . . it wasn't only those who voted for Europe but there was a core of people who began to work together and see a lot of each other, and we used to have monthly meetings in people's houses and so forth . . . it was a group to which some people came and went, but that was the first time . . . that I would identify anything within what was already, of course, a split in the right of the party.[26]

David Marquand further notes the importance of the 'charismatic leadership' of Roy Jenkins to the formation and internal cohesion of the Jenkinsite group and to its uncharacteristic position/trajectory in the Labour Party:

A very simple thing that held the Jenkinsite group together was admiration for Roy Jenkins . . . the core group thought that Roy Jenkins was the right person to lead the Labour Party . . . if you think of the Bevanites . . . in the 50s, you can't disentangle the Bevanite Group philosophically from Bevan's own personality and charisma . . . the Jenkinsites in the 70s were people who . . . when no longer associated with the leadership of the party were . . . regarded as being opposed to it by the actual leader Harold Wilson.[27]

There was also a wider attempt among key intimates to groom Jenkins as the future leader of the Labour Party. As noted, a wider Jenkinsite position and agenda, beyond the narrow issue of Europe, was presented in a series of speeches and subsequent collection of essays on wider themes of injustice and deprivation in society, aimed at expanding the base of Jenkins' support inside the party.[28] However, the parliamentary Labour right was far from united behind the Jenkinsite vehicle. Jenkins' resignation from the deputy leadership in April 1972 after the party's decision to adopt (Tony Benn's) proposal to hold a referendum on the European issue when returned to government, combined with his appearance of increasing general disillusionment with the Labour Party,[29] contributed to the disorganised and leaderless character of the parliamentary Labour right. Refuge for the wider Labour right was not to be found in a single (charismatic) personality. Other leading social democrats such as Crosland had demonstrated their ambivalence to the European cause and, in the name of party unity, willingness for some form of rapprochement with the left. It was clear from the presentation of Crosland's campaign in the deputy leadership election after Jenkins' resignation over the referendum proposal, that he was frustrated that 'the Labour Party cannot set aside its factional warfare', and possessed a keen desire, 'whatever our different views on Europe', to 'unite on a clear and positive domestic policy' in order to achieve the first priority of defeating the repressive and unpopular Conservative Government.[30] By this point, it was increasingly evident that the two leading Gaitskellite revisionists (and candidates for the succession) had undergone a significant parting of the ways – politically, strategically and, to some extent, ideologically. Crosland's priorities were now clearly different to those of Jenkins. He complained of Labour's debilitating European divisions and heightened factional activity that:

Just at the moment when grass-roots Labour opinion sees the over-riding aim as being to get rid of a reactionary and repressive Tory government, the Parliamentary Labour Party seems divided by personalities and polarised into factions. We are set on a course of self-destructive madness. I am standing in protest . . . not . . . to keep someone else out. I am running to win – on a non-sectarian ticket . . . It is desperately urgent to re-create Party unity on the basis of a radical, egalitarian socialist programme.[31]

Reservations over the desirability of factional organisation were common on the parliamentary Labour right. Partly, this derived from fear of accusations of trying to create 'a party within a party' and behaving in a way 'which might be regarded as divisive', an accusation usually levelled at the allegedly divisive and 'schismatic' left.[32] The recent memory of CDS had, perhaps, established such a precedent. Brivati suggests that one legacy of CDS was that, in its role as an 'overtly social democratic grouping loyal to Gaitskell and . . . as the organisational expression of revisionist ideology', it 'changed the nature of the internal party division. After CDS this was no longer between the leadership and a critical left, but between articulated groups on the left and right with self images as being socialists and social democrats, with the leadership in a sort of ill-defined centre role playing one group off against the other.'[33] For some in the party, the Jenkinsites represented the re-emergence of CDS in truncated form (as the articulation of a clearly defined social democratic identity and agenda).[34] Jenkins, himself, explains that 'the nucleus of a campaign organisation', as 'the continuous focus of the committed pro-Europeans in the parliamentary Labour Party', emerged out of a meeting of about twelve MPs on 25 June 1970, a week after Labour's 1970 election defeat. It was hosted by Dick Taverne and attended by, among others, Jenkins, Taverne, George Thomson, Bill Rodgers, David Owen and David Marquand.[35] The priority of the initial meeting was discussion of whether Jenkins should contest the deputy leadership of the party after George Brown had lost his seat at the general election and the likely attitude of the party to the Common Market in opposition. The core of this group became known as the 'Walston group' (after Lord Walston, whose home provided a regular meeting place), and continued to meet at least until the leadership election of March 1976, and even on a few occasions thereafter. Taverne traces the origins of the Jenkinsite group back even further to the core membership of the 1963 Club, a dining group established in memory of their former leader, Hugh Gaitskell, who died in 1963 (hence the direct link with CDS for some).[36] Taverne claims that it was essentially a Jenkinsite group:

there was a Jenkins section in the party no doubt about it, a strong section too. Jenkins provided the leadership . . . for sixty nine people to defy the three-line whip and vote for entry in 1971 . . . they took their lead from Roy Jenkins. He was their leader. That is why he had a strong position because he was seen as a leader. It is also why it gave him a lot of standing in the country, because although they didn't agree with him on the Common Market, they respected his toughness. It was definitely a group.[37]

Two weeks after the first 'formal' meeting, Jenkins was elected to the deputy leadership of the Labour Party. Jenkins' core supporters in the PLP included Marquand, Rodgers, Taverne, George Thomson, Tom Bradley, Roy Hattersley,

Dickson Mabon, Robert Maclennan and, after 1973, Giles Radice.[38] Owen claims that, although a supporter, he was not a natural Jenkinsite. In his memoirs, he explains that, like many of the Jenkinsite group, 'my political heart belonged to Tony Crosland. I did not make a wholehearted commitment to Roy as the future leader . . . until the summer of 1971, when it became clear . . . that . . . Crosland was not prepared to recognize that Britain's entry into the European Community was a major issue.'[39] Unusually for a figure of the Labour right, this parliamentary core was supplemented by a coterie of extra-parliamentary supporters and contacts. Although most of the Jenkinsites at this point were not politically important of themselves, the very existence of the close-knit group caused some unease in the Labour Party: insiders considered the Jenkinsite group to be 'serious, dedicated, even selfless'; but many outsiders considered it to be 'cliquish and stand-offish, almost too good to be true. Its high moral tone was widely regarded as a thin disguise for its leader's personal ambitions.' They complained that the prominence and media access of the group led to comparatively extensive and favourable coverage of Jenkins' particular ideas and activities: 'to find out what Jenkins was thinking you could talk to anyone of half a dozen people, each of whom had some reasonable claim to be his spokesman – and, if you did not talk to one of them, there was a very good chance one of them would talk to you. The Jenkinsites in this way constituted a formidable propaganda machine . . . Few other politicians could rival it.'[40]

Given their lack of formal organisation and membership, the Jenkinsites do not clearly satisfy the essential conditions of factional behaviour of standard models of factionalism, in the same way as, for example, the Tribune Group (or the Manifesto Group).[41] Bill Rodgers remembers the small scale and informality of the Jenkinsite set-up:

> it was a much smaller group of people . . . it consisted for example of David Marquand and David Owen and Bob Maclennan . . . Dickson Mabon . . . it had as a non-parliamentarian John Harris . . . We sometimes met in the flat of Harry Walston who . . . had been a Junior Minister in the Labour government, but mainly we met at my house and David Marquand's house, Bob Maclennan's house and I'm sure there were others as well.

However, Rodgers identifies a core membership of the Jenkinsite group who met frequently and worked closely together. At this stage, the essence of any Jenkinsite organisation owed more to a keen sense of kinship and shared values and priorities than any desire to rival the Tribune Group in technical factional terms: 'it was a close-knit group of around ten or a dozen people who shared the same views and judgments, and this was a core of what you might call [the] Jenkinsite centre.'[42] The Jenkinsites can be characterised by the informality of their parliamentary networks; they remained colleagues and friends in regular contact who shared common values and goals. Given the precedent of CDS and the similarity of personnel between the two groups, the Jenkinsites engendered suspicion and intrigue in the PLP in terms of hidden agendas and secretive campaigns (not least among those around the leadership of Harold Wilson). However, the Jenkinsites were relatively clear and candid about their twin goals to promote British membership of the Common Market and to establish Jenkins as leader of the Labour Party in succession to Wilson.[43]

The implications of a Jenkinsite factional identity

Rodgers has suggested that the Tribunite left was tempted to see in its opponents those structures mirroring their own. However, the majority of Jenkinsites were never natural apparatchiks, but Rodgers' particular reputation preceded him. His precision-like organisation of Labour's pro-European rebels in the vote of 28 October 1971, and his central coordinating role of the Jenkinsites, indicated for some the revival of CDS in the Labour Party.[44] Certain parallels can be drawn between CDS and the Jenkinsites in their respective contexts in opposition. As CDS were diverted from a wider 'modernisation' of the Labour Party by internal debates and disputes over defence, the Jenkinsites were diverted from the 'modernising' agenda that would follow Jenkins' succession to the leadership by debates and internal divisions over Europe. However, the particular pursuit of their European ideal appeared to be at the expense of party unity and Jenkins' leadership claims.[45] The European issue hastened a specific identity for the Jenkinsites in the Labour Party: if 'the revisionists had lacked an organised presence in the Labour Party after 1964, the European issue precipitated them once again as an identifiable intellectual tendency, the social democrats'.[46]

The pro-Market revolt of 28 October 1971 particularly, and their pro-Europeanism more generally, was an important factor in the longer-term marginalisation of the core Jenkinsite group in the PLP. Along with opposition to Labour's 'most left-wing' programme of economic and industrial strategy resulting from the policy process set up in the party in 1970 'under the auspices of the left', it reflected 'the political marginalization' of a core group of revisionist intellectuals that led directly to the 1981 schism in the party. It was an important dimension of the 'complex political and ideological conjuncture of the early 1970s which precipitated Labour's principal intellectuals in their final form – the social democrats'.[47] The attempt to trace a direct link between the various stages and expressions of Labour's post-war revisionist tradition and the creation of the SDP in 1981 is not without its problems. The task of locating the precise point of origin of the SDP and interpreting the individual commitments and motivations of 'those who went and those who stayed' is a hazardous one,[48] but the core of a pro-European Jenkinsite group had identified itself clearly with a particular cause that their factional opponents could argue held first call on their loyalty,[49] questioned their commitment to party unity and led to claims of the creation of a party within a party, usually an accusation reserved for the factional left.

In spite of the success of Jenkins and a number of pro-European colleagues in gaining election to PLP office during late 1971, the Jenkinsites soon began to lose ground in the party. In the recriminations of the aftermath of the October 1971 vote on the principle of entry, Rodgers, as the organiser of Labour's pro-European rebels, was removed from the Opposition front bench along with a number of pro-European colleagues in January 1972 (despite prior assurances by Wilson to the contrary). This was perceived to be a direct challenge to the authority of Jenkins.[50] This move against Rodgers and other supporters of Jenkins, together with a broad centre-left realignment on the Common Market issue, further signalled the wider marginalisation of the Jenkinsites within the party. The absence of majority pro-European sentiment in any of the party's key institutions compounded their difficulties: the Shadow Cabinet, PLP, conference, NEC and TUC all came out in opposition to membership on the terms negotiated by the Heath Government.[51]

The decision of the party to hold a special conference on the Common Market issue had been a further significant step (symbolically and strategically) in the marginalisation of the Jenkinsite group in the Labour Party. This development possessed important implications for the traditionally close relationship to the parliamentary leadership previously enjoyed by the Jenkinsites in their revisionist guise. Jenkins had still hoped that Wilson might adopt the 'hard, difficult, consistent, unpopular line' and remain with the pro-European policy of the previous Labour Government. However, the consequence of the decision to hold a special conference on the Common Market issue for the Jenkinsites was that it required a speech from Wilson that 'took him quietly out of intellectual hailing distance' with them and their principle of support for British entry.[52] Without the support of the party leader, the Jenkinsite position in the party was critically undermined. Moreover, the growing divergence of Jenkins and Callaghan (and Crosland) and their key supporters over Europe (along with significant differences between the two camps over the economic and industrial roles of trade unionism and the position of the trade unions in the Labour Party) was indicative of the emerging instability of the alliance of labourism and revisionism that had been the guiding force of Labour politics since the days of Gaitskell. Jenkinsite pre-occupation with, and intra-party marginalisation over, the European issue, determined that they did not see the left coming. This development and the subsequent rupture of Labour's dominant centre-right coalition transformed the immediate future of the Labour Party.[53]

The marginalisation of the Jenkinsites in the PLP and the wider organs of the party was compounded by Jenkins' decision to resign from the Shadow Cabinet and his position as deputy leader of the party in April 1972 over Labour's adoption of a referendum on the Common Market question. Other pro-Europeans such as George Thomson and Harold Lever also resigned their Shadow Cabinet posts. The gesture served only to remove both himself and his supporters from the centre of power and spheres of influence in the party. Additionally, he sacrificed his seat on the NEC and his influence in Labour's research and policy programme.[54] For the Jenkinsites, resignation made sense only if it held out the prospect of the party leadership and significant influence in the party's research and policy agenda. Initially, this appeared to be the underlying motive of the pre-resignation publication of Jenkins' 'Unauthorized Programme' for the Labour Party in *What Matters Now*, the collection of speeches that spelled out a broader Jenkinsite post-European agenda as the basis of a possible leadership challenge.[55] However, Jenkins' refusal to consider a challenge to Wilson for the party leadership, even if, in retrospect, he believed that in '1972–3 it might have been better for the future health of the . . . Party',[56] left him and his core supporters with nowhere to go in the Labour Party. Despite the broad sweep of the 'Unauthorized Programme', it lacked grounding and impact if Jenkins, as a means of enacting his programme, was unwilling to offer himself as potential leader of the Labour Party or senior representative of a future Labour Government.[57]

Jenkins' disinclination to compete with his factional opponents from within the Shadow Cabinet and the NEC was to have important implications for political alignments and the balance of power in the Labour Party. It allowed the left to cement their influence and policy gains in the party, while Jenkins' renunciation of the obligations associated with his position in the parliamentary leadership was resented by others on the Labour right who remained to combat the left in the various policy committees.[58] Moreover, Jenkins' post-resignation behaviour demonstrated a largely negative attitude to the Labour Party and its immediate electoral fortunes. Although he differed in this respect from some of his younger supporters, he neither expected nor wanted the Labour Party to win the next general election.[59] However, the Jenkinsites appeared to be collectively resolved on a course of action in pursuit of their European ideal that carried them beyond the rudiments of Labour Party politics, and the process of marginalisation was almost an inevitable one. The Jenkinsites were, perhaps, the only faction in a position to split the Labour Party in opposition and undermine its electoral prospects. In the circumstances, they became the most significant impediment to party unity and, ultimately, for this reason, they lost, temporarily at least, their place at Labour's high table.[60] In effect, an important strand of parliamentary Labour right opinion was excluded from the spheres of influence in the parliamentary leadership, which increasingly took the form of a centre-left coalition, with the pragmatic centrist influence of Callaghan and Healey to the fore. Their former Gaitskellite revisionist mentor, Crosland, had also deserted the Jenkinsite European cause. The latter was now primarily concerned to maintain the unity of the Labour Party as the only vehicle to defeat the Tories and to realise his egalitarian democratic socialist philosophy, and to occupy himself with the rudimentary issues of most concern to his working-class constituents rather than the lofty principles of the Jenkinsites. This was a further important breach, as Crosland made the transformation from 'revisionist *enfant terrible*' to 'sober, respectable departmental minister in the mainstream of the Labour movement'. The Jenkinsites caricatured him in the 1970s as little more than a loyalist Labour apparatchik, concerned only with the minutiae of housing finance and the workers of Grimsby.[61] The depth of Jenkinsite feeling over the Common Market issue, and the development of explicit group mentality and behaviour in support of their beliefs, divided and laid the foundations for the fragmentation of the Labour right and Labour Party revisionism in the 1970s. Crosland, for one, was not interested 'to be the mentor of a divisive and potentially heretical sect', for he believed that 'the pro-Marketeers had . . . divided the Labour right against itself and, in doing so, allowed the left into the citadels of party power'.[62]

The Jenkinsites as a faction of the parliamentary Labour right?

Returning to standard models of factionalism introduced previously, the Jenkinsites lacked the 'organisational solidity' important in Rose's distinction between factions and tendencies.[63] However, the Jenkinsites constituted more than a tendency or issue group of '*ad hoc* combinations of politicians in agreement upon one particular issue or at one moment in time'. Neither could they be clearly distinguished as 'a stable set of attitudes, rather than a stable group of politicians'.[64] Hine suggests that precisely because the distinction between faction and tendency 'is an analytical distinction there is an element of ambiguity. Factions may be based on people, and tendencies purely on ideas and attitudes, but . . . we cannot have a clear idea of which ideas and attitudes combine together to form a tendency, unless we observe the real-world behaviour of practising politicians.' Moreover, while the distinction between a political faction and a political tendency is useful to draw 'attention to the different levels of organisation which intra-party groups may display', quite 'what level of organisational cohesion and continuity a group actually has to display before it can be known as a faction is of course problematic'. The need of a group 'for organisation will depend on the rules and conventions governing party life', and 'there are substantial problems in measuring the solidity of factional organisation'.[65]

The intra-party status of the Jenkinsites falls somewhere between the analytical categories of faction and tendency. The group did not possess the technical factional attributes of solid organisation or self-administered disciplinary procedures (although the group was keen to punish former colleagues such as Crosland whom it perceived to have abandoned critical causes and associations).[66] However, it would appear that the Jenkinsites, given their increasingly marginal existence in the PLP, were a 'self-aware' group that enjoyed 'a relatively stable and cohesive personnel over time' and, in the central cause of European membership and the wider prospectus of Jenkins' 'Unauthorized Programme', pursued a range of political issues and policies inside the Labour Party in at least some form of consciously organised political activity.[67] Berrington questions the value of Rose's original distinction between factions and tendencies based on their formal organisational solidity. In a proviso applicable to the Jenkinsite group, he suggests that 'it is wrong to divide groups too starkly into the organised and unorganised, the formal and the informal. Organisation is a matter of degree. An informal network of friends in the House of Commons may co-ordinate their work as effectively (or more so) as a formally constituted group.'[68] Berrington argues that the 'study of cleavages within parties is likely to profit more from an examination of the inter-action between tendencies and issue-groups than from investigation into organised groups per se', as formal structure 'may actually dilute the parity, and perhaps the effectiveness, of a tendency'. It has been argued that the Tribune Group has become 'ideologically less distinctive as its ranks have been joined by Members who wish to display a badge of left-wing purity to their constituency party'.[69] On Rose's scale, the Jenkinsites can be said to represent the emergence of a minority revisionist social democratic faction within Labour's wider 'right-wing' revisionist tendency. The expression of a Jenkinsite current – and, increasingly, group identity and activity – in the party after 1970 reflected the wider organisational (and ideological and political) fragmentation of both Labour Party revisionism and Labour's traditionally dominant centre-right coalition and alliance. Inevitably, this wider development possessed important implications for the intra-party balance of power and direction of the party.

Parliamentary Labour right factionalism in the 1970s: the Manifesto Group

The 'loose and informal' Jenkinsite grouping, characterised by the existence of 'no minutes . . . no papers . . . no officers . . . no structure', was only one expression of group behaviour on the parliamentary Labour right in the 1970s. The formation of the backbench Manifesto Group of centre-right Labour MPs in December 1974 was intended primarily as a response to Tribune-led left-wing activity and gains in the PLP. In the absence of a single leader of the Gaitskell variety who might be able to unite the centrist and revisionist Labour right in the face of the left-wing onslaught, a number of concerned lieutenants took it upon themselves to initiate organised representation of the Labour right in the PLP. The election of Ian Mikardo as chairman of the PLP demonstrated the increasing organisational cohesion and effectiveness of the parliamentary Labour left and alarmed many of the traditional centre-right majority. It drew attention to the fact that, in important elections to PLP office, the Labour right vote was often split between two candidates and allowed the highly organised Tribune Group to elect their chosen candidate. In the various offices and significant channels of the PLP, the left-wing Tribune Group appeared to be at the height of its power. In addition to the chairman of the PLP, Tribune Group members dominated both the Liaison Committee of the PLP, the important channel of communication between Labour backbenchers and the Labour Government, and the leadership of backbench subject groups. Given the inroads already made in the research and policy spheres of the party, it looked increasingly possible that the programme of a Labour Government could be undermined by potential left-wing economic and anti-EEC measures.[70] Initially, a small group of centre-right MPs, among them David Marquand, Giles Radice, John Horam and Dickson Mabon, met soon after the election of Mikardo to establish a group that would support and campaign for a single candidate of the Labour right for the next election of the chairmanship of the PLP and to organise candidates for election to other major posts of the PLP.[71]

In addition to this immediate strategic aim, the wider objectives of the Manifesto Group were 'to work for the implementation of the policies set out in the [1974] Labour manifesto and to support the Labour Government in overcoming the country's acute economic difficulties'. It also encompassed an almost revisionist (and New Labour) ambition 'to act as a forum for constructive discussion designed to relate democratic socialist philosophy to the needs of the present age', and 'to endeavour to achieve a truly democratic socialist society through our representative Parliamentary system'.[72] Although there was significant overlap with the Jenkinsite group in terms of personnel, the Manifesto Group was not the same as, or merely a formal expression or extension of, the Jenkinsite group. Although support for the manifesto on which Labour was elected in 1974 was as far as the Manifesto Group was prepared to go, even this would have been too far for some Jenkinsites given the relatively left-wing tone and content of the document. Moreover, unlike the Tribune Group, it was an exclusively backbench organisation of the PLP, which precluded the involvement of Labour's frontbench representatives, largely on the grounds that 'only by being clearly independent of the Government will our voice be heard'.[73] The Manifesto Group, because of fear of left-wing reprisals in some CLPs, refused to publish its membership list,[74] but did constitute 'a formal group' in terms of organisation, structure and membership.[75] It 'met in . . . a committee room in the House of Commons and it did have officers and an agenda'.[76]

The Manifesto Group 'was formed to deal with a purely Parliamentary situation', and it remained a 'purely Parliamentary' organisation. Initially, 'its focus on PLP elections' meant that only Labour MPs were eligible for membership, but Labour Peers were then included as 'many of them showed interest in the Group and because the Group itself inevitably widened its interest to include discussion of Government policy and of democratic socialism in general'. The membership, which by early 1979 had reached 'about sixty backbench Labour MP[s] in addition to about fifteen Labour peers', paid an annual subscription, but, with the exception of the frontbench disqualification, there were 'no formal criteria of membership'. Original members 'got together because they shared views on relevant matters, and the Group is loose enough for the question of "suitability" not to arise'. In terms of officers, group members nominated and elected a chairman, three vice-chairmen, treasurer and secretary at the beginning of each parliamentary session in November. The Group also received funding from the Joseph Rowntree Social Service Trust to employ a full-time researcher/administrator. The organisational structure of the group was based around a weekly meeting, on a Wednesday evening in the parliamentary session, open to all group members. Occasional open meetings were also organised, open to all members of the PLP. Contact between the officers of the group was constant and informal, and it was suggested that 'the Group, like most Parliamentary bodies, works informally rather than through rigid procedures'. Apart from the Rowntree Trust grant, the main sources of income of the group came from membership subscriptions and small amounts from the sale of its periodic policy statements. With the exception of these occasional pamphlets, the group did not release regular publications and had 'no "internal documentation" . . . worth . . . reading'.[77]

The chosen name of the Manifesto Group possessed a certain irony, given the relatively left-wing nature of the manifesto upon which Labour had been elected in 1974, and it encouraged a number of interpretations of its meaning and significance.[78] From one such perspective, it was representative of the defensiveness of moderate opinion in the PLP and of their attempt to emphasise their loyalty to the moderate party leadership and to locate themselves broadly within the Labour Party tradition.[79] From another, it represented a reluctant acceptance of, rather than explicit support for, Labour's manifesto. Although it was as far as most members of the Manifesto Group were prepared to go, it offered something of social democracy to defend.[80] The role of the Manifesto Group was more than that of a mere 'rubber stamp for the Government': 'we see our role as that of reasserting the democratic socialist principles of the party.'[81] Initially, the Manifesto Group campaign to overturn Tribune Group victories in elections to important posts of the PLP met with a good degree of success. In the PLP elections held after the October 1974 general election, Cledwyn Hughes was elected to the chairmanship of the PLP as the single candidate of the Labour right. There was also a significant improvement in the election of its preferred candidates to the important Liaison Committee of the PLP. In fact, it was claimed that after 'the formation of the Manifesto Group its candidates were elected to all the backbench seats on the Liaison Committee and they have continued to have a clean sweep'.[82] Buoyed by such successes, the Manifesto Group broadened its purpose and objectives beyond the organisation of the right-wing slate in PLP elections. The elected officer posts within the group were established, and a full-time researcher was appointed to collate material for the purpose of publishing Manifesto Group statements of policy position 'intended to spread its ideas about democratic socialism much more widely' than its narrow parliamentary arena (while remaining a strictly parliamentary organisation).[83] The wider objective was to broaden the scope and role of the Manifesto Group 'to include discussion of Government policy and of democratic socialism in general' and to offer a contribution to the battle of ideas in the party, particularly in the critical areas of economic and industrial policy. Consequently, the group undertook to publish a number of statements and papers 'on matters of current interest' and as a 'contribution to debate in the party'.[84]

After the presentation of a number of reports on the current economic context, written by John Horam and David Marquand,[85] the first and most eclectic of such statements was published in March 1977 as *What We Must Do: A Democratic Socialist Approach To Britain's Crisis*. It presented the broad canvas of the Manifesto Group philosophy and approach, and provided the big picture of the 'kind of programme' of 'radical and constructive change' that it believed was required. Prepared 'by a sub-committee of the Manifesto Group', consisting of Bryan Magee, John Roper, Horam, Marquand, Radice and John Mackintosh, it set out an alternative, and potentially less divisive, 'democratic socialist' programme of economic *and* social change to the 'equally old-fashioned' schemes of Conservatism and the Marxist left:

> The Conservatives are unfitted by conviction, temperament and their traditions to be the party of change. The 'Marxists' . . . advocate a programme which has resulted in bureaucratic dictatorship wherever it has been tried. The democratic socialist approach alone can bring about the radical changes we need, while at the same time preserving the fundamental liberties of our people . . . only a democratic socialist approach has any prospect of securing and preserving the social harmony which is necessary for a fully civilised life in any community.[86]

The statement of philosophy and proposals demonstrated the twin aims of the Manifesto Group within the developing wider prospectus of the group to offer discussion of both current economic and political themes and the direction of social democracy more generally. In the context of the immediate and future economic situation, the group consistently 'emphasised the importance of wealth creation, restraining public expenditure and, most recently, holding down wage claims to within the Chancellor's limits'.[87] To this effect, the document restates its faith in *limited* planning and the mixed economy, but repudiates increased public expenditure and simple redistribution of wealth. Instead, it emphasises the importance of wealth creation as a stimulus to the economy: '[p]rogressive taxation and increased public expenditure have been pursued with too little regard for overall cost and too optimistic a view of the likely benefits.' Wealth creation must be given a new priority that it had never previously achieved in socialist thinking.

The pamphlet also worked as a wider attempt to update and promote support for the principles of moderate democratic socialism, and argued that only such an approach could deliver the radical, sweeping and integrated economic and social changes necessary to reverse the process of Britain's economic decline and its unanticipated social consequences, and still preserve the fundamental concept of civil liberties:[88]

> We approach these problems as democratic socialists, firmly committed to the central democratic socialist values of personal freedom and social equality. We want neither the devil-take-the-hindmost society of laissez-faire – in which the full fruits of life are enjoyed by a successful minority while the poor, the weak and the unlucky go to the wall – nor a totally planned society, with the destruction of individual initiative and choice, and therefore of freedom, which that brings with it.[89]

In effect, it represented a 'modernising' agenda – even a 'middle way' or 'a third possible course', if you like – within a broad social democratic framework.[90] Given the significant younger revisionist (and Jenkinsite) component of Manifesto Group membership, it was in no small way an attempt to update Crosland's seminal social democratic revisionism for the present context of unanticipated economic conditions of low economic growth and high inflation (which Crosland himself appeared unable or unwilling to do). In the adverse economic circumstances, it was Labour's traditional (and Crosland's seemingly unreconstructed) dependence on a 'high priority for public spending' and high and progressive levels of taxation in the pursuit of redistributive policies to achieve its aim of 'greater economic and social equality', which provided a major target of social democratic revisionism. While the Manifesto Group was generally in favour of high levels of public expenditure as the basis of 'a prosperous and civilised society' in conditions of stronger economic growth, it also warned of the potentially damaging consequences of high levels of public expenditure 'against a background of slow or stagnant growth'. Developing an emerging Jenkins theme on the potential dangers to freedom of increased public expenditure as a proportion of GDP, however, the group's general statement of intent took the analysis a stage further to question some of the wider principles of public expenditure: particularly, it questioned the unplanned and wasteful aspects of increases in public expenditure, and even the reliability of its redistributive effects and warned of the danger of a 'taxpayers' backlash . . . against the whole idea of the Welfare State'.[91] Some of the new generation of revisionists such as Giles Radice saw their attempts to promote new definitions of socialism appropriate to the 1970s as a means of rebuilding bridges with Crosland and reuniting Labour Party revisionism after the bitter divisions of the party in the EEC membership debates. However, Crosland appeared to remain unmoved in his commitments and unimpressed with their efforts to update his revisionist philosophy.[92] The emerging new or neo-revisionist contextual analysis of the basis and priorities of social democratic political economy exposed a further critical rift in Labour Party revisionism and the moderate centre-right of the PLP in the 1970s.[93]

The Manifesto Group represented a clear attempt at factional organisation on the parliamentary Labour right from late 1974. Although there was a clear overlap in personnel and some ideas between the two groupings, the Manifesto Group more clearly possessed standard factional attributes of formal organisation, structure, membership etc., but was less intellectually and 'ideologically' cohesive than the narrower, exclusive and more intimate Jenkinsites. It was, perhaps, this lack of ideological 'purity' or cohesion that would prove to be its 'Achilles' heel'. Although generally moderate in its ideas and proposals, attempting to steer an economic course between the extremes of left-wing collectivism and Thatcherite neo-liberalism, and founded initially as a focal point for 'moderate' unity and organisation against the Labour left in the PLP, the Manifesto Group was not a parliamentary Labour right faction in the conventional leadership-loyalist sense. It was also eager to display its relative independence from the government and voted against it on a number of occasions between 1974 and 1979, as it considered it important to be seen as conditional supporters of the government.[94] The Manifesto Group perceived itself to be only a 'critical friend' of the Labour Government. In the context of the acute economic difficulties of the mid-1970s, it urged the government to develop a firmer line on the need to review fundamental aspects of traditional social democratic political economy and the 'old . . . social democratic subsumption of labourist economism' in its support for 'a permanent but flexible incomes policy [and] a careful review of public expenditure and anti-inflation measures'. A range of internal Manifesto Group statements on economic policy provide clear support of government's strategy to reduce inflation in order to create economic stability and foster economic growth. Additionally, they stress the reduction of inflation as the key target of economic policy as the only way towards economic stability, growth and efficiency, and as the basis of stable employment and increased but *efficient* public expenditure.[95] The general direction of Manifesto Group economic policy statements was threefold: first, clear acknowledgement of the limitations of traditional social democratic economic tools and methods in post-OPEC conditions; second, explicit and extensive criticism of the general helpfulness and implicit dangers of left-inspired alternative economic strategies of 'unilateral' import controls or 'a large competitive depreciation of sterling'; third, tentative proposals for cautious 'internationally co-ordinated' growth and reflation In this respect, immediate priorities would be the control and further reduction of inflation by means of 'continuing restraint in wage bargaining' and the need for some form of institutionalised 'flexible incomes policy' and 'firm monetary control'.[96] In as far as the group offered positive policy ideas and proposals, it encouraged an increased emphasis in social democratic political economy on the control of inflation, clearer guidelines for the control of wage demands and public expenditure, and a new focus on wealth creation as opposed to wealth (re)distribution and wider issues of individual choice and freedom.[97]

The constraints and limitations of Manifesto Group organisation

The effects of the internal diversity and tensions of the Manifesto Group reflected the emerging divisions and fragmentation of the centre-right more widely. Manifesto Group ideas and proposals had relatively limited impact on the Labour Party and contemporary debate. In the contemporary press, for instance, the proposals were viewed as a return to the past, or as a recommendation 'that we go on doing what we are, with minor modifications and in a more aesthetically pleasing style'. Even relatively sympathetic commentators such as Peter Jenkins described the analysis and proposals contained in the group's 'manifesto' as 'Plus ça change', on the grounds that the same statement might have been made fifteen years previously.[98] By this stage, it appeared that both inside and outside the party the tide of ideas was against them. Lacking an overall and innovative intellectual perspective, the majority of the Manifesto Group membership was less concerned to develop a coherent set of ideas and proposals, within the context of a comprehensive statement of social democratic intent appropriate to the new conditions, than (perhaps inevitably) with the immediate priority to maintain the Labour Government and a moderate democratic socialist programme in office and to stem the left-wing tide in the party. Additional attempts were made to augment the radical Labour credentials of the Manifesto Group and to take up the wider battle of ideas with the publication of a clear anti-Conservative statement in June 1978 attacking new Conservative ideas and policies. *The Wrong Approach: An Exposition of Conservative Policies* was essentially an attempt to provide the Manifesto Group with an offensive anti-Thatcherite as well as a defensive anti-left position. However, the limited overall impact of Manifesto Group ideas reflected the consequences of its 'paralysingly diverse' centre-right membership, which itself was a reflection of the fragmentation of the centre-right in the context of the key political debates and intra-party alignments of the 1970s.[99] In this respect, it was hampered by institutional, ideological, organisational and political constraints and limitations.

In the first instance, at an institutional level the Manifesto Group found itself in a different position to that of CDS. Although the 'purely Parliamentary' Manifesto Group, which had 'no intention' of 'undertaking political organisation outside', was keen to emphasise clear differences between the group and CDS, some commentators drew similarities between them. However, there were critical institutional and contextual differences between the two organisations, which impacted on their relative intra-party influence. In the early 1960s revisionist social democracy had enjoyed a good degree of hegemony in the party and the patronage of the party leader, Hugh Gaitskell. By the mid-1970s the party political context was very different. Although the Manifesto Group in its original mission was formed to offer reinforcement to the beleaguered government, its relationship to the parliamentary leadership was never better than ambiguous. After his election to the party leadership in April 1976, Callaghan declared that he was opposed to the idea of intra-party groupings of all types and that he would 'not be willing to accept a situation in which minority groups in the Parliamentary Labour Party manoeuvre in order to foist their views on the party as a whole'.[100] Ambitious politicians in the group feared that explicit and active membership would jeopardise their prospects of promotion, but the obdurate response of the Manifesto Group was that it 'would be ready to disband the day after the Tribune Group did so'. The Manifesto Group was also much less ideologically distinctive and cohesive than CDS and, as a purely parliamentary organisation of the 'moderate' centre-right, possessed the unenviable task of attempting to (re)unite the diverse anti-left tendencies of the PLP.[101]

Although the Manifesto Group was able to achieve a good degree of success in one of its original aims to reverse the trend of Tribune Group success in electing its candidates to PLP office,[102] its wider limitations appeared to be built into its very structure and *raison d'être*. Intellectual and political differences between the Manifesto Group membership were clearly demarcated. In the post-Common Market environment of the Labour Party, there was clear distance between Jenkinsite revisionist social democrats, who held the European ideal as an 'article of faith', and pragmatic centrist politicians and the so-called 'old' or traditional Labour right who were opposed to, or at best ambiguous about, the European issue. Desai argues that:

> the very description of the Manifesto Group as 'moderate' revealed its basic irrelevance to the cause of the social democrats. It was at least partly a consequence of the existence of many social democrats on the backbenches who in different circumstances would have expected to be in Government. On the backbenches, they attempted to mobilise 'moderate' opinion divided and demoralised since the European split, against the left. However, right-wing unity could only be had by agreeing not to raise important issues such as the Common Market and any gains for the Manifesto Group could only be of dubious value to the social democratic cause.

Moreover:

> The social democrats who were engaged in this attempt at recreating this alliance of the revisionist right and the centrists in the Labour Party knew well enough that in the prevailing political climate it was of limited effectiveness. It was a half-hearted ... effort on the part of those who probably knew that their tenure in the Labour Party was now seriously in question – an exercise in premeditated futility not unlike Roy Jenkins' bid for the party leadership.[103]

Given its solely parliamentary and backbench composition, a further problem of Manifesto Group organisation arose when core members of the group were promoted to government positions or departed Parliament altogether, depriving the group of some its most active and able resources. The departure of Horam to the Department of Transport in 1976 and the resignation from Parliament of

Marquand to join Roy Jenkins as an adviser in Brussels in 1977, deprived the Manifesto Group of two key figures interested in ideas. The group retained some such as Radice who were interested in ideas but, for the most part, driven by the organisational ability of those such as Ian Wrigglesworth and John Cartwright, it focused on consolidating its early successes in organising and electing 'slates' of candidates for PLP committees and cultivating an effective media profile rather than engaging in a full frontal intellectual and ideological assault on the Labour left. The perceived need to withhold its list of members for fear of reprisals and deselection of right-wing Labour MPs at the hands of left-wing CLPs also prevented a more frontal challenge to the Labour left. The small number of Manifesto Group members such as Horam, Wrigglesworth, Marquand, Dickson Mabon and John Mackintosh who were prepared to adopt a high profile and risk the bitter criticism of the left, felt disappointed by others who did not. The impact of the group was also limited by the reluctance of influential representatives of the centre-right such as Roy Hattersley, John Smith, Gerald Kaufman and Bryan Gould to join its ranks. Although they might have privately supported the general aims of the Manifesto Group, they were careful to publicly distance themselves from the group and denounced its appeal as too 'right-wing'.[104]

Beyond the initial organisational success against the Tribune Group within the PLP, the constraints and limited impact of the Manifesto Group faction reflected the emerging ideological and political complexity and tensions of the wider Labour right tendency of the PLP in the 1970s. It contained within its (seventy plus) membership a diverse range of broadly centre-right Labour MPs and opinion, including both Jenkinsites and loyalist centrists. Beyond 'getting their slates elected to [backbench PLP] committees' and 'having "agonized discussions" about the government's series of public expenditure cuts', the Manifesto Group had little wider impact given the diversity and constraints of its internal organisation. It limited its 'critical friend' of the Labour Government role to discussion of the 'minutiae of anti-inflation policy – demanding more firmness and consistency' and, in the circumstances of 'new and unanticipated [economic] problems', focused on the need for 'careful review of public expenditure and anti-inflation measures' and the need for a flexible but permanent incomes policy.[105] Although invitations to speakers and the agendas of Manifesto Group meetings reveal a desire to expand the prospectus of political discussion on occasion (to issues such as devolution), the majority of meetings and all significant internal documentation were devoted to issues of inflation and public expenditure.[106] The limited concerns of the Manifesto Group were, perhaps, understandable given national priorities and the group's original limited ambition to support the Labour Government in the interests of right-wing unity against the challenge of the new Labour left. However, any wider aspiration to develop and propose positive policy alternatives, beyond the odd 'laudable modernising sentiment' and a defensive, moderate 'middle way' between the economic extremes of left and right, was severely curtailed by the complexity and tensions of its diverse membership. For this reason, the contribution of the Manifesto Group was notable for the absence of discussion of critical/divisive policy themes. The issue of EEC membership was a particularly thorny issue for the group (as was the question of devolution),[107] and the highly disappointing performance of Roy Jenkins in the 1976 party leadership contest (in a crowded field of candidates of the centre-right) highlights the fact that the group was unable to organise behind a single figurehead. The fragmentation of the Labour right was both cause and effect of the emerging strength of the Labour left in the party.[108]

Conclusion

The broad aim of this chapter has been to show that it was not the case that the parliamentary Labour right in the 1970s lacked group mentality and factional organisation, and that such group behaviour could not take 'oppositional' form within the context of Labour Party politics of the period, but, rather,that such behaviour took place within a party and political environment that was passing them by. The development and efficacy of factional activity on the parliamentary Labour right were constrained by a number of factors, not least among them an alien, unforgiving party environment and the ideological and political complexity and fragmentation of the wider source of membership. Consequently, attempts to cohere and organise on the parliamentary Labour right lacked significant impact on the internal politics of the Labour Party. Rather, for some, their experience of group organisation and activity consolidated their increasing frustration with the constraints and trajectory of Labour Party politics, and offered the prospect of an alternative vehicle and agenda of social democracy.

In opposition after 1970, the Jenkinsite faction took a stance that divided them not just from the Labour left, but also from the centrist leadership, who were committed to party unity and the priority of defeating the Conservative Government, and some former influential allies of the Gaitskellite revisionist tendency of the Labour Party. The 'oppositional' form of Jenkinsite behaviour further weakened the cohesion of the parliamentary Labour right in the face of enhanced left-wing activity and emphasised the increasing tensions and divisions of Labour's centre-right 'dominant coalition' and 'governing elite'. Moreover, it also offered an early indication of the potential (and promise) of a social democratic breakaway from the Labour Party.

The underlying complexity, divisions and potential fragmentation of the parliamentary Labour right were further illustrated from the mid-1970s in the internal organisation, dynamics and limitations of the Manifesto Group. Initially established to offer a critically supportive perspective of the Labour Government and to act as a counterweight to the Tribune Group in the PLP, its diverse membership reflected a broad range of centre-right opinion. While it was temporarily effective in stemming the flow of success of the Tribune Group in elections for PLP office, its inability to address critical and divisive policy themes reflected the diversity and tensions of its internal organisation and membership, and restricted the latitude and impact of its ideas and proposals. Again, the experience of the Manifesto Group for some confirmed the emerging constraints, divisions and limitations of Labour's centre-right coalition and the seemingly inalienable trajectory of the Labour Party further to the left.

The factional organisation and activity of the parliamentary Labour right in the 1970s does not correspond unconditionally to the conventional models of left–right factionalism outlined by Rose and others. Parliamentary Labour right forces did not coalesce in a clearly loyalist or supportive 'undifferentiated non-Left tendency'.[109] Nor did they give rise to a homogeneous, resolute revisionist faction in the mould of CDS, dedicated to the defence of the parliamentary leadership. The factional behaviour and impact of the parliamentary Labour right reveals, rather, the extent to which the wider tendency had fragmented ideologically, politically and organisationally by the 1970s.

Notes

1 British membership of the Common Market, for example, cut right across party lines and party political labels. It presented a particularly thorny issue for the Manifesto Group, which contained both pro- and anti-Europeans.

2 R. Rose, 'Parties, Factions and Tendencies in Britain', *Political Studies*, 12 (1), 1964, pp. 33–46; also see T. Bale, 'Towards a "Cultural Theory" of Parliamentary Party Groups', *Journal of Legislative Studies*, 3 (4), 1997, pp. 25–43; D. Hine, 'Factionalism in West European Parties: A Framework for Analysis', *Journal of West European Politics*, 5 (1), 1982, pp. 36, 37, 44–5.

3 See Hine, 'Factionalism in West European Parties', pp. 37, 38–9.

4 *Ibid.*, pp. 37, 38.

5 *Ibid.*, p. 37; Rose, 'Parties, Factions and Tendencies in Britain', pp. 37–8.

6 See Bale, 'Towards a "Cultural Theory" of Parliamentary Party Groups', pp. 25–7; J. Brand, 'Faction as its Own Reward: Groups in the British Parliament 1945 to 1986', *Parliamentary Affairs*, 42 (3), 1989, pp. 149–51; Hine, 'Factionalism in West European Parties', pp. 17, 44–5; also see V. McKee, *Right-wing Factionalism in the British Labour Party 1977–87*, unpublished M.Phil. Thesis, CNAA, 1988, pp. 7–8, 236–7.

7 See Hine, 'Factionalism in West European Parties', p. 39.

8 See S. Meredith, 'Labour Party Revisionism and Public Expenditure: Divisions of Social Democratic Political Economy in the 1970s', *Labour History Review*, 70 (3), 2005, pp. 253–73.

9 At the time Rose was writing in 1964, the moderate, leadership/loyalist faction of the Labour right was represented by the Gaitskellite CDS: Rose, 'Parties, Factions and Tendencies in Britain', pp. 41–2.

10 See D. M. Wood and W. G. Jacoby, 'Intraparty Cleavage in the British House of Commons: Evidence from the 1974–1979 Parliament', *American Journal of Political Science*, 28 (1), 1984, pp. 203, 207, 217, 221; also see McKee, *Right-wing Factionalism in the British Labour Party 1977–87*, pp. 3–4.

11 See S. Brittan, *Left and Right: The Bogus Dilemma*, London, Secker & Warburg, 1968; S. Brittan, 'Further Thoughts on Left and Right', *Capitalism and the Permissive Society*, London, Macmillan, 1973, pp. 354–73; A. Warde, *Consensus and Beyond: The Development of Labour Party Strategy since the Second World War*, Manchester, Manchester University Press, 1982, pp. 10, 12.

12 G. Daly, *The Crisis in the Labour Party 1974–81 and the Origins of the 1981 Schism*, unpublished Ph.D. Thesis, University of London, Birkbeck College, 1992, pp. 69–70.

13 P. Larkin, 'New Labour and Old Revisionism', *Renewal*, 8 (1), 2000, pp. 42–9.
14 J. E. Ryan, *The British Social Democrats: A Case Study of Factionalism in Left-of-Center Parties 1964–1981*, unpublished Ph.D. Thesis, Georgetown University, Washington, DC, 1987.
15 See Labour Party, *Labour and the Common Market*, Report of A Special Conference of the Labour Party Central Hall Westminster, 17 July 1971, London, Labour Party, 1971, pp. 42–9; *Report of the Seventieth Annual Conference of the Labour Party, Brighton 1971*, London, Labour Party, 1971; also see *Report of the Seventy-first Annual Conference of the Labour Party, Blackpool 1972*, London, Labour Party, 1972, pp. 195–217; B. Pimlott, *Harold Wilson*, London, Harper Collins, 1992, pp. 583–6.
16 Pimlott, *Harold Wilson*, pp. 586–7.
17 Roy Jenkins, cited in L. Minkin, *The Contentious Alliance: Trade Unions and the Labour Party*, Edinburgh, Edinburgh University Press, 1991, p. 231.
18 Labour Party, *Labour's Programme 1973*, London, Labour Party, 1973, pp. 13–39, 40–2.
19 *Ibid.*, p. 6.
20 See, for instance, D. Owen, *Time to Declare*, London, Michael Joseph, 1991, p. 172; Pimlott, *Harold Wilson*, pp. 594–5.
21 J. P. Mackintosh, 'Socialism or Social Democracy? The Choice for the Labour Party', *Political Quarterly*, 43 (4), 1972, p. 484.
22 R. Jenkins, *What Matters Now*, London, Fontana, 1972, pp. 21–2.
23 Brian Walden, cited in Daly, *The Crisis in the Labour Party 1974–81*, p. 75.
24 See D. Butler and D. Kavanagh, *The British General Election of February 1974*, London, Macmillan, 1974, p. 268.
25 Ryan, *The British Social Democrats*, pp. 1–5, 10, 11–12, 13.
26 Bill Rodgers, Interview with the author, 18 February 2001.
27 David Marquand, Interview with the author, 16 January 2001.
28 The series of speeches was delivered to Labour Party and trade union audiences between March and September 1972: see Jenkins, *What Matters Now*, pp. 13–15, 115; also see P. Bell, *The Labour Party in Opposition 1970–1974*, London, Routledge, 2004, pp. 190–209.
29 R. Jenkins, *European Diary 1977–81*, London, Harper Collins, 1989, p. 1.
30 A. Crosland, Speech to the Labour Political Studies Centre, 16 April 1972; A. Crosland, Press Statement, 17 April 1972, Crosland Papers 6/2; also see S. Crosland, *Tony Crosland*, London, Jonathan Cape, 1982, pp. 238–44.
31 A. Crosland, Statement, April 1972, Crosland Papers 6/2.
32 John Wakefield to Paul Adamson, 27 February 1978, Manifesto Group Papers, LP/MANIF/23; B. Brivati and D. Wincott (eds), 'The Campaign for Democratic Socialism 1960–64', *Contemporary Record*, 7 (2), 1993, p. 365.
33 Brivati and Wincott, 'The Campaign for Democratic Socialism', p. 365.
34 See, for example, Pimlott, *Harold Wilson*, p. 587.
35 R. Jenkins, *A Life at the Centre*, London, Macmillan, 1991, p. 310; also see pp. 315–21, 324–34; Bell, *The Labour Party in Opposition*, pp. 192–3; Owen, *Time to Declare*, p. 167; D. Taverne, *The Future of the Left: Lincoln and After*, London: Jonathan Cape, 1974, p. 102.
36 See S. Crosland, *Tony Crosland*, pp. 250–3.
37 Dick Taverne, Interview with the author, 18 January 2001; Rodgers, Interview with the author.
38 Bell, *The Labour Party in Opposition*, p. 193.
39 Owen, *Time to Declare*, p. 167.

40 Crewe and King, *SDP*, pp. 55–6, 529–30. They suggest that '[p]robably the only other modern British politician to have had a similar entourage for a time is Tony Benn'.

41 Taverne, Interview with the author.

42 Rodgers, Interview with the author.

43 See Bell, *The Labour Party in Opposition*, pp. 193–4.

44 B. Brivati and D. Wincott (eds), 'The Labour Committee for Europe', *Contemporary Record*, 7 (2), 1993, pp. 386–9; Rodgers, Interview with the author, 18 February 2001.

45 Bell, *The Labour Party in Opposition*, p. 194.

46 Desai, *Intellectuals and Socialism*, pp. 145–6; T. Benn, *Office Without Power: Diaries 1968–72*, London, Hutchinson, 1988, p. 358; T. Nairn, 'The Left Against Europe', *New Left Review*, 75, September–October, 1972, p. 75.

47 Desai, *Intellectuals and Socialism*, pp. 127–63; also see Jenkins, *A Life at the Centre*, pp. 329–32.

48 See Desai, *Intellectuals and Socialism*, pp. 136–41; also see B. Brivati, 'Revisionists', *Socialist History*, 9, 1996, pp. 109–14; Crewe and King, *SDP*, pp. 104–16.

49 Bell, *The Labour Party in Opposition*, pp. 195–6.

50 Desai, *Intellectuals and Socialism*, pp. 150–1; Owen, *Time to Declare*, p. 187.

51 Bell, *The Labour Party in Opposition*, pp. 196–7.

52 See Jenkins, *A Life at the Centre*, pp. 86, 310, 320; Labour Party, *Labour and the Common Market*, pp. 42–9; Pimlott, *Harold Wilson*, pp. 581–2.

53 See Bell, *The Labour Party in Opposition*, pp. 198–9, 200–2.

54 *Ibid.*, p. 206.

55 See Jenkins, *What Matters Now*, pp. 9, 22; Jenkins, *A Life at the Centre*, p. 339; also see Desai, *Intellectuals and Socialism*, p. 157.

56 Jenkins, *A Life at the Centre*, p. 621; also see Owen, *Time to Declare*, p. 190.

57 Bell, *The Labour Party in Opposition*, pp. 206–8.

58 *Ibid.*, pp. 208, 215; S. Crosland, *Tony Crosland*, p. 252.

59 Jenkins, *A Life at the Centre*, p. 364; H. Laser, 'British Populism: The Labour Party and the Common Market Parliamentary Debate', *Political Science Quarterly*, 91 (2), 1976, pp. 274.

60 See Bell, *The Labour Party in Opposition*, pp. 208–9.

61 Marquand, Interview with the author; D. Marquand, *The New Reckoning: Capitalism, States and Citizens*, Cambridge, Polity Press, 1997, pp. 11–12; D. Marquand, *The Progressive Dilemma: From Lloyd George to Blair*, revised second edition, London, Orion/Phoenix, 1999, pp. 166–7; R. Plant, 'Social Democracy', in D. Marquand and A. Seldon (eds), *The Ideas that Shaped Post-war Britain*, London: Fontana, 1996, pp. 165–6; Rodgers, Interview with the author, 18 February 2001; but see J. Nuttall, 'Tony Crosland and the Many Falls and Rises of British Social Democracy', *Contemporary British History*, 18 (4), 2004, pp. 68–9.

62 Marquand, *The Progressive Dilemma*, p. 170.

63 Rose, 'Parties, Factions and Tendencies in Britain', pp. 37–8; also see Hine, 'Factionalism in West European Parties', pp. 38–9.

64 Hine, 'Factionalism in West European Parties', p. 39; Rose, 'Parties, Factions and Tendencies in Britain', p. 37.

65 Hine, 'Factionalism in West European Parties', pp. 38–9; also see F. P. Belloni and D. C. Beller, 'The Study of Party Factions as Competitive Political Organisations', *Western Political Quarterly*, 29 (4), 1976, pp. 531–49.

66 The Jenkinsites claim to have marshalled the crucial forty or so centre-right votes in support of the eventual victor, Ted Short, in the deputy leadership contest of April 1972 following Jenkins' resignation, thereby 'sabotaging' Crosland's candidature: see S. Crosland, *Tony Crosland*, pp. 243–4; Jenkins, *A Life at the Centre*, p. 352; Marquand, *The Progressive Dilemma*, p. 169.

67 See Hine, 'Factionalism in West European Parties', p. 38; Rose, 'Parties, Factions and Tendencies in Britain', p. 37. In policy terms, the Jenkinsite group was not a one-trick pony. The core of the group held common or similar views on critical issues of public expenditure and industrial relations and trade union reform. It reflected the emergence of an ideologically cohesive core group of 'liberal' revisionist social democrats: see, for example, Meredith, 'Labour Party Revisionism and Public Expenditure'.

68 This appears to accurately describe the organisation and interaction of the Jenkinsite group in (and out of) Parliament: H. Berrington, 'The Common Market and the British Parliamentary Parties, 1971: Tendencies, Issue Groups ... and Factionalism', paper presented to the workshop, *Factionalism in the Political Parties of Western Europe*, European Consortium for Political Research (ECPR), Florence, 25–29 March 1980, p. 14; Marquand, Interview with the author; Rodgers, Interview with the author; Taverne, Interview with the author.

69 Berrington, 'The Common Market and the British Parliamentary Parties', pp. 2, 15.

70 See *Financial Times*, 9 March 1977, Manifesto Group Papers, LP/MANIF/18.

71 Neville Sandelson, Memo, n.d., Sandelson Papers, 6/1.

72 Manifesto Group, Committee Proposals, Sandelson Papers, 6/1; John Wakefield to Paul Adamson, 3 February 1978; John Wakefield to Paul Adamson, 27 February 1978; John Wakefield to Patrick Seyd, 13 March 1978, Manifesto Group Papers, LP/MANIF/23; John Wakefield to Patrick McSharry, 18 August 1978; John Wakefield to R. F. Atkins, 17 January 1979; John Wakefield to Roger Poole, 23 January 1979, Manifesto Group Papers, LP/MANIF/25; George Robertson to Ron Hayward, March 1980, Manifesto Group Papers, LP/MANIF/7.

73 John Wakefield to Paul Adamson, 3 February 1978; John Wakefield to Paul Adamson, 27 February 1978, Manifesto Group Papers, LP/MANIF/23.

74 John Wakefield to Paul Adamson, 3 February 1978; John Wakefield to Paul Adamson, 27 February 1978, Manifesto Group Papers, LP/MANIF/23; Letter from George Robertson to Manifesto Group members, January 1980?, Manifesto Group Papers, LP/MANIF/9; Dennis Canavan to Ian Wrigglesworth, 18 March 1979; Ian Wrigglesworth to Dennis Canavan, 20 March 1979, Manifesto Group Papers, LP/MANIF/25; also see Berrington, 'The Common Market and the British Parliamentary Parties', p. 14; Brand, 'Faction as its Own Reward', p. 152.

75 George Cunningham, Correspondence with the author, 21 November 2001.

76 Marquand, Interview with the author.

77 John Wakefield to Paul Adamson, 27 February 1978, Manifesto Group Papers, LP/MANIF/23; John Wakefield to Roger Poole, 23 January 1979, Manifesto Group Papers, LP/MANIF/25; Ian Wrigglesworth, Notes on Manifesto Group Meeting, 11 January 1978; Ian Wrigglesworth, *Tribune*, 30 December 1977, Manifesto Group Papers, LP/MANIF/4; George Robertson to Ron Hayward, March 1980, Manifesto Group Papers, LP/MANIF/7.

78 *Financial Times*, 9 March 1977.

79 *Ibid.*

80 John Horam, Interview with the author, 16 February 2001.

81 *Financial Times*, 9 March 1977.

82 John Wakefield to Paul Adamson, 27 February 1978, Manifesto Group Papers, LP/MANIF/23.

83 Letter from Neville Sandelson to Manifesto Group Members, n.d., Sandelson Papers 6/1; John Wakefield to Paul Adamson, 27 February 1978, Manifesto Group Papers, LP/MANIF/23.

84 John Wakefield to Paul Adamson, 27 February 1978, Manifesto Group Papers, LP/MANIF/23; John Wakefield to Roger Poole, 23 January 1979, Manifesto Group Papers, LP/MANIF/25; and see Manifesto Group, *What We Must Do: A Democratic Socialist Approach To Britain's Crisis*, March 1977, Manifesto Group Papers, LP/MANIF/18; Manifesto Group, *The Wrong Approach: An Exposure of Conservative Policies*, June 1978; Manifesto Group, *Priorities for Labour: A Manifesto Group Statement*, March 1979, Manifesto Group Papers, LP/MANIF/20; Manifesto Group, *The Future of Counter-Inflation Policy*, January 1979, Manifesto Group Papers, LP/MANIF/3.

85 David Marquand, 'Economic Situation'; Horam, 'The Present Situation'; John Horam, 'Economic Report by the Manifesto Group' for meeting with Denis Healey, 27 February 1975, Sandelson Papers, 6/1.

86 Manifesto Group, *What We Must Do*, pp. 4, 5–6, 36.

87 'Moderates in the Labour Party, 2: The Manifesto Group, Giving intellectual credibility to policies', *The Times*, 30 September 1977, Sandelson Papers 6/1.

88 Manifesto Group, *What We Must Do*, pp. 5–6; Horam, 'Economic Report by the Manifesto Group', Sandelson Papers, 6/1.

89 Manifesto Group, *What We Must Do*, pp. 10–12; *Financial Times*, 9 March 1977; *The Times*, 30 September 1977.

90 See *Daily Telegraph*, 9 March 1977, Manifesto Group Papers, LP/MANIF/18.

91 Manifesto Group, *What We Must Do*, pp. 22–4; also see Minkin, *The Contentious Alliance*, pp. 209, 231; P. Whitehead, *The Writing on the Wall: Britain in the Seventies*, London, Michael Joseph, 1985, p. 346.

92 G. Radice, 'Revisionism Revisited', *Socialist Commentary*, May 1974, pp. 25–7; K. Jefferys, 'The Old Right', in R. Plant, M. Beech and K. Hickson (eds), *The Struggle for Labour's Soul: Understanding Labour's Political Thought since 1945*, London, Routledge, 2004, pp. 77–8; K. Jefferys, *Anthony Crosland: A New Biography*, London, Richard Cohen, 1999, p. 176; also see C.A.R. Crosland, *Socialism Now and Other Essays*, London, Jonathan Cape, 1974, pp. 17–48; Statement by Rt Hon. Anthony Crosland MP, 21 March 1976, Crosland Papers, 6/4; Bruce Douglas-Mann to Betty Boothroyd, 22 March 1976, Crosland Papers, 6/4; D. Leonard, 'Memo on Leadership Election and its Implications for the Future', 1 June 1976, Crosland Papers, 6/3.

93 In the leadership election, Crosland drew more support from the 'non-Tribunite left' than from the revisionist Labour right: Jefferys, *Anthony Crosland*, pp. 193–5; P. Kellner, 'Anatomy of the Vote', *New Statesman*, 9 April 1976; Neville Sandelson to Bruce Douglas-Mann, 24 March 1976, Crosland Papers, 6/4; Leonard, 'Memo on Leadership Election', Crosland Papers, 6/3.

94 Horam, Interview with the author, 16 February 2001.

95 See Desai, *Intellectuals and Socialism*, pp. 156–7, 172; John Wakefield, Public Expenditure Cuts: the Chancellor's remarks and further comments, 12 July 1976; Manifesto Group, 'Keep on Course: A Statement on Economic Policy', 27 October 1976; Manifesto Group, Statement on the Budget, 11 April 1978; Manifesto Group, Statement Issued 15 November 1978, Manifesto Group Papers, LP/MANIF/3; also see D. Marquand, J. Mackintosh, D. Owen, 'Change Gear! Towards A Socialist Strategy', Supplement to *Socialist Commentary*, October 1967, John P. Mackintosh Papers, 323/138; David Owen Papers, D709/2/10/1, pp. iv–v.

96 Manifesto Group, 'Economic Policy', 13 March 1978, Mackintosh Papers, 323/139, pp. 4–5, 9–14.

97 This 'new' thinking in social democratic political economy not only set core members of the Manifesto Group apart from increasingly centrist 'egalitarian' social democrats such as Crosland and Roy Hattersley, but gives some credence to the idea, if not of a wholesale paradigm shift in economic policy in the direction of neo-liberal monetarism and therefore of the fracture of the post-war Keynesian social democratic consensus, of some sort of philosophical sea-change in the basis and purpose of social democratic economic policy. It was more willing to address intrinsic limitations of traditional social democratic political economy in the economic circumstances of the 1970s, to consider the need to adapt fundamental aspects of economic thinking to the new conditions, and even to reconceptualise the balance and priorities of guiding principles in the direction of a greater emphasis on individual freedom: see T. Clark, 'The Limits of Social Democracy? Tax and Spend under Labour, 1974–79', Working Paper 01/04, Institute for Fiscal Studies, 2001; Meredith, 'Labour Party Revisionism and Public Expenditure'.

98 *Financial Times*, 9 March 1977; *The Guardian*, 19 May 1977; Manifesto Group Papers, LP/MANIF/18.

99 Desai, *Intellectuals and Socialism*, p. 171.

100 *The Times*, 22 April 1976.

101 John Wakefield to Paul Adamson, 27 February 1978, Manifesto Group Papers, LP/MANIF/23; Desai, *Intellectuals and Socialism*, p. 170.

102 *Sunday Times*, 30 November 1975; *The Times*, 30 September 1977, Sandelson Papers 6/1.

103 Desai, *Intellectuals and Socialism*, pp. 170–1.

104 After 1979, for instance, Hattersley and Gould were said to want Bill Rodgers to remain in the Labour Party because there would always be someone to the right of them: Horam, Interview with the author; Rodgers, Interview with the author.

105 See Manifesto Group, 'Economic Policy', 13 March 1978, Mackintosh Papers, 323/139.

106 See Desai, *Intellectuals and Socialism*, pp. 171–2. In addition to its general policy statement, *What We Must Do*, see Marquand, 'Economic Situation', Sandelson Papers, 6/1; Sydney Irving, Notes on Manifesto Group Meeting, 9 February 1977; Notes on Manifesto Group Meeting, 15 June 1977, Manifesto Group Papers, LP/MANIF/4; Manifesto Group, 'Keep on Course: A Statement on Economic Policy', 22 October 1976; Manifesto Group, 'After Phase Two', June 1977; Manifesto Group, Statement on the Budget, 11 April 1978, Manifesto Group Papers, LP/MANIF/3; also see Ian Wrigglesworth, Notes of Manifesto Group Meeting, 1 December 1976; Notes of Manifesto Group Meeting, 8 December 1976; George Robertson to Bill Rodgers, Shirley Williams, David Owen, Roy Mason, Roy Hattersley, 7 July 1980; George Robertson to Manifesto Group Members, 7 July 1980, Manifesto Group Papers, LP/MANIF/4.

107 Its Assistant Secretary noted in January 1979 that the 'Group has never taken a clear pro or anti view . . . because its members, like the members of the Labour Party more generally, are divided over the question': John Wakefield to François-Xavier Camenen, 17 January 1979; Ian Wrigglesworth to Dennis Canavan, 20 March 1979, Manifesto Group Papers, LP/MANIF/25. David Owen (unconvincingly) suggested that 'differing attitudes to the Common Market, defence spending, public ownership and many social policies reflected . . . not a polarised Right but a broad span of Labour voters' attitudes': D. Owen, Speech at a meeting of CLV, 10 January 1980, Owen Papers, D709/2/17/1/2.

108 Desai explains that the absence of any discussion of the EEC in Manifesto Group statements was 'a problematic omission made necessary by the fact' that those who wrote them were 'not only [Jenkinsite] social democrats but other right-wingers in the Labour Party who were opposed to the Common Market'. Desai also notes that 'Callaghan's strongest rival for the leadership was the Labour left's Michael Foot, not the social democrats' Roy Jenkins', a reflection of new 'left-wing voting strength' and the discrepancies of the Manifesto Group and the disunity of the Labour right more broadly. The Manifesto Group was now struggling to contain the influence of the Tribune Group inside the Party: Desai, *Intellectuals and Socialism*, pp. 172–3; also see John Horam, 'After the Change', *Socialist Commentary*, May 1976.

109 Ryan, *The British Social Democrats*, pp. 26–8.

4

A prelude to secession?
The parliamentary Labour right
and Europe

Introduction

This study argues, somewhat against the grain, that a wider range of policy issues and underlying political philosophy, beyond the single issue of British membership of the Common Market, divided the parliamentary Labour right and Labour Party revisionism. However, the European issue remains a critical element of any analysis of the nature and dimensions of Labour right and wider party tensions and divisions in the 1970s. Arguments and perspectives in the debate over Europe 'cut across party lines, across party political labels', and it has been noted that 'the true story of the formation of the SDP begins here in early 1971' as 'the European Community became another issue for instant opposition' to the Conservative Government.[1]

The reluctant and shifting relationship of post-war British governments with the idea of European integration is well known.[2] It has been a central theme of recent British history and Britain's post-war, post-imperial experience.[3] Throughout much of the post-war period, the Labour Party has displayed complex and shifting attitudes towards European integration. For thirty years or more the party has experienced significant internal conflict, disputes and divisions over membership of the EEC, and the party itself has fluctuated back and forth, between pro and anti, when in and out of office.[4] The first two years of Labour's return to opposition in 1970 were overshadowed by protracted disputes over the party's attitude to the Common Market. A minority of pro-Market MPs, mainly from the 'revisionist' wing of the party, supported Heath to secure British entry, despite increasing scepticism at grass-roots level about the benefits of membership. In an attempt to reconcile divisions, 'Wilson adopted a compromise: Labour would renegotiate the terms of entry and hold a referendum on British membership – a formula which prompted the resignation from the front-bench of the Shadow Chancellor [and deputy leader of the party], Roy Jenkins'.[5]

Labour's European divisions represented more than a simple split on orthodox left–right party lines. Tom Nairn noted that:

> the Common Market schism is only partly between 'left' and 'right' in the classical Labourist sense. Far too many right-wing and centrist leaders joined the anti-Market

movement for this to be an adequate explanation. It corresponds more closely to a split between old 'party men' . . . and 'new men' of bourgeois origin less dependent on the party machine and the Old Labourist spirit.

One effect of divisions over the principle of entry to the Common Market in October 1971 was 'the formation of a new leadership for the social-democratic right wing – around Jenkins and [George] Thompson – and in a general strengthening of that faction's fibre and spirit'.[6] The split over Europe has been described as 'the most serious to wrack the party since the days of Bevanism'. It led to the first visible, organised 'revisionist' presence in the party since the days of CDS in 1964 and, without the patronage or wider support of the party leadership, precipitated the marginalisation in the party of an important element of parliamentary Labour right and revisionist social democratic opinion.[7]

The previous chapter noted the centrality of the European issue to the Jenkinsite cause and factional activity on the parliamentary Labour right in the 1970s. This chapter examines more broadly the differential attitudes and perspectives of European integration on the parliamentary Labour right, and the fault lines and divisions contained therein. First, it briefly addresses the context of the European debate within the Labour Party from Macmillan's original attempt to seek British membership of the EEC in 1961. From this moment, future relations with the EEC were presented as a matter of 'capital importance in the life of our country' as a major 'political as well as . . . economic issue'.[8] Second, it examines the nature and dimensions of earlier Gaitskellite revisionist tensions and disagreements over Europe. Third, it assesses the context and implications of the Wilson Government's second application to join the Community in 1967 as a prelude to the bitter divisions and conflict that overtook the party in opposition after 1970 as it reversed its position on British membership of the EEC. Finally, it addresses the clear emergence of disparate attitudes to the European question and the extent to which European divisions underpinned the fragmentation of Labour Party revisionism and the parliamentary Labour right in the 1970s.

The Labour Party and Europe

Labour's divisions reflected wider debates in British politics over the process of European integration. The essence of the Common Market question was the nature of Britain's relationship with the rest of the world. There were three main dimensions to this discourse. First, the peculiarity of Britain's post-war alignments, comprising of the sterling area as an economic unit, the Commonwealth as a political entity and the 'special relationship' with the United States, had to be balanced with its role as a European power. The potential conflict of its European and wider roles raised questions of Britain's likely commitment to the Community and, on the other hand, the potential losses to accrue from the failure to join the European dynamic. Second, questions emerged about the form the community of nations would, or should, take and how it would impact on British sovereignty. Many in the Labour Party viewed the Treaty of Rome as a capitalist association and a potential external force that might constrain the ability of a Labour

Government to plan the British economy.[9] As well as informing left-wing opposition to the European project, this view also influenced revisionist anti-Marketeers such as Douglas Jay and 'centrists' such as Peter Shore.[10] Only if the Labour Party could be harnessed to EEC institutions would it develop in a way compatible with the precepts of democratic socialism. Labour pro-Europeans came to regard 'limitations on sovereignty' arguments as 'curious'. They detected these and arguments about a remote bureaucracy as 'really political' and as having 'different motives'.[11] A third dimension of the debate concerned the danger that EEC membership presented to the Commonwealth and the rise of disproportional losses in Commonwealth trade.[12] This was a principal theme of the arguments of Gaitskell and other anti-European Labour revisionists such as Jay. On the other hand, pro-Marketeers urged that entry would open up European markets and that Commonwealth interests could be safeguarded.

Although membership of the EEC was not strictly ruled out in its policy statements, Labour became identified with an anti-European position.[13] Within the PLP there was a majority of anti-Marketeers, and opposition to the Community was also widespread in the party at large. With the small exception of those who came from an internationalist Independent Labour Party (ILP) background, those on the left were broadly anti-European. Among so-called Gaitskellite revisionists there was a majority of pro-Marketeers, but this grouping also contained a significant minority of anti-Marketeers.[14] Labour Party divisions over Europe were, in many ways, the antithesis of contemporary debates over defence. Moderate trade union MPs and the party leader were this time lined up with those who were suspicious of the nature and effects of the Community. In contrast to the defence debate, in which he could rely on a majority of the parliamentary party, if Gaitskell had come out openly in favour of the Common Market he would have faced opposition from all sides of the Labour movement. Alternatively, if he explicitly rejected the principle of the Common Market, he risked alienating the majority of his most loyal supporters.

Gaitskell's failure to approach the Community as an 'article of faith' can be understood partly as an attempt to unify the party in the face of the emerging fissure. He adopted a similarly pragmatic approach as party leader to Wilson's later attempts to maintain party unity in the face of serious intra-party divisions over membership of the Common Market.[15] Gaitskell's personal view of the Community was based on an acceptance of the underlying aspirations of the European movement, tempered by a profound suspicion of the implications of membership for Britain. This approach was expressed most clearly in a deep concern for the precise terms of entry that any British application for membership should make.[16] Gaitskell was 'not against the Common Market in principle, but he argued that the economic case was not proved and he was a great believer in the Commonwealth. He felt it was a factor of stability in the world.'[17] He thus insisted on rigid terms of entry and, believing that talks would ultimately fail, felt he had little to lose by representing vital British interests. The 'famous five conditions' of British membership outlined by Gaitskell included guarantees to British agriculture, a fair deal for European Free Trade Association (EFTA)

partners, the ability to plan national economic policy, the freedom of an independent foreign policy, and safeguards for Commonwealth trade.[18]

'Gaitskellite' divisions over Europe

Far from representing a clear left–right schism in Labour's internal politics or an
unambiguous cause of Labour Party revisionism, the European issue provoked a
range of opinion and some history of indifference and opposition among Labour
revisionists and the parliamentary Labour right more broadly. This included
Gaitskell's initial scepticism and Jay's outright opposition, which reflected 'general
ambivalence . . . to the place of Britain in the process of European integration' on
the basis of a 'concern for practical details rather than abstract principles'.[19]
Gaitskell famously expressed to Jean Monnet in 1962 that 'I don't believe in
faith. I believe in reason and you have not shown me any.' His attitude was to
be characterised by an 'economic rationalism' that was at odds with what he
considered to be the 'irrational' pro-European faith of 'flighty prophets'.[20] It also
included the later strategic manoeuvring, according to the relative intra-party
position and alignments, of Callaghan and Healey, and the studied ambivalence
in the face of more pressing priorities of Crosland.[21] This contrasted with the
enthusiastic support for entry of George Brown, and the 'article of faith' that British
membership represented to Jenkins and his supporters.[22]

As Gaitskell shifted from his initial position as 'a cautious supporter of entry'
as the issue surfaced during 1960, to one of 'public agnosticism' that he thought
should be the basis of Labour Party policy, signs of unrest among pro-European
revisionist colleagues who had been central to his victories in both the Clause IV
and unilateralism debates soon became apparent. In response to the conditions
that Harold Wilson laid down in the House of Commons as essential to Labour's
acceptance of EEC membership, Jenkins resigned his frontbench post.[23] While he
explicitly rejected the general argument of the left of the party, with Wilson to the
fore, that the EEC represented a capitalist cartel that would signal the end of
socialism, Gaitskell 'shared their generally sceptical, suspicious, very *British* attitude
. . . it was his enemies rather than his friends he finished up by pleasing'.[24]

A number of factors lay behind Gaitskell's shifting perspective. The question
of party unity and Labour's electoral fortunes were essential considerations. He
was very conscious of 'the prospect of another huge split in the Labour Party, so
soon after the 1960–61 battle over defence', which 'had the likelihood of ending
Labour's bid for electoral victory', and the 'anticipation of another five years in
frustrating opposition weighed heavily with the "government minded" Gaitskell'.[25]
He was also sensitive to the implications of EEC membership for 'the nature
of Britain's relationship with the rest of the world' because it demanded that
'Britain's relationship to the Commonwealth and the "special relationship" with
the United States would have to be reconsidered'. Gaitskell possessed 'a residual
belief in Britain's global responsibilities, especially where the Commonwealth was
concerned', and he 'regarded the . . . European Community as something of an
irrelevance in the context of this global role'. The continued belief in a global

perspective reflected 'two overriding' assumptions. First, 'much the greater part of our trade and investment overseas is conducted with countries outside Europe'. Second, 'our closest political and human links have been for generations . . . with those nations which were largely created by British emigration, capital, and economic development over the last two centuries', such as Australia and New Zealand. In this respect, he differed from younger Gaitskellites such as Jenkins who believed that 'the future lay in achieving closer links to the Community because . . . Britain could not sustain its international role and . . . needed to develop a more realistic sense of its position in the world'. It represented a 'powerful lobby in the Labour Party . . . arguing against the idea of Britain having a global leadership role and proposing a strategic readjustment: cutting the international cloth to fit the domestic economic reality'.[26]

Gaitskellite European divisions were made explicit in the wake of their leader's emotional anti-Community appeal to the 1962 Labour Party Conference. Famously, Gaitskell disappointed many of his pro-European revisionist supporters with his speech, which argued dramatically against the prospects of a federal Europe:

> We must be clear about this: it does mean, if this is the idea, the end of Britain as an independent European state . . . It means the end of a thousand years of history . . . And it does mean the end of the Commonwealth. How can one seriously suppose that if the mother country, the centre of the Commonwealth, is a province of Europe . . . it could continue to exist as the mother country of a series of independent nations? It is sheer nonsense . . . If we carry the Commonwealth with us, safeguarded, flourishing, prosperous, if we could safeguard our agriculture, and our EFTA friends were all in it, if we were secure in our employment policy, and if we were able to maintain our independent foreign policy and yet have this wider looser association with Europe, it would indeed be a great ideal. But if this is not possible . . . then we must stand firm by what we believe, for the sake of Britain and the World; and we shall not flinch from our duty if that moment comes.[27]

The ovation for the speech in the auditorium was 'unparalleled', but Dora Gaitskell remarked that all 'the wrong people are cheering'. Bill Rodgers, the pro-European organiser of the Gaitskellite CDS, remained firmly in his seat.[28] From an anti-Market perspective, Jay described the character and effect of Gaitskell's speech as 'unique among all the political speeches I ever heard; not merely the finest, but in a class apart . . . It can only be described as an intellectual massacre. Nobody had anything else to say. For its uniqueness rested in its ring of truth.'[29] The speech also revealed clear divisions in the interpretation of a central revisionist theme. The 'power-political creed' held that 'politics was primarily the art of attaining, maintaining and using power'.[30] Revisionist pro-Marketeers developed this theme in their argument, articulated forcefully by Jenkins at the Conference, that British interests would be severely curtailed if it did not attempt to exert influence in what was fast becoming a new centre of power. Part of this argument also suggested that Britain's world role would be better protected from within the Common Market.[31] Gaitskell, on the other hand, argued that British influence would decline markedly if Britain joined the EEC and would be subject to the overall control of policy by 'the Six': there is a possibility of 'majority decisions on political issues, just as we are to have majority decisions on economic issues . . . we would be able somehow or other to outvote those we disagree with. I would like to be very sure of that before I committed myself.'[32]

Before the 'emergence of the Common Market as a major political event revisionists had found themselves united on virtually all the practical policy decisions that had faced the Party both as a government and as an opposition since the war'.[33] Beyond different interpretations of the so-called 'power political creed', much of the argument consisted of economic analysis of the potential effects of entry on economic growth, efficiency and enterprise. Pro-European revisionists identified British entry to the Common Market as concomitant with the desire to promote a more dynamic, efficient and enterprising economy. Anti-European revisionists such as Douglas Jay argued that European protection of food and raw material imports would damage the British economy. Far from aiding the creation of a competitive domestic economy, Common Market entry would hinder the capacity of British industry to compete in certain areas of its home market.[34] They also emphasised the likely effects on equality and social justice, and argued that entry would mean a more regressive taxation system on the grounds of a comparison of the percentage revenue collected from direct taxation in member states. The capacity to control core social services was held to be important by anti-Marketeers, while pro-Market revisionists argued that the Treaty of Rome provided for progressive 'social harmonisation'. Jay's concern was that it depends on what you are harmonising to, but the pro-Europeans argued that levels of pensions and family allowances in Germany, for instance, were far higher than those in Britain.[35]

Revisionist European divisions also revealed different perspectives of the core concept of internationalism. The Gaitskellite CDS manifesto claimed that anything but Britain's membership of the EEC would represent conservative, inward-looking and regressive attitudes and would compensate for any perceived loss of sovereignty with a less insular, more international perspective. Anti-Market revisionists such as Jay claimed equally internationalist credentials, and argued that membership would result in the 'biggest step backwards towards protectionism in 100 years' rather than expand Britain's global perspective and relationships.[35] Others claimed that it was not so much a question of loss of British sovereignty, but whether the European context was the most appropriate in which to integrate. The important issue was not a settlement of British relations with Europe but agreement on arms control and disarmament between the major cold war states and integration of nations into the wider international system. The prospects of security and stability would be better served by the development of genuinely international groups and organisations than the emergence of a few super states, to which British membership of the Common Market would only contribute.[37] There were those who identified an inherent conflict in British membership of the EEC with a post-war Atlanticist mindset. Many of the revisionist Labour right 'were all very certainly pro-European as well', but some Labour social democrats, 'who were great supporters of NATO, were not in favour of it'. They 'took the view that entry into the Common Market . . . would cause transatlantic rifts . . . it was because we were pro-American on this issue that we were hostile to entry into the Common Market'.[38] Pro-Europeans such as Jenkins were far more sanguine about the prospects of British entry to the EEC as an addendum to its Anglo-American commitments. They contended that 'just as Britain had been forced to re-examine its post war attitudes to the Commonwealth and Europe, and reconsider the relative priorities that each should be given in terms of British thinking about foreign policy . . . the time had also come to reconsider the trans-Atlantic relationship'. Jenkins, himself, hinted at the 'inherently unequal nature' of the Anglo-American relationship, and suggested that there was 'a certain lack of enthusiasm, for exclusivity at any rate, on both sides of the Atlantic'. In fact, the US was generally supportive of British entry.[39]

Different internationalist perspectives and priorities and some disparity of approach to the question of the democratic character and deficit of EEC institutions among Labour revisionists informed contending responses to the Common Market question. One observer suggests of the divisions that 'those who agree upon first principles can . . . come to totally separate conclusions on matters of policy'.[40] Gaitskell's opposition to the 1962 negotiations marked a sense of departure with some of his political allies who were disappointed in the lack of enthusiasm towards Europe contained in official Labour policy. Some attempted to explain his approach in terms of the electoral popularity and party advantage to be gained from a hostile attitude to Europe. Gaitskell's anti-European Brighton speech managed to unite the party as a whole behind his leadership and established his reputation as a national leader, but at the expense of 'the comfort of the friendship of those who, on Europe, bitterly disagreed with him'. There was, possibly, the question of the generation gap between Gaitskell and 'his younger revisionist followers' who 'were impressed and excited by the modernisation and technological advance involved in European co-operation'. Gaitskell's patriotism, expressed in his 1962 Brighton speech with references to 'Vimy Ridge' and 'Gallipoli', offered his disappointed supporters the 'strange spectacle of a modernising radical appealing to . . . old-hat sentiment'.[41] In the wider PLP, pro-Marketeers were in a minority and, of those, few 'carried their opposition to Gaitskell's policy into the open by signing a pro-Market motion placed on the order paper by Jenkins, [Jack] Diamond and [Roy] Mason'. Revisionist support for Gaitskell in Labour's Shadow Cabinet could be identified among those such as Healey, Michael Stewart, Patrick Gordon Walker. Along with Callaghan and others such as Wilson, they provided a powerful enough grouping to ensure adequate votes against the adoption of a more enthusiastic approach to British entry. It was only George Brown, Ray Gunter and Douglas Houghton who offered opposition to the Gaitskell line.[42]

Gaitskell's verdict on the Common Market, culminating in his 1962 Brighton conference speech, exposed a serious political fissure of Labour Party Revisionism. Contrary to accounts of the Common Market question as essentially a left–right split in the Labour Party, European divisions were subsequently 'to cut right across the Labour right'.[43] Parliamentary Labour right divisions over Europe were to become entrenched and, in the shifting political and intra-party context of the late 1960s and 1970s, were to become a test of loyalty to the party itself.

The 1967 Wilson application

Divisions over Europe were evident as the Wilson Labour Government undertook to take Britain into the EEC. Initially, both major parties regarded a renewed application as impractical after de Gaulle's veto of Macmillan's bid for entry in January 1963. Labour had not ruled out EEC membership in principle, as long as the terms of entry were favourable. If Commonwealth interests were protected and Britain retained its independent foreign policy, Wilson acknowledged that the EEC offered access to a considerable market in which growth rates had recently far outstripped those of Britain. Eventually, the Wilson administration instigated a second application for British entry in 1967.[44]

By the end of 1966, the Wilson government had begun to explore the possibility of entry to the EEC. Wilson's inability to secure a close relationship with President Johnson, and the perilous state of the Commonwealth (because of Rhodesia) encouraged the belief that the British future was in Europe. The sterling crisis of July 1966 encouraged the view that a wholly independent policy would only result in continuing economic decline, and the idea of a North Atlantic Free Trade Area with the United States and Canada could never be considered practical politics. Politically, the general mood was swinging toward Europe: key ministers such as George Brown were ardent Europeans and the new intake of Labour MPs in March 1966 was also more generally disposed towards Europe.[45] Although he was not an enthusiastic European, Wilson supported the idea of a European 'technological community' that might enable Britain, in cooperation with European partners, to compete with the US in the technical arena.[46]

The various positions of Labour right Cabinet members on the Common Market became clear in the deliberations over British entry. The European Committee of the Cabinet, established by Wilson to consider the prospects of Britain joining the EEC 'within two or three years', consisted of George Brown, Callaghan, Healey, Jay, Bert Bowden, Fred Peart and George Thomson.[47] Of these, only Brown strongly supported entry at this stage. Healey, Peart and Jay were opposed and the others unclear or ambiguous in their views. Brown's move to the Foreign Office in August 1966 had increased the pressure within the government to take the initiative for entry. At a meeting of the Cabinet on 22 October 1966, the Foreign Office line of Brown and Stewart was that Britain needed to apply to join the EEC, 'not for economic reasons but to keep up its international status and its place "at the top table"'. They were looking for a 'declaration of intent' to join the Community. At the meeting, those who spoke in favour of entry included Brown, Jenkins, Crosland, Houghton, Hughes, Gordon-Walker, Lords Gardiner and Longford, and Benn, and those who spoke against included Jay, Healey, Peart, Bowden, Dick Marsh, Tony Greenwood, Ross, and Castle. Callaghan remained uncommitted to the idea of membership, and Crossman, adopting the view that the debate was a distraction as it was clear that de Gaulle would again use his veto, was willing to accept an application for entry only on the basis that 'the General will save us from our own folly'.[48]

Neither was there a consensus on the Common Market issue between the three rising stars of Labour Party revisionism. Healey explained that neither he nor

Crosland 'ever shared [Jenkins'] dedication to the Common Market – an issue which had also strained his relations with Hugh Gaitskell':

> Unlike Tony, I supported Douglas Jay's determined campaign against making a second application for membership in 1966, not least because I was certain that Wilson would be no more successful than Macmillan, so long as de Gaulle was alive . . . like Tony, I found the extremism . . . distasteful. Our agnosticism on the Common Market won us no friends in either camp. On issues which arouse strong feelings, like nuclear weapons or the Common Market, politics awards no prizes to pragmatists.[49]

Healey's pragmatism can be contrasted with the idealism of Jenkins' liberal internationalism in arguments over Europe and the wider social environment.[50] Even Gaitskell was prompted to describe Jenkins 'as an extremist . . . when it comes to the question of Europe'. Jenkins had published a short manifesto that expressed his commitment to the European project on the grounds that it would enable Britain 'to escape from our "great-power complex" which made us play at being in the same league as the United States and Russia while in reality being rapidly overtaken by the German and other lesser European economies'.[51] Alternatively, other Labour right revisionists maintained that Wilson's application to join the Common Market was misguided and only contributed to, or demonstrated, a much greater degree of 'agnosticism' on the issue. Some, such as Jay, believed that the Common Market controversy only contributed to the economic strain and downturn in the fortunes of the Wilson Government after July 1966. It represented an unnecessary distraction from more pressing domestic issues, and 'merely added to the stream of necessary administrative activities, and to several other explosive conflicts'. Respective arguments and differences over the likely economic consequences of membership, particularly the 'oppressive' impact of the Common Agricultural Policy (CAP) on the British economy and balance of payments, had the effect of dividing leading Labour Party revisionists personally and politically and aiding the process of fragmentation of 1950s Labour Party revisionism.[52]

After July 1966, it became clear to a number of senior Labour figures that British economic decline needed fresh impetus and new markets. Even Callaghan, who had never been an enthusiastic European, recognised along with Wilson 'the need for Britain's economic future to aim for a different and more secure course . . . Both Chancellor and Prime Minister were pragmatists on Europe as on most other issues, prepared to see how discussions would go.' Callaghan had previously accepted the insular Gaitskell line, but the majority of the Cabinet now 'saw the political, and perhaps economic, advantages of a new shift of policy'. Callaghan, along with Healey, Crosland and others, was sceptical, but 'he was happy to endorse an attempt to enter the Market – that is, if the terms were right'.[53] By the final week of argument in early May 1967, Stewart and Gordon-Walker had joined the pro-Market camp, Healey had adopted a similar position to that of Jay, and Callaghan was 'in the middle, though "wobbling"'. Those who came out in favour of an application included Wilson, Brown, Callaghan, Crosland, Jenkins, Crossman, Benn, Gardiner, Gunter, Hughes, Longford, Stewart and Gordon-Walker, while those against included Healey, Jay, Castle, Greenwood, Bowden,

Marsh, Peart and Ross. The narrow majority in favour of an application, which included Callaghan, Crossman and Benn, 'was decided by those who, having no firm views of their own, voted with the PM'.[54]

Labour's application for membership again hit the barrier of de Gaulle's veto on 27 November 1967 but, in light of the emerging belief that the British future remained with Europe, Wilson left the second membership application 'on the table'.[55] Formal negotiations for entry did not start again until after the June 1970 election, but the negotiations of the new Conservative administration were based on the briefs prepared by the Wilson Government. Labour revisionist and parliamentary Labour right divisions over the relative merits of British membership of the Common Market were already in evidence. These included distinct anti- and pro-European positions, together with the more 'agnostic' and pragmatic responses of Callaghan, Healey and Crosland. As official party policy and much of the Labour movement shifted against British membership in opposition after 1970, divisions over the European issue became entrenched and a test of loyalty to the party on the Labour right as the prospect of entry became a stark reality in the form of the Heath Government's negotiations for entry.

Labour in opposition after 1970: the Common Market debate and Labour's European divisions

The litmus test of attitudes and Labour Party unity over Europe arrived in the critical debate over the Heath Government's terms of membership, culminating in the vote on the principle of entry of October 1971. In opposition after 1970, the question of European membership inevitably proved problematic as members and organisations of the Labour party turned against British entry, particularly under a Conservative Government, and as the Wilson leadership developed a strategy of 'qualified opposition' to attempt to balance the competing factions and preserve party unity.[56] For Wilson and a substantial proportion of Labour MPs the issue was largely a pragmatic one. They possessed no strong emotional opinion on the question and the politics of opposition demanded that they challenge the Conservative Government come what may. Again, Labour's official approach in opposition was based on the terms of entry. Although Wilson was unable to reject the principle of membership, given his own 1967 application, he was able to argue that the terms of entry negotiated by Heath in 1971 were unsatisfactory. The large minority of pro-Market Labour MPs believed much more strongly in the principle of membership as a means 'to bolster British power . . . secure better access to European markets and bring the country into line with post-imperial realities'.[57] They regarded the twists and turns of Wilson on Europe as characteristic of his emerging contradictions and deviousness over a range of issues and questioned his suitability to lead Labour to victory in 1974 (but were also aware of the difficulties involved in the lack of agreement on a likely successor). Given his (and Labour's) similar reversals and prevarication on domestic policy issues such as 'incomes policy, inflation and industrial relations' reform, it boded for an unappealing party environment for those who desired 'positive' action in these respects.[58] On the other side of the polarised debate, a diverse grouping, including those on the left such as Foot and centrists such as Peter Shore, were opposed to the principle of British membership of the EEC on a number of grounds. These included the possible destruction of the Commonwealth, a challenge to parliamentary sovereignty and a threat to the pursuit of domestic socialist policies: 'it would make Britain part of a "capitalist club" where working-class interests would be harmed by higher food prices . . . and unemployment caused by the need to deflate.'[59]

In the heat of Labour's Common Market disputes after 1970, the divisions of senior representatives of Labour party revisionism and the parliamentary Labour right became explicit. In the second half of 1971, Europe provided the catalyst of a damaging split between the two leading figures of Gaitskellite revisionism, Crosland and Jenkins. Crosland, who had adopted a party strategy of attempting to broaden his political base to include the 'anti-European right + Centre' while moving away from the (Gaitskellite) '1963 Club', found European membership to be 'an issue on which it was impossible to remain on good terms with both the centre and the right of the party'. With Europe as the catalyst, Crosland was to gradually become further estranged from the strongly pro-European element around Roy Jenkins, to the extent to which Crosland was heard to proclaim that their 'idea of a Labour Party is not mine . . . Roy has come actually to dislike socialism'.[60] Clear lines of demarcation were developing between the respective perspectives and priorities of emerging strands of Labour Party revisionism. Crosland believed the European issue to be far 'less important than a host of other issues – incomes policy, devolution – and therefore could not use language of extreme pros'. Crosland stated that he was not prepared 'to "stand up and be counted"' in support of causes he didn't believe in such as Tavernite claims of an extremist left-wing takeover of the party, 'fanatical Europeanism' and 'virulent anti-trade unionism'.[61]

The European issue in the Labour Party after 1970 had both a divisive impact on Labour Party revisionism and a debilitative effect on the parliamentary Labour right. The bitterness of Europe divisions 'left deep scars, with a combination of policy and personality clashes occasioning a division that had been on the cards since 1967. Crosland and Jenkins had parted company irrevocably.'[62] The crisis over Europe which engulfed the party in 1971–72 was to 'fatally divide' Labour's key revisionist representatives. The

> summer of 1971 was a crucial moment. If Crosland, Jenkins and Healey had managed to agree on a modus vivendi over Europe, the history of the Labour Party in the 1970s and the 1980s might have been different . . . if the three men had stood together, the divisions in the party over Europe could well have been accommodated without isolating the Jenkinsites and without undermining the cohesion of the centre-right in the Labour Party. Their failure to work together fatally weakened the forces of revisionism and opened the door to the left.

Fragmentation on the Labour right meant that the Labour left was able to make the running in a way that had been impossible in the 1950s and 1960s.[63]

The Common Market special conference, July 1971: renewing the battle lines

A special conference of the Labour Party on the Common Market on 17 July 1971 presented a forum for the expression of Labour's European divisions. The special conference was called as 'the proper constitutional course to secure a test of opinion ... on the greatest single issue facing both our Movement and this country today'. The resolution for debate read that this 'Conference, while taking note of the N.E.C. statement on the Common Market ... opposes British entry to the Common Market on the terms negotiated by the present government and set out in the White Paper ... believes that the question of entry should be submitted to the British people at a general election'.[64]

In the period leading up to the parliamentary vote on the principle of entry in October 1971, Labour's pro-Europeans argued that the Conservative Government's application to join the Community was pre-empted and underpinned by the application for entry of the previous Labour administration.[65] The former Labour Minister for Europe, George Thomson, stated publicly that the terms of entry negotiated by the Heath Government were not very different from those that Labour might have obtained had his negotiations continued. The point was forcefully pursued by both Thomson and John Mackintosh in their speeches to Labour's special conference.[66] It was believed that it was

> morally wrong for Labour to take one view in government and then adopt a different position in opposition ... membership of the European Community was absolutely crucial, both economically and for Britain's role in the world. It was not only a vital element in the policies of a modernising, revisionist Labour Party; it had also become one of those great issues which transcend party. If it came to a clash between his party's short-term interests and Britain's European future, [some] would choose Europe.[67]

The anti-European perspective, less prominent in the previous period of Labour Government, increased in strength and voice, particularly among influential trade union leaders such as Jack Jones and Hugh Scanlon.[68] At the 1970 Labour Party Conference, delegates only narrowly rejected a resolution opposing British entry.[69] At the July 1971 special conference, Peter Shore represented the anti-Common Market view that the terms negotiated by the Heath Government were not just inappropriate to the needs of the country, but were negotiated against developments that were 'not there in 1967' when George Thomson and George Brown negotiated on behalf of the Labour Government.[70]

In addition to the 'extreme pros' and the 'extreme antis', there were those in the middle, including Wilson and Callaghan. Wilson had opposed Macmillan's original application in 1962, but had broadly favoured entry in government. In opposition 'his priority, given his style of leadership, was always likely to be to keep the party together and to maintain his leadership'. As hostility to the Common Market grew, Wilson gradually began to shift his position again.[71] Wilson's delicate attempt to balance the respective forces was, to a large extent, dependent on Callaghan. As his actions over *In Place of Strife* demonstrated, he was always a shrewd judge of the wider party mood and opinion. Although an Atlanticist by instinct, Callaghan had judiciously supported the attempts of the previous Labour Government to join the Community. However, his tone on Europe again changed according to the general shift of the party in opposition with a markedly anti-Market speech at Bitterne Park School, Southampton on 25 May 1971, followed by others in Bradford, Cardiff and Portsmouth in September 1971 (subsequently published by the Labour Committee for Safeguards on the Common Market). The gist of his argument was a sweeping (anti-French) appeal on behalf of British culture and traditions, opposition to the potentially detrimental economic consequences of a 'rigid relationship with the E.E.C.', the likely implications for British relationships with 'old friends' in 'the Commonwealth, old and new, and the United States' and wider problems with the Heath Government's strategy.[72] For some Labour pro-Marketeers, it was Callaghan who was 'the real villain of the piece on Europe', not Wilson.[73] It may not have been his finest hour, and Callaghan himself paid no retrospective attention to it in his memoirs, but 'Callaghan's move had a significant impact not just on Wilson but on Healey and Crosland as well'.[74]

Healey had developed a sceptical and antagonistic approach to British membership of the European Community. He had opposed both the 1962 and 1967 applications on the pragmatic grounds that they would be subject to de Gaulle's veto. Healey's appointment as Shadow Foreign Secretary in 1970 appeared to engender a more positive approach to Britain's role in the Community. On 11 May 1971, he was one of over a hundred Labour MPs who signed a pro-European letter to *The Guardian*. However, by July 1971, Healey had again swung against entry on the terms negotiated by the Heath Government, and announced his intention to vote with the anti-Marketeers in the crucial Commons vote on the principle of entry in October. To the partisans on either side of the debate, Healey's oscillation appeared to be highly opportunistic rather than merely pragmatic. Given his decision to join the pro-European *Guardian* signatories in May, 'it is difficult not to conclude that his July position was as much dictated by the swing of party opinion as by an analytic consideration of the terms'.[75] Another interpretation identifies more consistency in Healey's indifference to the Common Market question. In a similar sense to Crosland, Healey developed 'professional indifference' as a 'way of dealing with the passions that raged around him left and right. He thought Europe and the zealotries it induced were a distraction from what he regarded as the "real issues".' It was his line 'through all the arguments in the Labour Party for the decade following the 1967 application'. It also reflected the general 'agnosticism' of the British people in an attempt to 'find a way of fending off the wild obsessions over Europe which have been an enduring difference between the political class and the voters'. Either way, it suggested a further critical fissure in the leadership of the parliamentary Labour right as it represented an approach to the question 'almost as far removed from Jenkinsism as it would be possible to invent, short of outright Bennery'.[76]

Crosland, himself, had previously demonstrated pro-European credentials.[77] He had both argued strongly against the position adopted by Gaitskell in 1962 and supported the Labour Government's application for entry to the EEC in 1967.

However, Labour's internal debate in opposition after 1970 presented Crosland with something of a dilemma. While he still generally favoured entry, his core response was that the issue was a relatively minor one that detracted from the more important domestic priorities of his Grimsby constituents. He also believed that the Common Market argument should not be allowed to imperil Labour Party unity nor maintain the Conservative Government in office. Crosland's dilemma was not an uncommon one among Labour MPs: the question was should 'he line up with Jenkins who regarded British entry as a matter of high principle or should he back the majority who argued that opposing Heath came first?'[78] Crosland's perceived lack of commitment to the Common Market issue engendered resentment among Jenkins and his supporters, particularly as he had always 'been known as European and had equivocated' and 'wobbled over Europe in 1971–2'.[79] Although still a committed European, he was not prepared to maintain the Heath Government in power unnecessarily, and his long-term policy priorities of increased public expenditure, greater equality, the reduction of poverty, educational reform, housing policy and the environment would not 'be decisively affected one way or another by the Common Market'.[80] He was also increasingly aware of the danger to party unity posed by the formation of an elitist, potentially separatist, pro-European faction of the Labour right. For their part, the pro-European 'Jenkinsites' were less concerned with the perceived opportunism of Healey than Crosland's apparent 'apostasy' on Europe; his intellectual credentials, they felt, presented a significant threat to their case.[81]

Jenkins, himself, prevented from airing his views at the special conference on the Common Market, and in light of Wilson's anti-Market speech to close proceedings, attempted to redress the balance at a meeting of the parliamentary party on 19 July 1971. Wilson had narrated how he rejected 'assertions, wherever they came from, that the terms this Conservative Government have obtained are the terms the Labour Government asked for . . . the terms the Labour Government would have asked for, the terms the Labour Government would have been bound to accept'. He explained that 'the Labour Party will come to our decision', and that during 'the genuine, serious and important debate we are conducting, we shall not sacrifice our Party's basic unity. For even while our debate on this issue is proceeding . . . our main objective is, and must continue to be, the defeat of this Tory Government and a return of a Labour Government pledged to the ideals which all of us share.' He urged the conference to 'recognise that what divides us is an important policy issue, not an article of faith'.[82] Swimming against the tide, as he saw it, Jenkins offered an unapologetic, 'uncompromising, even inflammatory' contribution that made 'no attempt to paper over cracks'.[83] He disagreed openly with Wilson that a Labour Government would not have necessarily pursued the same terms as those accepted by the Heath administration. His 'personal and strong belief was that a majority of a Labour Government would have been willing to accept these terms'; the terms were 'about as good as those with direct knowledge of the situation believed were realistically possible to get in 1967 and almost equally so today'. He also rejected 'the argument that we could not go in with a Tory Government in power' on a number of grounds. These included the right of a Conservative Government to continue Labour initiatives, the need to trigger 'great reserves of capacity' and invigorate investment in the economy and, if the Tories could be removed from office by the autumn of 1974 at the latest, 'we would be responsible for 70% of the transitional period'. Jenkins believed that it was impossible to 'turn it down now and pick up the threads again in two or three years . . . If this opportunity were lost it would be gone for a decade or perhaps for a life time.' In a thinly veiled attack on the likes of Callaghan, he talked of the short-sightedness of those who focus on New Zealand 'to the exclusion of everyone else', and appeared contemptuous of Callaghan's argument to 'run the economy flat out for 5 years' and the 'narrow political considerations of the moment' at the expense of the wider aspiration of joining the Community.[84] Even opponents rhapsodised over Jenkins' speech, and interpreted it as a 'direct attack on . . . Wilson and also on Healey and Crosland, who had climbed off the fence against the Market'. Jenkins' defiant response even held out the prospect of factional conflict that 'took you right back to 1951 or 1961'.[85]

The Common Market parliamentary vote: a stake through the heart of the Labour right?

In the crucial parliamentary debate on the Common Market of 21–28 October 1971, Labour's European divisions were formalised. On 28 October, Jenkins led sixty-nine Labour MPs into the division lobbies in support of the Heath Conservative Government's attempt to ratify the principle of British membership. In the process the Labour rebels defied a three-line whip, imposed by a narrow vote in both the Shadow Cabinet and the PLP in spite of Rodgers' best efforts to gain for them a free vote in the critical division.[86] Labour's ardent pro-Europeans interpreted British membership of the EEC as more important than traditional party loyalty, and were not willing to use an issue of principle, as they saw it, as a cynical opportunity to defeat the Heath administration. According to Wilson, they were, perhaps, evolving into a faction within the party.[87]

A number of Labour right and revisionist pro-Europeans, including Fred Mulley, James Wellbeloved, and even David Owen, urged Jenkins and Rodgers to lead their troops to abstain in the critical division.[88] This would produce the effect of carrying the government motion in favour of entry, but with a much smaller majority and without the stigma of large-scale Labour dissension in the division lobbies. Crosland urged Jenkins to make his pro-European stand without voting explicitly for the Government, and accused him of irresponsibility for refusing to allow his supporters to consider the possibility of abstention. Crosland warned 'that in the long run you are damaging yourself as well as the Labour Party'.[89] Jenkins' response demonstrated both his historical sense and principled commitment to the issue. It ranked in importance with 'the first Reform Bill, the repeal of the Corn Laws, Gladstone's Home Rule Bills, the Lloyd George Budget and the Parliament Bill, the Munich Agreement and the May 1940 votes', and he was not prepared to have to continually reply to the question of what he did in one of the great divisions of the century with the answer that he abstained.[90]

Opening the debate for the Labour Party,[91] Healey argued that the case for entry was heavily dependent on economic considerations and had yet to be made. Particularly, the cost of tariff changes would be between £200 million and £300 million and the British contribution to the EEC budget would mean that it would have to carry a foreign exchange burden of £100 million in 1973 and £500 million in 1977. Healey posed the question of how the UK was to meet the foreign exchange burdens that the Government had imposed as a result of its Brussels negotiations against the background of rising costs, increasing unemployment and industrial stagnation. It could only be achieved through deflation or devaluation.[92] As was the case during Labour's special conference in July, Jenkins was unable to speak from the front bench in the debate because he did not now represent the official position of the Labour Party. A similar fate befell other pro-European Shadow Cabinet members, including Douglas Houghton, Harold Lever, George Thomson and Shirley Williams.[93]

However, Labour's pro-Europeans possessed a good number of surrogate speakers. In addition to active Jenkinsite organisers of the pro-Europeans such as 'Rodgers and Taverne, Marquand, Maclennan and Owen', these included 'a number of ex-ministers, such as Michael Stewart, Patrick Gordon Walker and Roy Mason, who remained staunchly on the side of the European commitment which had been entered into by the Wilson government'.[94] During the course of the six-day debate, a number of backbench MPs (on both sides of the House) rose to dissent from the front bench official party line. For Labour, Rodgers argued that the negotiated terms were likely to be the best available in 1971 and that they were unlikely to be improved even on a future date. Another former Gaitskellite, Charles Pannell, chose to emphasise the argument that membership of the Community would help to stimulate British industry and economic performance and that it 'would no longer be the sick man of Europe'. David Owen's motivations for entry were essentially political, as he argued that it would benefit the long-term economic interests of the country and 'our constituents' and Britain would be better able to offer a constructive influence in international and east–west relations than if it remained on the periphery of Europe.[95] Roy Hattersley suggested that the potential benefits of entry outweighed the drawbacks and, for David Marquand, the ideals of democratic socialism could only be realised through the further economic growth that membership of the EEC would bring. John Mackintosh tackled the sovereignty aspect of the argument. He argued that 'untrammelled' national sovereignty is largely an illusion; what matters more 'is not the legal power to act but whether the consequences may mean anything'.[96]

In the parliamentary vote of 28 October, Jenkins, along with Houghton, the chairman of the PLP, and sixty-seven other committed pro-European Labour MPs, entered the Conservative Government division lobby. The result of the crucial vote was a comfortable majority of 112 votes for the Government. Sixty-nine Labour votes were cast for the Government and 20 Labour MPs abstained.[97] Crosland, who 'thought so long and hard about complex issues that he was often in danger of falling between stools', decided to abstain in the vote and, having 'performed his double somersault, Healey voted with the Labour Opposition'.[98]

For Labour 'loyalists' among the pro-European rebels it was not an occasion to celebrate 'breaking ranks with the Labour Party'. The plan of some was now to 'gracefully submit to the will of the whips during the days and nights of detailed debate which followed', which reflected a 'need to balance conviction and loyalty'.[99] However, the arrangement was not accepted wholeheartedly by Labour's pro-European rebels. Jenkins did not exactly agree with the majority position of the group, who 'positively wanted to go back to voting with the Labour Party on the legislation': 'I knew that I was going to be miserable voting against the legislation, and I knew too that if by chance we defeated the Government on any aspect of the issue we would have made absolute asses of ourselves.'[100]

Underlying the respective preferences of strategy in the subsequent divisions following the major vote of principle were wider differences of attitude to the party and policy. Outside of a 'Jenkinsite' core, it was by no means clear that the sixty-nine European rebels were a united, cohesive group on other issues of policy or in their relationship to the wider party and Labour movement. Although brought together by a shared commitment to the principle of British membership, the post-vote hiatus and fragmentation of Labour's pro-European rebels reflected divergent responses to the wider post-vote political and party environment. Hattersley, for example, describes his increasing ideological departure from Jenkins:

> I agreed . . . with his position on the Common Market and . . . sympathised with his growing reluctance to vote against his conscience. It was his views on domestic policy which had begun to worry me. Although I did not know it at the time, the drift to the political centre had begun . . . I believed that comprehensive education – freed from the disability of a competing selection system – mattered a great deal more than he was prepared to allow.

Although the 'disagreement ended with a sterile dispute about the rival merits of "more equality" and "less inequality"', they remained 'expressions of deeply held feelings which are too painful to express openly. Roy and I were drifting apart.'[101]

More significantly perhaps, the Common Market debate and vote of October 1971 served to consolidate the increasing political distance between Jenkins and Crosland, a development that was to prohibit any serious challenge by 'the pro-European Jenkinsite faction' to the wider constituency of support of 'both . . . Callaghan and . . . Foot in a future leadership election'.[102] The Jenkinsite pro-Europeans claimed that Crosland had 'behaved like a shit' in the Common Market vote and that he must be punished. For his part, Crosland was determined that they would not win over the party: even 'if I was prepared to chuck my own values and strengthen their group, they still couldn't win over the Party – shouldn't win it over. The most that would happen is that the Party would be split for a generation. It is Roy's misfortune that because of his father, he's in the wrong Party. As a Liberal or Conservative, he might make a very good Leader.' Crosland had begun to heed Callaghan's advice that, however mixed his feelings about Europe, he 'should establish [himself] in people's minds as a Party man, forever distinct from the Jenkinsite Right'.[103] Although he claimed to 'believe that Britain should enter the Common Market', Crosland's priority was to remove a deeply unpopular Conservative Government that 'has already created a million unemployed and great social hardship and suffering' and represented a significant barrier to 'all the objectives . . . I have fought for and written about for twenty years'. The 'overriding political necessity' was to avoid the 'sort of dissensions that kept the Tories in power for so many long years' and 'jeopardize the control of the Party currently held by the moderate Right' and the 'desperate need to change this Government at the earliest possible moment'. From his perspective, it would be a grave danger for 'the Right' to 'isolate itself . . . from the moderate Centre' and for the 'extreme Europeans . . . not only to appear to be keeping a Tory Government in power, but to divorce themselves from the sort of opinion represented by Vic Feather, Bob Mellish and many moderate and even Right-Wing Trade Union M.Ps.'. Ultimately, he 'could under no circumstances desert my Party and vote with the Tory Government which is pursuing such disastrous domestic policies'.[104]

Neither was there much political love lost between Jenkins and Callaghan. Jenkins decided to stand to be re-elected as deputy leader (to resign five months later), at least in the spirit of attempting to build some bridges and retain some influence in the party. He managed only narrowly to defeat Foot in the second ballot because some Labour MPs, including Callaghan and his close allies, 'abstained so as to prevent [Jenkins] achieving too great a triumph'.[105] Healey was also now increasingly estranged from the Jenkinsite camp as they distrusted his inconsistency and apparent opportunism during the Common Market debates. Not only did Healey's 'blatantly opportunistic' change of tack offer 'the most damaging' episode of his 'entire career', it further added to the mutual suspicion and envy that prevented these two major representatives of the parliamentary Labour right from cooperating more successfully.[106] Healey's opportunism was anathema to the 'politics of principle' practised by the Jenkinsites over Europe. For Healey, Jenkins lacked the tribal instinct appropriate 'to the politics of class and ideology' of the Labour Party.[107] Increasingly explicit tensions associated with Labour's European debates in opposition after 1970 opened up 'the prospect of a damaging division on the right of the Labour Party' with potentially fateful consequences for the intra-party balance of power and the unity of the Labour Party and British social democracy.[108]

Decision on a European referendum and Jenkins' resignation: a Jenkinsite social democratic watershed?

The subsequent strategy of the Labour Party to adopt Tony Benn's proposal to hold a referendum in government, based on renegotiated terms of entry, to decide the future of British involvement with the EEC led to the resignation from Labour's front bench and further marginalisation of Jenkins and his core support. Wilson's decision to climb aboard the 'left-wing bandwagon' and support the referendum motion on British membership, as a possible solution to Labour's internal divisions, 'proved the last straw for Jenkins', who 'resigned the deputy leadership of the party in 1972 in protest'. Jenkins' decision severely weakened his position and influence in the parliamentary party as a potential unifying force of the Labour right and centre and future leader.[109]

Developments and decisions surrounding the referendum issue and Jenkins' resignation from Labour's front bench reflected the increasing fragmentation of the fabric of the parliamentary Labour right after the October vote, which was to have longer-term implications for both the Labour right and the Labour Party. Callaghan's Euro-pragmatism was again evident in Labour's post-October 1971 intra-party environment. He was 'careful not to let his opposition to Europe carry him too far' as, from 1 January 1973, British membership of the EEC would be 'a political and constitutional fact'. Callaghan was also predisposed to endorse the formula of a referendum to give the people the opportunity to decide Britain's European future after a Labour administration had 'renegotiated' the terms of entry. This strategy, it was hoped, would both 'preserve Labour's principled opposition and ensure party unity. It also made it more unlikely that British withdrawal from the EEC would in fact take place. However unenthusiastic, grudging and insular it felt, Britain was in and was likely to stay in.'[110] Healey acknowledges the fact that he paid the price for his own 'pragmatism' in the Shadow Cabinet elections that followed the October debates, which was, in part, a reflection of the fact that he did not belong to any of the respective group alignments in the European debate. Having replaced Jenkins as Shadow Chancellor after the latter's resignation, his priority was his challenging new post as he was launched, for the first time in his life, 'on the stormy and shark-ridden seas of economic policy'.[111] Crosland voted against the referendum motion in the Shadow Cabinet, but had no intention of resigning over the issue. In their appointment to their preferred posts of Shadow Chancellor and Shadow Foreign Secretary, respectively, in the subsequent reshuffle, it was Healey and Callaghan who were the immediate beneficiaries of Jenkins' resignation. Wilson was also able to 'rid himself of an increasingly troublesome deputy', and Callaghan witnessed the elimination of Jenkins, his main rival for the post-Wilson Labour leadership, from the Labour Party game.[112]

The dilemma of Jenkins' post-July 1971 position was that the 'more he upped the stakes on Europe, the more he endangered his own position and that of the pro-European minority within the party'.[113] Not only did Jenkins resign, complaining bitterly about the inconsistency of key organs of the party on Europe and the referendum, he was joined by Thompson and Lever from the Shadow Cabinet and Owen, Taverne and Dickson Mabon from Labour's front bench.[114] Rodgers had already been removed by Wilson as a punishment for his effective organisation of Labour's pro-European rebels during the October 1971 debates, although Hattersley and Shirley Williams remained to take up the positions in the Shadow Cabinet vacated by Thompson and Jenkins.[115] Williams was not opposed to the (democratic) principle of a referendum, and Hattersley, increasingly disenchanted with fundamental Jenkinsite philosophy, was anxious about the impact of Jenkins' resignation on the unity of the Labour Party.[116] In fact, he reflected that Jenkins' decision to resign the deputy leadership in April 1972:

was not the day on which the Social Democrats were born. It was not even the morning when they were conceived. But it was the moment when the old Labour coalition began to collapse. I did not realise it at the time, but once the envelope landed on the Chief Whip's desk, the creation of a new Centre party was inevitable. I do not think Roy Jenkins realised that he was acting as a catalyst to a cataclysm . . . no doubt he anticipated . . . a reconciliation before the election – as indeed there was. But our meeting in the Members' lobby remains in my memory as the turning point in Labour's history . . . the Labour Party was never the same again.[117]

The degree of separation of Labour's leading revisionists engendered by the European issue is reflected in the decision of the Jenkinsite group, with the possible exception of David Owen, to vote *en masse* for Ted Short in the ensuing deputy leadership election. It was a strategy designed to prevent Crosland from winning the contest as a 'punishment' for his actions over Europe, and to undermine his position as a potential future leadership rival to Jenkins.[118] As noted, Crosland's general strategy in elections to party office in the post-October 1971 intra-party environment was to offer himself as a non-sectarian, party unity and explicitly anti-Conservative candidate 'on the basis of a radical, egalitarian socialist programme' of 'full employment, housing, education, redistribution of wealth and an attack on social and economic privilege and inequality'.[119] Although Crosland had failed to establish a substantial support base in the party, he possibly lost as many as fifty pro-European votes 'controlled' by Jenkins as a result of the Jenkinsite sabotage of his candidature.[120] The result of the initial ballot for the election of deputy leader for the remainder of the session 1971–72 was 111 votes for Short, 110 votes for Foot and 61 votes for Crosland. He was eliminated from the contest as Short defeated Foot in the second ballot.[121]

From the moment of the pro-European resignation from Labour's Shadow Cabinet over the decision to hold a referendum on Europe, 'Labour Europeans were to be outsiders in the party'. It 'weakened the party's ability to resist the dangerous drift to the left during the 1970s. The vote of 28 October 1971 and Roy's subsequent resignation had rearranged the pieces on a chessboard of the Labour Party, separating the European knights from the anti-European bishops of the right and centre. It took a long time to put them back together again.'[122] The explicit fracture of the parliamentary Labour right and Labour party revisionism, over the relative merits and priority of the European cause from the summer of 1971, possessed important consequences for the position and future of a core element of pro-Europeans in the Labour Party. Although, as Hattersley suggests, it cannot be understood unambiguously as the point at which the SDP was conceived, the depth of feeling and significant, multi-dimensional divisions surrounding the issue galvanised and set apart a core grouping who regarded it as an 'article of faith' and one that transcended the banalities of tribal party loyalties and personal ambition. Ultimately, there was little attempt within the 'Wilson-Callaghan-Healey position . . . to accommodate the pro-Europeans in the party, an omission that was to have highly damaging consequences for the future':

What happened at the vote of 28 October 1971 and then over Roy's resignation in April 1972 and the subsequent deputy leadership election highlighted the split on the centre-right of the Labour Party between those who gave priority to Europe and those who were either anti-European or at least prepared to put their party loyalties and personal ambitions before their European beliefs. The fracture of the old Gaitskellite coalition on the European issue (already foreshadowed at Labour's 1962 party conference) was to have momentous consequences, leading to a dramatic increase in the influence of the left in the early 1970s and early 80s and, arguably, in 1981to the SDP breakaway.[123]

The 1975 referendum and beyond

There was a . . . cause which united politicians from all three main parties in the 1970s and which produced far deeper divisions within parties than between them. It was, of course, Britain's membership of the EEC.[124]

This was not the end of Labour's European travails. Following the earlier commitment by the party in opposition, Wilson agreed to hold a national referendum in 1975 to decide whether to remain in the EEC on the Labour Government's renegotiated terms.

Campaigning in the referendum allowed cross-party collaboration on either side of the argument after Wilson suspended collective Cabinet responsibility for the duration of the campaign. Although Jenkins and Thomson had resigned from the Shadow Cabinet in 1972 in response to the acceptance by the party of Tony Benn's referendum proposal, others on both sides of the debate accepted the idea of a referendum to decide the outcome of Britain's relationship with the EEC. Peter Shore supported the referendum as 'one of the five so-called "defence ministers" . . . of the Wilson Cabinet in the 1974–76 period who had faith in the referendum against the terms brought back by . . . Callaghan and endorsed for staying in the Common Market'.[125] Unlike Jenkins and Thomson, Shirley Williams did not resign in response to the referendum proposal because she believed that Benn 'was quite right to say that people should be consulted, and . . . it also gave us the opportunity to get across a lot of the arguments in a way that we would not have had another way of doing it . . . we did not agree about the referendum; that was a major disagreement between us because I did not resign . . . it was not for reasons of personal advance, it was because I really thought we were going wrong and judging from there.'[126] From Jenkins' perspective, she was 'torn between disapproval of the tactical cynicism of the reversal of the previous decision and her democratic populist feeling that it was difficult to oppose a referendum'.[127] Although regarded as an 'obscure' and 'curious commitment' of Labour's election manifesto and campaign among pro-Europeans, a referendum on British membership of the EEC was regarded as inevitable 'once negotiation is completed'. Williams redeemed herself in the eyes of her pro-European allies with her statement (along with Jenkins) that she would either leave politics or resign from the Cabinet if Britain had to withdraw as a result of a referendum. The priority now was 'to concentrate on winning the referendum in the country and, before that, of winning the battle to get the Cabinet to agree to recommend acceptance [of the Common

Market]'.[128] Whatever the philosophical merits of the argument, the whole debate and rift of the referendum 'was a great, ghastly and shaping experience', in the wake of which 'the party would never be the same again'.[129]

The referendum campaign and the implications of cross-party collaboration

The referendum itself was a radical constitutional departure in British politics. It had first been mooted by the Gaitskellite anti-Marketeer, Douglas Jay, in 1970, and was later taken up by Benn as a freshly converted anti-Marketeer,[130] but the outcome of the referendum campaign was not the one the anti-Marketeers expected. Wilson's renegotiated terms of entry were approved by nearly two-thirds of the electorate. A well-financed and well-organised pro-Market 'Britain in Europe' campaign, supported by the majority of the press, helped to secure victory. The anti-Market campaign was composed of a more disparate grouping from the extremes of British politics that lacked a 'convincing alternative to the EC if Britain were to remain a secure, influential power'.[131]

An apparent paradox lay at the heart of the referendum issue and campaign for the Labour Party. Principally, the referendum was a management device to maintain party unity. Callaghan described the instrument of the referendum as 'a life raft which we would all have to climb aboard' as the only means by which the Labour Party could be held together over Europe.[132] Paradoxically, the cross-party formula of the referendum campaign encouraged the belief of some Labour pro-Europeans that they possessed more in common with the pro-European Liberals (and even some Conservatives such as Heath, Peter Walker or Ian Gilmour) than with many of their own Labour Party colleagues (of both left and right).[133] It led to the perception in the Labour Party that Labour's Euro-enthusiasts 'cared more about Europe than they did about socialism'. As he announced the press launch of the 'Britain in Europe' campaign in St Ermin's Hotel, Jenkins was flanked by a coalition of Willie Whitelaw, Reginald Maudling, Cledwyn Hughes and Jo Grimond.[134] The experience of sharing the 'Yes' platform with traditional political opponents such as Heath and David Steel was significant for Jenkins, Williams and other Labour pro-Marketeers in reinforcing their 'own innate centrism' or converting them 'to the idea of coalition politics' in the context of the perceived sterility of the two-party system.[135] In his initial opposition to the idea of a referendum in 1972, Jenkins had warned that it would have 'a loosening effect upon the tribal loyalties of British party politics'. After the European referendum of June 1975 things 'were never quite the same for the Labour Party'. Previously, 'peacetime cross-party co-operation could never be discussed without raising the spectre of Ramsay MacDonald. After then it called up for about a third of the party the much more benevolent image of referendum success.'[136] These were the unforeseen consequences for the Labour Party when it agreed to hold a referendum on Britain's future in Europe in the cause of maintaining party unity, strength and identity.

Conclusion

Although the referendum was intended as a device to keep the party together, and the decisive popular verdict served to resolve the question of Europe in British politics for a time,[137] the damage of Labour's European divisions had largely been done and it failed to heal the rift in the way that Wilson had hoped. A number of anti-Marketeers such as Benn, Foot and Shore remained in the Cabinet, Jenkins left British politics to take up the post of President of the European Commission and the reliance of the Callaghan administration on pro-European Liberal support to maintain its governing majority complicated matters further. The parliamentary party divided fifty-fifty in the vote on direct elections to the European Parliament in 1977.[138] Further controversy soon surrounded 'green currencies', fisheries and the increase in Britain's net financial contribution to the Community, largely as a result of the CAP which, as an industrial nation, benefited Britain to little effect, and which had reached a figure of almost £800 million by 1979. Callaghan, himself, became more predisposed to the principle of a system of stable exchange rates than some of his Cabinet colleagues, but further tension was fostered as his Government avoided membership of the Exchange Rate Mechanism (ERM) as it was launched in 1979.[139]

After the 1979 general election defeat, Labour changed its European 'position of qualified acceptance to one of outright rejection' as the party swung unmanageably to the left. The Bennite initiative of 1980 to withdraw from the EEC, as part of a general repudiation of the Wilson-Callaghan years from the left, became a key issue in Labour's post-1979 intra-party conflict.[140] Although it is difficult to quantify the precise influence of Labour's European divisions in the Labour Party split and formation of the SDP and its breakaway from the Labour Party, its relative role in serving to expose the complexity and divisions of the parliamentary Labour right and in the formation of 'the collective consciousness of the social democrats in the Labour Party' was an important one.[141]

The European membership debate in the Labour party was not, as many saw it, a simple division between left and right. The European issue also divided the parliamentary Labour right within itself.[142] It is also problematic to conceive of a 'revisionist'–'labourist' divide on the Labour right over Europe. To some extent, there was a distinction between the 'principled' approach of revisionist social democrats led by Jenkins, including the likes of Marquand, Rodgers and Taverne, who were 'very much motivated by pro-European sentiment', and the more phlegmatic approach of 'the whole group around . . . Callaghan, Merlyn Rees' who were 'not particularly interested in Europe [n]or particularly keen on it'.[143] However, there were also significant divisions within the respective 'revisionist' and 'labourist' camps. With the likes of Mason and Brown also in the pro-European camp and, for the most part, Healey and, to a lesser extent, Crosland (and earlier, of course, both Gaitskell and Jay) adopting relatively detached pragmatic and ambivalent perspectives, neither was it a clear division between the intellectual revisionist right and the old trade union right.

Issues of such political significance are routinely presented as theological choices or articles of faith. The question is posed simply as for or against and divisions are characterised as those between pro- and anti-European camps, but the picture is often more complicated. 'Agnosticism' has often been as much in evidence as faith or atheism in debates over Europe. Motivations have often included political expediency as much as the principles or merits of the issues themselves. Although Labour leaders have revealed moderate pro- or anti-European preferences, political choices have often 'been made on good old-fashioned party political advantage'. Behind the emotional rhetoric of Gaitskell's Conference speech and the political expediency, lay a core of ambivalence. Gaitskell's approach revealed an underlying agnosticism on the substantive question and a political decision by which he could unite the party in opposition, after the earlier battles over Clause IV and unilateralism. The Labour Party appeared to be more strongly united by Gaitskell's speech on Europe than it had previously been under his leadership, and Gaitskell found that his career reached its height in the weeks after Labour's 1962 Brighton Conference.[144]

'Agnosticism' was as much in evidence as distinct pro- and anti-European positions in Labour right divisions over Europe through the 1960s and 1970s. The pro-Europeanism of Jenkins, Owen, Rogers, Taverne and Williams was counter-acted on the revisionist Labour right by the profound anti-Europeanism of Gaitskell, Jay and, to some extent, Healey and centrists such as Peter Shore. Varieties of agnosticism ranged from the arch-pragmatism of Callaghan, to the initial scepticism and pragmatic 'opportunism' of Healey, to the studied ambivalence of Crosland in the face of more pressing priorities. The pro-European position was 'unfashionable' in the context of Labour's politics of 'opposition' after 1970, and the Jenkinsite core of pro-Europeans found themselves increasingly alienated not just from the anti-Europeanism of the Labour left, but also from colleagues of the parliamentary centre-right who, anxious about party unity, refused to treat the issue as an article of faith and as one that transcended the (tribal) loyalties and adversarial character of party politics.

This chapter has attempted to demonstrate that the pivotal issue of Britain's relationship with Europe was immensely significant in dividing Labour Party revisionism and the parliamentary Labour right within itself. European divisions helped to undermine the fragile alliances of the parliamentary centre-right, and precipitated the marginalisation of a committed group of Jenkinsite pro-Europeans within the Labour Party. Given the emergence of relatively distinct positions in a number of key policy areas and an emerging wider critique of social democratic philosophy, the Jenkinsites were increasingly alienated from both the general mood and disposition of the Labour Party after 1970 and from erstwhile revisionist and centre-right colleagues. Although it is problematic to attempt to identify the precise origins of secessionary activity in the Labour Party, there is a sense in which the seeds of the SDP split were sown earlier than conventional accounts of the consequences of the post-1979 intra-party constitutional and power struggles allow. The cumulative effect of parliamentary Labour right and revisionist divisions in a number of critical policy spheres – Europe, industrial relations and trade union reform and issues of public expenditure and redistribution in a changing political economy – were conducive to a longer gestation period for the creation of the

SDP.[145] Arguably, its roots can be traced back to the emergence of explicit divisions over industrial relations reform and Europe in the 1969–71 period. It is to further contentious themes of industrial relations and trade unionism, and the role of public expenditure and redistribution in social democratic political economy in the 1970s that the study now turns.

Notes

1 D. Owen, 'A Socialist Case for Joining the E.E.C.: Speech by Dr David Owen, M.P.', Extract from *Hansard*, 26 October 1971, Owen Papers, D709/2/4/1/3; D. Owen, *Time to Declare*, London, Michael Joseph, 1991, p. 172.

2 See S. George, *An Awkward Partner: Britain in the European Community*, Oxford, Oxford University Press, 1998; J. W. Young, *Britain and European Unity 1945–1999*, Basingstoke, Palgrave, 2000; J. W. Young, 'Introduction', in R. Broad, M. D. Kandiah and G. Staerck (eds), 'Britain and Europe', Witness Seminar, Institute of Contemporary British History, 2002, pp. 15–16.

3 R. Broad, *Labour's European Dilemmas: From Bevin to Blair*, Basingstoke, Palgrave, 2001; P. Daniels and E. Ritchie, '"The Poison'd Chalice": The European Issue in British Party Politics', in P. Jones (ed.), *Party, Parliament and Personality: Essays Presented to Hugh Berrington*, London, Routledge, 1995, pp. 84–98.

4 B. Brivati, 'Hugh Gaitskell and the EEC', *Socialist History*, 4, 1994, pp. 16–17; B. Brivati, *Hugh Gaitskell*, London, Richard Cohen, 1996, pp. 405–8; Daniels and Ritchie, '"The Poison'd Chalice"', pp. 84–5, 86–7; L. J. Robbins, *The Reluctant Party: Labour and the EEC 1961–75*, Ormskirk, G. W. & A. Hesketh, 1979.

5 K. Jefferys, *The Labour Party since 1945*, Basingstoke, Macmillan, 1993, p. 85.

6 T. Nairn, *The Left Against Europe?*, Harmondsworth, Penguin, 1973, p. 94.

7 R. Desai, *Intellectuals and Socialism: 'Social Democrats' and the Labour Party*, London, Lawrence & Wishart, 1994, pp. 145–6.

8 Harold Macmillan, 'European Economic Community (Government Policy)', *Parliamentary Debates*, Fifth Series, 1960–61, Vol. 645, 31 July 1961, pp. 928–31.

9 H. Berrington, 'The Common Market and the British Parliamentary Parties, 1971: Tendencies, Issue Groups … and Factionalism', paper presented to the ECPR Workshop, 'Factionalism in the Political Parties of Western Europe', Florence, 25–29 March 1980; Daniels and Ritchie, '"The Poison'd Chalice"', p. 86.

10 Peter Shore, Interview with the author, 3 March 1999.

11 J. P. Mackintosh, MS notes on subjects for lectures, 'The EEC and the UK', 1977–78, John P. Mackintosh Papers, 323/34.

12 Brivati, *Hugh Gaitskell*, p. 406; D. Owen, Draft of election speech as prospective parliamentary candidate for Torrington constituency, 1962, David Owen Papers, D709/2/1/1/1; J. W. Young, 'Foreign, Defence and European Affairs', in B. Brivati and T. Bale (eds), *New Labour in Power: Precedents and Prospects*, London, Routledge, 1997, p. 149.

13 Young, 'Foreign, Defence and European Affairs', p. 149.

14 See Brivati, *Hugh Gaitskell*, pp. 407–8; S. Haseler, *The Gaitskellites: Revisionism in the British Labour Party 1951–64*, London, Macmillan, 1969, p. 228; E. G. Janosik, *Constituency Labour Parties in Britain*, London, Pall Mall, 1968, p. 42; U. Kitzinger, *The Challenge of the Common Market*, Oxford, Blackwell, 1961, pp. 150–1.

15 Young, 'Foreign, Defence and European Affairs', pp. 150–1.

16 P. Williams, *Hugh Gaitskell*, London, Jonathan Cape, 1979, p. 705.

17 G. Goodman, *Awkward Warrior: Frank Cousins, His Life and Times*, London, Davis Poynton, 1979, p. 337.

18 Brivati, *Hugh Gaitskell*, pp. 408–9; Haseler, *The Gaitskellites*, p. 230.

19 Brivati, 'Hugh Gaitskell and the EEC', p. 16; D. Jay, *After the Common Market: A Better Alternative for Britain*, Harmondsworth, Penguin, 1968, pp. 11–15; D. Jay, *Change and Fortune: A Political Record*, London, Hutchinson, 1980, pp. 339.

20 Brivati, *Hugh Gaitskell*, p. 404; Williams, *Hugh Gaitskell*, p. 708; H. Young, *This Blessed Plot: Britain and Europe from Churchill to Blair*, Basingstoke, Macmillan, 1998, pp. 149–50, 151–2; also see Jay, *Chance and Fortune*, p. 282; R. Jenkins, *A Life at the Centre*, London, Macmillan, 1991, p. 145.

21 Brivati, 'Hugh Gaitskell and the EEC', p. 16; D. Healey, *Time of My Life*, London, Michael Joseph, 1989, pp. 210–12, 329–30; Young, *This Blessed Plot*, p. 148.

22 See D. Marquand, 'Europe', in B. Whitaker (ed.), *A Radical Future*, London, Jonathan Cape, 1967, pp. 21–35.

23 Brivati, 'Hugh Gaitskell and the EEC', p. 17; Jenkins, *A Life at the Centre*, pp. 143–4; Young, *This Blessed Plot*, pp. 150–1.

24 Young, *This Blessed Plot*, p. 151.

25 Brivati, *Hugh Gaitskell*, pp. 404–5; Williams, *Hugh Gaitskell*, pp. 706, 777–8.

26 Brivati, 'Hugh Gaitskell and the EEC', pp. 17–19; also see Healey, *Time of My Life*, pp. 210–11; Jay, *After the Common Market*, pp. 13–14; D. Owen, Speech to public meeting in Torrington, n.d, Owen Papers, D709/2/1/1/5.

27 Labour Party Annual Conference Report (LPACR), London, Labour Party, 1962, pp. 155, 159, 166.

28 P. Williams, *Hugh Gaitskell*, revised and abridged edition, Oxford, Oxford University Press, 1982, p. 390.

29 Jay, *Change and Fortune*, p. 286; Owen, Draft of election speech as prospective parliamentary candidate for Torrington constituency; D. Owen, Draft of speech of thanks on his selection as prospective parliamentary candidate for Torrington, 1962, Owen Papers, D709/2/1/1/2.

30 Haseler, *The Gaitskellites*, p. 234.

31 LPACR 1962, p. 173.

32 *Ibid.*, pp. 158–9; also see H. Gaitskell, *Parliamentary Debates*, 1962–63, Vol. 666, Col. 1018, 7 November 1962.

33 Haseler, *The Gaitskellites*, p. 231.

34 See D. Jay, *The Truth About the Common Market: Three Articles Reprinted from the* New Statesman *and* Statist *in 1961 and 1962*, London, Forward Britain Movement, 1962.

35 D. Jay, 'The Real Choice', *New Statesman*, 25 May 1962.

36 *Ibid.*

37 Haseler, *The Gaitskellites*, pp. 233–4; D. Healey, 'Political Objections to British Entry into the Common Market', *The Observer*, 25 May 1961; Owen, Draft of election speech as prospective parliamentary candidate for Torrington; D. Owen, Notes for speech discussing Labour policy on British membership of the EEC, n.d., Owen Papers, D709/2/11/26.

38 Stephen Haseler, Interview with the author, 23 January 2001; also Leo Abse, Interview with the author, 20 June 2001; L. Black, '"The Bitterest Enemies of Communism": Labour Revisionists, Atlanticism and the Cold War', *Contemporary British History*, 15 (3), 2001, pp. 26–62; P. Jones, *America and the British Labour Party: The Special*

Relationship at Work, London, I. B. Tauris, 1997; K. O. Morgan, *Callaghan: A Life*, Oxford, Oxford University Press, 1997, pp. 252–4; Shirley Williams, Interview with the author, 25 June 2002.

39 Jones, *America and the British Labour Party*, p. 164.
40 Haseler, *The Gaitskellites*, pp. 234–5.
41 *Ibid.*, pp. 235–6; Morgan, *Callaghan*, p. 254.
42 Haseler, *The Gaitskellites*, pp. 229–30.
43 Shirley Williams, Interview with the author.
44 Young, 'Foreign, Defence and European Affairs', pp. 149–50; also see B. Castle, *The Castle Diaries 1974–76*, London, Weidenfeld & Nicolson, 1980, p. 12; Daniels and Ritchie, '"The Poison'd Chalice"', p. 86; B. Pimlott, *Harold Wilson*, London, Harper Collins, 1992, pp. 432–42; C. Ponting, *Breach of Promise: Labour in Power 1964–1970*, Harmondsworth, Penguin, 1990, pp. 204–6.
45 Marquand, 'Europe', p. 21.
46 Young, 'Foreign, Defence and European Affairs', p. 150.
47 Roy Jenkins was a significant omission.
48 Ponting, *Breach of Promise*, pp. 206–7; also see G. Brown, *In My Way*, Harmondsworth, Penguin, 1972, pp. 197–218.
49 Healey, *Time of My Life*, pp. 329–40; D. Healey, Interview with the author, 9 February 1999; also see Jay, *After the Common Market*, p. 104.
50 Jenkins, *A Life at the Centre*, p. 143.
51 See R. Jenkins, *The Labour Case*, Harmondsworth, Penguin, 1959, pp. 10–11; Jenkins, *Life at the Centre*, pp. 105, 109, 117.
52 Jay, *After the Common Market*; Jay, *Change and Fortune*, pp. 339–408.
53 Morgan, *Callaghan*, pp. 252–4.
54 Jay, *Change and Fortune*, pp. 387, 389.
55 Ponting, *Breach of Promise*, pp. 212–13.
56 See D. Taverne, *The Future of the Left: Lincoln and After*, London, Jonathan Cape, 1974, pp. 102–4.
57 J. P. Mackintosh, 'Britain and Europe: New *Opportunities*', *Socialist Commentary*, February 1970, pp. 5–6; G. Thomson, 'Socialism, Schisms and the Common Market', *Socialist Commentary*, September 1971, pp.3–6; Young, 'Foreign, Defence and European Affairs', pp. 150–1.
58 R. Jenkins, 'Labour in the Seventies – Retrospect and Prospect', *Socialist Commentary*, November 1970, p. 5; J. P. Mackintosh, 'The Shadow Emperor has No Clothes', n.d. [but probably written at the beginning of the parliamentary session, 1973–4], John P. Mackintosh Papers, 323/46; *The Observer*, 30 September 1973. They claimed that Wilson had 'master-minded Labour's determined effort to join the Common Market but today . . . conveys a generally anti-European tone'. His volte-face would be a great handicap to Britain's relations with the other nations if he became Prime Minister again. In Europe:

> his relations with Willy Brandt and the governing party in Germany will probably never recover from the bitterness created by his change of front on Europe. Between 1967 and 1970 he constantly twisted the arms of his German socialist comrade, urging him to put pressure on the French to let Britain into the EEC and they cannot forgive him, once the French veto was removed, for turning against not just the terms, but so many essential aspects of European integration.

59 Mackintosh, 'The Shadow Emperor has No Clothes'; Shore, Interview with the author.

60 S. Crosland, *Tony Crosland*, London, Jonathan Cape, 1982, p. 229; K. Jefferys, *Anthony Crosland: A New Biography*, London, Richard Cohen Books, 1999, pp. 152–3, 160; Dick Leonard, 'The Case for Abstention', 22 October 1971, Crosland Papers, 4/9; Marquand, *The Progressive Dilemma*, pp. 167–9.

61 David Lipsey, 'Panorama Profile', 4 March 1976; David Lipsey, Memorandum, 29 March 1976, Crosland Papers, 6/3.

62 Jefferys, *Anthony Crosland*, pp. 160–1. Jenkins had been promoted to the Chancellorship ahead of Crosland after Callaghan's resignation from the post as a result of the forced devaluation of sterling in 1967.

63 Radice, *Friends & Rivals*, pp. 186, 189–91, 195; K. Jefferys, *The Labour Party since 1945*, Basingstoke, Macmillan, 1993, p. 85.

64 Labour Party, *Labour and the Common Market*, Report of a special conference of the Labour Party, Central Hall Westminster, 17 July 1971, London, Labour Party, 1971, p. 4.

65 Radice, *Friends & Rivals*, pp. 190–3; Young, *This Blessed Plot*, pp. 223–5.

66 See Labour Party, *Labour and the Common Market*, pp. 11–12, 28–9; *The Economist*, 17 July 1971.

67 Radice, *Friends & Rivals*, pp. 191; Phillip Whitehead, Interview with the author, 20 January 2001; also see Young, *This Blessed Plot*, pp. 260–5, 305.

68 Taverne, *The Future of the Left*, pp. 103–4.

69 Radice, *Friends & Rivals*, pp. 190–1.

70 Labour Party, *Labour and the Common Market*, pp. 18–19, 44.

71 Pimlott, *Harold Wilson*, p. 585; also see Jenkins, *Life at the Centre*, pp. 319–20.

72 J. Callaghan, *James Callaghan on the Common Market*, London, Labour Committee for Safeguards on the Common Market, 1971; Morgan, *Callaghan*, pp. 394–5.

73 Pimlott, *Harold Wilson*, p. 585; Taverne, *The Future of the Left*, pp. 102–7.

74 Radice, *Friends & Rivals*, pp. 191–2; also see Morgan, *Callaghan*, p. 395; Young, *This Blessed Plot*, p. 273.

75 Radice, *Friends & Rivals*, pp. 192–3; also see Crosland, *Tony Crosland*, p. 220; Healey, *Time of My Life*, pp. 359–60.

76 Young, *This Blessed Plot*, pp. 267–70.

77 C. A. R. Crosland, *The Conservative Enemy: A Program of Radical Reform for the 1960s*, London, Jonathan Cape, 1962, p. 8.

78 Jefferys, *Anthony Crosland*, pp. 153–6; Radice, *Friends & Rivals*, p. 193.

79 Rodgers, Interview with the author, 18 February 2001; Crosland, *Tony Crosland*, pp. 221–2.

80 A. Crosland, The speech that was never delivered!, early July 1971 – after talking to Hatt, Owen, Leonard, July, 1971, Crosland Papers, 4/9; also see Crosland, *Tony Crosland*, pp. 218–20; Jefferys, *Anthony Crosland*, pp. 154–5.

81 Crosland, *Tony Crosland*, pp. 220–2; Jefferys, *Anthony Crosland*, pp. 155–6; Radice, *Friends & Rivals*, pp. 194–5.

82 Labour Party, *Labour and the Common Market*, pp. 42–9.

83 Jenkins, *Life at the Centre*, p. 322.

84 Minutes of a Party Meeting, 19 July 1971, PLP Papers/Minutes 1970–71.

85 T. Benn, *Office Without Power: Diaries 1968–72*, London, Hutchinson, 1988, p. 358.

86 U. Kitzinger, *Diplomacy and Persuasion: How Britain Joined the Common Market*, London, Thames & Hudson, 1973, pp. 328–9; W. Rodgers, *Fourth Among Equals*, London, Politico's, 2000, pp. 128–31.

87 Radice, *Friends & Rivals*, pp. 198–9; Taverne, Interview with the author.

88 Radice, *Friends & Rivals*, p. 199; Rodgers, *Fourth Among Equals*, pp. 128–9.

89 Crosland, *Tony Crosland*, p. 221; Rodgers, *Fourth Among Equals*, p. 131.

90 Jenkins, *Life at the Centre*, p. 329; Owen, 'A Socialist Case for Joining the E.E.C.'; also see R. Hattersley, *Who Goes Home? Scenes from a Political Life*, London, Little, Brown, 1995, pp. 105–7; Kitzinger, *Diplomacy and Persuasion*, pp. 372, 400.

91 After prior discussion with a number of Labour pro-Europeans on the precise wording to maximise potential votes, the Foreign Secretary, Alec Douglas-Home, moved the motion that 'this House approves Her Majesty's Government's decision of principle to join the European Communities on the basis of the arrangements which have been negotiated': Kitzinger, *Diplomacy and Persuasion*, p. 371.

92 D. Healey, *Parliamentary Debates*, 1970–71, Vol. 823, Cols 2211–18, 21 October 1971.

93 See Radice, *Friends & Rivals*, pp. 199; Rodgers, *Fourth Among Equals*, p. 130; also see Jenkins, *Life at the Centre*, pp. 329–30.

94 Jenkins, *Life at the Centre*, p. 330; also see Brown, *In My Way*, pp. 11–12; Kitzinger, *Diplomacy and Persuasion*, p. 372; R. Mason, *Paying the Price*, London, Robert Hale, 1999, pp. 117, 140–1.

95 Owen, 'A Socialist Case for Joining the E.E.C.'.

96 *Parliamentary Debates*, 1970–71, 823, 2211–18; also see J. P. Mackintosh, 'The Battle for Entry', in D. Marquand (ed.), *John P. Mackintosh on Parliament and Social Democracy*, London, Longman, 1982 [1971], pp. 244–8; Owen, 'A Socialist Case for Joining the E.E.C.'; Radice, *Friends & Rivals*, pp. 199–200.

97 Kitzinger, *Diplomacy and Persuasion*, pp. 372–3, 400–5.

98 Radice, *Friends & Rivals*, pp. 200–1.

99 See Hattersley, *Who Goes Home?*, pp. 104–6, 107. Hattersley, not without reservation, declared that he would be willing 'to vote for every amendment that the Labour Party composed – absurd though some of them were'. This was similarly the position of those such as Houghton and Joel Barnett.

100 Jenkins, *Life at the Centre*, pp. 332–4.

101 Hattersley, *Who Goes Home?*, pp. 104, 106–9.

102 Radice, *Friends & Rivals*, p. 201.

103 Crosland, *Tony Crosland*, pp. 224–30; Jefferys, *Anthony Crosland*, pp. 156–7; B. Douglas-Mann to A. Crosland, 6 January 1974, Crosland Papers, 12/2; Radice, *Friends & Rivals*, pp. 200, 201–2.

104 A. Crosland to Philip Stewart, 13 July 1971; A. Crosland to T. E. M. McKitterick, 13 July 1971; A. Crosland to Frank Pickstock, 13 July 1971, A. Crosland, 'My Views about the Common Market are and long have been as follows', Statement on the Common Market, 29 October 1971, Crosland Papers, 4/9.

105 Radice, *Friends & Rivals*, pp. 203–4.

106 Healey, *Time of My Life*, pp. 359–60; Healey, Interview with the author; P. Whitehead, *The Writing on the Wall: Britain in the Seventies*, London, Michael Joseph, 1985, p. 66.

107 Healey, *Time of My Life*, p. 329.

108 See Radice, *Friends & Rivals*, pp. 101, 163–5, 202.

109 Jenkins, *Life at the Centre*, p. 350; D. Lipsey, 'Roy Jenkins', in K. Jefferys (ed.), *Labour Forces: From Ernest Bevin to Gordon Brown*, London, I. B. Tauris, 2002, p. 111; Radice, *Friends & Rivals*, pp. 204–8; Young, *This Blessed Plot*, pp. 277–8.

110 Morgan, *Callaghan*, p. 397.

111 Healey, *Time of My Life*, pp. 359–60; E. Pearce, *Denis Healey: A Life in Our Times*, London, Little, Brown, 2002, p. 397.

112 Crosland, *Tony Crosland*, pp. 239–40; Jefferys, *Anthony Crosland*, pp. 163–4; Radice, *Friends & Rivals*, pp. 208–10.

113 Radice, *Friends & Rivals*, pp. 197–8, 206–7.

114 D. Owen to Jack Harriman, 18 April 1972; D. Owen to Mrs M. Lightwood, 19 April 1972; D. Owen to Mervyn Stockwood, 19 April 1972, Owen Papers, D709/2/4/2/1. In spite of the uncertainty of the consequences of resignation and risk of 'giving up the "levers of power" for the pro-European social democrats', the 'situation was rapidly becoming intolerable'. At least 'we are slightly freer to campaign for a continued European commitment within the Labour Party' and to concentrate on the problem of preventing the 'Labour Party Conference in October [making] a commitment to come out of the Common Market if we win the election'.

115 Hattersley, *Who Goes Home?*, pp. 110–11; Rodgers, *Fourth Among Equals*, pp. 133, 134.

116 Lipsey, Interview with the author; Radice, *Friends & Rivals*, p. 208; Williams, Interview with the author.

117 Hattersley, *Who Goes Home?*, pp. 107–9.

118 A. Crosland, 'Note on talk with Bill Rodgers in Italy', 6 September 1973, Crosland Papers, 6/2; Jenkins, *Life at the Centre*, pp. 352–3; Dick Leonard, Interview with the author, 23 January 2001.

119 A. Crosland, speech to a conference of the Labour Political Studies Centre, 16 April 1972, Crosland Papers 6/2; William Hamilton, Press Statement, 17 April 1972, Crosland Papers 6/2; Jefferys, *Anthony Crosland*, pp. 165–6.

120 Jefferys, *Anthony Crosland*, p. 166; Radice, *Friends & Rivals*, p. 210.

121 PLP Papers/Minutes, 20 April 1972.

122 Rodgers, *Fourth Among Equals*, pp. 134–5; Rodgers, Interview with the author.

123 Radice, *Friends & Rivals*, pp. 210–11.

124 I. Bradley, *Breaking the Mould? The Birth and Prospects of the Social Democratic Party*, Oxford, Martin Robertson, 1981, p. 31.

125 Shore, Interview with the author.

126 Williams, Interview with the author.

127 Jenkins, *Life at the Centre*, pp. 343–4.

128 J. P. Mackintosh, 'The Case Against a Referendum', *Political Quarterly*, 46 (1), 1975, p. 73; J. P. Mackintosh, 'Do we want a referendum?', *The Listener*, 22 August 1974; John Macintosh to Shirley Williams, 22 October 1974; John Mackintosh to George Thomson, 22 October 1974, Mackintosh Papers, 323/74. To this end the Labour Committee for Europe and its journal, *Europe Left*, played a formative role in galvanising and organising Labour's pro-Europeans and promoting the relative benefits of membership against the arguments of the left and anti-Europeans: Jim Cattermole to John Mackintosh, 14 October 1974; John Mackintosh to Jim Cattermole, 23 October 1974, Mackintosh Papers, 323/74; *Europe Left*, July/August 1977; Labour Committee for Europe, 'The Europe Argument: Brief Notes', n.d.; European Movement, 'Britain in Europe since 1973: The Benefits of Membership', n.d.; D. Marquand, J. Cattermole and N. Hart, *The British Labour Party and Direct Elections to the European Parliament: A Discussion Paper*, London, Labour Committee for Europe, n.d., Mackintosh Papers, 323/90.

129 Lipsey, Interview with the author.

130 See P. Goodhart, *Referendum*, London, Tom Stacey, 1971, pp. 59–66.

131 Young, 'Foreign, Defence and European Affairs', p. 151; also see Bradley, *Breaking the Mould*, p. 34; R. Broad and T. Geiger (eds), 'The 1975 British Referendum on Europe', *Contemporary British History*, 10 (3), 1996, pp. 82–105; D. Butler and U. Kitzinger, *The 1975 Referendum*, London, Macmillan, 1976; Young, *This Blessed Plot*, pp. 286–99.

132 Broad and Geiger, 'The 1975 British Referendum on Europe', p. 83.

133 Bradley, *Breaking the Mould*, pp. 33–4; also see D. Marquand, 'Inquest on a Movement: Labour's Defeat and its Consequences', *Encounter*, July 1979, pp. 8–18.

134 Broad and Geiger, 'The 1975 British Referendum on Europe', pp. 82–3, 105; Jenkins, *Life at the Centre*, pp. 405, 407.

135 Bradley, *Breaking the Mould*, pp. 35–6; Jenkins, *Life at the Centre*, pp. 399–418; Morgan, *Callaghan*, p. 426.

136 Jenkins, *Life at the Centre*, p. 418.

137 Young, *This Blessed Plot*, p. 299.

138 The 'prospect of Direct Elections to the European Parliament' was seen as the 'main hope for the improvement of the links between the Community institutions and those whom they were set up to serve': D. Owen, Notes for a speech 'The Community with a Human Face', Owen Papers, D709/2/10/3. Although they proposed to conduct the matter in private 'for the sake of party unity', a number of Labour's pro-European social democrats were concerned at the lack of progress n the issue and declared to make representation to the Prime Minister, Jim Callaghan, and to 'discuss further action if necessary'. Callaghan 'noted' that there were 'strongly held feelings in the Party on Direct Elections': Roderick MacFarquhar to John Mackintosh, enclosing copy letter from James Callaghan, 17 May 1977; John Mackintosh to Roderick MacFarquhar, 19 May 1977; Mackintosh Papers, 323/92.

139 David Marquand to John Mackintosh, 13 March 1978, Report on Labour Committee for Europe Lunch, 6 February 1978, Mackintosh Papers, 323/54; D. Marquand, *The New Reckoning: Capitalism, States and Citizens*, Cambridge, Polity Press, 1997, pp. 93–109; G. Radice, *Offshore: Britain & the European Idea*, London, I. B. Tauris, 1992, p. 165; Young, *This Blessed Plot*, pp. 300–2. It resulted from Jenkins' initiative to re-launch the Community's monetary project in the creation of the European Monetary Union System (EMS), and was the 'forerunner . . . of the system that was to come to full flower in the 1990s, leading . . . to many of the developments which ensured that "Europe" would remain for the duration a festering source of division in British politics'.

140 Radice, *Offshore*, p. 165; Young, 'Foreign, Defence and European Affairs', pp. 151–2.

141 See Bradley, *Breaking the Mould*, pp. 31–6, 53–4, 54–6; Crewe and King, *SDP*, pp. 106–7; Taverne, *The Future of the Left*, p. 50.

142 David Marquand, Interview with the author, 16 January 2001; Williams, Interview with the author.

143 Williams, Interview with the author.

144 See Brivati, *Hugh Gaitskell*, pp. 410–11, 413–19.

145 In the context of wider concerns about the general ideological and political direction of the party, Labour Party attitudes and divisions over the European question produced considerable disquiet in some of Labour's avid pro-Europeans. John Mackintosh, for instance, had considered standing down as a Labour MP as early as 1972 after the Common Market debate at the Labour Party conference in October. Correspondence with similarly minded Labour MPs such as Marquand, Taverne and Robert Kilroy-Silk reveals the clear discomfort of Mackintosh and others with the Labour Party over

a six-year period from 1972: Robert Kilroy-Silk to John Mackintosh, 17 October 1972; John Mackintosh to Robert Kilroy-Silk, 18 October 1972, John P. Mackintosh Papers, 323/46; David Marquand to John Mackintosh, 21 August 1977; John Mackintosh to David Marquand, 31 August 1977; David Marquand to John Mackintosh, n.d. [but approximately September–November 1977], Mackintosh Papers, 323/10; also see J. P. Mackintosh, 'Socialism or Social Democracy? The Choice for the Labour Party', *Political Quarterly*, October–December 1972, pp. 470–84.

5

In Place of Strife?
The parliamentary Labour right
and the 'trade union question'

Awareness of Britain's relative economic decline led Social Democrats to a series of economic questions, each of which involved trade unionism ... It was in seeking answers to these questions that ... 'The Old Order' – the post-war consensus – 'crumbled' and the first crack occurred in its weakest area – namely over the role expected of trade unions ... Where once Gaitskell and Crosland had urged that legislation should be kept out of industrial relations, now a significant section of Labour Ministers became quietly sympathetic to a range of permanent legislative solutions to industrial problems. Constrained by a newly assertive trade unionism within the Labour Party in the early 1970s, the ex-Labour Ministers were unable to pursue either the industrial relations reforms or the detailed incomes policy commitments that they favoured.[1]

Social democratic policies ... must be backed by a renewed emphasis on parliamentary democracy and debate. The current drift to government by sit-in, confrontation and defiance of the law only aids those with special positions of power in the community and is utterly at variance with the social democratic belief that priority goes to those with a just case established by open debate and the process of representative government. As part of this, the Labour Party should try to eliminate any position of special power accorded to pressure groups within its own constitution and should give each citizen who joins the Labour Party an equal chance of influencing its policies.[2]

Introduction

The previous chapter explored the complexity and divisions of the parliamentary Labour right in terms of attitudes to British membership of the European Common Market. In contrast to orthodox interpretations of the left–right dimensions of Labour's intra-party conflict, it identified critical Labour right and revisionist divisions that ranged from distinct pro- and anti-European positions to varying degrees and expressions of 'agnosticism'. These possessed important implications for the cohesion and unity of the parliamentary Labour right within Labour's intra-party politics of the 1970s, particularly the marginalisation and alienation of the Jenkinsite group and the constraints imposed by European divisions on the solidity

of Labour right attempts to organise against the left. This chapter examines
parliamentary Labour right attitudes to a similarly contentious issue for the Labour
Party and Labour Governments after 1964, that of industrial relations policy and
trade union reform.[3]

In their retrospective of the limitations of Labour's history, the position and
role of the trade unions are perceived by New Labour 'modernisers' as
representative of some of the worst excesses of 'old' Labour governance during
the Wilson and Callaghan administrations and as justification for reconfiguration
of party management and leadership.[4] However, argument over the position and
influence of the trade unions in the Labour Party and British politics is hardly a
novel exercise. Given the socio-economic context of the 1970s and debates over
the means by which to arrest long-term British economic decline, 'the trade union
question', as it became known, became a fundamental aspect of contemporary
British political argument and the statecraft of both Labour and Conservative
governments. The bitter internal divisions of the Labour Party that accompanied
the Wilson Government's proposed reform of industrial relations, the further
industrial unrest that accompanied the Heath Government's Industrial Relations
Act, and the critical role of trade unions in both the production and implementation of government economic and industrial policy and in the internal dynamics
of the Labour Party, guaranteed the trade union question a central position in
contemporary political discourse.

In terms of the labour movement relationship, the historic centrality of trade
union constraint and the implicit division between the political and the industrial
wings made the formal domination of the party by the unions compatible with
the parliamentary leadership's pursuit of electoral majorities and government
in the national interest.[5] It was when one or other of the partners crossed this
line that conflict increased. *In Place of Strife* represented an example of perceived
intrusion, and neither did the 'labour alliance's internal settlement produced
in the "social contract" and the creation of a new TUC-Labour Party Liaison
Committee' completely resolve the tensions created by *In Place of Strife* and
problems arising from the centrality of incomes policy to Keynesian social
democratic economic strategy.[6] Minkin's 'centrality of constraint' argument and
the wider role and influence of the trade unions certainly came to the fore in
the period after 1969, and nowhere were discussion and debates over the trade
union question more profound than on the parliamentary Labour right. One close
observer of the labour alliance identifies aspects of trade union power and
collectivism that posed a fundamental challenge to the emerging liberal political
philosophy of elements of the Labour right in the 1970s. Moreover, the '"rules"
of the Labour Movement' and seeming irresolution of the 'trade union question'
was a crucial factor behind the 'fundamental estrangement' of the 'Social
Democrats' from the Labour Party and their subsequent departure to the SDP.
Although a number of factors and developments contributed to their growing
disillusionment, it 'was the trade union role in society and in the Party which
formed a crucial sub-text of their departure. Only when they came to shape their
own public policies towards the unions as the SDP would it become clear just

how far this alienation had gone.'[7] In the respective political testaments that supported their decision to leave the Labour Party, each of the so called 'gang of three' (Owen, Williams and Rodgers) considered the reform of industrial relations, decentralisation of political power and expansion of the mixed economy as central tenets of their political philosophy.[8]

Previously, points of disagreement over the party and wider role and influence of trade unions were obscured by some degree of consensus around 'the post-war settlement and 1950s revisionism', but the problems of a moribund economy undermined such an agreement 'as a broad crisis of revisionist social democracy stimulated and coincided with a crisis over power within the Party'. Moreover, the general political terrain had been reshaped by left-wing trade union militancy and the political expression of a 'new Rightwing Conservatism', to the extent that the 'politics of ideology, class and industrial conflict, thought to have been buried by the post-war consensus . . . emerged as a dominating element in political life'. Faced with the new economic and political problems and a further 'reappraisal of means and ends', some Labour revisionists appeared 'much readier to shed the socialist ascription, some of the main commitments and ultimately the fundamental values and "rules" of the Labour Movement'. As a group of the 'now more consciously Social Democratic . . . Right made its continuing reappraisal, so "the trade union question" began to loom large as the source of problems and as an obstacle to their solution', and the 'pull and push of [other] pressures traversed time and time again the terrain of trade unionism, its defects and culpabilities'.[9]

This chapter considers key themes and developments of industrial relations and trade union reform in order to explore the roots and implications of differential attitudes and divisions of the parliamentary Labour right over the 'trade union question' in British politics. Contextually, it begins with Labour's ill-fated attempt to impose a legal framework on the context of industrial relations in *In Place of Strife*. The leading actors of the parliamentary Labour right divided on relatively unorthodox lines. While Callaghan inevitably defended the voluntarist nature of industrial relations, the issue 'divided Jenkins and Crosland, though Healey was on Jenkins' side of the argument'. It also 'laid bare' for some a pertinent 'structural fault . . . which, over the next two decades, was to call into question its credibility as a governing party . . . how could the Labour Party, so closely tied to the unions, also claim to represent the national interest?'.[10] The chapter further considers responses to the Heath Government's Industrial Relations Act and the nature and evolution of the subsequent Labour Government's 'social contract' with the trade unions in the context of concerns over the primacy of representative parliamentary government and the crucial tension between trade union power and collectivism and questions of individual freedom. The chapter addresses the question of to what extent did disputes around the 'rules of the Labour Movement' and 'the trade union role in society and the Party' foster and accentuate divisions and further marginalise an emerging liberal revisionist element of the parliamentary Labour right. To what extent does it support Minkin's claim that it was the trade union question that formed the 'crucial sub-text' of the departure to the SDP?

The context of Labour's industrial relations: *In Place of Strife*?

The White Paper of January 1969, *In Place of Strife: A Policy for Industrial Relations*, was the first (recent) attempt 'to confine industrial relations within a framework of law'.[11] It represented a serious threat to the internal politics of the Labour Party and to the struggling Wilson administration in particular. Many in the PLP – which was 'viscerally opposed to "penal sanctions on trade unions"' – feared that the continued dispute between the Labour Government and the TUC could only end in electoral disaster.[12] One observer of the 1964–70 Labour Governments has written that it is 'difficult to understand why a Prime Minister with a reputation for adroit handling of awkward political issues and a minister well-known for her left-wing sympathies ended up with an agreement with the TUC which even Wilson himself regarded as "not worth the paper it was written on" and in the process caused the most bitter and damaging divisions yet in the party and the Cabinet'.[13]

The proposed reform of industrial relations was part of Labour's wider desire to 'modernise Britain's institutions' and to 'humanise the whole administration of the state', not least as a solution to the country's recurrent economic difficulties, after it returned to power in 1964.[14] Increasing strain in the relationship between the Government and the trade unions over wage restraint and the generally poor state of British industrial relations, particularly the debilitative level of unofficial strikes, led to the creation of a Royal Commission on Trade Union and Employers' Associations under the chairmanship of Lord Donovan. Wilson had 'decided on union reform because he had given up hope of making incomes policy work'.[15] The subsequent report, firmly rooted in the 'British laissez-faire style', rejected any idea of a legal framework or state intervention for industrial relations. It recommended a purely voluntary reform of industrial relations on the shop floor. The only move towards intervention was the proposal to establish a Commission for Industrial Relations (CIR), 'which would be a voluntary body to prod the system into self-reform by disseminating ideas about good practice'.[16]

The voluntarist nature of the report of the Donovan Commission was welcomed by some leading figures in the Labour Cabinet such as Callaghan. However, Barbara Castle, the newly appointed Secretary of State for Employment and Productivity, believed that the Donovan recommendations represented a missed opportunity in industrial relations and did not provide the basis for a sensible industrial policy.[17] The central issue was whether the Donovan recommendations were adequate, given the increasing number of unofficial strikes in key industries and the inflationary pressures of the British economy. An interventionist by instinct, she decided that something more substantial was necessary. The added pressure of a forthcoming general election and the opportunity to outflank the Tories on the issue meant that Wilson offered Castle enthusiastic support in her attempt to reform industrial relations.[18] The outcome was the publication of the draft White Paper, *In Place of Strife*, at the end of 1968. It adopted some of the Donovan themes, but also included proposals for pre-strike ballots in disputes that could threaten the economy or national interest, an enforced conciliation period of twenty-eight days in unofficial disputes and the referral of unofficial action arising from inter-union disputes to the TUC, and ultimately the CIR, to impose a settlement, with appropriate financial penalties if the order was breached. The rationale was to develop a labour relations framework that 'would both provide the unions with legal recognition and protection, and also ensure that industrial discipline would be imposed on them to avoid unofficial strikes, irresponsible wage demands, disruptions caused by inter-union disputes, and the other plagues endemic to British labour relations'.[19] The White Paper offered 'a charter for tackling the causes of strikes . . . to tackle these causes in ways which will strengthen the trade union movement's authority'. Rather than advocating greater ministerial intervention in disputes, it wanted 'unions themselves to face up to their responsibilities in preventing unnecessary disputes which can do wanton damage to other members of the community'. This approach 'lies behind . . . proposals for a "conciliation pause". This has one purpose only: to ensure that workers do not down tools before they have used the procedure for examining disputes which their own union have negotiated.'[20]

In the hostile trade union response to Castle's White Paper and the subsequent divisions of the Labour Cabinet and PLP, the balanced nature of the proposals was overlooked, containing as they did a number of pro-trade union measures in 'a charter of trade union rights'. It was 'grounded in a well-thought-out philosophy of trade union rights and responsibilities' and 'designed to protect and enhance the standing of the trade union movement'.[21] In addition to the 'punitive' paragraphs, it contained proposals for the recognition of trade unions and trade union rights in the workplace, the creation of a development fund, with government support, to encourage and assist in union mergers and measures to combat unfair dismissal by employers. It further rejected the idea that collective bargains should be legally enforceable and that unofficial strikers could be sued for any damages that they incurred.[22] It was the penal aspects, providing the government with increased powers to limit the scope of trade unions to engage in industrial action, which led to dismay within the trade union movement and elsewhere.[23] The significance of the proposed legislation and the catalyst for trade union hostility was that for 'the first time since 1927, a government – a Labour Government – was proposing to interpose the force of the law into hitherto unfettered collective bargaining. For the TUC . . . this was the ultimate heresy, a betrayal of hard-won union freedoms going back to the mythical heroism of the Tolpuddle martyrs. The fact that almost all the applause came from the right-wing press intensified their fury.'[24] The subsequent intransigence of the trade unions for some 'came close to challenging the government's right to govern' and to 'represent the interests of the wider community'.[25]

While Castle's proposals incorporated measures that would strengthen the position of the trade unions, they simultaneously 'provided for an unprecedented degree of government power to intervene directly in industrial relations'. Jack Jones was clearly opposed to a framework of government intervention and legal sanctions: the idea of legally enforced 'conciliation pauses', and official ballots on strikes, provides further opportunities for delay and frustration within a system of bureaucratic state intervention. In particular, the idea that fines may be enforced by allowing employers to deduct them from the pay packet may well spark off further strikes even when the original strike has been settled . . . We need faster settlement of disputes, not more Ministerial intervention, which can often be influenced by employer-backed alarmist press campaigns on a particular dispute. The sort of costly, time-consuming, harmful intervention by punitive measure and legal sanction is certainly likely to cause many more strikes than they prevent.[26]

Within the party itself, the proposals also aroused bitter opposition and led to significant Cabinet divisions. In the enforced series of Cabinet meetings of early January, opposition to the proposals initially took two forms. The first, led by Callaghan, with support from Crosland, Dick Marsh and Judith Hart, was opposed to the proposed legislation in principle. Callaghan explained to Castle that 'it is absolutely wrong and unnecessary to do this . . . what you ought to do is set up the Commission, put the trade unions on their honour and do what you can'. It was a 'minimalist position that would have provided some actions on trade unions whilst not alienating the TUC and the Labour party', but it was not enough and would not satisfy public expectations of the Government 'to do something about industrial relations'.[27]

The second form of 'opposition', expounded by Jenkins and Crossman, focused on the tactical handling of the issue rather than the fundamental philosophy behind the reforms. It would be politically disastrous to publish firm proposals in a White Paper in January and wait to the late autumn to legislate, as it would allow enough time to establish a campaign of opposition and necessitate having to defend the legislation 'at every trade union conference in the early summer, followed by the TUC and Labour conferences in September and October'. Legislation that would have to be passed in the months leading up to a general election could also be damaging to Labour's electoral prospects. The alternative was either a White Paper of possibilities rather than firm proposals that could be put forward for consultation until the autumn or to rush through a shorter bill before the summer and hope to dispose of the issue quickly.[28]

Callaghan's opposition was far more intransigent. As the so-called 'keeper' of Labour's 'cloth cap', he was fundamentally opposed to legal controls and penal sanctions from the outset.[29] He regarded Castle's (and Jenkins') insistence in April that 'a Bill be passed during the remaining months of the current Session . . . as a fallback position when the Prices and Incomes legislation should expire later in the year' as representative of a broken promise of several months of discussion of the proposals. *In Place of Strife* 'was suddenly to be turned into instant government'. Callaghan regarded the issue as one of fundamental principle, reinforced by his long personal links with the trade union movement. He welcomed the Donovan report 'as a safeguard for free collective bargaining and for industrial freedom . . . Donovan had rightly endorsed a voluntary system; the only reform possible of the industrial system must necessarily come from the unions themselves'. He agreed with Jack Jones that 'rather than the heavy-handed pressure of the courts', it 'was the only way to control unofficial strikes. Legal penalties would make the temper of labour relations much worse, and make a successful attack on the balance of payments impossible'. He believed that Castle and Wilson were ill-informed about the nature of industrial relations and 'oblivious to the intensity of the TUC's reaction'. Callaghan has explained that, from 'the moment I set eyes' on the White Paper, 'I knew that such a proposal, which ran counter to the whole history of the trade union movement and to the ethos of the Donovan Report, could not succeed . . . I declared my opposition to the legal sanctions . . . on three grounds'. They 'would not stop unofficial strikes', they 'would not pass through Parliament' and the 'proposals would create tension between government and unions at a time when morale was low, to no real effective purpose'.[30] At an unprecedented meeting of Labour's NEC on 26 March, Callaghan's refusal to accept the conventions of collective responsibility led to a significant public display of Cabinet division over the issue. Callaghan, the Home Secretary, cast his vote publicly against the policy proposals of his Cabinet colleague on a motion which proposed that the NEC reject 'legislation designed to give effect to all the proposals contained in the White Paper'.[31] Although accounts of the strength of Wilson's admonishment of Callaghan for his public departure from principles of collective Cabinet responsibility differ, colleagues such as Jenkins and Healey 'spoke of Callaghan's "shabby" behaviour'.[32] In practice, however, Callaghan was too powerful to be forced out of Cabinet.[33] His opposition to *In Place of Strife* and role as the 'principled defender' of the trade unions was also soon to acquire support in the PLP as well as the TUC and NEC. In early March, eighty-seven Labour MPs had refused to support Castle's White Paper.

Jenkins (and his 'dedicated . . . band of desperados from the right of the . . . Party', such as Marquand, Christopher Mayhew and Gordon Walker), on the other hand, had been willing to engage 'in an unlikely alliance' with Castle. As Chancellor, preoccupied with the restrictive economic situation, Jenkins was 'convinced that the economy could not recover without an effective wages policy and machinery to enforce it'.[34] Although he was unhappy with 'the leisurely timetable of consultation followed by legislation in the following session proposed by Wilson and Castle', Jenkins had offered strong support to Castle's proposals from the outset, 'partly because of his Cabinet alliance with Barbara Castle and partly because he saw the need for action on industrial relations'. He later reflected that the 'problem which became acute over the turn of the year 1969–70 was that of wage inflation', and the 'form which it took was to a considerable extent a result of the sad failure of Mrs Castle's trade union policy'.[35]

Although it was not a formal Jenkinsite cause and 'they kept their heads down' as a group over the issue, Dick Taverne explains that his break with his local party in Lincoln had 'as much to do with the attitude to the unions as it did with the Common Market': 'I was in favour . . . and they were violently opposed to *In Place of Strife* . . . a very strong left-wing trade union constituency and my stand on *In Place of Strife*, which was not public but was private inside the party, was one of the things that made them very bitter towards me.' The unions needed reform and 'the arguments that Barbara Castle produced were correct . . . it was an important issue ... that and the Bennite plan for massive nationalisation, increasing emphasis on CND, the anti-Market theme all combined ... to say ... the Labour Party is going in a direction that I will not support ... I felt a great sense of liberation when I did resign. I could speak my mind because when you are a member of the party you don't speak your mind.'[36] For others of a similar persuasion, Castle was 'absolutely right' to attempt *In Place of Strife*. Given the rise of the radical shop stewards movement and some of the excesses of the 1970s, it 'would have saved the unions from themselves' and would not have 'helped to destroy the Labour Government of Jim Callaghan and helped to destroy the Labour Party': 'what we actually did ... was to produce the situation where Mrs Thatcher was able to come in on the back of trade union abuse and essentially get rid of much trade union power, and there was an awful lot of support for her among the public and some in the Labour movement who had not had the guts to do what she did.'[37] Two themes concerned with the trade union role were emphasised from this perspective: the 'closeness' of the trade unions to the Labour Party and the general question of trade union reform. It had reached the conclusion that the 'trade unions had a too dominant position in the Labour Party ... it was ridiculous that they were often casting votes in the Labour National Exec[utive] Committee or the Conference which were votes ... determined by people who were not members of the Labour Party'. It advanced a view shared by a number of Jenkins' supporters on the question of trade union reform that indicates the emerging divisions of the parliamentary Labour right over key party and governing themes. From this perspective, 'the need for reform was clear from that time, and then, of course, was clear from the report which led to *In Place of Strife* ... we were all in favour of reform at the time of *In Place of Strife* and Roy Jenkins ... did support her a long way on reform and that was the revisionist right supporting the soft left at a time, of course, when Callaghan had gone off to say no change'.[38]

However, not all erstwhile Gaitskellite revisionists shared the Jenkinsite perspective on the urgency for a review of the party and wider role of trade unionism. Leading revisionist figures were at loggerheads over a critical theme of party management and governing strategy. Crosland was sceptical of the timing of the proposed reform. His attitude to Castle's White Paper was pragmatic. In light of increasing industrial unrest, he was not personally opposed to the need to modernise the trade unions, but considered it politically imprudent to legislate on the issue late in a parliamentary term. He expressed this concern in the Cabinet discussions of early January, proposing instead that the minority recommendation to the Donovan report, that the CIR be awarded powers in relation to unofficial strikes, be considered. He was further concerned that the proposals, as drafted, would be ineffective and could possibly lead to a situation in which the intended penal clauses would fail to achieve their intended objectives and unofficial strikes would continue to grow.[39] There may also have even been an underlying personal motive. Although not uncritical of Callaghan's public defiance of Wilson, his abdication of collective Cabinet responsibility and personal meetings with trade union leaders, Crosland supported his opposition to *In Place of Strife* in Cabinet. In combination with Douglas Houghton, the chairman of the PLP, Crosland and

Callaghan formed a triangle that threatened Wilson's position over *In Place of Strife*. Crosland appeared to be increasingly allying himself with Callaghan as a potential successor to Wilson, perhaps in the hope of replacing Jenkins as Chancellor.[40] Like Jenkins, Healey accepted the broad philosophy of *In Place of Strife*. Healey's initial attitude was that it would be better to attempt to get at least some of it on the statute book during 1969 rather than wait until the following year. As party and trade union opposition grew more open and confrontational, Healey, ever the pragmatist, developed a more circumspect approach to the issue. In Cabinet, he advised of the need for discussions with the TUC, and remarked that 'if he had realised the impact the proposed Bill would have on party morale he would not on balance have supported it in the first place'. He developed the view that the Labour Government 'had wasted six months on a hopeless fight, which had caused permanent damage to our relations with the trade unions, without making them any less necessary to our survival. *In Place of Strife* did for Wilson what the hopeless attempt to delete Clause Four from the Party Constitution had done for . . . Gaitskell', although he was aware that the 'trade unions were now emerging as an obstacle both to the election of a Labour Government and to its success once . . . in power'.[41]

Beyond his public denunciation of Callaghan's 'shabby' behaviour, ambiguity and a 'lack of excitement on the question' pervaded Healey's stance. He considered the trade unions to be a restrictive force on a Labour Government but appeared unwilling to support radical proposals in the face of hostile and potentially divisive opposition. He also viewed the protracted debates and Callaghan's public campaign against the proposals as an attempt to garner 'enough trade union support to force Wilson out and take his place' when the opportunity arrived, and as part of a general atmosphere of plotting against Wilson in the parliamentary party.[42] Roy Hattersley, Castle's deputy during the *In Place of Strife* episode, identifies a similar desire on the part of key Jenkinsites to promote their champion as a potential replacement for Wilson. Given the divisions of the Cabinet and PLP over *In Place of Strife* and talk of Wilson's resignation over the issue, Hattersley, along with other 'plotters' such as Tom Bradley, Jenkins' parliamentary private secretary (PPS), was keen to persuade Jenkins that this was his opportunity to succeed Wilson, if only he would abandon his support for Castle and her hugely unpopular Bill.[43]

There were now two rival camps of the parliamentary Labour right competing to replace Wilson as the leader of a post-*In Place of Strife* Labour Party (and even a very brief flirtation with the idea of a leadership challenge from Denis Healey, which failed to secure recognition from Callaghan).[44] Kenneth Morgan, Callaghan's biographer, offers an assessment of the alleged conspiratorial groupings – 'Callaghanites' and 'Jenkinsites' – that surfaced to replace Wilson. He concludes that explicit evidence of a specific Callaghanite conspiracy is impossible to identify, not least because it is by no means clear that such a group existed. Some senior colleagues such as Douglas Houghton and Merlyn Rees and his PPS assistance of Roland Moyle and Gregor MacKenzie were an undoubted source of support, but they did not constitute any kind of coherent group. Cabinet colleagues such as Crosland and George Thomson were, perhaps, even less open to this kind of group identification. It was the more readily identifiable Jenkinsite cluster, those Callaghan himself identified as the 'Mackintosh/Alan Lee Williams group of 1964/66 "intellectuals"', who were more identifiable in intra-party group terms than any recognisable Callaghan grouping. Jenkinsite identity and positioning was much more in evidence: this group 'included a number of very able younger members like Taverne, Mackintosh, Marquand, Owen, Rodgers, Maclennan and Hattersley, with some senior figures like . . . Mayhew and . . . Gordon Walker'.[45]

Despite the treacherous mood of the PLP and considerable discontent with Wilson's leadership, neither party was quite sure how to proceed. Some wanted a meeting of the parliamentary party to debate the leadership, but 'the Callaghanites wanted the Jenkinsites to move first and vice versa'.[46] Callaghan saw himself as a possible pawn in a Jenkinsite challenge for the leadership. He reports that John Mackintosh asked him if he would be willing to stand for the leadership, not because they necessarily wanted him to succeed Wilson but as a stalking horse 'in opening up a contest' for the benefit of Jenkins.[47] For his part, Jenkins refused to abandon his principled support for Castle for the sake of a leadership challenge. He felt that he was unable to challenge for the leadership using 'Wilsonite' tactics of which he was so critical: 'I was not tempted to renege on the Bill in order to replace Wilson . . . this would be fatal for the future. The real count against Wilsonism was that it was opportunistic and provided leadership by manoeuvre and not by direction. To replace him by outdoing his own deficiencies would make a discreditable nonsense of the whole enterprise.'[48] The rivalry and mutual suspicion of Jenkins and Callaghan, as well as the growing personal and political chasm between Jenkins and Crosland and the detached, pragmatic furrow ploughed by Healey, stood in the way of a determined, coherent attempt from the parliamentary Labour right to usurp Wilson in the window of 'opportunity' provided by the divisions and dissent of *In Place of Strife*. Jenkins revealed to Bill Rodgers, for instance, that he was unwilling to serve under Callaghan's leadership. Despite the evident weakness of his position during *In Place of Strife*, Wilson's leadership was salvaged by significant political and personal differences of the principal representatives of the parliamentary Labour right and their inability to cooperate to mount a challenge to replace him.

The *In Place of Strife* controversy also had the effect of consolidating emerging divisions between erstwhile Gaitskellite revisionist colleagues, Crosland and Jenkins. Whether in pursuit of Callaghan's patronage as a means of achieving his aim to become Chancellor, or because of his increasing disillusionment and disassociation with the Jenkinsite group, Crosland had clearly identified himself with the Callaghan camp during the *In Place of Strife* debates. His approach engendered criticism from both left and right of the parliamentary party.[49] Crossman suggested that he had switched 'from demanding stronger anti-trade union measures to being 100 per cent pro-Callaghan'. Former devotees on the Jenkinsite right, such as Bill Rodgers, suggested that he had 'lost some of the fearless, visionary independence of his earlier years' and that he was now 'more calculating in his political judgments, often making the opinions supposedly held by his working-class constituents in Grimsby the touchstone of his own'. For the

Jenkinsites, Crosland's populism soon became an excuse for awkwardness, petulance and retreat from the idea of political principle and group loyalty.[50] *In Place of Strife* reflected Crosland's gradual shift towards the (Callaghanite) centre of the party and his further deviation from the emerging Jenkinsite revisionist Labour right. Parliamentary Labour right divisions over *In Place of Strife* also provided a source of impasse within the Cabinet and party during the critical period of discussions and contributed to the eventual climb down from the proposed legislation. Callaghan's 'purely voluntarist position may have been popular with the unions but was hardly a viable long-term response to the UK's industrial relations problem'. Crosland's 'argument about the detail and timing . . . was more tenable, while Jenkins can be criticised for not holding out to the last, though at least he was the last rat to leave an already sinking ship'.[51] In a similar vein to the Common Market issue, *In Place of Strife* divided the parliamentary Labour right within itself. It revealed something of its inherent complexity, ambiguities and emerging ideological, political and organisational fragmentation, largely absent or contained in the earlier period of cohesive Gaitskellite revisionist development, at a crucial juncture of Labour Party and British politics.

'Undemocratic and unconstitutional'? Opposition to the Heath Government's Industrial Relations Act

Following Labour's subsequent election defeat in 1970, the reform of industrial relations was left to the incoming Conservative Government, although the relationship between the unions and party and wider 'community' remained a crucial aspect of intra-party debate.[52] This came in the form of the Heath Government's Industrial Relations Act. The Conservatives 'believed that, if Britain was to be modernised, to achieve real economic growth in the bracing climate which awaited its industry in Europe, they needed simultaneously to reform industrial relations and to break away from the muddled compromises, restrictive practices and wildcat strikes which, in their view, had characterised the Wilson era'. Robert Carr, the new Secretary of State for Employment, explained that:

> we were an old country in desperate need of physical renewal. We could only do this if we could get economic growth, and the Industrial Relations Bill fitted into this pattern because we believed we would not succeed in getting growth going. One of the conditions was to bring a greater degree of stability and orderliness into the conduct of . . . industrial relations . . . It wasn't too much trade union power; it was really too little constitutional trade union power. The shop floor had taken over.[53]

The substance of the Bill offered trade unions a combination of benefits and restrictions, but sought to introduce legal controls of industrial relations by the compulsory 'registration' of trade unions and the regulation of union–employer agreements, enforceable by fines or imprisonment. It included both the right to belong to a trade union and the right not to, a development 'which struck at the heart of the pre-entry closed shop which many unions had established'. Under the Bill, trade unions also won the right of recognition and improved protection against unfair dismissal, but these had to be pursued as 'registered' unions through the new National Industrial Relations Court (NIRC) and the CIR. Unregistered unions lost tax concessions and were left open to unlimited claims for damages if they were accused of the 'unfair industrial practices' established in the Bill.

Inevitably, it again aroused great hostility within the Labour movement. The trade union leadership felt that it struck at the very heart of the gains and immunities fought for over seventy years of industrial struggle. At best, the advantages would place them in no better position than the trade union leaders of the 1950s, but 'clamped in corporatist embrace and legal restraint' as they were informed that the central pillars of the Bill were non-negotiable. The concept of registration in exchange for benefits or favours, and in favour of penalties, was bitterly opposed by the unions and interpreted as 'state-licence'. The TUC consequently organised a 'Kill the Bill' demonstration in February 1971, and at a special conference the following month advised member unions to de-register.[54] The Labour Party was also generally hostile to the proposed legislation. Much of the dense, 'complex package' of the Industrial Relations Bill, initially published in 1970, was forced through the guillotine procedure in Parliament without debate. On one occasion, the Labour opposition, led, perhaps ironically, by Barbara Castle, voted solidly through twenty-four divisions against a mass of clauses contained in the Bill that there had been no time to discuss. Some pro-reform members of the parliamentary party were highly critical of Labour's tactics in opposition to the Bill, given that it reflected and 'partially implemented . . . Labour's own In Place of Strife'.[55] Nevertheless, the Industrial Relations Act was duly placed on the statute book against a cacophony of opposition against the new legal framework. In the context of the background of states of emergency, the industrial sector witnessed an intensive period of unrest and conflict from the autumn of 1971 that ultimately undermined and discredited important elements of the Conservative industrial relations legislation.[56]

'The Keeper of the Cloth Cap': pragmatic Labourism reconfigured?

As spokesman on employment issues in succession to Barbara Castle between 1971 and 1972, Callaghan was again a prominent force in directing Labour's opposition to the penal sanctions of the Heath Government's industrial relations legislation. As he had demonstrated during Labour's own recent attempt to reform the context of industrial relations, Callaghan believed that the issue was not one for the courts and 'the full panoply of the law', and he attacked the new Government's approach as one that would make 'for greater divisions on the shop floor'. Given what he now considered to be the ineffective character of the solemn and binding covenant agreed in the wake of the collapse of In Place of Strife, however, Callaghan combined his attack on the Industrial Relations Act with an appeal for still greater voluntary discipline on the part of the trade unions. He believed that they should operate a proper framework for the conduct of collective bargaining and avoid self-seeking and unruly stoppages that were resented by the public. The potential dangers of the political victory he had won in 1969 were becoming all too apparent. Like other Labour leaders he maintained a prudent distance from the miners' strike of

January–February 1972. Although he sympathised with the claim that they had fallen behind in the pay stakes and welcomed the significant increase in their wages following the Wilberforce arbitration, the perceived excesses of the strike came as an unappealing reminder of the problems of any government in the face of unfettered trade union power.[57]

Although old guard 'Labourist centre-right' figures such as Callaghan were obvious targets of the 'powerful new forces of industrial, political and generational revolt', he 'was a pragmatic politician, less concerned with ideology than with common sense solutions . . . perhaps more so than any previous Labour leader'.[58] Within the context of industrial policy of the time, he appeared to be moving broadly to the left, and it was 'remarkable to see a former Home Secretary defending the right of workers to resist the operation of "bad laws", constitutionally passed through parliament'. His general shift to the left was accompanied by a move to a more explicit anti-European position. He always 'positioned himself in such a way that he could strike out in a number of different directions', which 'brought him some rather unexpected alliances, notably when in the period of opposition when he does . . . tactically appear to move to the left both on trade union matters and on Europe in 1971–2'. For Callaghan, as for other Labour leaders, 'this was a relatively unfocused and unattractive period, in which it seemed difficult for the party to define its objectives or its strategies effectively while in Opposition'. Some speculated that he was realigning himself with the new grass-roots radicalism in the party and trade unions, possibly with the intention of a future leadership bid.[59] However, Callaghan had long been perceived to belong to 'the generation of Labour leaders which had come to depend on the trade union block vote for protection against extremism in the constituencies', and 'the trade unions had provided his main political base in the previous decade'.[60] He was representative of that 'whole trade union task-based' tradition, which 'particularly people like Attlee relied upon'. It was 'not unradical, but not revolutionary in any sense'. It was an 'incremental social democrat tradition, but it wasn't [an] intellectual tradition'.[61]

The continuing trade union dilemma: a point of departure?

Others on the parliamentary Labour right lacked the natural outright hostility to trade union reform, and emphasised the similarity of the Industrial Relations Act to Labour's own proposed *In Place of Strife* legislation and a 'constitutional' line for their lack of opposition to the Conservative legislation. Jenkins' general position can be read off from his response to Castle's 'irrational' opposition to the Conservative Government's Industrial Relations Bill. He 'considered that she had just been making a most appalling ass of herself, and of the Labour Party, by frenziedly opposing the Government's Industrial Relations Bill as a monstrous piece of class oppression, despite the fact that it owed about 80 per cent of its inspiration to her own *In Place of Strife*'.[62] Similarly, John Mackintosh suggested that:

> [w]hilst the spirit of the document is fundamentally different from that of the Labour Government's White Paper . . . it contains a number of important recommendations

which to a large extent coincide with or resemble those of the Labour Government (e.g. on a Code of Industrial Practice, on information to be supplied by the employer, to some extent on protection against unfair dismissal, and on recognition). It would be a mistake to reject it in toto. It should be fought on the essential points to which objections must be raised.[63]

The Industrial Relations Bill was also the source of Dick Taverne's first major dispute with his constituency party after the 1970 election defeat. He was initially prepared to keep his disagreement with Labour's response to the Bill quiet, but when his local party announced a one-day strike in opposition to the Conservative legislation he made his views explicit: 'I said you can't strike against a measure which is adopted by an elected government and they said we've got no time for this middle class constitutionalism and we are going ahead with our strike.' Therefore, 'I said to them if you go on strike I will denounce it as your MP in public [and] they didn't strike, but in return I agreed to go on an anti-trade union Bill march which was ridiculous but I was one of the few MPs that actually marched against the Bill. I did that as a compromise.' Taverne explains that he:

was totally and utterly opposed to strike action . . . To strike on this issue would be undemocratic and unconstitutional. However much they disagreed with the Bill, industrial action was totally unjustified because the Government was carrying out policy which had been part of the election manifesto. Strike action would increase, not diminish, public sympathy for the Bill . . . it was a method of protest that in the end could only lead to Fascism . . . Having attacked unconstitutional forms of protest, the least I could do . . . was to support a peaceful protest march. But the row confirmed the feelings of the leaders of the Lincoln Labour Party that I did not see politics primarily as a class struggle. Increasingly they did.[64]

Although many believed that the penal severity of the 1971 Industrial Relations Act was not considered to be an effective or enforceable means by which to conduct industrial relations,[65] they did not enjoy tribal or sectional opposition for its own sake. The principle of trade union reform was still considered to be necessary. It 'didn't mean not having a decent, proper working relationship' with the trade unions. It 'was simply a matter of [them] being . . . far too dominant in the Labour Party . . . You only have to look back now to see how dominant they were and how much the Labour government tended to cringe in front of them'. Labour's own failure to reform the context of trade union activity was a significant factor in the later conduct of industrial relations and the difficulties of the Labour Government after 1974.[66]

From 'revisionist *enfant terrible*' to pragmatic 'populism'
Other influential revisionist figures of the parliamentary Labour right appeared to adopt the standard party line on the issue. Apart from identifying the power and influence of local shop stewards and 'pressures from local trade union activists' in trade union affairs, Healey's memoirs present an ambiguous, inconclusive approach to trade union reform.[67] He believed that trade unions possessed too much power and influence in the 1970s, with powerful trade union leaders immune to the democratic control of their members, and represented a danger to the

election and success of a Labour Government. However, he also recognised the potential damage of reform to Labour's mutually beneficial relationship with the trade unions.[68] Crosland was more attached to the important trade union relationship than some of his erstwhile revisionist colleagues and supporters. He certainly 'never advocated breaking with the trade unions', and considered the trade union link to be very 'important in keeping the party rooted in ... what was then called the working-class movement, which he believed in'. In the context of Labour Party of the time, he 'basically took a Callaghanite view, which was that the trade unions might be awful but they were the only real balance to keep the ship upright and if it were not for the trade unions we would be at the mercy of the activist left'.[69]

In the wake of Labour's own failed attempt to reform industrial relations, the parliamentary Labour right remained divided on the trade union question in the new radicalised industrial and political environment of the early 1970s. Old trade union centre-right figures such as Callaghan remained wedded to the unions as an irrevocable element of the historic Labour alliance and as a potential bulwark against extremist left-wing activity. Arch pragmatists such as Healey acknowledged some of the excesses and hazards of trade union power, but also recognised the problems implicit in any attempt to reform the context of industrial relations. Crosland viewed the trade unions as representative of Labour's political culture and working-class credentials, and, again, as an effective safeguard against increased left-wing influence in the constituencies. For the emerging Jenkinsite liberal strand of the parliamentary Labour right, the expression of trade union power and collectivism was increasingly incompatible with issues of personal freedom, and the increasingly explicit role of the trade union movement in the conduct of government economic and industrial policy represented a fundamental test of the democratic process. The period of Labour Government after 1974 increased the force and tensions of the respective views and positions. It witnessed an enhanced role for the trade unions through the establishment of the Labour Party-TUC 'social contract', agreed with the trade unions in opposition to improve unity and electoral credibility and provide a credible wages pact to help 'control inflation and achieve sustained growth in the standard of living'.[70]

The Labour Government, the 'social contract' and government by trade union

The experience and particular arrangements of the 1974–79 Labour Government reinforced misgivings about the industrial role of trade unions and about trade union political leverage through the Labour Party for those most concerned with the dangers of trade union collectivism. The

> loose and general social contract appeared ... to be incapable of dealing with escalating wage claims and spiralling inflation. For a period, 1975–8, the TUC's co-operation brought a degree of control but the accommodation was always predicated, on the union side, on the assumption of a return to free collective bargaining. This assumption was not shared by some of Labour's Ministers for whom it now

represented a dated perspective inconsistent with the pursuit of policies conducive
to the prosperity of the economy.[71]

Originating from 1971 in the new Labour Party-TUC Liaison Committee, the
arrangement represented the internal settlement of the Labour alliance after the
disaster of *In Place of Strife*. Both parties agreed to adopt 'a wide-ranging agreement'
over inflation and the cost of living under a Labour Government. In exchange,
the Labour Government would pursue economic and social policies congenial to
the trade unions and their members in terms of conciliation and arbitration
procedures in industrial disputes, the redistribution of wealth and progressive
social policies such as higher pensions.[72]

The Labour-TUC 'contract' represented 'a somewhat uneven agreement' in
that, while a potential Labour Government detailed its future programme, 'and
in a way that perhaps compromised its role as voice for the entire nation', the
trade union side of the bargain was more ambiguous. It was viewed by some as
a one-sided arrangement, by which the Government fulfilled 'its obligations
under the Social Contract to the letter, while the unions did little or nothing to
respond', and an agreement that 'was taken to imply that the unions must never
be criticised'.[73] There 'was no mention of incomes policy . . . no reference to
productivity, industrial efficiency, or economic modernization, little attention
to the generation of wealth rather than its redistribution'. Even, Callaghan,
chairman of the NEC Home Policy Committee in the discussions leading to the
inception of the social arrangement was initially sceptical of some aspects of its
likely value. Particularly, he questioned the likely success of a 'tripartite incomes
policy', feeling that it would be better to rely on 'fiscal and monetary' policy
instruments. It was 'an attempt to give political flesh and blood to the skeletal
agreement between the party and the unions sketched out during the crisis over
In Place of Strife in 1969. It was corporatism in its most undiluted form.' It was
in the context of the collapse of Heath's industrial relations policy during 1973–74,
the three-day week and the national miners' strike that the 'social contract' with
the trade unions appeared as 'a better way' and 'Labour's only strategic option if
it hoped to win the next election'. However, 'on the right there was grumbling
that we had handed the economy over to the unions', adding pressure to public
spending expectations and commitments in a highly problematic economic
environment.[74]

Retrospectively, Labour's social democratic critics have suggested that 'one of
the disasters' of the trade union role and influence of the period of Labour
Government 'was the social contract'. It represented a 'product of Labour's . . .
perceived failure between '64 and '70, and it gave a Labour Government coming
in in '74 a horrific manifesto which there was no chance at all of delivering in
those circumstances'. Some even believed that 'Labour did not deserve to win' in
1974, 'given its behaviour on Europe and the inflationary Social Contract it had
agreed with the trade unions'. They 'questioned the party's institutional links with
the unions and [were] critical of the role of Hugh Scanlon and Jack Jones'.[75] In
addition to moving further to the left in opposition, Labour had become far more

dependent on the trade unions. It was 'inevitable that Labour would be committed to repealing the Conservative Industrial Relations Act', although it owed many of its clauses to Labour's own *In Place of Strife*. This rapprochement continued well beyond the industrial sphere, and the joint declaration of aims published in February 1973 included 'a wide-ranging system of price controls, big increases in public spending on pensions, health, housing and transport and substantial extensions of public ownership'. Although Wilson declared it a 'great compact' between a future Labour Government and the trade unions, 'it was a deal on the union's terms. Labour was promising to deliver on a whole range of costly items; the unions merely agreed to take these commitments into account when bargaining for their members.'[76]

Both Crosland and Healey shared some of the misgivings about trade union power. The increased significance of the trade unions in the party's and Government's general strategy concerned Crosland, who commented that it was not Marxism that presented the problem, because no one really believed in Marx, but the question of whether the Labour Party should be so closely linked to the trade unions. Crosland had been one of the first senior Labour ministers to advocate a prices and incomes policy after the 1970 election defeat, arguing that it was essential to secure higher growth as a basis to pursue egalitarian policies. Healey, too, was concerned that trade union power might undermine the prospects of a Labour Government. As noted, however, both Crosland and Healey, in their different ways, were more generally predisposed to the cultural and political significance of the trade unions in the Labour Party. In his role as Shadow Chancellor, Healey saw it as one of his main responsibilities to be on good terms with the most powerful trade union leaders, especially Jack Jones of the Transport Workers and Hugh Scanlon of the Engineers. During the so-called 'Winter of Discontent', when even Callaghan 'was so disenchanted with the behaviour of the unions that he was contemplating legislation to control them, Healey, only half in jest, told him 'in that case I would "do a Callaghan" on him', a reference to Callaghan's own role in the party's *In Place of Strife* conflict ten years previously. Healey explains that even the Thatcher Governments'

> draconian curbs on union freedoms have been no more effective in curbing excessive pay . . . In Britain it is difficult to operate a pay policy even with the co-operation of the union leaders . . . the real power lies not in the union headquarters but with the local shop-stewards, who tend to see a rational incomes policy as robbing them of their functions. Moreover, the TUC has no real power over its constituent unions, unlike its equivalents in Scandinavia, Germany and Austria.[77]

Other less union-oriented politicians, such as Jenkins, regarded some of the rearguard Cabinet battles against pro-union and nationalisation measures as the 'last scene of "Labourism", for such it was much more than socialism or radicalism . . . played out by one of the most experienced and intelligent Cabinets of recent British history . . . with an amazing lack of imagination combined with a dogged but unconvinced determination'. He was particularly exasperated by Michael Foot's role as Employment Secretary, whose 'plans for trade union legislation continued as an overhanging menace'. Jenkins reports that he had earlier 'got him in bilateral discussions to retreat from his worst proposals which would have given strike pickets the same authority as the police, and one possessed by no one else, to stop vehicles on the highway'. Jenkins and his 'beleaguered minority' in Cabinet were further disturbed when Foot 'brought forward closed-shop provisions which were dangerously inimical to press freedom' in autumn 1975. In Jenkins' view, Foot's 'own editorial background seemed to count for nothing compared with his union worship. In his pantheon the dead Lord Beaverbrook had been superseded by the living Jack Jones.' More generally, he believed that the 'leaders of the Government' were in thrall to, or fearful of, 'a number of dangerous beasts' living further up the mountain; the bigger of these 'were known as union leaders and the smaller ones as constituency parties'.[78]

Trade union collectivism and the question of individual freedom: a 'small "l" liberal . . . social democrat' cause

The trade union question in the politics of the 1970s helped to amplify the emerging philosophical tension between the relative positions of freedom and equality in social democratic thought and practice. The issue of individual freedom across a range of policy spheres had been a key tenet of Gaitskellite revisionism in the 1950s, which 'turned into one of the few clear success stories of the 1964–70 Labour Government'.[79] In the industrial sphere, 'there was always an unresolved problem of reconciling this individual-focused and negative concept of freedom – absence of restraint – with trade union collectivism and the culture that sustained it . . . One strand of revisionism always defined freedom in positive terms as something that needs to be enlarged . . . rather than as simply the absence of restraint. Such a perspective could more readily appreciate the benefits to the individual of collective capacity in the face of the power of the employers.'[80] This conceptual dilemma was accentuated for Labour's social democrats in the 1970s as they reflected on 'the electoral liabilities of varying labour institutions'. A 'new and introspective awareness grew on the Right of the Labour Party of the trade-off between equality and liberty – a trade-off the older revisionist leaders, "children of the successes of war-time collectivism", had not fully appreciated', and if 'a choice had to be made between freedom and equality, then . . . revisionists would plump for freedom'.[81]

Central to the dilemma now was the behaviour of the trade unions, as they were provided with new facilities through 1974 and 1976 Acts that 'made it legal for employers who were party to a closed shop agreement to refuse to employ or to dismiss employees who refused to join a trade union'. In light of some highly publicised cases of 'closed shop victimisation', a protracted struggle developed within the Labour Government over the application of the legislation to the case of the National Union of Journalists (NUJ). In the Cabinet, both Jenkins and Shirley Williams were highly prominent in contesting this aspect of the legislation on the basis that it contravened principles of freedom.[82] Right-wing attacks on the trade union closed shop and collectivist values as a threat to personal freedom also 'found an anxious sensitivity on Labour's Right', as it was acknowledged that the question of freedom was now high on the political agenda across Europe 'with the ethical credentials of Socialism under scrutiny'. Although it remained 'unproven that the Labour Party will be incapable of redressing the balance between collectivism and individualism', that it 'required redressing was not in doubt'. For some, the next priority 'should be to reassert the value of the freedom of the individual'.[83]

A particular concern for liberally minded social democrats, not always shared by centre-right colleagues, was that, because of an 'overly intimate relationship with the trade unions, the government was moving in illiberal directions that were potentially dangerous to the principles of democratic government'.[84] Two particular developments were resonant in this respect. The first concerned the issue of the so-called 'Shrewsbury Two', Warren and Tomlinson, who were jailed for picketing offences in December 1973. On the left, there was widespread belief that Jenkins, in his second stint as Home Secretary, should automatically release them. Against opposition that included the TUC, meetings of the PLP and even some difference of opinion within Cabinet, however, he 'believed that the "Shrewsbury Two" were claiming to be above the law at a time of great trade union power':

> I could not go round the country fulminating about the rule of law and even contemplate taking a purely political decision to commute these sentences . . . I had the impression that the bulk of the [TUC] deputation was not so much angry as amazed that I would not accede. The climate of the time was that of ministers finding out what the TUC wanted and giving it to them . . . Foot, with whom as Employment Secretary they dealt most frequently, was totally of this disposition, but he was not alone.[85]

Jenkins, as Home Secretary, adopted 'a line that really incensed the trade unions and got very little support from his Cabinet colleagues. I think we all felt Jenkins was right about that'.[86] It is perhaps also revealing that Jenkins' speech in Haverfordwest in 1974, in which he explained that no one 'is entitled to be above the law', was 'an implied reproof to his erstwhile friend Anthony Crosland – who had lifted the penalties on the rebel Clay Cross councillors, imposed on them for their defiance of the Conservatives' Housing Finance Act – as well as to the Labour Left'. In the same speech, he argued that Labour would only find new support to break the stalemate of British politics by looking to the middle ground, an appetite for non-sectarian, cross-party politics increased by his role in the Britain in Europe Campaign during the 1975 referendum on British membership.[87]

The second issue concerned the important question of a closed shop in journalism, which developed out of the repeal of the Conservative Industrial Relations Act. It remained a significant theme for Labour's social democrats who deemed the protection of liberal freedoms to be a priority:

> Arguably, in the end, it was all a bit of a storm in a teacup, but it didn't look so at the time because it did look as though the way in which the Bill was drafted was going to make it possible to establish a closed shop not only amongst the print unions, which

of course have always had to have it, but amongst journalists as well. The NUJ would have a closed shop . . . (which was at this point very much under Trotskyite influence) . . . that seemed to us to be a very serious denial of . . . the . . . life-blood of the free society, and we formed . . . a deputation to . . . Foot, who we thought was absolutely dreadful and simply tamely followed the line of the TUC and, in fact, we did, in the end, because the government was so weak, actually force them to accept a modest amendment . . . straight away. I'm not trying to claim it was a huge and major issue, but it did loom quite large at the time and . . . it was important for us. For those involved in this, it was actually quite a touchstone issue.[88]

Others, similarly, were 'very, very opposed to the Trade Union Labour Relations Bill . . . in the sense that, among other things, it included control over editors and I thought that was an absolutely unacceptable invasion of freedom of information and civil liberties'. Along with critical European divisions, the whole issue of trade union power, particularly over a democratically elected government, remained a corrosive and divisive influence on the parliamentary Labour right:[89]

> I did not think the trade unions anymore than . . . the CBI had any right to be part of a committee which determines the legislative programmes of government. I am . . . purist on that. I think it is dangerous and corrupting. By the late Wilson, '75–'hat legislation they would accept and what they wouldn't . . . What they wouldn't accept was treated as an almost un-overturnable veto, and I . . . thought this was a very dangerous road to go . . . The central issue of the constitutional responsibility of the executive to parliament and not to any other body is something I hold as a very central principle . . . So the old trade union right did not see the point of people like Roy Hattersley and me who were saying that you mustn't have complete trade union power.

The economic role of trade unions remained important for the 'small "l" liberal wing of social democrats'. Some 'were very much in favour of an incomes policy and thought . . . that there needed to be more effective policing of wage claims etc. to make an incomes policy effective . . . it certainly was important when you reflect on the huge rate of inflation . . . when the government came into power, which was then of course greatly exacerbated by the way in which the miners' strike was ended in 1974, and it really did look as though the country was heading for . . . hyper inflation for a while'. But more serious to some were the 'libertarian aspects of trade union power', and it reflected a clear distinction of priorities and philosophy on the parliamentary Labour right. In addition to their passionate pro-Europeanism, this tension represented a touchstone issue for an emerging group of liberal social democrats:

> The trade unions got into an extremely bad attitude in that period from the point of view of freedom of speech and conscience, and . . . the attitude of a large number of members of the Cabinet on the right . . . what I used to think of as the Callaghan right didn't care about all this . . . they were anxious to get the approval of Jack Jones and Hugh Scanlon to the incomes policy and they didn't mind how many concessions they made to illiberal policies in other fields . . . I think that was quite an important distinction between Crosland and Jenkins too.[90]

Trade union power and Liberal freedoms: a 'brooding oppressive shadow'?

Although more extreme social democratic positions could 'overstate the power of union leaders and . . . ignore the extent to which Scanlon and Jones played by the old "rules" of the relationship', perceptions of trade union influence and 'claims of "solidarity"' among some Labour ministers continued to represent 'a brooding, oppressive shadow whose approval was as undesirable as it was deeply resented' and a real dilemma for Labour's 'social democrats'.[91] The 'brooding shadow' over the advancement of wider individual rights and freedoms manifested itself in a further minor, but portentous, episode. It concerned the proposal for a Bill of Rights, a long-term Liberal cause, which was given a new lease of life in December 1974. It was also supported by Lord Hailsham as a potential check against the 'elective dictatorship' of a Labour Government, who 'referred specifically to trade union legislation as likely to be caught by any Bill of Rights'.[92] The conflict over the Bill of Rights was fought out largely in private in the Human Rights Sub-committee of the NEC. For those 'concerned as in the past with personal freedom from the State but now as much concerned . . . at the threat to freedom thought to be posed from the Left by trade union practices, including the closed shop', a Bill of Rights became progressively more attractive. Jenkins, as Home Secretary, encouraged by his Home Office advisor, Anthony Lester, was known to be sympathetic. The Home Office produced a Green Paper, *Legislation on Human Rights: With Particular Reference to the European Community*, in June 1976.[93]

Inevitably, there was strong reaction to the idea of passing power from a democratically elected parliament to the judiciary, and the social democratic Labour right was equally torn over the issue. Roy Hattersley was strongly opposed and the Home Office Minister, Alex Lyon, objected on the grounds of handing 'the English judiciary more power'. On the NEC, however, the Sub-committee on Human Rights was dominated by sympathisers of a Bill, with Shirley Williams in the chair. In fact, the majority of these sympathisers on the sub-committee between 1975 and 1977 would eventually defect to the SDP in 1981. In addition to Shirley Williams, these included Jenkins, Lord Harris, Bruce Douglas-Mann, Edward Lyons, John Lyttle and Ian Wrigglesworth, as well as Anthony Lester, the Home Office advisor.[94]

The proposal for a Bill of Rights ultimately fell on the sword of the NEC Home Policy Committee, based on the lack of wider support in the party. Although the NEC agreed to the publication of a discussion document, Labour's general programme for 1976 established that the party 'will not finally commit . . . to this step until and unless we are satisfied that it has the support of the Party'.[95] This support was not forthcoming in resolutions to the 1976 and 1977 party conferences: in 1976 there was only one supporting resolution and, in 1977, none at all. Moreover, as right-wing elements in the press wrote of the evils of collectivism and welcomed a charter 'specifically as a means of dealing with the victims of trade union legislation', alarm bells were ringing at the TUC over the potential implications of such a development.[96] A TUC memo on the subject counselled caution 'crucially on issues relating to the right to join or not to join a trade union' and the difference between the positive rights of such a charter and '"the immunities" . . . central to the present "highly acceptable framework of British labour law"'. It also noted inherent 'dangers from the judiciary, given "their social background" and "mistrust of collective action"'. The TUC, therefore, thrust its weight decisively against the proposals of the NEC Sub-committee on Human Rights. On the NEC Home Policy Committee, the majority and minority positions of the Human Rights Sub-committee were reversed, and Shirley Williams found herself without allies from the trade unionists and out-voted by the left led by Michael Foot. The senior committee decided not to submit evidence to the House of Lords Select Committee that had invited evidence on a Bill to incorporate the European Convention into British law. Consequently, Labour's pro-Bill of Rights lobby found itself in a political cul-de-sac: the TUC

> had spoken; its word . . . conveyed to the NEC. The NEC with its left-wing majority agreed that there was a potential threat to party policy and to trade unionism from court intervention. This was decisive. But to change the composition of the NEC required trade union co-operation. Catch 22. Furious at the rebuff, and at their own imprisonment within Labour's power structure, the sub-committee majority broke all precedents and sent their memorandum to the House of Lords under their own names.[97]

There was also significant opposition from those such as John Mackintosh and Brian Walden in Parliament to the Labour Government's attempt to extend the provisions of the Dock Labour Scheme and the dockers' closed shop, embodied in the Dock Labour Bill, on the grounds that it catered for a special group rather than the population as a whole. Like many other liberal social democrats, Mackintosh favoured a statutory incomes policy and opposed uncontrolled collective bargaining. During the period of Labour Government, he 'spoke out for a return to statutory wage controls at a time when it was still heresy to question the social contract, tried to emasculate . . . Foot's proposals to legalize the closed shop in journalism . . . and, together with Brian Walden, sabotaged the so-called Dock Labour Bill with a brilliantly-timed last minute abstention'.[98] The latter was mockingly described as an attempt to ensure that 'anybody who worked within three miles of a dockyard had to be a member of the dockers' closed shop', and Mackintosh defended his actions on the basis that the 'Dock Work Regulation Bill was never in the election manifesto and nor was it passed by the Labour Party Conference. It was an agreement reached by Mr Foot and Mr Jack Jones and I have no intention of accepting this agreement when it is contrary to the interests of my constituents in their fishing ports and contrary to the interests of the bulk of the people in this country, as has been made clear by the support Brian Walden and I have received.' He further explains that 'I cannot accept that Jack Jones has the right to push matters into the social contract when Members elected for marginal seats like myself see why fishermen adversely affected by such dock regulations are not entitled to make their point'. He was clear that he did not do it 'simply because the Tribune Group defeated the Government on public expenditure cuts . . . I voted that way because I believed . . . that the reservation of new jobs for people organised under a previous Labour regulations scheme is not the method of proceeding that is most suitable' and certainly this is the view taken by many trade unionists in other occupations. At the heart of his opposition to the extended provisions was his disbelief that the 'Labour Party exists to give bribes to special people to achieve special objectives when these are damaging to the national interest'.[99] He was congratulated, among other things, for his exhibition of 'radical libertarian independence' in response to the 'illiberal and sectional' character of the Bill. He attracted support from those who rejected the 'exercise of naked power by entrenched groups' and who welcomed the sight of MPs 'prepared to put the interests of the country before those of narrow party political dogma'.[100]

Frustrated with the apparently unlimited expression of trade union control within the party apparatus and wider industrial and economic role, the 'trade union question' remained a fundamental and consistent dilemma for Labour's liberal social democrats, not least because it possessed critical policy implications and symbolised a narrow, sectional, class-based outlook and commitments:

> the 1974–9 Government . . . for the Right . . . was a Government where too often they would 'wander through the Lobby . . . in a reluctant position' . . . the Liaison Committee . . . for many on the Right of the PLP . . . remained a disturbing new arrangement – a new way of institutionalising union power and a potential threat to Parliamentary accountability . . . for the Right it continued to be a Government tied in a connection to the unions by which they were at the beck and call of vested interests and of further excessive demands for public expenditure commitments, while being unable to firm up a certain and lasting arrangement over industrial productivity and inflation. This assertive trade union presence within the Labour Party was experienced by the social Democrats not only in the obligations of policy but as an expression of class, style, and culture. The preoccupation with manual worker trade unionism was seen by some on the intellectual Right as . . . 'a strange, inward-looking proletarianism' whose proponents imagined that the Movement could 'rely exclusively on the strong right arm of the working class'.[101]

Conclusion: a 'framework of defection'?

Collectively, these various episodes and issues formed part of a wider social democratic critique of the trade union role and influence in British industrial and economic culture. The critique of free collective bargaining was extended to its impact on unemployment. Reflecting an almost neo-liberal critique, for example, the Manifesto Group argued that there had been a failure to distinguish between unemployment from lack of sufficient demand and unemployment due to 'organised Labour using its bargaining power to push wages beyond what the economy could stand'. There also was a view that the assertive power of the trade unions in industrial relationships had shifted too far in their favour. Management, it was argued, had become too weak and defensive, and too willing to believe that it would lose an industrial confrontation. According to the critique, the unions represented a particular reflection of 'the national cultural weaknesses of conservatism and resistance to change'. It was the trade unions who were taking the Labour Government 'down the path of a "half-hearted statism" where intervention was, more often than not, directed towards the subsidy of the inefficient' and, in their present state, were a considerable constraint on industrial modernisation.[102]

The trade union question eventually became one of how the Labour Party was to prise itself free of the constraints of trade unionism which, in turn, became 'linked with a second question of how to achieve a realignment of British politics and a change in the adversarial two-party system'.[103] It was partly a reaction to the development of the 'political role of the unions as "an estate of the realm" within a set of neo-corporatist arrangements', which made it important to have a more representative trade union leadership and to regulate on behalf of the public interest.[104] Some still insisted that government with consent had to develop these processes and involve the trade unions as 'social partners', but in 'any pluralist society, the leaders will have to win the agreement of their followers, and this is the central issue'.[105] However, another view interpreted corporatism, with its emphasis on consultation and consensus, as a significant aspect of British decline and, for any sort of revival, the primacy of corporatism must be discarded and democracy allowed to flourish.[106] The question remained as to whether this could be accomplished within the Labour Party, or whether it would require an alternative, 'modernised' vehicle of social democracy to 'open up' participation in the political sphere. It was the experience of Labour Governments since the late 1960s which encouraged some to believe that an inherent danger to democracy, liberty and economic efficiency lay in the ability of the trade union movement to bend governments to their will: in 'the ten years from 1969 to 1979, the rumbling concern on the Right . . . about trade union power over Government moved to a climax . . . the Callaghan Government was the third to have been destroyed, essentially, by the trade unions . . . [and] it raised a spectre which haunted the Social Democrats'.[107]

Debilitating divisions of the Labour right occurred across a range of key themes and issues of industrial relations and trade union reform. As with the European issue, it was not merely a simple labourist–revisionist division over the 'trade union question'. The Gaitskellite revisionist Labour right of the 1950s and early 1960s was fundamentally split between emerging and competing liberal and egalitarian conceptions of political and industrial arrangements and goals. Led by Callaghan, the Labour's 'Keeper of the Cloth Cap', there were the obvious defenders of the 'rules of the Labour movement' who viewed the Labour alliance in almost cultural terms.[108] Callaghan was, perhaps, most representative of 'traditional Labour', and valued the historic partnership of the trade unions and the Labour Party, as expressed in 'the traditional moderate, centrist role [the TUC] had exercised in the pre-Frank Cousins days in the 1940s and early 1950s'. Callaghan's instinct was for party unity and he believed that 'the business of creating socialism was also the business of subordinating individual views to those of the party'.[109] It was against all their instincts 'to create a situation in which the trade unions movement was not regarded as the flesh and bone of the Labour movement'. Although they may have balked at left-wing infiltration and extremist elements of trade unionism in the 1970s, they deemed the relationship to be essential to their preferred vision of central control of the Labour Party through the parliamentary leadership in conjunction with the trade unions. A close liaison with the unions was an essential stabilising force for the party, particularly against the advent of a resurgent radical left in the 1970s. Attempts to reframe and regulate the context and conduct of industrial relations would undermine traditional trade union rights and privileges, and potentially lead to a damaging split in the Labour alliance.[110] A pragmatic and populist element of the 'revisionist' Labour right, represented in their own ways by Healey and Crosland, which might have lacked the cultural appreciation and attachment to the Labour alliance, also foresaw the need to maintain the 'special link' with the trade unions as the representatives of the 'organised working class'. They recognised some need to reorder priorities and rework more distinctive institutional roles, but within the existing framework of the rules of the Labour movement. In terms of the reform of industrial relations, they largely adopted pragmatic perspectives according to political and party context and timing. To some extent, they upheld the earlier Gaitskellite revisionist position of Crosland and Allan Flanders, who argued that the central problem and the primary responsibility for industrial success lay with management, intent as they were on maintaining party unity and the essence of its Labourist spirit.[111] A third view was that the major problem of British industry lay in the cumulative assertive and confrontational power of the trade unions. This was the perspective of the emerging and relatively cohesive Jenkinsite pro-European, liberal revisionist strand of the parliamentary Labour right, and appeared 'much readier to shed ... the fundamental values and "rules" of the Labour Movement'.[112] A clear liberal-egalitarian/collectivist dimension had emerged within Labour Party revisionism, which indicated a shift from the Croslandite ideological revisionism of the Gaitskellite heyday to the Jenkinsite political revisionism of the 1970s. From this perspective, Gaitskell and Crosland's earlier social democracy possessed '[n]o working out of the freedom problem, limits of state action. Trade off between compulsion & freedom. Value of independence.' It also offered '[n]o consideration of Labour Party structure & national pol[itical] machinery'.[113] The seemingly irresolvable 'trade union question' in Labour and British politics in the 1970s became a central feature of their thinking about the party and on policy. Increasingly, they were to feel frustrated and constrained within these 'rules', and it was this confinement, apparently confirmed by the intra-party disputes after 1979 which emphasised the constitutional significance of the trade unions in the party, which provided a crucial sub-text of the departure of some of their number to the SDP.[114]

As the problems and divisions of the party and movement engulfed the Labour Government in the period leading to the 'Winter of Discontent' and subsequent general election defeat in 1979, they found it both an embittering and formative experience that exemplified their most profound fears about the structural attachment to the trade unions. Some still argued that the association with the trade unions remained one of the party's greatest assets and that there were continental role models for a successful partnership, and some even argued that only more rather than less trade union participation in the party would offer a ballast against an increasingly left-wing NEC and constituency parties. For others, there remained an irreconcilable underlying tension 'between the economic objectives of trade unionism with their emphasis on self-help, free collective bargaining and rampant individualism and the wider Socialist perspective of Labour with their appeal to fraternity and equality. These features of trade unionism filled out a growing disenchantment on the Right of the PLP, provoking discreet but urgent discussions on their future within the Labour Movement.'[115] The distance between the preferences of moderate but radical social democracy and the 'rules' of the Labour movement now represented perhaps the deepest gulf in British politics. The aim of the former would be to create a permanent shift of power from organised labour to democratic government, which might necessarily involve a departure from the present party system to strengthen the 'radical centre'.[116]

Increasingly unwilling to dance to the tune of the party's paymasters, a number of factors further alienated the 'radical' liberal social democratic Labour right from the party mainstream after 1979. These included having to vote against the trade union legislation of the first Thatcher administration, elements of which they supported; the fact that the party leadership appeared unwilling to do little but to 'seek accommodation with the advancing Left and with the "unacceptable" union voting arrangements' after the 1980 conference decisions and announcement of a Special Conference to discuss the process of election for the party leader; and the subsequent election of Foot as leader served to suggest that a similar pattern of political subservience was inescapable. The 'faults in the Labour Movement appeared endemic, incurable and worsening fast. At every turn they felt constrained by the "rules" of the relationship. They could not initiate the industrial relations policies nor the incomes policy they felt to be necessary; nor could they produce a Bill of Rights. Each in some way breached the "rules" of freedom', and they were 'convinced that the Labour Party was beyond salvation for the sort of things that [they] believed in'.[117] The wider constitutional changes in the party appeared to represent 'command democracy . . . it was all about trying to replace parliamentary control with party control', the 'attempt to try to gain party control over responsibility for Parliament'.[118] With their defection to the SDP the new Social Democrats could make the question of trade union power a central tenet of the political framework and policies outlined in the Limehouse Declaration, which emphasised the deeper, longer-term concerns and principles underlying their discomfort with the immediate constitutional changes in the party: the 'calamitous outcome of The Labour Party Wembley Conference demands a new start in British politics. A handful of trade union leaders can now dictate the choice of a future Prime Minister. The Conference disaster is the culmination of a long process by which the Labour Party has moved steadily away from its roots in the people of this country and its commitment to Parliamentary government.'[119]

Notes

1 L. Minkin, *The Contentious Alliance: Trade Unions and the Labour Party*, Edinburgh, Edinburgh University Press, 1991, pp. 209–10.

2 J. P. Mackintosh, 'Socialism or Social Democracy? The Choice for the Labour Party', *Political Quarterly*, October–December 1972, pp. 483–4; also see J. P. Mackintosh, 'The case for a realignment of the Left', *The Times*, 22 July 1977. Writing on the prospects of the 1977 Lib-Lab pact for a centre-left realignment of British politics, Mackintosh believed that such a party, freed from the institutional constraints and limitations of the trade unions, 'would be free to press for what it saw as the national interest' and could be 'far more radical on many issues'.

3 See S. Ludlam, 'Norms and Blocks: Trade Unions and the Labour Party since 1964', in B. Brivati and R. Heffernan (eds), *The Labour Party: A Centenary History*, Basingstoke, Macmillan, p. 220.

4 See T. Bale, 'Managing the Party and the Trade Unions', in B. Brivati and T. Bale (eds), *New Labour in Power: Precedents and Prospects*, London, Routledge, 1997, pp. 159–60, 166–7, 174–5.

5 Affiliated unions traditionally set the party's industrial relations policy and nothing else.

6 See Minkin, *The Contentious Alliance*, pp. 3–22; also see Ludlam, 'Norms and Blocks', pp. 223–4.

7 Minkin, *The Contentious Alliance*, pp. 208–13. For David Marquand, the trade union role in the Labour Party was responsible for a host of ills in the 1970s and, ultimately, for Labour's failure to transform itself into a fully fledged social democratic party in the European sense. He wrote to John Mackintosh that when he joined the Labour Party in the late 1950s it looked as if Gaitskell might do for it what Brandt and Schmidt did for the German SPD. The 'experience of two ghastly Labour Governments . . . show . . . what a mess a party which is tied to the trade unions . . . basically hostile to the mixed economy and fundamentally anti-European, is bound to make when it tries to run the country . . . in the last 20 years its become clear that the Labour Party simply isn't going to transform itself into a social-democratic party in the way that the SPD did'. He concluded that the 'idea that the Labour Party can ever become a non-doctrinaire, non-class radical party of the sort Gaitskell tried to turn it into no longer seems . . . remotely possible'. The 'only hope of rescuing the country from the doldrums of the last 20 years is a realignment of the Left': David Marquand to John Mackintosh, 21 August 1977; David Marquand to John Mackintosh, n.d. [approximately September–November 1977], John P. Mackintosh Papers, 323/10.

8 See D. Owen, *Face the Future*, Oxford, Oxford University Press, 1981, pp. 97–113, 114–27; W. Rodgers, *The Politics of Change*, London, Secker & Warburg, 1982, pp. 94–106, 107–24; S. Williams, *Politics is for People*, Harmondsworth, Penguin, 1981, pp. 126–40.

9 Minkin, *The Contentious Alliance*, pp. 208–9.

10 G. Radice, *Friends & Rivals: Crosland, Jenkins and Healey*, London, Little, Brown, 2002, pp. 172–3.

11 R. Hattersley, *Who Goes Home? Scenes from a Political Life*, London, Little, Brown, 1995, p. 67; Leo Abse, Interview with the author, 20 June 2001.

12 Hattersley, *Who Goes Home?*, pp. 68–9; D. Healey, *Time of My Life*, London, Michael Joseph, 1989, pp. 341, 407; Radice, *Friends & Rivals*, pp. 172–3; R. Tyler, '"Victims of our History"? Barbara Castle and *In Place of Strife*', *Contemporary British History*, 20 (3), 2006, p. 462.

13 C. Ponting, *Breach of Promise: Labour in Power 1964–1970*, Harmondsworth, Penguin, 1990, p. 351.
14 Labour Party, *The New Britain*, London, Labour Party, 1964; Ponting, *Breach of Promise*, pp. 257, 350–1.
15 Healey, *Time of My Life*, p. 341; G. Radice, *The Industrial Democrats: Trade Unions in an Uncertain World*, London, Allen & Unwin, 1978, p. 67; Radice, Friends & Rivals, p. 175.
16 K. O. Morgan, *Callaghan: A Life*, Oxford, Oxford University Press, 1997, pp. 330–1; Ponting, *Breach of Promise*, pp. 351–2.
17 B. Castle, *Fighting All The Way*, London, Macmillan, 1994, pp. 413–14.
18 B. Castle, *The Castle Diaries 1964–70*, London, Weidenfeld & Nicolson, 1984, p. 625; Morgan, *Callaghan*, pp. 331–2; B. Pimlott, *Harold Wilson*, London, Harper Collins, 1992, p. 528; Ponting, *Breach of Promise*, p. 354.
19 Morgan, *Callaghan*, p. 332; Ponting, *Breach of Promise*, pp. 352ff.; also see Cmnd 3888, *In Place of Strife: A Policy for Industrial Relations*, London, HMSO, January 1969.
20 Cmnd 3888, pp. 25, 35; *Tribune*, 7 February 1969.
21 Tyler, ' "Victims of our History"?', pp. 461–2, 474.
22 Cmnd 3888, pp. 9–12, 18–21, 22–4; P. Jenkins, *The Battle of Downing Street*, London, Charles Knight & Co., 1970, pp. 26–43; Ponting, *Breach of Promise*, pp. 353–4.
23 Jenkins, *The Battle of Downing Street*, pp. 44–74; Minkin, *The Contentious Alliance*, pp. 114–15.
24 Morgan, *Callaghan*, p. 333.
25 Tyler, ' "Victims of our History"?', pp. 461, 474.
26 *Tribune*, 24 January 1969; also see Ponting, *Breach of Promise*, p. 354; Radice, *Friends & Rivals*, pp. 173–4.
27 Castle, *The Castle Diaries 1964–70*, pp. 582–3; Tyler, ' "Victims of our History"?', p. 474.
28 Ponting, *Breach of Promise*, pp. 354–6; D. Taverne, *The Future of the Left: Lincoln and After*, London, Jonathan Cape, 1974, pp. 42–3.
29 J. Callaghan, *Time and Chance*, London, William Collins, 1987, pp. 272–7; Jenkins, *The Battle of Downing Street*, pp. 79–97.
30 Callaghan, *Time and Chance*, pp. 40–64, 274; Morgan, *Callaghan*, pp. 20–39, 333–4; also see Tyler, ' "Victims of our History"?', pp. 461, 469, 474.
31 LP/NEC Minutes, 26 March 1969; Morgan, *Callaghan*, p. 334; Ponting, *Breach of Promise*, pp. 356–7.
32 Wilson's memoirs are not effusive on the matter, and Castle herself was not convinced by Wilson's delivery of a 'constitutional homily' on the duties and responsibilities of being a minister: Castle, *The Castle Diaries 1964–70*, pp. 625–6, 630–2; Morgan, *Callaghan*, pp. 334, 357; Ponting, *Breach of Promise*, p. 357.
33 R. Jenkins, *A Life at the Centre*, London, Macmillan, 1991, p. 288; Radice, *Friends & Rivals*, p. 174.
34 Callaghan, *Time and Chance*, p. 274; Jenkins, *A Life at the Centre*, pp. 287–9; Morgan, *Callaghan*, pp. 331–2.
35 Jenkins, *A Life at the Centre*, p. 287; Radice, *Friends & Rivals*, pp. 174–5; Bill Rodgers, Interview with the author, 18 February 2001.
36 Dick Taverne, Interview with the author, 18 January 2001; Taverne, *Lincoln and After*, pp. 42–3.
37 Shirley Williams, Interview with the author, 25 June 2002; Phillip Whitehead, Interview with the author, 20 January 2001.

38 Rodgers, Interview with the author.

39 A. Crosland, 'Notes For Cabinet on Industrial Relations Bill', n.d., Crosland Papers, 5/4.

40 See S. Crosland, *Tony Crosland*, London, Jonathan Cape, 1982, pp. 202–3; K. Jefferys, *Anthony Crosland: A New Biography*, London, Richard Cohen Books, 1999, pp. 137–9; D. Owen, *Time to Declare*, London, Michael Joseph, 1991, p. 157; Radice, *Friends & Rivals*, p. 175.

41 Healey, *Time of My Life*, pp. 341, 345–6; also see S. Haseler, *The Tragedy of Labour*, Oxford, Blackwell, 1980, p. 121; R. Mason, *Paying the Price*, London, Robert Hale, 1999, p. 110.

42 Healey, *Time of My Life*, p. 341; E. Pearce, *Denis Healey: A Life in Our Times*, London, Little, Brown, 2002, pp. 378–9.

43 Hattersley, *Who Goes Home?*, pp. 67–70; R. Hattersley, 'Barbara the brave – a woman to reckon with', *The Observer*, 5 May 2002; R. Hattersley, 'He would have made a great PM', *The Guardian*, 6 January 2003. He also reveals that, while it is now very difficult to understand why Castle's essentially modest proposals aroused 'so much passion', like other politicians of moderation and common sense, such as Callaghan and Houghton, he 'believed that industrial relations should be regulated by good intentions, enlightened self-interest and the occasionally flexed muscle, not the law'. Clear 'association with the Luddites' helped to secure his release to join Healey as his deputy at the Ministry of Defence.

44 Owen, *Time to Declare*, pp. 155, 156–7; Radice, *Friends & Rivals*, p. 176.

45 Morgan, *Callaghan*, pp. 339–41, 475; Kenneth Morgan, Interview with the author, 17 October 1997; also see R. Heffernan, 'Leaders and Followers: The Politics of the Parliamentary Labour Party', in B. Brivati and R. Heffernan (eds), *The Labour Party: A Centenary History*, Basingstoke, Macmillan, 2000, p. 261; Radice, *Friends & Rivals*, p. 234.

46 Owen, *Time to Declare*, p. 156; also see Jefferys, *Anthony Crosland*, p. 139; C. Mayhew, *Time to Explain: An Autobiography*, London, Hutchinson, 1987, p. 187; Morgan, *Callaghan*, p. 339.

47 Callaghan, *Time and Chance*, p. 275; Owen, *Time to Declare*, p. 155.

48 Jenkins, *A Life at the Centre*, pp. 288–9; Owen, *Time to Declare*, pp. 156–7.

49 It also reinforced Crosland's reputation for indecision, a criticism he would have to endure on a frequent basis from the Jenkinsites, particularly in relation to his (shifting) stance on the Common Market issue.

50 See Castle, *The Castle Diaries 1964–70*, p. 351; Crosland, *Tony Crosland*, pp. 205–6; Jefferys, *Anthony Crosland*, pp. 138–40; Owen, *Time to Declare*, pp. 156–7; Radice, *Friends & Rivals*, pp. 176–9; W. Rodgers, *Fourth Among Equals*, London, Politico's, 2000, pp. 113–15.

51 Radice, *Friends & Rivals*, p. 329.

52 G. Radice, 'Trade Unions and the Labour Party', *Socialist Commentary*, November 1970, pp. 7–10.

53 P. Whitehead, *The Writing on the Wall: Britain in the Seventies*, London, Michael Joseph, 1985, p. 70.

54 Radice, *The Industrial Democrats*, pp. 71–5; Whitehead, *The Writing on the* Wall, pp. 71–2.

55 Rodgers, *Fourth Among Equals*, p. 121; Rodgers, Interview with the author; also see Hattersley, *Who Goes Home?*, pp. 96–8; Dick Leonard, Interview with the author, 23 January 2001; D. Marquand, *The Progressive Dilemma: From Lloyd George to Kinnock*, London, Heinemann, 1991, pp. 195–6.

56 E. Heffer, *The Class Struggle in Parliament*, London, Gollancz, 1973, p. 231; Whitehead, *The Writing on the* Wall, pp. 72–80.

57 Morgan, *Callaghan*, p. 383.

58 K. Jefferys, *The Labour Party since 1945*, Basingstoke, Macmillan, 1993, pp. 93–7; D. Howell, *British Social Democracy: A Study in Development and Decay*, London, Croom Helm, 1976, p. 297; Morgan, *Callaghan*, pp. 384–5.

59 Morgan, *Callaghan*, pp. 383–4; Morgan, Interview with the author.

60 Healey, *Time of My Life*, p. 467.

61 Williams, Interview with the author.

62 Jenkins, *A Life at the Centre*, p. 322; J. P. Mackintosh, Typescript of the 1977 Fawley Lecture, 'Britain's Malaise: Political or Economic?', Mackintosh Papers, 323/8.

63 J. P. Mackintosh, 'Memorandum on the Consultative Document on Industrial Relations', 1970–71, Mackintosh Papers, 323/123; R. Prentice, 'Recollections of a Trade Unionist', unpublished manuscript, Prentice Papers, 6/5, p. 9; *The Guardian*, 'The law and the prophets', 3 December 1970.

64 Taverne, *Lincoln and After*, pp. 52–5; Taverne, Interview with the author; also see J. Mackintosh, 'Anybody Still for Democracy? Troubled Reflections of a Westminster M.P.', *Encounter*, November 1972, p. 24.

65 See Marquand, *The Progressive Dilemma*, p. 196; Morgan, *Callaghan*, p. 383; Radice, *The Industrial Democrats*, pp. 71–5; Taverne, *Lincoln and After*, pp. 52, 54.

66 Rodgers, Interview with the author.

67 See Healey, *Time of My Life*, pp. 399, 406, 467.

68 *Ibid.*, pp. 341, 346; Denis Healey, Interview with the author, 9 February 1999; Mason, *Paying the Price*, pp. 109–10.

69 David Lipsey, Interview with the author, 17 January 2001.

70 See Ludlam, 'Norms and Blocks', pp. 223–4.

71 Minkin, *The Contentious Alliance*, p. 210.

72 Ludlam, 'Norms and Blocks', p. 223.

73 Prentice, 'Recollections of a Trade Unionist', pp. 12–15; also J. Horam, 'The Present Situation', Sandelson Papers, 6/1; Manifesto Group, 'Economic Report by the Manifesto Group', Sandelson Papers, 6/1, p. 10; G. Radice, 'Social Contract and Community', *Socialist Commentary*, September 1976, pp. 13–14.

74 See J. Barnett, *Inside The Treasury*, London, Andre Deutsch, 1982, p. 49; J. P. Mackintosh, Notes headed 'Finance Bill' with attached list of major wage claims and settlements, 7 April–7 May 1975, Mackintosh Papers, 323/117; also see Callaghan, *Time and Chance*, pp. 416–17; Morgan, *Callaghan*, pp. 389–90; R. Taylor, *The TUC: From the General Strike to New Unionism*, Basingstoke, Palgrave, 2000, pp. 201–2. For further discussion of the construction, detail and development of the 'social contract' see Ludlam, 'Norms and Blocks', pp. 223–9; Taylor, *The TUC*, pp. 201–33; Whitehead, *The Writing on the Wall*, pp. 116–28.

75 Rodgers, Interview with the author; Rodgers, *Fourth Among Equals*, pp. 136–7.

76 Radice, *Friends & Rivals*, p. 213.

77 A. Crosland, *A Social Democratic Britain*, London, Fabian Society, 1971, p. 7; Healey, *Time of My Life*, pp. 346, 398–9; Jefferys, *Anthony Crosland*, pp. 168–9; Radice, *Friends & Rivals*, pp. 213–14, 278.

78 Jenkins, *A Life at the Centre*, pp. 427–8; Prentice, 'Recollections of a Trade Unionist', pp. 12–13. Prentice suggests that after Foot became Employment Secretary, 'the country was increasingly governed by the Jones/Foot axis. It was Jones who called the tune'. His 'divorce proceedings [from the Labour party] were gathering momentum'.

79 Minkin, *The Contentious Alliance*, pp. 212–13; also see R. Jenkins, *The Labour Case*, Harmondsworth, Penguin, 1959, pp. 135–46; LPACR, 1956, pp. 82–96.

80 Minkin, *The Contentious Alliance*, pp. 212–13; also see S. Haseler, *The Gaitskellites: Revisionism in the British Labour Party 1951–64*, London, Macmillan, 1969, p. 93; *Socialist Union, Socialism: A New Statement of Principles*, London, Lincolns-Prager, 1952, pp. 32–7; *Socialist Union, Twentieth Century Socialism*, Harmondsworth, Penguin, 1956, pp. 38–50.

81 Haseler, *The Gaitskellites*, p. 93; Minkin, *The Contentious Alliance*, p. 212; P. L. Sykes, *Losing from the Inside: The Cost of Conflict in the British Social Democratic Party*, New Brunswick, NJ, Transaction Publishers, 1990, pp. 39, 90–1; Williams, Interview with the author.

82 David Marquand, Interview with the author, 16 January 2001; Williams, Interview with the author.

83 See *The Guardian*, 16 September 1977; J. P. Mackintosh 'Liberty and Equality: Getting the Balance Right', in D. Marquand (ed.), *John P. Mackintosh on Parliament and Social Democracy*, London, Longman, 1982, pp. 182–9; Minkin, *The Contentious Alliance*, p. 213.

84 Marquand, Interview with the author.

85 Jenkins, *A Life at the Centre*, pp. 391–3.

86 Marquand, Interview with the author; Prentice, 'Recollections of a Trade Unionist', p. 9; R. Prentice, 'The Rubicon Papers', unpublished manuscript, Prentice Papers, 6/17, Chapter 8. Such issues represented a 'test case' for some who were increasingly concerned about the 'rule of law'. Although they may have been critical of some of the more extreme 'legalistic' provisions of the Industrial Relations Act, observation of the rule of law remained paramount: in 'a democracy we have the right to campaign for changes in the law'. In the meantime, 'we should obey the law, however bad it may be. This is the only basis on which democracy can survive. Large sections of the Labour Party and the Trade Union Movement rejected this basic concept during the early 1970s.'

87 Whitehead, *The Writing on the Wall*, pp. 344–5.

88 Marquand, Interview with the author.

89 Williams, Interview with the author; also see Minkin, *The Contentious Alliance*, pp. 212, 214; S. Williams, 'The New Authoritarianism', *Political Quarterly*, 60 (1), 1989, p. 6.

90 Marquand, Interview with the author; Williams, Interview with the author; also see W. Rodgers, *The Politics of Change*, London, Secker & Warburg, 1982, pp. 107–8, 124. Marquand contends that it was the point at which Shirley Williams began to consider the need for some sort of ideological and political realignment, or at least became more closely associated with Roy Jenkins. Earlier she would have probably been 'a bit suspicious of Jenkins . . . thinking of him as not really her kind of radical egalitarian'. In the 1976 leadership election, when the centre-right vote divided between the candidatures of Callaghan, Healey, Jenkins and Crosland, she voted for Jenkins, primarily as a staunch pro-European against a left-wing anti-European threat. She explains that Europe 'was becoming a major issue everyday. We have had the 1975 referendum, the country voted two to one to remain in, but already . . . the left was moving away from accepting the referendum that they themselves had actually sworn they would live by, and so you could see the new battleground opening up and that meant that there was no question I would not have voted for Roy'.

91 J. P. Mackintosh, 'Has Social Democracy Failed in Britain?', *Political Quarterly*, 49 (3), 1978, p. 264; Minkin, *The Contentious Alliance*, pp. 213–14, 220–5; *The Observer*, 8 October 1972.

92   Minkin, *The Contentious Alliance*, pp. 214, 233; *The Times*, 19 May 1975.
93   Jenkins, *A Life at the Centre*, p. 375; Minkin, *The Contentious Alliance*, pp. 214, 233.
94   Minkin, *The Contentious Alliance*, pp. 215, 233.
95   Labour Party, *Labour's Programme 1976*, London, Labour Party, 1976.
96   *Sunday Times*, 15 February 1976. Commentators such as Paul Johnson described trade union collectivism and 'the brute power of the group' as a totalitarian threat to freedom. He wrote of the great division between 'those who put their trust in the individual and those who insisted on the moral righteousness of the collective': *New Statesman*, 11 February 1977; also see Minkin, *The Contentious Alliance*, pp. 213, 215–16. Much of this critique found a reflective audience among Labour's liberal social democrats.
97   'Memorandum Submitted by Some Members of the Labour Party to the Select Committee of the House of Lords on a Bill of Rights', n.d., Mackintosh Papers, 323/139; Minkin, *The Contentious Alliance*, pp. 215–16, 233. The memorandum from Labour's Human Rights Sub-Committee stated that it is 'precisely because in general the Labour Party believes in . . . social justice through state action that it is concerned also to provide effective guarantees to individuals against the abuse of power by public authorities'. It argued that '[m]inorities and ordinary men and women in the modern world have suffered a loss of control over their lives through the inevitable growth of the powers of great institutions. It is because we favour some modest redressing of this balance that we urge the select Committee [of the House of Lords] to recommend the incorporation into English law of the European Convention on Human Rights.'
98   J. P. Mackintosh, 'The Shadow Emperor has No Clothes', n.d. [probably the beginning of the parliamentary session 1973–4], Mackintosh Papers, 323/46; J. P. Mackintosh, 'Is Labour Facing Catastrophe?', in Marquand (ed.), *John P. Mackintosh*, p. 177; D. Marquand, 'Introduction', in Marquand (ed.), *John P. Mackintosh*, p. 12; Whitehead, Interview with the author.
99   J. P. Mackintosh to member of the public on his abstention from voting for the Dock Workers Regulation Bill, 23 November 1976, Mackintosh Papers, 323/152; also see *Daily Express*, 12 November 1976; *Sunday Times*, 14 November 1976; *The Scotsman*, 11 November 1976.
100 Letters from members of the public to J. P. Mackintosh, 10 November 1976; 11 November 1976, Mackintosh Papers, 323/152.
101 Minkin, *The Contentious Alliance*, p. 214; also see D. Marquand 'Inquest on a Movement: Labour's Defeat and its Consequences', *Encounter*, July 1979, pp. 13–14; Williams, 'The New Authoritarianism'.
102 Manifesto Group, *What We Must Do: A Democratic Socialist Approach to Britain's Crisis*, 1977, Manifesto Group Papers, LP/MANIF/18, p. 14; also see B. Brivati and R. Cockett (eds), *Anatomy of Decline: The Political Journalism of Peter Jenkins*, London, Cassell, 1995, pp. 86–102; *The Guardian*, 9 March 1977; J. P. Mackintosh, 'Britain's Malaise: Political or Economic?', in Marquand (ed.), *John P. Mackintosh*, pp. 215–17; Rodgers, *The Politics of Change*, pp. 94–106.
103 Minkin, *The Contentious Alliance*, p. 210; also see Mackintosh, 'Is Labour Facing Catastrophe?', pp. 177–8; D. Marquand, 'Trying to Diagnose the British Disease', *Encounter*, December 1980, p. 78; Owen, *Face the Future*, pp. 179–80.
104 Minkin, *The Contentious Alliance*, p. 211; also see Manifesto Group, *What We Must Do*, p. 33.
105 D. Marquand, *The Unprincipled Society: New Demands and Old Politics*, London, Jonathan Cape, 1980, pp. 242–3; Williams, *Politics is for People*, p. 134.

106 Owen, *Face the Future*, p. 55.

107 Minkin, *The Contentious Alliance*, pp. 211–12, 222–3; also see *The Guardian*, 30 March 1979.

108 Abse, Interview with the author.

109 A. Michie and S. Hoggart, *The Pact: The Inside Story of the Lib-Lab Government, 1977–8*, London, Quartet Books, 1978, pp. 87–8.

110 Morgan, Interview with the author; Morgan, *Callaghan*, pp. 333–4, 389–90, 744–5. From Callaghan's 'traditional' perspective, the 'ideological roots' of the 'new spokesmen' of New Labour, some of whom advocate the end of Labour's 'formal ties with the unions', 'appeared to lie more with the SDP defectors of the early 1980s than with traditional Labour'.

111 See Crosland, *Tony Crosland*, pp. 202–4; Healey, *Time of My Life*, pp. 341, 406–7; Jefferys, *Anthony Crosland*, pp. 137–8; Lipsey, Interview with the author; Minkin, *The Contentious Alliance*, pp. 209, 210, 211.

112 J. P. Mackintosh, 'Jockeying for Position', Mackintosh Papers, n.d. [but shortly after Labour's Blackpool conference following the 1970 election defeat], Mackintosh Papers, 323/291; Manifesto Group, *What We Must Do: A Democratic Socialist Approach to Britain's Crisis*, Sandelson Papers, 6/1, pp. 7–9, 20–1; Manifesto Group, *Priorities for Labour: A Manifesto Group Statement*, Sandelson Papers, 6/1, pp. 11, 12. Mackintosh attempted to sum up the respective and distinctive views of the purpose and objectives of the Labour Party of the major Labour right protagonists, Callaghan and Jenkins. Callaghan's view of politics was a 'power struggle between interest groups'. He considered the Labour Party to be 'the political weapon of the working classes so that its leaders must never get too far away in sentiment or objective from the mass of wage-earners. Perhaps for this reason . . . Callaghan is on the right on social issues and was the author of the Commonwealth Immigrants Bill, but his view of politics keeps him closely tied to the trade unions, even when they are in a Jones/Scanlon mood'. Jenkins, on the other hand, 'sees the Labour Party more as a radical party in the great tradition of gradual British reform and considers . . . its task is a reduction of class conflict and the creation of a more civilised society. This, he believes, should appeal to a wider group than organised labour alone and demands should be judged by the same criteria that are applied to all pressure groups.'

113 J. P. Mackintosh, MS draft of Hugh Gaitskell Memorial Lecture, 'Has Social Democracy Failed?', 15 March 1978, Mackintosh Papers, 323/9; Mackintosh, 'Has Social Democracy Failed in Britain?', pp. 269–70; D. Marquand, *The New Reckoning: Capitalism, States and Citizens*, Cambridge, Polity Press, 1997, pp. 11–25; W. Rodgers, Speech to the launch meeting of the Campaign for Labour Victory (CLV), 19 February 1977, Mackintosh Papers, 323/140; Owen Papers, D709/2/17/1/1; Rodgers to David Owen, 21 February 1977, Rodgers, Interview with the author.

114 See Mackintosh, 'Britain's Malaise', pp. 215–17; Marquand, 'Inquest on a Movement'; Marquand, 'Trying to Diagnose the British Disease'; Minkin, *The Contentious Alliance*, pp. 209, 210, 216–20.

115 Minkin, *The Contentious Alliance*, pp. 216–18; Marquand, Interview with the author; G. Radice, 'Labour and the Unions', in D. Lipsey and D. Leonard (eds), *The Socialist Agenda: Crosland's Legacy*, London, Jonathan Cape, 1981, pp. 117–31; Rodgers, Interview with the author; Williams, Interview with the author.

116 Marquand, 'Inquest on a Movement', pp. 16–17; Marquand, 'Trying to Diagnose the British Disease', p. 81; Minkin, *The Contentious Alliance*, p. 217.

117 Marquand, Interview with the author; Minkin, *The Contentious Alliance*, pp. 218–20.
118 Williams, Interview with the author.
119 D. Owen *et al*, 'The Limehouse Declaration', 25 January 1981, Owen Papers, D709/2/17/1/3; D. Owen *et al.*, reproduced copy of open letter to *The Guardian*, 1 August 1980, Owen Papers, D709/2/17/1/3; H. Stephenson, *Claret and Chips: The Rise of the SDP*, London, Michael Joseph, 1982, pp. 185–6; Rodgers, Speech to the launch meeting of CLV.

6

The 'frontiers of social democracy': public expenditure, redistribution and divisions of social democratic political economy

Introduction

Two abiding themes of British politics in the 1960s and 1970s were the European membership debate and British economic decline. Both played crucial roles in the dialogue and uneven progress of Labour Governments of the period, and in the wider debates of the Labour Party and British politics. These critical aspects of political debate also reveal the inherent complexity and emerging divisions of Labour's post-war revisionist tradition, which possessed important (if under-developed) implications for Labour's intra-party politics and the subsequent trajectory and divisions of the Labour Party and British social democracy. The issue of European membership has conventionally been seen as a major cause of tension in Labour Party politics during the 1960s and 1970s. It was an issue that cut across traditional left–right party lines. Not only did it divide left and right in the Labour Party, it provoked disabling divisions both between and within the dimensions of the so-called 'old' and 'revisionist' Labour right.[1] Similarly, central themes of economic policy, particularly the continued level and role of public expenditure within the context of economic decline, were divisive for Labour revisionism in the 1970s. 'Declinism', as an increasingly influential thesis of British political discourse, based on the general issue of economic performance and efficiency, possessed resonance for some Labour revisionists. Endemic features of British economic decline – low economic growth and the problem of inflation – were seen to undermine traditional assumptions of 'Croslandite' social democracy. The implications of 'decline' were to give a much greater priority to the attainment of faster economic growth than Crosland envisaged, and to imply a shift away from 'egalitarianism as a key objective of Labour policy, declinism offering more to the poor through growth rather than redistribution'.[2] As Minkin suggests, within revisionism '[o]ptimism about economic management turned to pessimism in the context of persistent inflation, diminishing international competitiveness and repetitive problems with the balance of payments. Social engineering via the state encountered new difficulties and produced new dilemmas.'[3]

An emerging liberal strand of Labour revisionism favoured greater emphasis on economic growth and wealth creation as part of a wider contextual appraisal of social democratic political economy. Revisionist divisions of political economy turned on the question of the role and commitments of the state through the mechanism of public expenditure. By January 1976, Roy Jenkins was questioning the wisdom and implications of increased public expenditure in relation to gross domestic product (GDP). Revealingly, he reflected in his Anglesey speech that you cannot 'push public expenditure significantly above 60% and maintain the values of a plural society and freedom of choice. We are here close to one of the frontiers of social democracy.'[4] Although this figure appears to have been exaggerated, others such as John Mackintosh wrote about the culture and control of public expenditure. He was concerned by 1977 that government now 'spends 50% plus of G.D.P.'. He argued that the figure had risen from 41 per cent in 1952 to 55 per cent by the mid-1970s, and areas of weak control existed in local government, the nationalised industries and inflation in the period 1974–77.[5] Minkin writes that this became a major point of division on the Labour right. Jenkins (and his supporters) appeared 'much readier to shed the socialist ascription, some of [its] main commitments and ultimately . . . fundamental values'.[6] Divisions over the limits and relative merits of public expenditure represented a shift in emphasis in social democratic political economy from wealth distribution to wealth creation, and reflected wider attempts to address the perceived imbalance between ideas of equality and personal freedom in social democratic thought and policy.[7] Central themes of political economy divided Labour revisionism in the 1970s, and added to further debilitating divisions over Europe and the 'trade union question'.[8] A portfolio of critical policy divisions and underlying philosophical tensions offer a more substantial basis for understanding the emergence of the SDP and even something of the historical roots of the emergence of New Labour in the 1990s.

Crosland, Labour Party revisionism and the crisis of social democratic political economy

It would first be instructive to locate the pivotal role of Crosland in the development of revisionist social democracy and subsequent revisionist divisions of social democratic political economy. Given his seminal contribution to the original revisionist paradigm, the role and ideas of Crosland provided an essential reference point for successive generations of Labour revisionists. Although more of a state of mind than a coherent ideological doctrine or body of thought, 'revisionism' achieved a degree of consensus on the centre-right of the Labour Party in the 1950s under the political leadership of Hugh Gaitskell and in the political thinking of Anthony Crosland.[9] Radice has written that Crosland's thinking 'influenced a whole generation'.[10] This sentiment is echoed by others such as David Marquand, Bill Rodgers and David Owen, who were to form the spine of liberal revisionism in the 1970s.[11] Crosland argued that to define socialism purely in terms of ownership was to confuse ends and means. Public ownership was only one, and not necessarily the most effective, *means* among many, including taxation, public/social expenditure and educational reform, that could be used to achieve fundamental socialist objectives. For Crosland, socialism was about equality in its widest sense, requiring major 'egalitarian changes in our educational system, the distribution of property, the distribution of resources in terms of need, social manners and style of life and the location of power in industry'. He believed that the pursuit of these revised socialist objectives could be better achieved through the means of progressive taxation and high levels of public expenditure within the context of consistent economic growth rather than dogmatic doses of public ownership.[12] Crosland's revisionism represented a detailed theoretical analysis of socialism as equality, and a clear programme around which Labour's social democrats could cohere.[13]

However, by the mid-1970s there was discomfort among some former disciples that his earlier revisionist analysis and prescriptions had not kept pace with the limited performance of the British economy. He did not appear to substantially readdress these structural limitations or adapt his analysis to the twin dilemmas of low economic growth and persistent inflation. Crosland's final substantial work largely reiterated the theory, priorities and methods of his initial analysis.[14] Crosland's revisionist social democracy was founded on an optimistic view of economic developments, and, to some extent, was dependent for continued support on healthy and consistent economic growth to underpin a sustained programme of social expenditure and egalitarian redistribution. John Mackintosh, perhaps the most able of the 'neo-revisionist' social democratic theorists of the 1970s and, had he not died prematurely in 1978, perhaps the most likely to offer a systematic critique and renewal of Croslandite revisionism for the circumstances of the 1970s, claims that he had realised by 1976 that 'something had gone wrong with the [Croslandite] assumptions . . . which I had held at the time of my election in 1966'. He believed that subsequent economic developments had revealed 'the relative failure of his position' and that 'further revisions are now needed'. It was indicative of an emerging critique of Crosland's theoretical position, not just from the 'Marxist' left, but also from those such as Mackintosh and Marquand 'who accepted many of Tony's original assumptions'.[15] Mackintosh reveals the emergence of a more pessimistic 'declinist' analysis of British economic performance, in which low economic growth and inflationary pressures were much greater problems than the previously optimistic revisionist narrative had predicted.[16] In the context of the economic malaise of the 1970s, in the face of minimal growth, high inflation and pervasive trade union activity, Jefferys argues that by the time of Labour's return to office in the spring of 1974 'Crosland had become almost a one-man champion of egalitarian socialism'.[17]

This is probably an exaggeration of the isolation and redundancy of Crosland's social democratic philosophy even in the economic conditions of the 1970s. Crosland and his unreconstructed egalitarian position continued to attract a small band of dedicated disciples such as Roy Hattersley, Dick Leonard, John Tomlinson and Bruce Douglas-Mann.[18] Douglas-Mann believed that redistributive social justice should remain the key to Labour's economic approach even in the face of the 'threatening dangers of inflation'. An incomes policy to combat spiralling inflation would only be acceptable if it were combined with 'a rapid change in the distribution of both incomes and wealth' to achieve a measure of social justice.

Any incomes policy would need to be 'coupled with redistributive tax policies' and 'in exchange for a greater share of national income going to wages'. Labour's objectives should not be just 'to run the economy better, so as to secure an increase in the National Income, and only in that way to increase the share going to the public services'. He suggests that there are those on the 'Right of the Party' who have accepted without much question the existing distribution of wealth and income with 'some tinkering here and there'. While not ignoring the prerequisite of economic growth 'to cushion the effects, to ensure that the redistribution does not involve any sharp drop in living standards for the relatively better off', he suggests that a future Labour Government 'must go for social justice first, if it is to achieve either growth or economic success'. This needs to involve a process of 'rapid change in the distribution of both incomes and wealth within society, regardless of the pressures from those who wish to preserve their differentials'.[19]

The emerging liberal strand of revisionism began to question the universal wisdom of Labour's almost instinctive attachment to high public expenditure as the basis of its egalitarian principles and priorities. High levels of taxation and public expenditure (to further shift the balance of income and wealth in society) within the context of conditions of low growth and associated economic problems, together with the perceived dangers of unrestricted trade union power and collectivism brought starkly to bear during the decade, were believed to increasingly undermine the essence of individual freedom and stifle the opportunities and benefits of wealth creation that could underpin economic growth.[20] In this sense, they appeared willing to confront the sacred ends as well as means of Labour's historic aims and values. Egalitarian revisionists continued to advocate classic Keynesian expansionary policies of utilising redistributive taxation and public expenditure to alleviate social inequalities within the context of the economic cycle of boom and recession (and to underpin economic growth itself).[21] Given the contemporary economic climate, liberal revisionists emphasised economic growth and wealth creation as the first priority of 'sound economic management' and a balanced economy before thinking about what to do with it in terms of public expenditure and the redistribution of wealth and income in the cause of greater equality. For Mackintosh, Crosland's 'reformist, egalitarian approach' had been 'discredited by the experience of the 1963–77 period', and there was the need to further revise and modernise the Croslandite revisionism fostered under Gaitskell. Its failure was largely due to a single fundamental flaw: that it possessed 'no adequate theory of how the mixed economy should work' and no rationale for the operation of a thriving private sector within it. Consequently, there had been little thought or appreciation of how far the 'Gaitskell-Crosland philosophy' 'depended on the kind of growth we had claimed was possible once the Tories were out of office'. The 'basic error' of Croslandism was that it focused exclusively on 'the distribution of wealth, its taxation and use for this . . . but [said] very little about the creation of wealth . . . [and] the central task of justifying and producing a thriving mixed economy remains'. The apparent failure of Crosland's programme inevitably provoked attacks from critics of both left and right, but there were also those former Gaitskellite revisionists of whom some were now 'on the defensive in the Labour Party, some have left politics, and those who remain are unclear about which way to turn'.[22]

Emerging divisions of revisionist social democracy in the 1970s

The previous section addressed the formative influence of Crosland's original revisionist analysis. It further considered the emergence of seeds of a schism in Labour Party revisionism between Crosland's egalitarian revisionism and an emerging liberal revisionist response to the perceived limitations of the static Croslandite analysis in the context of the unanticipated problems of the under-performing British economy. The limitations of his original revisionist thesis in adverse economic conditions provided the basis and departure point of a new liberal revisionist economic and conceptual analysis. The following sections look to further locate and develop the nature, substance and implications of disabling revisionist divisions over core tenets and issues of social democratic political economy in the 1970s.

As noted, the classic Croslandite revisionism of the 1950s stated that socialism was essentially about equality, a theme he was to reiterate more defensively perhaps in later writings.[23] However, his original revisionist doctrine was to undergo a degree of revisionism itself from the mid-1970s, particularly the apparently rigid emphasis on high levels of public expenditure in the pursuit of equality. Some of the new generation of revisionists, such as Giles Radice, saw their attempts to promote new definitions of socialism appropriate to the 1970s as a means of rebuilding bridges with Crosland and reuniting Labour Party revisionism after the bitter divisions of the party in the EEC membership debates. Crosland, it seemed, remained unimpressed with their efforts to update his own revisionist thinking.[24] Crosland's continued alienation of former revisionist allies had obvious implications for his poor performance in the 1976 Labour leadership election. Already facing a difficult proposition in a contest in which 'the centre-ground was crowded' and because 'some of his views did not fit neatly with the simple left-right labels favoured by backbenchers', his paltry total of seventeen votes reflected the difficulty of establishing a clear identity for a 'radical moderate'. In the final analysis, Crosland drew more support from the 'non-Tribunite left' than from the revisionist Labour right.[25] As noted, by this point Crosland was openly appealing to the wider centre of the party in the name of party unity. He offered himself as someone 'both idealistic and realistic', combining 'a very strong commitment to socialism through economic equality and improvement in public services' with the recognition of the importance of an incomes policy to both 'defeat inflation and achieve social justice'. He described his platform as a 'distinctive brand of Democratic Socialism', based on a dynamic mixed economy supporting full employment; an incomes policy *with* the trade unions to combat inflation; a 'more equal and less class-ridden Britain, in which people get what they really earn', and a 'high priority for public spending on our vital social services'. He stated that in 'present circumstances the economy must come first, however harsh the measures needed to put it right', *but* 'the Party must retain a clear vision of its ideals and seize every opportunity to advance them'.[26]

The seeds of revisionist economic divisions appeared evident as soon as Labour entered opposition after 1970. In January 1971 Crosland published a Fabian pamphlet that was 'primarily a restatement of Croslandism' and 'represented an attempt to stake out a middle ground in the Labour Party between what he saw as Jenkinsite economic orthodoxy and the so-called "new politics" of Benn'. Crosland argued against 'some great shift of direction', and for a reaffirmation of 'those agreed ideals' such as high priority for the relief of poverty, a wider ideal of social equality and strict social control over the environment, although he appeared to be less complacent about economic growth which was 'an essential condition of any significant re-allocation of resources': the key to growth, 'if squeeze and deflation were to be avoided, was a prices and incomes policy agreed between party and unions'. However, he restated, largely unchanged, the basic egalitarian principles and goals of Labour's social democratic economic policy: 'an exceptionally high priority . . . for the relief of poverty, distress and social squalor – Labour's traditional " social welfare" goal'; the 'more equal distribution of wealth'; and 'a wider ideal of social equality . . . such that the less well off have access to housing, health and education of a standard comparable, at least in the basic decencies, to that which the better off can buy for themselves out of their private means'.[27]

Jenkins attempted to set out his own agenda for tackling problems of injustice in a collection of 'promotional' speeches published under the title, *What Matters Now* (1972). It was significantly different in tone and approach to that of Crosland, and focused on wider issues of injustice than the more typically narrow egalitarian themes of redistribution and social welfare. Largely written by political allies such as David Marquand, David Owen and John Mackintosh, it was presented as an attempt to build a coalition of support beyond traditional class origins, loyalties and past political affiliations. Arranged around a broader concept of injustice, and adopting a greater emphasis on 'individual freedom of choice' (in a positive, 'meaningful sense'), it offers a wider perspective of political advance and 'social progress, capable of winning support, not only from our own ranks, but from a majority of the society around us'. The wider rationale of the collection could also be seen as an attempt among key intimates to reclaim and groom Jenkins as the future leader of the Labour Party after the divisive effects of their stand over EEC membership. To this end, it represented a Jenkinsite position and agenda beyond the narrow issue of Europe and around wider social democratic themes of injustice and deprivation in society, aimed at expanding the base of Jenkins' support inside the Labour Party.[28]

However, the parliamentary Labour right was far from united behind the Jenkinsite vehicle. Jenkins' European commitment and his resignation from the deputy leadership in April 1972, combined with his appearance of increasing disillusionment with the Labour Party, contributed to the disorganised and leaderless character of the revisionist Labour right in Parliament. In terms of political economy, Jenkins' emerging view that neither the economy and national prosperity nor the concept of freedom could withstand or stretch to further increases in public expenditure as a proportion of GDP was not a view shared by all on the Labour right. It was anathema to the Labour left, and for 'the Crosland faction in the party it marked a[nother] point of departure, a time to drop the pilot'.[29] Hattersley, for example, cited the speech as evidence of the emerging ideological difference that prevented him from voting for Jenkins in the 1976 leadership election. Hattersley relayed to Jenkins that he was experiencing a 'growing lack of sympathy with [his] political position', reinforced by his recent speech on the illiberal implications of high public expenditure, which was 'quite the opposite of what Tawney and Crosland had written and Hattersley himself believed'.[30] Refuge for Labour's revisionists was not to be found in a single personality. Crosland had demonstrated his ambivalence to the European cause and, in the name of party unity, his willingness for some form of compromise with the left. Aspirations of party office further prevented close factional identification with the Jenkinsites, and partly explains his reluctance to act as a figurehead of the emerging, explicitly social democratic Labour right.[31]

The public expenditure debate and the IMF crisis: a revisionist watershed?

Although the question of the levels and role of public spending was a generally divisive issue of social democratic political economy during the decade, the key set-piece debates over public expenditure occurred from the mid-1970s onwards in the face of mounting economic difficulties and, eventually, within the context of the 1976 IMF crisis. The nature and consequences of the IMF crisis, and the party and government debates that surrounded it, have been the subject of considerable academic literature and argument over the extent to which it represented a shift in post-war British economic policy and a move towards the neo-liberal monetarism associated with the Thatcher era.[32] Hattersley, for instance, a self-proclaimed Croslandite egalitarian, captures the significance of these events:

> Labour was no longer the party of public expenditure . . . The whole idea of public expenditure – both its social merits and its economic advantages – was suddenly challenged. Labour began to examine precepts that it had previously taken for granted. And for a political party that is only one step away from acknowledging the possibility that its long-held beliefs are wrong.[33]

The conventional view is that the events and consequences of this episode broke social democratic trends in tax and spend, and that the later years of the 1974–79 Labour Government witnessed 'the abandonment of social democratic policy' in this respect.[34] Mullard suggests the 1974–79 period of Labour Government generated 'an alternative discourse of public expenditure' that brought about its public transformation from the 'healer of the nation' to economic 'villain'. In its place was substituted a new emphasis on the control of inflation rather than the maintenance of full employment and policies of wealth redistribution based on high levels of taxation and public expenditure.[35] Contrary to some received academic wisdom, Hickson has recently argued that the 1976 IMF crisis did not, in fact, instigate a basic shift of economic policy in the general direction of some sort of neo-liberal monetarist consensus. On this reading, the post-IMF economic policy of the Labour Government was, at the least, little different to that pursued before the visit of the international financiers, and its macroeconomic strategy, with a continued emphasis on incomes policy, remained distinct from that of the early Thatcher years.[36] However, a nascent liberal revisionist strand of the Labour right had already begun to question the continuing viability of Croslandite social democratic political economy in the restrictive economic circumstances of the 1970s, and appeared to be more responsive to 'new' thinking on the possibilities and priorities of economic policy within the changing economic context. This can be seen as a reflection of related developments in the structural economy and the wider ideational response of the Labour Party to the crisis of social democratic political economy in the 1970s, which took a number of ideological forms and directions.[37]

The process of the Labour Government's apparent macroeconomic conversion 'created Labour's most bitter internal disputes'. The uneasy alliance of the Labour Party in 1974 at least gained some succour and cohesion from its general association with enhanced social provision through public expenditure financed by high taxation of wealth, but by 1979 the scale and direction of public spending cuts had been the subject of fierce internal party debates and divisions.[38] Within intra-party deliberations, particularly arguments over whether spending cuts or tax rises should provide the main instrument for the reduction of the public deficit, the emerging liberal revisionists ceased to believe that the Labour Government necessarily had to spend more than their predecessors, and had abandoned high tax and spend as an *article of faith* even for the long-run. Some of their number had become anxious about the rapid spending growth of 1974–75, and Jenkins' 1976 Anglesey speech signalled a note of 'Hayekian alarm' about the creeping threat to pluralism and liberty implicit in uncontrolled public expenditure. Bill Rodgers comments that Jenkins' warning that even a 50 per cent rate of public expenditure was too high spoke for an increasing number of those on the social democratic Labour right who argued for sensible restraint in the growth of government and were gradually shifting away from Labour's Keynesian tax-and-spend tradition.[39] Rodgers reveals that during the prolonged IMF Cabinet debates he 'was not a fully paid-up member' of 'what was emerging as the Crosland-Lever group' because he 'needed to be persuaded that the Crosland analysis could be sold to the IMF, thus ensuring the loan without the strings'. At the Cabinet meeting of 23 November, Healey announced his proposal for meeting the IMF demands for cuts amounting to £3 billion, of which £1 billion would come from public expenditure. Initially, Rodgers found the Crosland case, that the July savings measures of £1 billion were working and that further cuts would bring on higher unemployment and could not be defended on any reasonable grounds, compelling. However, he was eventually lost 'on the impracticality of [Crosland's] game of bluff with the IMF', and it became clear that his proposals did not present a credible alternative. In any case, following Callaghan's example of declaring his personal support for

Chancellor Healey's package of cuts, Crosland 'tamely' came into line, as did other moderate rebels, Lever, Ennals and, less willingly, Shirley Williams and Hattersley. Rodgers declares that he was 'hard headed enough to do the sums' and 'hard-headed enough to recognise that in the end we had to find a solution that the IMF found acceptable . . . you have to have balance'.[40]

Clark suggests that it was during the IMF debates that the extent and depth of the conversion of a liberal revisionist strand of the Labour right became clear, and that '[u]nderlying [their] abandonment of statism was their rejection of what had earlier been its chief rationale, egalitarianism'.[41] However, Shirley Williams sounds a note of caution concerning the apparent abandonment of egalitarian principles and the economic tools of equality among liberal revisionists. She argues that discussion of the issues at stake during the IMF Cabinet debates was not a simple left–right division. Williams was generally supportive of the Crosland position during the debates and was also sympathetic of the position held by Peter Shore:

> I did not go along with . . . Healey or . . . Callaghan from the beginning . . . I thought that the IMF was asking for more than they needed to have . . . Benn's position was impossible because it was based on import restrictions, and those . . . would have hit the Commonwealth hardest of all . . . it would have hit some of the poorer countries and I did not think there was justification for that, which . . . you could say was left in position . . . it certainly wasn't a purely right-wing position.[42]

Shore explains the nature of the crisis and the positions held. He argued for 'a protective state', but also suggests that it was unavoidable that assistance was sought from the IMF 'to simply pay for our imports'. The major problem at the time was the oil shock which served to quadruple the price of oil a few weeks before the first general election of 1974. Therefore, coming to office in February 1974, we 'faced the largest trade deficit in our history . . . our imported oil bill had gone up . . . from £800 million in the previous year to £3,200 million the following year . . . we did our utmost but we ran out of money, so we had to finance necessary imports'. While Benn supported the idea of a siege economy more generally, Shore was in favour of import controls 'not as a permanent feature of our economy but simply to tide us over because we could see the element in the North Sea and we knew that in two to . . . four years at the most . . . tremendous strengthening of our economy would take place'. Crosland was anxious to avoid cuts in public expenditure, but 'if you did not do something pretty drastically and directly with imports . . . the IMF would not lend you the money if you invent particular public expenditure'.[43] Williams further explains that the original Shore position 'was essentially what we wanted, import restrictions and controls back in a big way, even at the level of rationing'. However, the final compromise was somewhere between Crosland's 'middle position' that the IMF was asking too much and should be confronted – 'make part of what you give them, cut what you can reasonably afford . . . without really major damage and then add to that the BP shares, which is . . . largely what happened', and the basic leadership position that 'you have got to meet what they have asked for'.[44]

On the principle of public expenditure more generally, however, Williams explains that 'we were much influenced by Roy having been the Chancellor'.

It represented 'recognition that because we were a Labour government we had to maintain a balance of payments, at least equilibrium, because the world financial markets just jump on any Labour government that does not do that . . . that is why I think Gordon Brown is right'.[45] The issue of international confidence appeared to play a significant role in the thinking of liberal revisionists in relation to the economic crisis and the IMF intervention. Rodgers had been arguing that the question of confidence represented the crucial economic justification for supporting spending cuts rather than tax rises. By the time of the IMF crisis, even Crosland accepted that the sole case for government expenditure cuts was that of international confidence.[46]

The wider implications of the general loss of liberal revisionist enthusiasm for traditional social democratic redistributive tax and spend policy was reflected in the nature of proposals for spending cuts during the IMF debates. Proposals for benefit and pension cuts revealed the emergence of a 'more general inegalitarianism'. According to the left, support for more controversial aspects of the 'leadership position', such as the untapped potential of benefit cuts for meeting IMF terms and the focus on the unchecked rise in pensions, directly contravened key commitments of the 1974 manifesto, and has been seen to represent the abandonment and replacement of core tenets of social democracy with a pragmatic managerialism or some sort of 'Conservative-style promise of competence'.[47] One minister

> admitted the passing of Croslandism but 'confessed that a new philosophy was not available from the Labour revisionists. What distinguished Labour from the Conservatives he could best define as a "feeling".' This neatly sums up the post-ideological position of the Labour Right in these years: it might now be called 'Blairite'.[48]

Crosland, himself, possessed reservations about the intrinsic value of indeterminate public expenditure. Crosland was never the uncomplicated and unreconstructed high-spending egalitarian of some (recent) Labour Party mythology, and he acknowledged some of the limits of public expenditure to achieve egalitarian aims. He increasingly advocated more discriminate use of public social expenditure and developed a distinction between its progressive and regressive dimensions:

> the principle [of high public expenditure] remains valid . . . We need to reform the practice; we need in our public spending decisions to ask not only; how much? But also: to whom? In particular, we must give a higher priority to social expenditure which is unambiguously progressive – for example, cash benefits to the old, the sick and the unemployed – and restrain that which is regressive – for example, some forms of indiscriminate subsidy, or excessive highway construction, or (in Europe) higher education. Only then will public expenditure play the progressive role which we expect of it.[49]

Certainly, Crosland turned to the emerging social democratic dilemma of the political space available for the traditional goals of social democratic political economy in the face of restrictive structural economic constraints and limits.[50] In a speech tackling this dilemma at the height of the economic difficulties of the

1974–79 Labour Government, Crosland presented the case for a wider inter-pretation and compass for the pursuit of equality. He suggested that there 'is a growing realization that government alone cannot solve the nation's problems' and that the 'gulf between people's expectations of what government can deliver, and what in the real world it can actually deliver, has always been one of the greatest threats to our democratic system'. In the face of the inevitable limits imposed by the current economic crisis, he proposed a more general remit to Labour's programme for progress towards a more equal society: when the purse strings are tight and restrictions on public expenditure prohibit a more focused idea of redistributive economic equality, a Labour Government should pursue measures of social equality 'to outlaw racial or sexual discrimination [that] cost little in terms of public expenditure'. This should be accompanied by 'a better sense of priorities within public expenditure. Total public expenditure is inevitably limited. So it is all the more vital that we concentrate . . . on those areas where it redistributes most sharply in favour of the less well-off.' In this respect, '[l]ocal Government as well as Central Government must be relentless in pursuit of maximum value for money'. It is also not good enough to simply increase taxes on the wealthy; rather, the priority is 'to build on the progress . . . already made towards creating a fairer tax system . . . [which] might well lead to increased revenue and a lower PSBR; and could therefore positively help our economic situation'. In difficult circumstances and within certain constraints, it 'encapsulates a sense of purpose within the bounds of the practical'.[51]

He always remained a 'committed believer in high public expenditure and would strongly oppose any general and indiscriminate cut', but he was also acutely aware of the need 'to consider relative priorities' and to get the priorities right.[52] Crosland's former political adviser, David Lipsey, explains Crosland's reservations about indiscriminate uses of public expenditure, but also emphasises the emergence of important philosophical differences underpinning divergent revisionist attitudes to public expenditure in the 1970s:

> Tony revised his view on public spending . . . in the 1970s for two chief reasons . . . One, it was pretty evident why we had the domestic reason for stagflation . . . because living standards have barely risen for people; people's basic take home pay had barely risen in real terms because they had put a lot of money into public expenditure and they didn't like that. The second and more sophisticated reason was that there was an increasing weight of academic evidence that a lot of the public spending was not going to the worst off, which was the idea from his point of view, but to the better off . . . from both these points of view he had revised his view on public expenditure. What he hadn't done was to go to the Jenkinsite extreme and raise some ludicrous hotch-potch figure of 60% of GDP going on public spending; absolutely misleading and must be cut back and was a threat to liberty . . . Tony didn't believe any of that . . . Basically people who believed that have been in charge ever since.[53]

Crosland's original 'egalitarian' revisionist thesis continued to influence successive generations of Labour's social democrats.[54] However, Marquand contends that it was neither a particularly radical nor durable strategy. Croslandite revisionism presupposed no need for a revolutionary transformation, but there was every need for steady incremental improvement . . . Life chances could be equalized; class distinctions could be eroded; public expenditure could be increased; welfare could be enhanced; society could be made more just and more contented . . . In retrospect . . . [i]t took the institutions and operational codes of the British state for granted, and assumed that if revisionist ministers pulled the right Whitehall levers, the desired results would follow. It presupposed continuing economic growth on a scale sufficient to produce an adequate fiscal dividend.[55]

Another former Gaitskellite revisionist, Bill Rodgers, adopted a critical view of both the Croslandite position and of Crosland as a political strategist during the IMF negotiations. Rodgers, himself, comes from 'a school that believes in public expenditure', because it is difficult to 'deal with problems of social justice unless you are prepared to have levels of taxation consistent with proper levels of public expenditure'. He believed that the IMF terms were too stringent and felt unhappy with Healey's initial proposals, but he argues that it became clear that Crosland's 'policies were not credible as the alternative' and, after leading us 'all up the top of a hill', Crosland capitulated rather than fighting to the end.[56] By early 1977, Rodgers was urging that 'the debate on policy must go on – about the right levels of public expenditure and priorities within it; the problems of price and incomes policy and how best to achieve economic growth'.[57]

Hattersley reports that it was Crosland himself, for the sake of party unity and the political survival of both the Chancellor and the Labour Government, who persuaded him to back down during the IMF Cabinet debates once it emerged that the Prime Minister had decided to recommend the Chancellor's proposals to Cabinet.[58] If anything, Crosland's eventual 'capitulation' was consistent with Marquand's (perhaps sardonic) retrospective of him as 'The Progressive as Loyalist' and his deep-rooted commitment to the wider Labour movement. While he was extremely anxious both during and after the outcome of negotiations about the implications of the IMF agreement for the very foundations of his political philosophy, in the final analysis his priority was the survival of the Labour Government. If it fell, it would result in the worst case scenario of a Conservative Government. The IMF crisis offers a useful vignette of the limits of Crosland's egalitarian philosophy. Hattersley stuck doggedly to his mantra that 'Socialism is about equality and we cannot have greater equality if we cut public spending' to the bitter end and, ultimately, appears to have been more 'Croslandite' than Crosland himself.[59]

Conclusion

This chapter has observed diverging attitudes of Labour Party revisionism to public expenditure in the 1970s, which was indicative of wider divisions over the very tools and goals of traditional social democratic political economy. The IMF episode, and issues and debates of public expenditure more broadly, revealed the emerging divisions of Labour's revisionist tradition in the 1970s between the egalitarian social democratic 'left', the so-called 'Keynesian dissenters', Crosland,

Hattersley, Lever and, to some extent, Shirley Williams, and the liberal social democratic 'right', schooled in Jenkinsite 'economic orthodoxy' and willing to countenance a re-evaluation of public expenditure in Labour's economic and political pantheon.[60] The Crosland position, shared with that of some of the centre-left, retained, in principle at least, a commitment to 'the long-run goal of higher spending', and 'remained clear that the eventual aim should be a return to steady public spending growth, which would probably have seen it grow further in GDP'. This common goal helped to produce a 'shared alarm at the apparent philosophical shift which the Labour Right had undergone', some of whom now believed that cuts were 'positively socially desirable'.[61]

Respective attitudes to public expenditure represented a further critical point of division and fragmentation of Labour Party revisionism and the parliamentary Labour right more broadly in the 1970s. Crosland reflected on the cost of 'the detested cuts and the wider economic climate' in his commonplace book. He suggests that the surrender of ideological conviction to a pragmatic, empiric, safety first attitude had bred a horrible, illiterate and reactionary attitude to public expenditure.[62] This was a belief that also underpinned Hattersley's strong reaction to Jenkins' critique of the (adverse) implications of high levels of public expenditure and his decision to sever a long-standing alliance with the Jenkinsites on these ideological grounds.[63] Given the similar denunciation of Crosland by the Jenkinsites during the earlier intra-party struggles over Europe, it would appear that a critical series of ideological and policy divisions was emerging within Labour Party revisionism to scupper 'whatever slight opportunity there might have been of a Gaitskellite inheritance, even in the 1970s'.[64]

Underlying revisionist divisions of political economy in the 1970s were diverging responses to the egalitarianism of Labour's traditional social democracy implied by high levels of public expenditure. In spite of his own qualifications for public expenditure in 'hard times', Crosland's essential egalitarianism cajoled him to find alliance with the left in December 1976 to oppose benefit cuts, and he continued to argue for greater state redistribution in the form of a 'fairer tax' that represented one of the priorities that must be pursued even more urgently now that times were hard.[65] In the debates over spending cuts in November 1975, the key Gaitskellite ideologist had found his 'strongest ally' to be the devoted Bevanite, Barbara Castle. Both argued that it was not clear that the public 'would automatically prefer cuts in public expenditure to higher taxes' and, together, 'they came within two votes of defeating . . . Healey'.[66] In this sense, Tomlinson has suggested that Crosland was someone who did not fit easily into the left–right political spectrum. If public spending is considered to be 'the touchstone of the left, then . . . Crosland was a hard left radical'.[67]

However, Jefferys remarks that the post-IMF period witnessed the gradual demise of the Croslandite 'revisionist notion of achieving equality via economic growth and redistributive taxation'. This was not because the basis of British economic policy was necessarily transformed after the visit of the international financiers, but because 'the number of articulate exponents of the social democratic cause dwindled further' after Crosland's premature death in February 1977.[68] The remaining core of Labour Party revisionism had shifted the focus and balance of its priorities, and those such as Mackintosh and others among the Manifesto Group of Labour MPs were now engaged in an attempt to refurbish Croslandite revisionism with more explicit recognition of the need for a clear theory of a dynamic and productive mixed economy as the basis of economic growth. They saw the 'basic error' of Croslandism as an excessive focus on wealth distribution, its taxation and usages at the expense of wealth creation. Ultimately, they were concerned to redress some of the balance between equality and individual freedom in social democratic theory. Their analysis also contained an emerging critique of the centralising and corporatist tendencies of Labour's (and Crosland's) social democracy, and introduced ideas of community and the possibility of a less 'mechanistic' route to social justice that prefigured some of the defining philosophical themes of the construction of New Labour in the 1990s.[69] By the late 1970s, liberal revisionists, such as Marquand and Mackintosh, were questioning whether a further revision of social democracy would be possible in the Labour Party (and considering a 'realignment of the Left'). As such, their position reflected as much an abandonment of Croslandite revisionism as an attempt to revise it.[70] For his part, Crosland preferred the description of 'democratic socialist' to distinguish him from the 'right-wing' and possibly secessionist tendencies of Labour's 'social democrats'.[71]

This essential division of revisionist social democracy was evident in later respective attempts to offer contemporary reconceptualisations of its underlying philosophy. Marquand was concerned to emphasise the libertarian basis of a rejuvenated social democracy, moving away from what he saw as an outdated state-based bureaucratic form towards a new decentralist, participative social democracy, based on values of community and civic morality (an embryonic 'communitarian public philosophy'). Hattersley later attempted his own synthesis of the problematic relationship between ideas of equality and liberty in social democratic thought. Although he recognised the important place of 'freedom' to any understanding of a 'modernised' social democracy, it was premised on Croslandite notions of a 'more equal distribution of resources'. Like Radice's argument to accept in principle, as well as for pragmatic reasons, the merits of a competitive market economy (adequately regulated) as an effective means of allocating goods and services, Hattersley was broadly willing to endorse the place and role of markets, but adopted a more cautious, traditionally social democratic, approach to their practical limitations. In certain spheres of public services, such as health and education, limited resources needed to be distributed according to need not purchasing power. The concept of freedom needed to be given a much more prominent position at the heart of democratic socialist philosophy, which needed to be associated more explicitly with the extension of choice and opportunity, but the 'extension of freedom' would be delivered by 'a more equal distribution of resources' that would result in the 'emancipation of previously powerless citizens'. Hattersley's attempt to locate freedom at the heart of democratic socialist analysis was recognition of its integral and positive relationship to equality. The 'new' revisionist attempts to reformulate the ideological context of British social democracy suggest efforts to synthesise 'egalitarian' and 'liberal' perspectives of Labour Party revisionism in the 1970s, perhaps now with the latter in the box seat.[72] Jeremy Nuttall has noted that the politics of 'synthesis' has a long, if relatively unexplored, history in the Labour Party. Attempts to synthesise apparently contradictory intellectual and political traditions was a central aspect of the work of previous generations of Labour revisionists such as Evan Durbin and Crosland himself. Nuttall encapsulates this approach as an attempt to escape traditional political loyalty to a '"depth" of ideological commitment, whether to equality or the free market', to incorporate a wider 'breadth' of ideological commitment.[73]

More immediately, the chapter has attempted to demonstrate that debates over the relative use of public expenditure in social democratic political economy divided 'egalitarian' and 'liberal' revisionists in the 1970s. This division reflected a wider underlying ideological tension between ideas of equality and liberty within Labour Party revisionism, which involved the implicit rejection of elements of the original Croslandite revisionist analysis by the emerging liberal strand of Labour revisionism. The diverging priorities and associations of the two strands of revisionism were clear. The priorities of the former were firmly established as the defence and maintenance of public expenditure in the cause of their wider egalitarian aims and objectives, and reflected a relative disinterest in Jenkinsite liberal and civil liberties concerns.[74] The latter were, from the mid-1970s, questioning the very principles of injecting large doses of public expenditure into the economy. With their emphasis on the 'values of a plural society and freedom of choice', they appeared willing to undergo a further revision of socialist principles and to rethink the traditional role of public expenditure and Labour's egalitarian commitments. It marked the formal fracture of Labour Party revisionism in the 1970s, and the shift of egalitarian revisionists away from an increasingly liberal revisionist identity towards the centrist mainstream of Labour Party opinion. In combination with significant discord over EEC membership and industrial relations and trade union reform, public expenditure and wider issues of equality represented a further critical point of division and de-stabilisation of the Labour Party revisionism in the 1970s. A range of critical divisions of policy and principle presented an emerging group of liberal revisionists with a point of departure from the Labour Party, and further encouraged a belief in the need for an alternative political vehicle of 'modernised' social democracy. On the wider question of the end of the so-called post-war (social democratic) consensus, and whether the Labour Government of these years instigated a paradigmatic shift in economic management, the jury inevitably remains open. The degree of ideational change within the Labour Party in the direction of the 'new' economic thinking was limited, but an emerging liberal revisionist strand appeared more responsive to new concepts and goals of economic management. They appeared more willing to restore the balance between economic growth and public expenditure, between wealth creation and wealth distribution and, ultimately, between concepts of liberty and equality in social democratic political thought and political economy.

Notes

1 See K. Jefferys, 'The Old Right', in R. Plant, M. Beech and K. Hickson (eds), *The Struggle for Labour's Soul: Understanding Labour's Political Thought since 1945*, London, Routledge, 2004, p. 77; also see B. Brivati, 'Hugh Gaitskell and the EEC', *Socialist History*, No. 4, 1994, pp. 16–32; B. Brivati, *Hugh Gaitskell*, London, Richard Cohen, 1996, pp. 405ff.; R. Desai, *Intellectuals and Socialism: 'Social Democrats' and the British Labour Party*, London, Lawrence and Wishart, 1994, pp. 141–52.

2 Tomlinson is 'sceptical of the wisdom of using [a universal concept of] economic "decline" to describe the trajectory of post-war Britain'. Nevertheless, he recognises that it has been a pervasive approach to recent British history. Concern over the relative performance and levels of growth of the British economy was a permanent feature of British political discourse in its particular form from the late 1950s and early 1960s. After a long pre-history, 'the career of declinism' reached its apex in the 1970s and 1980s. This was 'the period of maximum and major impact of such beliefs', and 'they played a very important part in the "panic" that characterised so much debate about the present performance and future prospects of British society in the first of these decades': see J. Tomlinson, *The Politics of Decline: Understanding Post-war Britain*, Harlow, Longman, 2000, pp. 1–7, 30–7; J. Tomlinson, 'Inventing "Decline": The Falling Behind of the British Economy in the Postwar Years', *Economic History Review*, 49 (4), 1996, pp. 731–3, 748–52; J. Tomlinson, 'Economic Policy', in R. Floud and P. Johnson (eds), *The Cambridge Economic History of Modern Britain*, Volume 3, Cambridge, Cambridge University Press, 2004, pp. 205–12; also see C. A. R. Crosland, *The Future of Socialism*, London, Jonathan Cape, 1956, pp. 375–85; 'Economic Report by the Manifesto Group' (for meeting with Denis Healey), 27 February 1975, Neville Sandelson Papers, 6/1, pp. 1–3, 11.

3 L. Minkin, *The Contentious Alliance: Trade Unions and the Labour Party*, Edinburgh, Edinburgh University Press, 1991, pp. 208–9.

4 See Minkin, *The Contentious Alliance*, p. 231; P. Whitehead, *The Writing on the Wall: Britain in the Seventies*, London, Michael Joseph, 1985, p. 346.

5 J. P. Mackintosh, MS notes on subjects for lectures, 'Public Expenditure and its Control', 1977–78, John P. Mackintosh Papers, 323/34.

6 Minkin, *The Contentious Alliance*, pp. 209, 231.

7 'Moderates in the Labour Party, 2: The Manifesto Group', *The Times*, 30 September 1977; Manifesto Group, *What We Must Do*, Manifesto Group Papers, LP/MANIF/18.

8 The economic consequences of unrestricted trade union power and collectivism, particularly its contribution to low growth and high inflation, formed part of a wider (liberal) social democratic critique of trade unionism and industrial relations policy in the context of an increasing awareness of British economic decline. For some, the assertive power and priorities of trade unionism in the 1970s was a major block on the potential for industrial modernisation and national economic development: see Minkin, *The Contentious Alliance*, pp. 209–10; J. P. Mackintosh, 'Britain's Malaise: Political or Economic?', Typescript of the 1977 Fawley Lecture, University of Southampton, 23 November 1977, Mackintosh Papers, 323/8; also see D. Marquand (ed.), *John P. Mackintosh on Parliament and Social Democracy*, Harlow, Longman, 1982, pp. 202–20; Manifesto Group, *What We Must Do: A Democratic Socialist Approach To Britain's Crisis*, 1977, Labour Party Manifesto Group Papers, LP/MANIF/18, p. 14.

9 See D. Lipsey, 'Revisionists Revise', in D. Leonard (ed.), *Crosland and New Labour*, Basingstoke, Macmillan, 1999, pp. 13–17.

10 G. Radice, 'Revisionism Revisited', *Socialist Commentary*, May 1974, p. 25.
11 D. Marquand, Interview with the author, 16 January 2001; Bill Rodgers, Interview with the author, 18 February 2001; D. Owen, *Time to Declare*, London, Michael Joseph, 1991, p. 167; also see R. Hattersley, *Choose Freedom: The Future for Democratic Socialism*, London, Michael Joseph, 1987, p. xix; D. Marquand, *The New Reckoning: Capitalism, States and Citizens*, Cambridge, Polity Press, 1997, pp. 11–12; D. Marquand, *The Progressive Dilemma: From Lloyd George to Blair*, revised second edition, London, Orion/Phoenix, 1999, pp. 166–7.
12 Crosland, *The Future of Socialism*; also see C. A. R. Crosland, *The Conservative Enemy: A Program of Radical Reform for the 1960s*, London, Jonathan Cape, 1962; C. A. R. Crosland, 'The Transition from Capitalism', in R. H. S. Crossman (ed.), *New Fabian Essays*, London, Turnstile Press, 1952, pp. 33–68.
13 Radice, 'Revisionism Revisited', p. 26.
14 C. A. R. Crosland, *A Social Democratic Britain*, London, Fabian Society, 1971; C. A. R. Crosland, *Socialism Now and Other Essays*, London, Jonathan Cape, 1974, pp. 17–48; Jefferys, 'The Old Right', pp. 77–8; G. Radice, 'What About the Workers?', *Socialist Commentary*, February 1971, pp. 6–7; Radice, 'Revisionism Revisited', p. 26.
15 John Mackintosh to Mrs Audrey Coppard, *The Political Quarterly*, 19 May 1977; John Mackintosh to David Marquand, 25 May 1977; John Mackintosh to Bernard Crick, 27 May 1977; David Marquand to John Mackintosh, 15 June 1977, Mackintosh Papers, 323/54; also see J. P. Mackintosh, 'Has Social Democracy Failed in Britain', *Political Quarterly*, 49 (3), 1978, pp. 259–70.
16 Neither was Mackintosh convinced of Crosland's claim that EEC membership was relatively unimportant, interpreting it as a populist response on Crosland's part to garner advantage over Roy Jenkins within the PLP: Mackintosh, ' Britain's Malaise', Mackintosh Papers, 323/8, p. 1; also see Marquand (ed.), *John P. Mackintosh*, pp. 203–4; G. Rosen, 'John P. Mackintosh: His Achievements and Legacy', *Political Quarterly*, 70, 2, April 1999, pp. 215, 216; Tomlinson, *The Politics of Decline*, pp. 36–7; 'Inventing "Decline"', pp. 732–3, 750–1, 752.
17 Jefferys, 'The Old Right', p. 77.
18 Hattersley has written extensively of his continuing allegiance to the egalitarian basis of Crosland's ideas and their continuing relevance to the wider philosophy of the Labour Party: see Hattersley, *Choose Freedom*; R. Hattersley, 'Why I'm no longer loyal to Labour', *The Guardian*, 26 July 1997; R. Hattersley, 'It's no longer my party', *The Observer*, 24 June 2001; R. Hattersley, 'Crosland died 25 years ago: But his definition of a good society is still the best I know', *The Guardian*, 18 February 2002. Tomlinson argues that Crosland's support of public spending as the basis of his programme of greater social equality took him much closer to one of the touchstones of the left than other, more liberally minded revisionist colleagues: John Tomlinson, Interview with the author, 27 March 2001.
19 B. Douglas-Mann, 'Social Justice is the Key', *Socialist Commentary*, January 1971, pp. 3–5.
20 J. P. Mackintosh, Notes headed 'Finance Bill' with attached list of major wage claims and settlements, 7 April–7 May 1975, Mackintosh Papers, 323/117; J. P. Mackintosh, 'Liberty and Equality: Getting the Balance Right', in Marquand, *John P. Mackintosh*, pp. 182–9; Manifesto Group, Economic Report for the Manifesto Group by John Horam, Neville Sandelson Papers, 6/1; Manifesto Group, 'Keep on Course: A Statement on Economic Policy', 27 October 1976, Manifesto Group Papers, LP/MANIF/3; Manifesto Group, Notes for Wednesday's PLP Meeting on the Budget, 8 February 1978;

Manifesto Group Papers, LP/MANIF/4; Manifesto Group, 'Economic Policy', 13 March 1978, Mackintosh Papers, 323/139; Manifesto Group, *What We Must Do*, Manifesto Group Papers, LP/MANIF/18, pp. 14–16, 22–4; D. Marquand, J. Mackintosh and D. Owen, *Change Gear! Towards A Socialist Strategy*, Supplement to *Socialist Commentary*, October 1967, David Owen Papers, D709/2/10/1, pp. iv–v. It was a position increasingly identified with an explicitly 'social democrat' (as opposed to 'democratic socialist') or 'left-wing liberal' element of revisionism, whose particular outlook went 'beyond the central issue of wages and equality'. As they 'are interested in individual rights and social justice, they will accept liberal legislation ... when much of this is alien to working-class group feeling which thinks of liberty more in terms of what *groups* can do and of what status they have in society': see J. Gyford and S. Haseler, *Social Democracy: Beyond Revisionism*, London, Fabian Society, 1971; J. P. Mackintosh, 'Socialism or Social Democracy?', *Political Quarterly*, October–December 1972, pp. 470–5.

21 See Manifesto Group, *What We Must Do*, Manifesto Group Papers, LP/MANIF/18, pp. 14–15; Douglas-Mann, 'Social Justice is the Key', pp. 4–5; S. Haseler, 'Don't soak the rich – they're doing their best', *Tribune*, 17 March 1972.

22 Mackintosh, 'Britain's Malaise', Mackintosh Papers, 323/8, pp. 1–3; Mackintosh, 'Has Social Democracy Failed in Britain?', pp. 259–63, 266–70; also see Rosen, 'John P. Mackintosh', p. 216.

23 See Crosland, *Socialism Now*; C. A. R. Crosland, *Social Democracy in Europe*, London, Fabian Society, 1975, p. 5; C. A. R. Crosland, 'Equality in Hard Times', *Socialist Commentary*, October 1976.

24 D. Leonard, 'Memo on Leadership Election and its Implications for the Future', 1 June 1976, Crosland Papers, 6/3; also see Jefferys, 'The Old Right', p. 78; K. Jefferys, *Anthony Crosland: A New Biography*, London, Richard Cohen, 1999, p. 176; Radice, 'Revisionism Revisited', p. 27.

25 Jefferys, *Anthony Crosland*, pp. 193–5; P. Kellner, 'Anatomy of the Vote', *New Statesman*, 9 April 1976; Neville Sandelson to Bruce Douglas-Mann, 24 March 1976, Crosland Papers, 6/4. In his analysis of the implications of Crosland's performance in the leadership election, Leonard recommended that Crosland might be able to appeal to the intellectual pretensions of the Jenkinsite group by acknowledging the intellectual substance of their contribution to party theory and debates. If that fails, 'there is not much which you can do with them' as some were 'already flirting with Healey, and quite a number are already talking openly of backing Shirley Williams' as their future candidate of choice in the post-Jenkins Labour Party: Leonard, 'Memo on Leadership Election', Crosland Papers, 6/3.

26 A. Crosland, Statement by Rt Hon. Anthony Crosland MP, 21 March 1976, Crosland Papers, 6/4; D. Lipsey, 'Main Points Arising from Secretary of State's Meeting with Economists, 20 May 1975, Crosland Papers, 4/19; Bruce Douglas-Mann to Betty Boothroyd, 22 March 1976, Crosland Papers, 6/4.

27 Crosland, *A Social Democratic Britain*; C. A. R. Crosland, 'The Anti-growth Heresy', *New Statesman*, 8 January 1971; also see Radice, *Friends & Rivals*, pp. 188–9.

28 R. Jenkins, *What Matters Now*, London, Fontana, 1972, pp. 9, 13–15, 22, 115; Jenkins, *A Life at the Centre*, London, Macmillan, 1991, p. 339; also see P. Bell, *The Labour Party in Opposition 1970–1974*, London, Routledge, 2004, pp. 190–209.

29 Minkin, *The Contentious Alliance*, p. 231; also see E. Dell, *A Hard Pounding: Politics and Economic Crisis 1974–1976*, Oxford, Oxford University Press, 1991, p. 185; M. Mullard, *The Politics of Public Expenditure*, London: Croom Helm, 1987, p. 6;

P. Whitehead, *The Writing on the Wall: Britain in the Seventies*, London, Michael Joseph, 1985, p. 346.

30 Although Hattersley also famously provoked Crosland's contempt by explaining to his mentor that he would have to vote strategically for Callaghan in the leadership election for fear of letting in Michael Foot: see S. Crosland, *Tony Crosland*, London, Jonathan Cape, 1982, pp. 315–16; R. Hattersley, *Who Goes Home? Scenes from a Political Life*, London, Little, Brown, 1995, p. 162; Jefferys, *Anthony Crosland*, p. 191; R. Jenkins, *A Life at the Centre*, London, Macmillan, 1991, pp. 430–1; G. Radice, *Friends & Rivals: Crosland, Jenkins and Healey*, London, Little, Brown, 2002, p. 236.

31 See R. Jenkins, *European Diary 1977–81*, London, Harper Collins, 1989, p. 1; Statement by the Rt Hon. Anthony Crosland MP, n.d., Crosland Papers, 6/2; also see Crosland, *Tony Crosland*, pp. 238–44.

32 K. Burk, 'The Americans, the Germans and the British: The 1976 IMF Crisis', *Twentieth Century British History*, 5 (3), 1994, pp. 351–2; K. Coates, *The Social Democrats: Those Who Went and Those Who Stayed: The Forward March of Labour Halted?*, Nottingham, Spokesman, 1983, pp. 9–11; also see K. Burk and A. Cairncross, *'Goodbye, Great Britain': The 1976 IMF Crisis*, London, Yale University Press, 1992; Dell, *A Hard Pounding*; M. Harmon, 'The 1976 UK-IMF Crisis: The Markets, the Americans, and the IMF', *Contemporary British History*, 11 (3), 1997, pp. 1–17; M. Harmon, *The British Labour Government and the 1976 IMF Crisis*, Basingstoke, Macmillan, 1997; K. Hickson, *The IMF Crisis of 1976 and British Politics: Keynesian Social Democracy, Monetarism and Economic Liberalism: The 1970s Struggle in British Politics*, London, I. B. Tauris, 2005; S. Ludlam, 'The Gnomes of Washington: Four Myths of the 1976 IMF Crisis', *Political Studies*, 40 (4), 1992, pp. 713–27; M. J. Oliver, 'From Anodyne Keynesianism to Delphic Monetarism: Economic Policy-making in Britain, 1960–79', *Twentieth Century British History*, 9 (1), 1998, pp. 139–50.

33 Hattersley, *Who Goes Home?*, pp. 178–9; Hattersley, 'Crosland died 25 years ago'.

34 See, for instance, T. Clark, 'The Limits of Social Democracy? Tax and Spend under Labour, 1974–79', Working Paper 01/04, Institute for Fiscal Studies, 2001, pp. 1, 3, 5–12; M. Holmes, *The Labour Government 1974–1979: Political Aims and Economic Reality*, London, Macmillan, 1985, p. 182.

35 Mullard, *The Politics of Public Expenditure*, pp. 149–50.

36 See Hickson, *The IMF Crisis of 1976*; also see C. Allsopp, 'Macroeconomic Policy: Design and Performance', in M. Artis and D. Cobham (eds), *Labour's Economic Policies 1974–79*, Manchester, Manchester University Press, 1991, pp. 19–37; Burk and Cairncross, *'Goodbye, Great Britain'*, p. 228.

37 See Clark, 'The Limits of Social Democracy', pp. 1–4, 5–12; Tomlinson, Interview with the author.

38 Clark, 'The Limits of Social Democracy', pp. 3–4, 35; also see Dell, *A Hard Pounding*, p. 13; B. Donoughue, *Prime Minister: The Conduct of Policy under Harold Wilson & James Callaghan*, London, Jonathan Cape, 1987, p. 51.

39 Clark, 'The Limits of Social Democracy', pp. 4, 23, 35–6; Rodgers, Interview with the author; Shirley Williams, Interview with the author, 25 June 2002.

40 Rodgers, Interview with the author; W. Rodgers, *Fourth Among Equals*, London, Politico's, 2000, pp. 164–7; Peter Shore, Interview with the author, 3 March 1999.

41 See Clark, 'The Limits of Social Democracy', p. 36.

42 Williams, Interview with the author. Shirley Williams perhaps most conspicuously straddles the emerging division of egalitarian and liberal revisionism. She describes herself as 'radical social democrat . . . Jenkinsite maybe . . . the closest description,

though I think I was probably always more egalitarian than Roy, and that's the bit that was more Croslandite . . . comprehensive schools and all that. So, egalitarian radical but moderate nonetheless'. She also usefully points to a further distinction between the libertarian (Labour) right and authoritarian (Labour) right within the context of the simple left–right classification of political attitudes in the Labour Party.

43 Shore, Interview with the author.

44 Williams, Interview with the author; also see P. Whitehead, *The Writing on the Wall: Britain in the Seventies*, London, Michael Joseph, 1985, pp. 189–201.

45 Williams, Interview with the author. Again, she appears to advocate a middle position between a balanced budget and generally progressive taxation to finance public services: 'but then within that framework where you cannot allow yourself to have a huge deficit, you have got to look at the taxation which enables you to maintain public services out of deficit and make sure it is generally progressive'. Of New Labour, she suggests 'that it is not a sufficiently progressive taxation position because it starts to bite too soon. People earning £10,000 are paying tax and we think that is crackers; they should not pay before £15,000, and you get that by charging fifty per cent on people who are over £50,000. I would have thought that was what I call a social democratic policy, but it is our policy not Labour's at the moment.'

46 Rodgers, Interview with the author; Clark, 'The Limits of Social Democracy', p. 23; Crosland, *Tony Crosland*, pp. 307, 343, 377; Dell, *A Hard Pounding*, p. 227; Whitehead, *The Writing on the Wall*, p. 201.

47 T. Benn, *Against the Tide: Diaries 1973–76*, London, Hutchinson, 1989, pp. 596, 668–9, 672–3.

48 See Clark, 'The Limits of Social Democracy', p. 37; J. Cole, *As it Seemed to Me*, London, Weidenfeld & Nicolson, 1995, p. 166. Of course, we should be cautious of drawing too close a parallel between 1970s liberal revisionism and New Labour. Although liberal revisionists noted the limitations of Crosland's economic (and to some extent philosophical) analysis and prescriptions in the changing economic and social context of the 1970s, they had not deserted the notion of the importance of the 'public domain', in which the integrity of principles of 'citizenship, equity and service' is 'essential to democratic governance and social well-being', and its centrality to policy spheres such as health and education: see, for example, D. Marquand, *Decline of the Public*, Cambridge, Polity Press, 2004, pp. 1–5.

49 Crosland, *Social Democracy in Europe*, pp. 4–9; also see Crosland, *The Conservative Enemy*, pp. 28–9; Crosland, 'Equality in Hard Times'; S. Fielding, *The Labour Party: Continuity and Change in the Making of 'New' Labour*, Basingstoke, Palgrave, 2002, pp. 70, 177–8, 204; D. Lipsey, 'Revisionists Revise', in D. Leonard (ed.), *Crosland and New Labour*, Basingstoke, Macmillan, 1999, pp. 13–17.

50 For further theoretical and empirical discussion of the 'structural constraints' model of social democratic political economy, see A. Przeworski, *Capitalism and Social Democracy*, Cambridge, Cambridge University Press, 1985; M. Wickham-Jones, *Economic Strategy and the Labour Party: Politics and Policy-Making, 1970–83*, London, Macmillan, 1996, pp. 23–6. A wide-ranging analysis of the economic policies of the 1974–79 Labour Government in the context of structural economic pressures and constraints can be found in M. Artis and D. Cobham (eds), *Labour's Economic Policies 1974–79*, Manchester, Manchester University Press, 1991; also see M. Artis, D. Cobham and M. Wickham-Jones, 'Social Democracy in Hard Times: The Economic Record of the Labour Government', *Twentieth Century British History*, 3 (1), 1992, pp. 32–58.

51 Crosland, 'Equality in Hard Times'; also see Jefferys, *Anthony Crosland*, p. 207.

52 A. Crosland to Dick Ross, 31 October 1975; A. Crosland to Harold Wilson, 'Public Expenditure', 31 October 1975, Crosland Papers, 5/8.

53 David Lipsey, Interview with the author, 17 January 2001.

54 See Hattersley, *Choose Freedom*, p. xix; Hattersley, *Who Goes Home?*, pp. 173, 179; Hattersley, 'Crosland died 25 years ago'; R. Plant, 'Social Democracy', in D. Marquand and A. Seldon (eds), *The Ideas that Shaped Post-war Britain*, London, Fontana, 1996, pp. 165–6.

55 Marquand, *The New Reckoning*, pp. 11–12; also see Marquand, *The Progressive Dilemma*, pp. 170–1, 174–5, 176–8; Plant, 'Social Democracy', pp. 165–6, 173–4.

56 Rodgers, Interview with the author; also see Marquand, *The Progressive Dilemma*, pp. 175–8.

57 W. Rodgers, Opening Statement of CLV, 19 February 1977, Mackintosh Papers, 323/14.

58 Hattersley, *Who Goes Home?*, pp. 176; also see Dell, *A Hard Pounding*, p. 285; Jefferys, *Anthony Crosland*, pp. 211–13.

59 Marquand, *The Progressive Dilemma*, pp. 166–78; also see Jefferys, *Anthony Crosland*, pp. 214–15.

60 See Crosland, *Tony Crosland*, p. 343; Dell, *A Hard Pounding*, pp. 226–8; Donoughue, *Prime Minister*, pp. 89–90.

61 Something they were perceived to hold in common with the emerging 'new Right-wing philosophy': see B. Castle, *The Castle Diaries 1964–1976*, London, Macmillan, 1990, p. 678; Clark, 'The Limits of Social Democracy', p. 40; Lipsey, Interview with the author.

62 Crosland, *Tony Crosland*, pp. 355–6, also see p. 34.

63 See Clark, 'The Limits of Social Democracy', p. 41; Crosland, *Tony Crosland*, p. 315; Jenkins, *A Life at the Centre*, p. 431.

64 A. Howard, 'Exciting Friend', *New Statesman*, 3 May 1999.

65 See Benn, *Against the Tide*, p. 684; Crosland, 'Equality in Hard Times'; Crosland, *Tony Crosland*, p. 357.

66 There were differences in their respective analyses: Crosland 'accepted some short-term cuts as the largesse of the mid-1970s offended his gradualism . . . This view lay behind his famous warning to local government that current spending growth was too fast – "the party's over" . . . This gradualism ultimately made even the IMF cuts acceptable: they were not "a refutation of Croslandism" if seen as a short-run measure. His chief concern in fighting cuts was thus to preserve demand (and so jobs), not to protect social spending: Keynesianism was integral to his approach, and he rejected inflation control through unemployment as unjust.' Castle 'consistently supported higher tax-and-spend even in the short run, as she sought rapid, rather than gradual, change . . . unlike Crosland, her chief interest was increasing tax-and-spend, not demand. She fought all tax cuts' as 'a loss of revenue for public expenditure': Castle, *The Castle Diaries 1964–1976*, pp. 633–4; Clark, 'The Limits of Social Democracy', pp. 41–2; Crosland, *Tony Crosland*, pp. 307–8, 355–6; Lipsey, Interview with the author.

67 Tomlinson, Interview with the author; Williams, Interview with the author.

68 Jefferys, 'The Old Right', p. 79.

69 See Mackintosh, 'Liberty and Equality'; Mackintosh, 'Britain's Malaise'; Mackintosh, 'Has Social Democracy Failed in Britain?', pp. 267–70; also see P. Diamond, *New Labour's Old Roots: Revisionist Thinkers in Labour's History 1931–1997*, Exeter, Imprint Academic, 2004, pp. 137–82; G. Foote, *The Labour Party's Political Thought: A History*, Basingstoke, Macmillan, 1997, pp. 259–60; E. Luard, *Socialism Without the State*, London, Macmillan, 1979; Taverne, *The Future of the Left*.

70 Marquand argues that 'the idea that the Labour Party can ever become a non-doctrinaire, non-class radical party of the sort Gaitskell tried to turn it into no longer seems to me remotely possible': David Marquand to John P. Mackintosh, n.d. [approx. September–November 1977]; David Marquand to John P. Mackintosh, 21 August 1977; John P. Mackintosh to David Marquand, 31 August 1977, Mackintosh Papers, 323/10; also see J. P. Mackintosh, 'Liberals and Social Democrats', *The Scotsman*, 28 March 1977, in Marquand, *John P. Mackintosh*, pp. 190–3; J. P. Mackintosh, 'The case for a realignment of the Left', *The Times*, 22 July 1977, in Marquand, *John P. Mackintosh*, pp. 193–6; D. Marquand, 'Inquest on a Movement: Labour's Defeat and its Consequences', *Encounter*, July 1979, pp. 8–18.

71 For a clear indication that Crosland, had he lived, would not have been tempted by the alternative social democratic vehicle of the SDP, and a synopsis of the fortunes of the now minority Croslandite 'democratic socialist' position in the Labour Party, see Lipsey, 'Revisionists Revise', p. 13; D. Lipsey, 'Crosland's Socialism', in D. Lipsey and D. Leonard (eds), *The Socialist Agenda: Crosland's Legacy*, London, Jonathan Cape, 1981, pp. 21–43.

72 See Hattersley, *Choose Freedom*, p. 148; D. Marquand, *The Unprincipled Society*, London, Heinemann, 1988; G. Radice, *Labour's Path to Power: The New Revisionism*, London, Macmillan, 1989; also see Diamond, *New Labour's Old Roots*, pp. 164–82, 192–209, 209–24.

73 J. Nuttall, '"Psychological Socialist": "Militant Moderate": Evan Durbin and the Politics of Synthesis', *Labour History Review*, 68 (2), 2003, pp. 235–7, 248–9; also see J. Nuttall, 'Tony Crosland and the Many Falls and Rises of British Social Democracy', *Contemporary British History*, 18 (4), 2004, pp. 52–79; J. Nuttall, 'Big Ideas and Synthesised Ideas in British Social Democracy since 1931', paper presented to the Rethinking Social Democracy Conference, Social Democracy, Culture and Society: Historical Perspectives, Centre for Contemporary History, Institute of Historical Research, University of London, 15–17 April 2004.

74 See Jefferys, *Anthony Crosland*, pp. 169–70; also see Gyford and Haseler, *Social Democracy*; Nuttall, 'Tony Crosland', pp. 70–1.

7

The parliamentary Labour right, Labour Party revisionism(s) and the roots of New Labour

Introduction

One important consequence of the failure to acknowledge the complexity, divisions and fragmentation of the 'old' Labour right in the 1970s has been an inability to conceive of parallels and continuities between so-called 'Old' and 'New' Labours. As noted at the outset, much of the recent literature on the Labour Party has been concerned to identify and explain the origins, ideological and political character and trajectory of New Labour from different perspectives. One strand has emphasised a Thatcherite 'accommodationist' explanation of New Labour.[1] Others have adopted a 'revisionist' perspective of the gradual evolution and transformation to New Labour from within Labour's own evolutionary social democratic tradition.[2] Others still attempt to combine these uni-dimensional explanations and describe the contemporary Labour Party as 'post-Thatcherite'[3] or, from within 'the project', as a modernised social democracy in radically changed economic and social circumstances, incorporating the concept of the 'Third Way'.[4] Within this debate, a small body of literature has emphasised New Labour's social democratic revisionist and even wider 'progressive' antecedents. Fielding traces a lineage from pre-1914 New Liberalism, through Labour's post-war revisionist tradition *and* interrupted 1970s 'neo-revisionism' to New Labour, which indicates the incidence and development of socialist-liberal 'intermingling' in the party. Broadly, 'revisionists . . . distinguished between time-bound means and fundamental ends; asserted that public ownership was not necessary to achieving equality; broadly accepted the market; and disavowed class appeals'.[5] Key themes of the Blair-led organisation 'have a long pedigree within the party. That he has been so successful in setting the agenda . . . has more to do with emasculated internal opposition than with any inherently novel approach.'[6] Importantly, unlike more general presentations of this argument, this perspective does not propose an uncomplicated, continuous evolution and course from a homogeneous 1950s social democratic revisionism to New Labour. It also notes the importance and influence of more immediate 'neo-revisionist' antecedents, which were a product of the emergent social democratic response to the problems of the 1970s and indicative of an emerging schism of Labour Party revisionism and 'old' and 'new' Labour rights. In this sense, the context and intra-party developments of the 1970s are very important to understanding New Labour, at least as important as Thatcherism in the 1980s.[7]

The 'old' Labour right and New Labour: complex political cultures and intra-party competition

If we conceive of the Labour Party as a complex organisation and political culture, incorporating within it a number of 'ways of life' that continuously interact and compete for dominance or hegemony, we are less likely to explain New Labour in terms of a definite break or departure with the past, or as 'year zero' in New Labour modernising terms.[8] It will help to avoid some of the amnesia and caricature current in the study of Labour politics and history and help to 'historicise' New Labour.[9] Rather than signifying a complete break with the past, (the ascendancy of) New Labour represents the present (and possibly temporary) dominance of just one of the 'ways of life' or competing 'segments' and 'strategies' of Labour's complex and competitive intra-party political culture. We are then likely to be more sensitive to the patterns weaved into Labour's complex internal political organisation and dynamics and the continuities inherent in Labour history and politics.[10]

If we acknowledge the importance of systematic intra-party competition and conflict between rival perspectives of how the party should organise and what it should stand for ('competing conceptions of Labour'), it will affect how we approach the question of relative continuity and change in the Labour Party and of New Labour's place within it. From this perspective, 'change in the direction of policy has little to do with ideological change per se but a change in the internal configuration of power within the party'. If we accept that the changes made to the revisionist model that emerged during the 1950s have been consistent with the broad ideology of the social democratic segment of the party, 'the ideological newness of New Labour has as much to do with the demise of currently viable alternatives within the Party and the social democrats' ability to determine the direction of the Party unencumbered as it does with ideological renewal'.[11] In this sense, the emergence of New Labour calls to mind Rose's observation that policy groups and factions within 'electoral parties' are often the crucial factor in policy change.

If we reject the simplistic conception of an unambiguous idea of 'Old' Labour, establish the need for a more profound examination of Labour's past as a means of locating New Labour's place within it, and acknowledge the contest between competing 'segments' and 'strategies' in the party, 'certain similarities between the modernisers and the revisionists . . . emerge'. Labour's post-war revisionist tradition and New Labour modernisers emanate from the same cultural tradition within the party, which includes a 'shared conception of the "hierarchical" way in which the Party should be organised with a strong leader and minimal public dissent'. There are significant similarities in the way that Gaitskell and Blair have approached the issues of discipline and decision-making in the party. This similar hierarchical line represents a shared concern and reasonably responsive approach to the perceived wishes of the public, together with the determination to get tough with the party in order to maintain discipline and unity. New Labour's party reforms, then, amount less to a new style and character per se than to an emasculated left-wing opposition, and we should treat with some scepticism the New Labour claim that they have transformed the party and left behind the traditions and 'stale left/right divisions of the past'.[12] In addition to perceived party management and leadership similarities, there is some notable continuity between revisionist and New Labour modernising elements at an even more fundamental level, which reflects similar conceptions of what the party should be and what it should represent. A 'social democratic ethos' has, 'for the time being, replaced the labourist ethos'.[13] In terms of notions of what the party should stand for and how it should organise itself, there are 'just too many systematic similarities': the Labour Party 'should aim not to change society fundamentally, but to correct market failure by long term supply-side intervention ... its parliamentary representatives must not allow their individual opinions to undermine either party unity or the leadership'.[14]

From this particular theoretical perspective, Labour's complex political culture has always been (and is) a combination of mutually dependent, continuously competing 'ways of life' each in search of dominance or even hegemony.[15] The Labour Party represents an 'organization sheltering a mixture' of cultures and traditions, 'whose divergent interests and aspirations frequently brought them into conflict' and were often incompatible. There is a 'systematic basis of intra-party cleavage' and internal conflict is 'neither unusual nor eradicable'. Most studies of factionalism and internal party divisions treat cleavage as 'a pathological condition, a deviation from some ideal party unity, engineered by organized cabals'. Rather, 'cleavage is a perfectly normal state of affairs, particularly in a two-party system, and is most often loosely co-ordinated'.[16]

Therefore, it is, perhaps, inaccurate to conceive of Labour's recent history and development as a simple dichotomy and departure between homogeneous 'Old' and 'New' Labours. Obviously, this distorted narrative owes much to the marketing strategy of New Labour modernisers in their haste to patent a new, dynamic and, most of all, electable party.[17] New Labour, rather, represents the manifestation or expression of the (possibly temporary) hegemony of one 'way of life' or 'segment' and 'strategy'. The other 'ways of life' continue in more or less attenuated form:

> no one way of life is capable of fully capturing a reality which is only completely described by all ways of life in combination. As we have seen in the past, the decisions made by the adherents of the temporarily dominant strain will at some point result in structures, practices, rhetoric and acts which prove incapable of coping with novel and unforeseen circumstances. At that point both the party and the public are likely to begin listening to the 'I-told-you-so's' of those ways of life that currently seem to make so little sense. Not for no reason are the most successful parties often the broadest churches.[18]

Misreading revisionism? Redistribution, public expenditure and equality

There remains a sense in which there is a tendency to subscribe to the rudimentary left–right orthodoxy of explaining Labour's intra-party competition and development. Analysis of constituent elements of these dimensions has generally been subordinated to a prime concern with the intra-party dynamics and balance between the two broad coalitions. In this case, there is a tendency to posit relatively uncomplicated, unambiguous parallels and continuity or to emphasise the stark differences between apparently homogeneous and hegemonic post-war Gaitskellite revisionism and New Labour. It appears to ignore the complexity, inconsistencies and tensions of the 'old' Labour right and Labour Party revisionism as they emerged during the 1970s. It is important to recognise Labour's inevitable and recurrent experience of intra-party debate and divisions both between and within the broad contours of left and right, and the tensions and gradual divergence of post-Gaitskellite revisionism in the intra-party and wider context of the 1970s.[19] If we acknowledge the complex and disputatious character of the parliamentary Labour right in the 1970s, we can identify both the emerging fissure of Labour Party revisionism and some nascent themes and thinking that pre-empted the development of 'New' Labour twenty years later (which was temporarily submerged and diverted in the post-1979 intra-party disputes and the formation of the SDP).

Divergent and divisive attitudes to the continued application of high levels of taxation and public expenditure in pursuit of egalitarian goals represented a particularly thorny issue, and reflected something of a public shift away from the social democratic primacy of 'tax and spend' and commitment to an unreconstructed 'Croslandism' among some erstwhile Gaitskellite revisionists and their successors. In the crisis years of Keynesian social democracy in the 1970s, nascent thinking around more tempered interpretations and applications of Labour's core principle of equality emerged on the Labour right and in organisations initially established to champion the cause of traditional moderate 'Keynesian socialism', which appeared to lack something of the original 'Croslandite' egalitarian spirit. The major policy statement of the Manifesto Group of centre-right Labour MPs, for instance, restated its faith in *limited* planning and the mixed economy but rejected increased public expenditure and simple redistribution of wealth. It argued that '[p]rogressive taxation and increased public expenditure have been pursued with too little regard for overall cost and too optimistic a view of the likely [redistributive] benefits', and advocated a new emphasis on economic growth, control of inflation and wealth creation:

> If our economy were growing faster, there would be a strong case for big *increases* in public expenditure in some areas. However, as democratic socialists we have to face facts as they are. The explosion in public expenditure over the last few years, occurring against a background of slow or stagnant growth, has potentially damaging economic consequences which . . . make industrial change more difficult. It has been in part unplanned. Some of it has been wasteful. Some of it is highly uncertain in its redistributive effects.

It was, therefore, a priority to look at more efficient ways to increase government control over (wasteful) public expenditure and to monitor the redistributive effect of public spending programmes. It also suggested that the 'feeling that we are over-taxed is growing strongly', and warned of 'a taxpayers' backlash – especially amongst those earning average wages or less – against the whole idea of the Welfare State'. It pointed to evidence that suggested that 'we are taxed inefficiently, not to say chaotically. In particular the incidence of personal taxation is damaging and unfair. And income tax has accounted for an ever larger share of tax revenue.' As well as the effect on incentives and doubtful redistributive impact of high marginal rates of taxation, compared to a 'more broadly based tax system with top rates of 50 per cent [that] would redistribute income more effectively than the more narrowly based tax system', problems for low wage earners were particularly acute. The Manifesto Group argued that the tax burden of average wage earners had risen substantially by 1975–76 and the tax threshold had fallen considerably in terms of average earnings, 'with the consequence that taxation is . . . hitting low income earners very hard':

> Many low paid workers who earn less than some people on Supplementary Benefit are paying income tax. If we take into account the withdrawal of means-tested benefits as income rises – the so-called poverty trap – many workers receive little net benefit from each extra £1 earned, and in some cases actually become worse off as they earn more . . . here is an additional disincentive effect: only [those] with above average earnings [are] more than £5 a week better off in work than unemployed.

The group statement recommended that tax thresholds should be raised and that there was a need to view taxation and benefits together. It recognised the destructive effects of inflation 'on the burden and incidence of taxation', and concluded that 'there is no room for further increases in direct taxation – though there may be a case for some rises in indirect taxes and in employers' contributions'. Without 'faster economic growth, it will not be possible to increase the overall level of public spending for a few years. It is . . . all the more essential that we get our priorities right, and use resources in the most effective way.'[20] The control of inflation, tax reform and economic growth remained central themes of the Manifesto Group analysis, and they rejected alternative 'ideological' approaches in favour of 'practical, workable policies' and concerns of how to make the industrial economy work and creating the new jobs that were needed. In themes that pre-date New Labour by fifteen years or so, it argued that the 'principal object of economic and industrial policy is to produce an atmosphere in which innovation thrives, risks are worth taking, profitability is satisfactory, and efficiency is a habit'. In doing so, it believed that under a Labour Government, Britain could become 'a more equal society, a less divided society, a society in which people gain more control over their lives, more choice over how they spend their time and their money'.[21]

It rejected both Conservative monetarist policies and the idea of a *laissez-faire* society and the Labour left's notion of a significantly planned economy and society and the 'destruction of individual initiative and choice, and therefore of freedom, which that brings'. It further attacked the 'inept use' of weapons on which democratic socialists have traditionally placed too much reliance. Focusing on the problems of economic growth and wealth creation rather than wealth distribution, the proposals represented new ground in democratic socialist thinking and attempted to revise the priorities of Crosland's earlier work which had presented economic growth as a given. In attacking the 'over-simplifications' of the 'neo-Marxist' demand economy and the Conservatives' vicious free market, it claimed to offer a 'middle course' or 'third way' towards economic recovery and social and democratic prosperity, and offered an emergent social democratic response to the problems and changing conditions of the 1970s.[22] Jenkinsite members of the Manifesto Group were particularly prominent in emerging opposition to high public expenditure and habitual egalitarian measures on the Labour right, which some claimed should be 'dependent on achieving economic growth and rising personal living standards *first*'. Bill Rodgers argued that individuals desired more control of their own lives and that this demanded greater attention to individual liberty, including lower personal taxation and clearer roles for individuals in greater industrial democracy. Reflecting an earlier (perhaps recurrent) anxiety of the social democratic left about the likely impact of affluence and consumerism on Labour's future electoral success, it argued that Labour should recognise the fact that most individuals now placed personal consumption above the pursuit of equality. Regardless of the merits of the approach, it 'lacked any sense of Crosland's commitment to equality as the central feature of Labour's vision of the future'.[23]

There has also been something of a general misconception about (differences in) the respective meanings attached to the core concept of 'equality' of first generation revisionists and New Labour, judgements about which have been a central aspect of debates over the relative social democratic credo of New Labour and the degree of continuity between so-called 'Old' and 'New' Labours.[24] Particularly, these have taken the form of arguments over the relative obeyance of the latter of a general standard of equality established by Labour Party revisionists of the 1950s led by Anthony Crosland. Crosland's work was central to establishing the core revisionist distinction between means and ends and the dictum that socialism is about equality rather than outmoded ideas of public ownership. In the pursuit of equality, it is ultimately the ends or values that matter and not the means to those ends. It is the precise nature of this equality that has been the subject of intense debate and controversy in attempting to establish the right to pin one's colours to the social democratic mast. Fielding argues that the original revisionists, including Crosland, 'were much nearer equality of oppor- tunity than that of outcome'. Although he was opposed to the pure 'meritocracy' of Michael Young's satirical nightmare, he was certainly never an advocate of equality of outcome because of its likely disincentive effects and the need to reward talent and hard work. Income tax rises were not viewed as the best means of achieving greater equality and a more equitable distribution of income. Again, the disincentive effects were too great and potentially damaging to individual liberty. Rather, economic growth was seen as the means by which revenues could be increased relatively painlessly to fund welfare and other schemes to reduce inequality.[25] He was conscious from a relatively early stage of the importance of economic growth and efficiency to the effective pursuit of 'greater equality' through public expenditure, and was careful to distinguish between earned or meritocratic and inherited income and wealth.[26] Crosland was also increasingly circumspect about the limits and uses of public expenditure. The optimistic and universalistic mood of his original defining tract appears to have dissipated by 1974, when he wrote that 'we must ruthlessly select priorities. We must prepare in advance a limited programme of radical measures which do not promise more than we can actually perform.' The pragmatic aspects of Crosland's revisionist thinking have been underplayed, particularly in the comparisons of the social democratic critique of New Labour.[27]

The general misreading of first generation revisionism, or at least neglect of Labour's 'interrupted neo-revisionism' of the Callaghan administration, 'something that was itself a critical response to post-war revisionism',[28] inevitably draws too stark a contrast between classic Croslandite and New Labour social democracy and between so-called 'Old' and 'New' Labours. It ignores or denies the essential *revisionist* aspect of social democracy and the role of (and link provided by) the emergent liberal social democratic strand of the Labour right, which had already begun to depart from some of the core tenets of Croslandism in the unanticipated circumstances of the 1970s, and to anticipate some of the key themes that were to tortuously work themselves through the Labour Party in the 1980s and 1990s (some via the SDP). By the mid-1970s the social democratic journey to a more equal society had 'reached an impasse'. It was responses to critical issues and developments of the 1970s that coaxed out and made explicit the inherent tensions and differential priorities of revisionist social democracy. Increasingly explicit debates and divisions over the political sensibility of increased public expenditure and taxation, the role and freedom of the private sector and the wider relationship and balance between the state, and the individual and core concepts and issues of equality and liberty were indicative of the emergence of an identifiable liberal strand of social democratic revisionism. While they generally remained committed to the goal of reducing poverty and greater redistribution and equality where possible, these 'neo-revisionists stressed that this could only come about with a greater role for the market and the decentralization, if not contraction, of government'.

Those such as Mackintosh in the Labour Party of the latter years of the floundering Callaghan administration and before his untimely death in 1978, and subsequently the developing ideas of David Owen, largely through the alternative vehicle of the SDP, predicted some of the key themes and ideas that (re)emerged in the Labour politics of the late 1980s and 1990s. Broadly, they were concerned to develop a traditional social democratic concern with equality and social justice within the context of a new emphasis on notions of individual liberty, decentralisation and participation and shifting trends and demands of the electorate, and the requirements of economic competitiveness.[29] Owen has been described as a 'proto-New Labour politician' on the basis that his emerging 'social market' ideas embraced a revisionist social democratic rather than neo-liberal perspective. Although not without its own tensions, if 'the

Gaitskellite-Croslandite revisionist right of the 1950s and 1960s is the progenitor of the SDP, then the SDP are New Labour's parents. Policy prescriptions aside, the SDP . . . provided New Labour with an intellectual inheritance of markets, nuclear deterrence, decentralisation and a scepticism for the inherent value of trade unions in the policy-making process.' New Labour can be interpreted as 'part of an [interrupted and revisionist] intellectual history within the Labour Party that reaches back [to] the Gaitskellite-Croslandite revisionist approach to democratic socialism', and which includes the SDP.[30] Mackintosh's 'incisive' and 'wide-ranging' attempts to 'modernise Gaitskellite revisionism' have also been clearly associated with the ideas and politics of both the SDP and New Labour.[31] Thirty years later, the proposals of 'radical social democrats' such as Owen, Mackintosh and David Marquand – 'devolution, a minimum wage, the establishment of "educational priority areas", road pricing and welfare reform' – have been 'key planks of the Blair agenda'.[32] The essential development and importance of this new social democratic thinking was to attempt to provide a 'new synthesis' of political concepts and ideas in combinations of 'what are too often assumed to be incompatible objectives'.[33] In this sense, a link can be established between emergent revisionist social liberal themes and combinations of thought, continued or diverted through the SDP, and those of New Labour. It is not the case that the Blairite modernisers were responsible for 'thinking the unthinkable' by combining notions and rhetoric of 'tough and tender, competitiveness and compassion, social concern and market realism, profit and service, the social market . . . and social justice'. The conjuring trick was to make the pursuit of these dual objectives finally acceptable through the Labour Party.

It can be a hazardous business to compare adherence to political philosophies and concepts unconditionally across time and space. The different context in which traditional values have to be applied inevitably leads to some reconfiguration of core concepts or, at least, some rethinking about their relationship to other important concepts. A new preoccupation with issues of personal freedom and the balance between equality and liberty in social democratic thought and practice from the mid-1970s was part of a wider sea change in political ideas and priorities. New Labour might be described as 'post-Croslandite' rather than 'post-Thatcherite' in the sense that it has continued and developed the synthesis of themes and ideas in the context of changing circumstances, demands and dilemmas initiated by 'neo-revisionist' social democrats of the 1970s and strands of thought diverted through the SDP. David Lipsey explains that it is part of an inevitable process of revisionism:

> I think it's a terrible mistake to adhere to a set of policies and views that applied . . . when Crosland died in 1977 and say those apply wholesale . . . Roy [Hattersley] identified himself with a certain period and he won't say revisionists revise and they go on revising . . . certain things have changed – the scale of globalisation, for example, which means that you just can't believe and sensibly implement certain things that you could have then. You can't have huge taxation on high incomes without destroying your economy now in a way you probably could [then] . . . The old values, basically . . . that socialism is about equality, remain, but New Labour is less statist about how that is achieved.[34]

New Labour has demonstrated a 'willingness to challenge accepted ways of doing something', such as a 'willingness to accept the private sector into the NHS', within the context of 'the differences . . . of . . . class divides [and] divides between public and private sectors [that have] changed in society'. While 'pure Blairism' may be different because 'it is happy to get very close to the private sector and . . . looks over its shoulder at middle England rather than working-class England', there remains a similar concern within the Government with issues of poverty to that faced by previous generations of Labour revisionists.[35] While members of the present Government may appear 'less explicitly egalitarian', or some may be 'less ferocious egalitarians' than earlier social democratic revisionists, New Labour has combined the 'neo-revisionist' critique of the limits of Croslandism in an underperforming economy and in the face of the demands of powerful interest groups with important egalitarian policy choices:

> it does again look as if you can have a mixed economy with a successful and stable non-inflationary growth and progressive social and expenditure policies and that basically is what New Labour is deliberating . . . the one thing that has turned out to be very difficult to combine with that is very strong labour unions because that's what tends to blow out when you're too optimistic when that balance could be shifted by incomes policy and voluntary self-restraint . . . in the end, the Thatcherite defeat of the unions . . . has made social democracy possible again.[36]

Although not without their controversies, he argues that policies of long-term care of the elderly and even student loans possess essential egalitarian elements within particular parameters:

> the long-term care of the elderly . . . an interesting case where there is an egalitarian policy which is to give money to the poor and a popular policy which is to give it to the better-off people to pay for their care and you can do one or the other, you can't do both, and this government bravely opted to give the money to the poor – an important egalitarian choice . . . and even . . . student loans . . . was designed, it was meant to actually stop giving public money to the middle classes, that's what the design of it was.[37]

Conclusion

Where once the Labour Party appeared to be 'beyond salvation' for 'the sort of things [they] believed in', 'radical' social democrats of the 1970s, who were 'actioning to differentiate [themselves] from . . . the . . . hard right . . . or . . . trade union right', have found some deliverance in New Labour, and the experience of the SDP was a 'very important catalyst for what later happened'.[38] One of the key 'motivating forces' for splitting the Labour Party and founding the SDP, along with the persisting question of Europe and attempts from the left to impose 'party control' over 'parliamentary control', was the pervasive general feeling that the Labour Party was 'getting completely out of touch'.[39] Influential 'neo-revisionist' thinkers such as John Mackintosh provided a 'prototype of a lot that happened in the Labour Party', including its embrace of devolution and Europe.[40] There were those among them who regarded themselves as neither left nor right, and 'thought that a lot of the old right and indeed some of the left were rather old fashioned in their views'. Rather, they saw themselves as 'modernisers', as the 'New Labour of the time': 'we saw ourselves as New Labour not as right wing reactionaries, which some of our trade union allies were – some of the older members of the group, people like Bob Mellish who at one stage were sort of allies – because we wanted to see reform, we wanted to see reform of institutions, we wanted to see Labour as a modern, radical, reforming, egalitarian party.' They believed that Labour in the 1970s 'was not going to be the vehicle for radical reform any more because . . . the party was in due course bound to fall under the due influence of the unelectable left'. Although Labour 'very unexpectedly' won the election in 1974 and 'in power . . . acted rather differently', it was a 'very divided and not very effective' government. The radical, reforming credentials of the present Labour Government, unencumbered by the demands of undemocratic and powerful trade unions and a resurgent left, appear much more to their liking.[41]

In an important sense, the history of the Labour Party is a history of 'new Labours'.[42] The idea of being new 'has always been part of the mental furniture of the Labour movement'. The Labour Party from its very beginnings has developed and adapted as society and politics has evolved. There is 'nothing new in the idea of being new. There's nothing new in saying we are modernisers, that we have a unique claim to power because we understand the nature of the modern world in a way that nobody else does.' From Ramsay MacDonald's strategy as leader of the party in the 1920s 'to build up a broad-based progressive coalition extending beyond the frontiers of the Labour Party' to Harold Wilson's 'white hot heat of technology' rhetoric and strategy to mobilise the 'new class of technicians and scientists to produce the second great Labour victory . . . of 1966', it is New Labour's success rather than its pursuit of creating an 'election-winning social coalition' that is new.[43] Crosland's original revisionist analysis was presented on the dust jacket of the first edition of his classic work, *The Future of Socialism*, as 'An answer to the demands for "new thinking on the Left"'.[44]

However, if comparison of New Labour ('modernisation') with 1950s Labour revisionism remains especially problematic,[45] given the hazards of attempting to compare philosophies and politics unconditionally across time and space, more recent comparison with those who were, themselves, attempting to update Croslandite revisionism to meet the demands and restrictions of the changing global political economy and the challenge of new intellectual and political dilemmas in the 1970s, might appear more apposite. One fundamental aspect of change that has inevitably impacted upon the ideological and programmatic formation of social democratic parties has been their relationship with the global political economy.[46] In the changing global economic environment, the challenge for social democratic parties has been 'not to fight old battles but to show there is a third way, a way of marrying together an open, competitive and successful economy with a just, decent and humane society'. It has involved the need to discard a significant amount of traditional dogma 'or die'.[47] In the prevailing conditions, European social democratic parties have undergone a gradual transformation in terms of the emergence of a new kind of 'liberal socialism' – a merger between 'the classical values of social democracy with the triumphant neoliberalism of the 1970s and 1980s'.[48] Under the auspices of 'modernisation', social democratic parties have 'reclaimed some of their forgotten traditions'. New Labour has attempted to demonstrate that it has successfully 'ended the legacy of the late 1970s and early 1980s and . . . returned to the reformist traditions of the party'. In a similar vein to their reformist predecessors:

> liberal socialists refute any fundamental opposition towards capitalism. Instead they seek regulatory frameworks in which capitalism can be made to work for the good of the greatest possible number . . . liberal socialists stress their commitment to social-democratic norms and values – nowhere more so than in Britain. They talk about increasing life chances, equality of opportunities . . . social justice, reviving the spirit of solidarity, a fair deal and giving a new ethical basis to society . . . Liberal socialists . . . are trying out, in Blair's words, 'permanent revisionism'.[49]

The different context in which traditional values have to be applied inevitably leads to a reassessment of means and even some reconfiguration of the relationship between core and related concepts and values. A new preoccupation with issues of personal freedom and the balance between concepts of equality and liberty in social democratic thought and practice from the mid-1970s was part of a wider sea change in political ideas and priorities. Many of the themes supposedly novel to New Labour and indicative of a retreat from its social democratic heritage – economic prudence, enthusiasm for the market, dynamic engagement of the private sector, a far less privileged role for powerful interest groups and institutional and constitutional renewal – were central to the embryonic programme of Labour's embattled minority social democratic revisionists in an unforgiving intellectual and political environment in the 1970s. They have re-emerged by route of the tortuous trajectory of the Labour Party and British social democracy in the 1980s to be championed in a more conducive party and intellectual context by a social democratic modernising tendency in the ascendancy.

Notes

1 See C. Hay, 'Labour's Thatcherite Revisionism: Playing the "Politics of Catch-Up"', *Political Studies*, 42 (4), 1994, pp. 700–7; C. Hay, *The Political Economy of New Labour: Labouring Under False Pretences?*, Manchester, Manchester University Press, 1999; R. Heffernan, 'Accounting for New Labour: The Impact of Thatcherism 1979–1995', in I. Hampsher-Monk and J. Stanyer (eds), *Contemporary Political Studies 1996*, Exeter, Political Studies Association, 1996, pp. 1280–90; R. Heffernan, *New Labour and Thatcherism: Exploring Political Change*, Basingstoke, Macmillan, 1999.

2 See T. Jones, *Remaking the Labour Party: From Gaitskell to Blair*, London, Routledge, 1996; M. J. Smith, 'A Return to Revisionism? The Labour Party's Policy Review', in M. J. Smith and J. Spear (eds), *The Changing Labour Party*, London, Routledge, 1992, pp. 13–28; M. J. Smith, 'Understanding the "Politics of Catch-Up" The Modernisation of the Labour Party', *Political Studies*, 42 (4), 1994, pp. 708–15.

3 S. Driver and L. Martell, *New Labour: Politics After Thatcherism*, Cambridge, Polity Press, 1998; S. Driver and L. Martell, *Blair's Britain*, Cambridge, Polity Press, 2002; S. Driver and L. Martell, *New Labour*, Cambridge, Polity Press, 2006.

4 T. Blair, *Let Us Face the Future: The 1945 Anniversary Lecture*, London, Fabian Society, 1995; T. Blair, *New Britain: My Vision of a Young Country*, London, Harper Collins, 1996; T. Blair, *The Third Way: New Politics for the New Century*, London, Fabian Society, 1998; A. Giddens, *The Third Way: The Renewal of Social Democracy*, Cambridge, Polity Press, 1998; P. Mandelson and R. Liddle, *The Blair Revolution: Can New Labour Deliver?*, London, Faber and Faber, 1996; P. Gould, *The Unfinished Revolution: How the Modernisers Saved the Labour Party*, London, Little, Brown, 1998.

5 S. Fielding, 'New Labour and the Past', in D. Tanner, P. Thane and N. Tiratsoo (eds), *Labour's First Century*, Cambridge, Cambridge University Press, 2000, pp. 367–92; S. Fielding, *The Labour Party: Continuity and Change in the Making of 'New' Labour*, Basingstoke, Palgrave, 2002.

6 P. Larkin, 'New Labour and Old Revisionism', *Renewal*, 8 (1), 2000, pp. 42–9; P. Larkin, *Revisionism & Modernisation in the Post-war British Labour Party*, unpublished D.Phil. Thesis, University of Sussex, 2000.

7 See Fielding, *The Labour Party*, pp. 70–2; K. Jefferys, *Anthony Crosland: A New Biography*, London, Richard Cohen Books, 1999, p. 195.

8 See T. Bale, *Sacred Cows and Common Sense: The Symbolic Statecraft and Political Culture of the British Labour Party*, Aldershot, Ashgate, 1999; T. Bale, 'Broad Churches, Big Theory and One Small Example: Cultural Theory and Intra-party Politics', in M. Thompson, G. Grendstad and P. Selle (eds), *Cultural Theory as Political Science*, London, Routledge, 1999, pp. 77–89; also see N. Ellison, *Egalitarian Thought and Labour Politics: Retreating Visions*, London, Routledge, 1994; A. Warde, *Consensus and Beyond: The Development of Labour Party Strategy since the Second World War*, Manchester, Manchester University Press, 1982.

9 T. Bale, 'The Logic of no Alternative? Political Scientists, Historians, and the Politics of Labour's Past', *The British Journal of Politics and International Relations*, 1 (2), 1999, pp. 192–204; M. Powell, 'Something Old, Something New, Something Borrowed, Something Blue: The Jackdaw Politics of New Labour', *Renewal*, 8 (4), 2000, pp. 21–31.

10 Bale, *Sacred Cows and Common Sense*, p. 250; Larkin, 'New Labour and Old Revisionism'; Warde, *Consensus and Beyond*.

11 Larkin 'New Labour and Old Revisionism', p. 45; Larkin, *Revisionism & Modernisation in the Post-war British Labour Party*, pp. 13, 21, 180.

12 Larkin, *Revisionism & Modernisation in the Post-war British Labour Party*, pp. 182–3; also see T. Bale, 'Struggling out of the Straitjacket? Culture and Leadership in the British Labour Party', paper presented to the ECPR Workshop, 'Cultural Theory in Political Science: Comparisons and Applications', Bern, 27 February–4 March 1997, p. 12; Bale, *Sacred Cows and Common Sense*, p. 27.

13 Larkin, *Revisionism & Modernisation in the Post-war British Labour Party*, p. 183.

14 Bale, 'Struggling out of the Straitjacket', p. 12.

15 Bale, 'Broad Churches, Big Theory and One Small Example', pp. 77–8.

16 Warde, *Consensus and Beyond*, pp. 1, 9–24.

17 See E. Shaw, 'From Old Labour to New Labour', *Renewal*, 4 (3), 1996, p. 52; E. Shaw, *The Labour Party since 1945*, Oxford, Blackwell, 1996, pp. 206, 212, 217–18.

18 Bale, *Sacred Cows and Common Sense*, pp. 250–1; also see D. Coates, 'Labour Governments: Old Constraints and New Parameters', *New Left Review*, 216, September–October 1996, p. 68; R. Toye, '"The Smallest Party in History"? New Labour in Historical Perspective', *Labour History Review*, 69 (1), pp. 83–103.

19 Through the conceptual lens of equality as 'Labour's central organizing principle', Ellison identifies both a post-war 'Keynesian socialist' tradition and the bifurcation of this tradition into 'socialist' and 'liberal' strands, 'the first signs of which emerged

in the 1950s, though the major split occurred in the early 1970s'. In his analysis of the main ideological currents and the development of strategy in the post-war Labour Party, Warde similarly identifies a tradition of 'social reformism', which fragmented and broke down in the period 1970–78: Ellison, *Egalitarian Thought and Labour Politics*, pp. x, 73–4, 187–200; Warde, *Consensus and Beyond*, pp. 9–24, 43–5, 125–40.

20 Manifesto Group, *What We Must Do: A Democratic Socialist Approach to Britain's Crisis*, 1977, Manifesto Group Papers, LP/MANIF/18, pp. 15–16, 27–30.

21 Manifesto Group, 'Priorities for Labour: A Manifesto Group Statement', 1979, Manifesto Group Papers, LP/MANIF/20, pp. 1–4, 11–12.

22 Manifesto Group, 'What We Must Do'; *Daily Telegraph*, 9 March 1977; *The Guardian*, 9 March 1977; also see Fielding, *The Labour Party*, pp. 67–73.

23 Ellison, *Egalitarian Thought and Labour Politics*, pp. 199–200; W. Rodgers, *Fourth Among Equals*, London, Politico's, 2000, pp. 291–2; W. Rodgers, Interview with the author, 18 February 2001.

24 A sustained social democratic critique of New Labour's apparent shift away from Croslandite egalitarian principles has emerged, largely in the writings of his unreconstructed and 'unrepentant' disciple Roy Hattersley: see R. Hattersley, 'Why I'm no longer loyal to Labour', *The Guardian*, 26 July 1997; R. Hattersley, 'It's no longer my party', *The Observer*, 24 June 2001; R. Hattersley, 'Crosland died 25 years ago: But his definition of a good society is still the best I know', *The Guardian*, 18 February 2002; R. Hattersley, 'Meritocracy is no substitute for equality', *New Statesman*, 6 February 2006; R. Hattersley, 'Is Equality Outdated?', *Political Quarterly*, 77 (1), 2006, pp. 3–11. The stock response has been that New Labour's commitment to equality and pursuit of social justice remains, but has been adapted to meet the challenges and dilemmas of radically changed circumstances: G. Brown, 'Why Labour is still loyal to the poor', *The Guardian*, 2 August 1997; G. Brown, 'Equality – Then and Now', in D. Leonard (ed.), *Crosland and New Labour*, Basingstoke, Macmillan, 1999, pp. 35–48; D. Leonard, 'Would Crosland feel betrayed by Blair and Brown?', *The Observer*, 17 February 2002; D. Lipsey, 'Revisionists Revise', in D. Leonard (ed.), *Crosland and New Labour*, Basingstoke, Macmillan, 1999, pp. 13–17; D. Lipsey, Interview with the author, 17 January 2001.

25 Fielding, *The Labour Party*, pp. 69, 70.

26 See C. A. R. Crosland, *The Future of Socialism*, London, Jonathan Cape, 1956, pp. 322–32; C. A. R. Crosland, *The Conservative Enemy: A Programme of Radical Reform for the 1960s*, London, Jonathan Cape, 1962, pp. 28–9. In the more defensive tone of *The Conservative Enemy*, he stated that inequalities should be tackled not in a 'bull-headed' way, 'but with circumspection, bearing soft on those which are relevant to growth and efficiency and hard on those which are not. Especially, we must bear soft on those which derive from personal effort and hard on those which derive from inheritance.'

27 C. A. R. Crosland, *Socialism Now & Other Essays*, London, Jonathan Cape, 1974, pp. 53–9; C. A. R. Crosland, 'Equality in Hard Times', *Socialist Commentary*, October 1976; Lipsey, Interview with the author; S. Meredith, 'Mr. Crosland's Nightmare? New Labour and Equality in Historical Perspective', *British Journal of Politics & International Relations*, 8 (2), 2006, pp. 238–55; S. Meredith, 'New Labour and Equality: A Response to Hickson', *British Journal of Politics & International Relations*, 9 (1), 2007, pp. 169–70.

28 Fielding, *The Labour Party*, p. 73.

29 *Ibid.*, pp. 68–70, 71–3; J. P. Mackintosh, 'Has Social Democracy Failed in Britain', *Political Quarterly*, 49 (3), 1978; J. P. Mackintosh, 'Liberty and Equality: Getting the Balance Right', in D. Marquand (ed.), *John P. Mackintosh on Parliament and Social Democracy*, London, Longman, 1982, pp. 182–9.

30 M. Beech, 'The Political Thought of David Owen: From Social Democrat to Neo-Liberal?', Working Paper No. 21, University of York, Department of Politics, 2005, pp. 14–16.

31 See G. Rosen, 'John Mackintosh: His Achievements and Legacy', Political Quarterly, 70 (2), 1999, pp. 210, 216, 217.

32 Ibid., p. 214; D. Marquand, J. Mackintosh and D. Owen, 'Change Gear! Towards A Socialist Strategy', Socialist Commentary, October 1967.

33 See T. Hames, 'At last it can be told: David Owen was Tony Blair's secret political father', The Times, 13 June 2005.

34 Lipsey, Interview with the author; Lipsey, 'Revisionists Revise'; R. Plant, 'Crosland, Equality and New Labour', in D. Leonard (ed.), Crosland and New Labour, Basingstoke, Macmillan, 1999, pp. 19, 34. Although he may have had severe doubts about the essentially 'market-driven, "flexible", deregulated economy which Labour retained after 1997' (the means), Kenneth Morgan argues that even Nye Bevan, the supposed antithesis of revisionist social democracy, would have welcomed the Labour Government's anti-poverty measures such as the minimum wage and child poverty programme and Brown's 2002 budget to revive the NHS. In this respect, he concludes that Labour retains 'its socialist ingredient, however well disguised': K. O. Morgan, 'Aneurin Bevan', in K. Jefferys (ed.), Labour Forces: From Ernest Bevin to Gordon Brown, London, I. B. Tauris, 2002, p. 98.

35 D. Newby, Interview with the author, 12 December 2001.

36 Lipsey, Interview with the author.

37 Ibid.

38 D. Marquand, Interview with the author, 16 January 2001.

39 S. Williams, Interview with the author, 25 June 2002.

40 P. Whitehead, Interview with the author, 20 January 2001.

41 D. Taverne, Interview with the author, 18 January 2001.

42 See E. Biagini, 'Ideology and the Making of new Labours', International Labour and Working Class History, 56, Fall 1999, pp. 93–105; N. Kinnock, 'New? We've always been new', New Statesman, 28 February 2000; Toye, '"The Smallest Party in History"?'.

43 D. Marquand, 'History today', Fabian Review, 112 (1), 2000, pp. 2–3. The same can be said of the idea of a 'third way' in politics. The 1945 Labour Government thought that it was pursuing a third way, and Labour's 1950s revisionists thought they 'were offering a Third Way between old style, boring, fundamentalist socialism and old style, boring, class bound Toryism'. A 'third way' has been 'part of the psyche of the Labour movement in this country for a very long time'. It also has a distinct historical lineage in processes of 'social democratic renewal', and represents the 'present-day version of the periodic rethinking that social democrats have had to carry out quite often over the past century': also see A. Giddens, The Third Way: The Renewal of Social Democracy, Cambridge, Polity Press, 1998, pp. vii–viii.

44 C. A. R. Crosland, The Future of Socialism, London, Jonathan Cape, 1956.

45 See, for example, Toye, '"The Smallest Party in History"?', pp. 84, 88–90.

46 Marquand, 'History Today'.

47 T. Blair, Speech to the Party of European Socialists Congress, Malmo, Sweden, 6 June 1997.

48 See H. Kitschelt, The Transformation of European Social Democracy, Cambridge, Cambridge University Press, 1994.

49 S. Berger, 'Labour in Comparative Perspective', in D. Tanner, P. Thane and N. Tiratsoo (eds), Labour's First Century, Cambridge, Cambridge University Press, 2000, pp. 330–3; S. Fielding, 'New Labour and the past', in D. Tanner, P. Thane and N. Tiratsoo (eds), Labour's First Century, Cambridge, Cambridge University Press, 2000, pp. 375–84.

8
Conclusion

[Labour's self-proclaimed] 'radical right' was actively actioning to differentiate [itself] from what [it] saw as the . . . hard right . . . or . . . trade union right.[1]

Fragmentation on the Labour right helped to open the way for the left to make much of the running inside the party.[2]

If the Labour left has been notoriously schismatic, neither has the Labour right been a homogeneous, loyalist unit. For much of the post-war period the complex ideological and political predispositions of the Labour right were concealed within the loose cohesive framework of Keynesian and Croslandite social democracy. However, as this framework crumbled in the 1970s, giving rise to a new range of political and policy concerns, including Europe, the character of industrial relations, the appropriate role of public expenditure, a new radicalised realignment of influential trade unions, and a more organised, confident Labour left, the relative ideological and political complexity and tensions of the parliamentary Labour right were exposed. The lack of intellectual and organisational cohesion in the face of divisive policy and political issues fundamentally weakened and undermined the parliamentary Labour right in Labour's intra-party politics, which underpinned the party's subsequent shift leftwards and long(er)-term gestation of the SDP. The roots of the latter reached further back than the immediate intra-party constitutional disputes after 1979, nor was it merely a split over European divisions in the party.[3] It was, rather, the culmination of a gradual process of alienation from both the wider party and more traditional 'labourist' colleagues of the Labour right. Seemingly irrevocable divisions over a range of core themes and developments in the 1970s exposed the emergence of profound philosophical and long-term policy differences within Labour Party revisionism and the parliamentary Labour right.

Case studies of key political and policy contexts, selected for their centrality to intra-party discourse and dissonance beyond that of general left–right dimensions, reveal some of the detail of the intrinsic ideological and political complexity and divisions of the parliamentary Labour right previously concealed within the loosely cohesive governing framework of Keynesian social democracy. The European debate in the Labour Party was not a simple reflection of left–right divisions, nor was it simply a reflection of a basic distinction between 'revisionist' and 'labourist' social democrats. Labour right and revisionist divisions over Europe reflected both pro- and anti-European positions, which were combined with varying degrees and expressions of agnosticism as the debate and circumstances progressed. A particularly harmful division was that within its so-called Gaitskellite revisionist strand. It ran right through from Macmillan's initial application for membership and the polarised divisions between Gaitskell himself, Jay, and his younger supporters such as Jenkins, Rodgers and others, to the critical period of opposition in the 1970s. The Jenkinsites, who took European membership to be an article of faith and one that transcended the crudities of adversarial party politics and Labour's government–opposition dichotomy, were fatefully divided and alienated from the respective pragmatic, opportunistic and ambivalent 'agnosticisms' of Callaghan, Healey and Crosland, which they so despised.

Similarly, the 'trade union question' in Labour politics in the late 1960s and 1970s cut right through the parliamentary Labour right. Led by Callaghan, there were the obvious defenders of the Labour alliance, who regarded the '"rules" of the Labour movement' as non-negotiable. It was against all of their instincts to create a situation in which the trade unions movement was not regarded as the flesh and bone of the Labour movement. They deemed the relationship to be essential to their vision of central control of the Labour Party through the parliamentary leadership in conjunction with the trade unions. A close liaison with the trade unions was an essential stabilising force for the party, particularly against the advent of a resurgent radical left in the 1970s. Attempts to reframe and regulate the context and conduct of industrial relations would undermine traditional trade union rights and privileges and potentially lead to a damaging split in the Labour alliance.

An emerging pragmatic and populist element of Labour revisionism, represented in their own ways by Healey and Crosland, who might have lacked the instinctual understanding and attachment to the Labour alliance, also sensed the need to maintain the 'special link' with the trade unions as representatives of the 'organised working class'. They recognised some need to reorder priorities and rework more distinctive institutional roles, but within the framework of the '"rules" of the Labour movement', and adopted a pragmatic, adaptive attitude to the reform of industrial relations according to political and party context and timing. A third perspective was that of the emerging and relatively cohesive Jenkinsite pro-European, liberal strand of Labour revisionism, who regarded a major problem of British industry and British economic decline to lie in the cumulative assertive and confrontational power of the trade unions. Consequently, they felt 'much readier to shed . . . the fundamental values and "rules" of the Labour Movement'. The seemingly irreconcilable 'trade union question' in the Labour Party and British politics became a central feature of their thinking about the party and on policy. Increasingly, they were to feel frustrated and constrained within the '"rules" of the Labour movement', and it was their confinement within these rules that provided a crucial sub-text of the departure of some of their number to the SDP.[4]

In the economic climate of the 1970s, public expenditure and traditional tools and goals of social democratic political economy more widely provided a further point of division. A pragmatic party leadership accepted the need, in principle, to undertake a review of the extent and commitment to public expenditure in light of recurrent economic difficulties, but a crucial division over the priority awarded to, and implications of, high levels of public expenditure in social democratic thought and practice emerged between evolving strands of 'egalitarian' and 'liberal' social democratic revisionism. Egalitarians such as Crosland and Hattersley continued to proclaim the prerequisite role of high public expenditure to Labour's redistributive egalitarian project. Liberal revisionists associated with Roy Jenkins were, from the mid-1970s, questioning the very principles of injecting large doses of public expenditure into the economy. With their emphasis squarely on the 'values of a plural society and freedom of choice', they appeared to be willing to undergo a further revision of socialist principles and to rethink the traditional role of public expenditure and Labour's egalitarian commitments.

To a large extent, group and factional organisation and behaviour reflected the lack of cohesion and divisions of the parliamentary Labour right and Labour Party revisionism in the 1970s. It was not the case that the parliamentary Labour right in the 1970s lacked group mentality and factional organisation, or even that such group activity could not take 'oppositional' form. Rather, attempts to cohere and organise on the parliamentary Labour right lacked significant impact on Labour's internal politics. The experience of group activity and organisation, for some, consolidated their increasing frustration with the constraints and trajectory of Labour Party politics and offered up the prospect of an alternative social democratic vehicle and agenda. In opposition, the Jenkinsite faction took a stance that divided them not just from the Labour left, but also from the centrist leadership. The 'oppositional' form of Jenkinsite behaviour maginalised an important strand of Labour right opinion, further weakened the cohesion of the parliamentary Labour right in the face of enhanced left-wing activity and emphasised increasing divisions within Labour's centre-right 'governing coalition'. It also provided an indication of the potential (and promise) of a social democratic breakaway from the Labour Party.

The limitations of Labour right factional activity were further illustrated in the internal dynamics and narrow concerns of the Manifesto Group. Its diverse membership reflected a broad range of centre-right opinion and, while it was temporarily effective in stemming the flow of success of the Tribune Group in elections for Labour Party office, a number of contentious policy themes were beyond its scope and restricted the latitude and impact of its policy agenda and statements. Again, the experience of the Manifesto Group only appeared to confirm for some the debilitating divisions of Labour's centre-right coalition and the inalienable trajectory of the Labour Party further to the left. Factional organisation and activity of the parliamentary Labour right in the 1970s did not correspond unconditionally to standard left–right/oppositional-loyalist formations outlined by Rose and others. Parliamentary Labour right forces did not coalesce in a purely loyalist 'undifferentiated non-Left tendency', nor did they give rise to a focused revisionist faction in the mould of CDS, 'authorised' by, and dedicated to the defence of, the parliamentary leadership. The 'unorthodox' factional behaviour and efficacy of the parliamentary Labour right, rather, reveals the extent to which it had fragmented ideologically, politically and organisationally by the 1970s.

Parliamentary Labour right divisions and the schism of revisionist social democracy

Increasingly explicit and wide-ranging tensions and divisions possessed important implications for the fragile unity and cohesion of the parliamentary right and the intra-party balance of power. The mounting antagonism of Labour's three leading revisionist figures, Jenkins, Crosland and Healey, inevitably divided and weakened the purchase of Labour Party revisionism and unity of the parliamentary Labour right in the party political context of the 1970s. In spite of increasing differences between them, friends and advisers frequently counselled some sort of *rapprochement,* if only 'in the name of a united opposition to the Left. But attitudes to Europe, personal rivalries and attitudes to the Party prevented unity on the Labour Right.'[5] By the 1980s, 'revisionist social democracy of the 1950s' Gaitskellite vintage, under whose banner Crosland, Jenkins and Healey, in their different ways and styles, had marched, was threadbare'. Although the reasons for its failure inside the Labour Party were complex, the undoubted rivalry and divisions of the three leading 'revisionist' protagonists, which reflected clear differences of approach and priorities, 'contributed to the decisive defeat of social democracy in the 1980s':

> if Jenkins and Crosland in the 1970s, and Jenkins and Healey in the 1970s and 1980s had been able to sink their divisions, then the situation inside the Labour Party might not have deteriorated so alarmingly and the SDP split might never have occurred . . . greater co-operation between them would have made a crucial difference . . . to the social democratic position inside the Labour Party and to the fate of Labour itself. But the three men did not work together . . . In the 1970s Tony and Denis believed that Roy was wrong to put the European issue above party. In 1976 they did not see why Jenkins, who had severely damaged his chances by resigning the deputy leadership in 1972, should be allowed a clear run in the leadership election.[6]

Divisions over a range of key policy and political themes more widely reflected the philosophical divergence of Labour Party revisionism and emerging differences and conflicting priorities in the nature of respective 'socialisms', which privileged either collective, comprehensive and egalitarian, or pluralistic, decentralist, anti-corporatist and individual principles and concerns. The latter signalled a radical departure and break with 'old-style revisionism'.[7] Crosland argued that there was little need to redefine socialism based on a concern with equality and welfare. He was unwilling to reject his initial belief that capitalism no longer presented a fundamental danger to socialist objectives of equality and believed that government action could meet and overcome any potential dangers. Crosland emphasised the original revisionist dictum that the ultimate objectives of any Labour Government must be an overriding concern with the poor and deprived working class and to promote greater social and economic equality. The key problem in pursuit of this aim had been the failure of the 1964–70 Labour Governments to obtain the increasingly elusive goal of higher production and growth levels, which he ascribed to its deflationary policies caused by initial obsession with the parity of sterling. Thus he still advocated 'a move to the left ... not in the traditional sense of a move towards old-fashioned Clause IV Marxism but in the sense of a sharper delineation of fundamental objectives, a greater clarity about egalitarian priorities, and a stronger determination to achieve them'.[8] Crosland (and initially Jenkins in the aftermath of the 1970 election defeat) refused to fundamentally 'question their own Keynesian beliefs'.[9]

For other Labour revisionists, the general mood of the Labour Party and the disappointment and perceived limitations and failures of the 1974–79 Labour Government 'only reinforced the glaring need for a break with the revisionist politics of a bygone era'.[10] Throughout the 1970s there were calls from the social democratic right to go beyond traditional revisionism in protest at the rise of the new left and increasing trade union power. They argued for the old Gaitskellite revisionist element of the Labour right to adopt a new, more populist strategy that would help to come to terms with the new desire for participation. They described themselves as 'Social Democrats' to differentiate their approach from that of traditional revisionism, and emphasised the point that inequality in power and status should be reduced by a more local, grass-roots approach. Some, further, took up the call for Labour to rethink its relationship with the large trade unions and to endeavour to develop community politics and small business relationships. They emphasised the guiding principles of pluralism, independence and freedom, and further argued for the Jenkinsites to establish a new, breakaway political party as Labour had, beyond redemption, become too left-wing and union-dominated.[11]

John Mackintosh, perhaps, became the most notable theorist of an acute anti-left, anti labourist and anti-corporatist position of the social democratic Labour right. Before his untimely death in 1978, he had become convinced that the failures of Labour in power were an indication that the revisionist politics of the 1950s were now outdated and irrelevant.[12] His basic critique of traditional revisionist social democracy was the claim that it lacked a sophisticated economic understanding of the mixed economy and its problems. Central to this analysis was the case that Labour's failure, and British decline generally, were defects of the very growth of corporatism that Labour had done so much to bring about and which led to a feeling of impotence and indifference in the electorate and its governing institutions. He suggested that traditional revisionist social democracy had contributed to the devaluation of parliamentary democracy in favour of corporate pressure groups such as the CBI and the TUC. Crosland's libertarian rejection of nationalisation had not gone far enough. It had been unable to break sufficiently from the statist strategy of the corporate socialists and the Fabians in its demands for equality and welfare. Principles of democracy, participation and citizenship were being compromised by the corporate interests that 'governed' the country, including the very trade unions upon which the Labour Party was dependent. He was fundamentally opposed to the primacy of the interests of those with a monopoly-hold on economic power, whether they were key financiers, multinational corporations, or unions controlling key sectors of the labour force, regardless of party political considerations.[13] In his critique of 'the corporate power of organised labour, Mackintosh was developing the anti-labourism implicit in revisionist thinking to a new and more dangerous stage. The social democratic wing of the Labour Party, as it was now called, was reaching a point where the "revisionists" could find no home in the Labour Party.'[14]

Although divisions of the parliamentary Labour right more broadly manifested themselves across a range of critical political and policy themes as described in the case study chapters,[15] the most debilitating rift developed in the rupture of Labour's post-war revisionist social democracy. The schism reflected emerging and seemingly irreconcilable philosophical and political differences between egalitarian and often Labourist, 'consolidationist' and 'populist' (often more of an accusative than analytical classification) 'democratic socialists' and liberal, pro-European, 'radical' 'social democrats'.[16] The latter objected to both the perceived illiberal conservatism and corporatist inclinations of the pragmatic, Labourist 'anti-Common Market and pro-trade union' 'old' Labour right and the ostensible unwillingness of egalitarian, increasingly defensive, revisionists to revise their strategy and priorities in light of the changing circumstances of the 1970s and apparent failure of the related programmes of recent Labour Governments.[17] Of course, there remained some cross-fertilisation of principles and views that owed something to common roots. Hattersley was a prominent pro-European supporter of Jenkins before his views on public expenditure and equality took him away from the emerging Jenkinsite position.[18] Shirley Williams, perhaps, retained more recognisably fundamental egalitarian and redistributive values. In the pursuit of social justice, she continued to 'believe in relatively high taxation to pay for good public services', but her self-perception was one of being a 'modern' 'radical social democrat' with clear liberal and libertarian principles and priorities:[19]

Social Democracy grew out of the revisionist movement of the 1950s in terms of ideology and even personnel . . . However, the differences between revisionism and social democracy, often reflected in differences between Jenkins and the new leaders, were profound . . . The old demands for equality were replaced with new demands for freedom, and the old belief in economic growth led by large and socially responsible corporations had been replaced by the new belief that 'small is beautiful' . . . It was in their calls for freedom that the specific nature of the Social Democrats was revealed most starkly. In harking back to the decentralist traditions of . . . Cole and William Morris, they were throwing a veil over the class nature of those traditions . . . [the] response that the market should be freed from the fetters of state control was an indication of the retreat from the revisionist values of social equality and welfare. It was an almost inevitable result of the divorce of freedom from its social context of a class-divided society . . . Their direct political influence was relatively short-lived, but in the longer term the new ideas of Mackintosh, Williams and Owen, elaborated by writers such as . . . Marquand, were to exert a major influence over New Labour theory.[20]

Fragmentation of the parliamentary Labour right and intra-party politics

The immediate consequences of the fragmentation of the parliamentary Labour right and Labour Party revisionism for the internal politics of the Labour Party were profound. The relative fragmentation and weakness of the Labour right in the 1970s were both cause and effect of the rise of the Labour left in the internal structures of the party. Talented representatives and competent administrators of the parliamentary Labour right, who were often able to naturally flourish in government,

> couldn't flourish in the Labour Party at the beginning of the 1970s because the left had control of the party. In opposition they were lost because the mood was too strong against them . . . The battles against the left could be won, were being won, if people stood firm and were courageous, but by the earlier 1970s it was too late. The Party had gone the wrong way; it was the Bennite way of control by then.[21]

While some Labour revisionists such as Crosland did not appear to perceive the left as such a threat, a number of prominent Jenkinsites recognised, from a relatively early stage, the potential damage to the Labour Party in the form of a likely (social democratic) split.[22]

The Labour right, perhaps with the exception of the relatively successful organisational and lobbying period of CDS in the early 1960s, was organisationally ineffective.[23] Although much of the power in the Labour Party 'was on the right . . . they weren't a united group'.[24] The parliamentary Labour right in the 1970s lacked the comfort of their central position in the 'nexus' of 'the trade union leadership plus the parliamentary leadership which controlled the Labour Party' of Hugh Gaitskell in the 1950s. The Labour right 'were not used to playing internal Labour Party politics . . . they didn't have to, nor were they very used to playing conference politics . . . All they had to do was to phone up Arthur Deakin, or have dinner with Arthur Deakin, and decide on what they were going to do, and then Arthur Deakin had the vote. But that changed.' Changes in the nature of the trade union movement and position of the trade union leadership, and reaction to the 1964–70 Labour Governments, in which leading representatives of the Labour right were perceived to be the ministers responsible for failing the working-class, left them with 'a weak hand . . . in terms of internal Labour politics given all that history'.[25]

Then, of course, came the disruptive split over Europe, which provoked the mutual antagonism of Crosland and the pro-European social democrats. Crosland accused the Jenkinsite core of pro-Europeans of being frivolous and of hawking their consciences around from conference to conference, achieving only the outcome of letting the left in. The 'unity of the right was broken in the post-1970 period about Europe', which also had the effect of contributing to its loss of intellectual primacy in the party:

> also it was psychologically and intellectually . . . on the defensive, it didn't have a story to tell . . . People like me . . . and . . . John Mackintosh . . . would . . . have liked to have managed somehow to find a story to tell. That's why we were keen on calling

ourselves the radical right, so not lining up with the old, centrist right . . . not lining up with Michael Foot, not lining up with the increasingly left-wing Benn, but at the same time also making it clear that we too were very dissatisfied by much of what the Wilson government had done. But we never managed it . . . probably that was our biggest failing . . . we didn't find a satisfactory story to tell . . . it was partly because of all the Common Market business . . . that overwhelmed us . . . it's very hard in politics to fight two battles at once, and if one of the battles is an immediate one where you are really fighting for your life politically speaking and the other one is a much more theoretical and long-term battle, of course one is always going to take precedence.[26]

As the adhesive ideological framework of Keynesian social democracy and core tenets of the post-war consensus and Labour's governing ethos collapsed around them, the Labour right had the fundamental problem that they 'didn't have anything to say'. They were left high and dry, divided and 'really without any ideological base'.[27] The general shift to the left in both the trade unions and the constituencies after the unsatisfactory experience of the 1964–70 Labour administrations and excess activity of the Labour left as the party entered opposition after 1970, found the Labour right with little to offer as an alternative, particularly in relation to the country's persistent economic difficulties.[28] Bill Rodgers reflects that 'we all felt and admitted that, and then on Europe the right of the party was fragmented'. These factors – 'disillusionment with the 1964–70 government and then the split and fragmentation of the Labour right on Europe' – were the 'two things that gave the left their opportunity'.[29] Reinforced by previous and subsequent divisions over industrial relations reform and the privileged status of the trade unions and key themes of social democratic political economy, which further distanced the emerging 'social democrat' grouping from both the party mainstream and fellow revisionists, Labour's European divisions of the early 1970s helped to divide the parliamentary Labour right within itself. Cumulatively, the 'split in the Labour Party had been a long time coming'. There was a shift to the left after the 1970 election defeat, as there was (an even greater) one after 1979, and on both occasions 'part of the right was slow at getting organised and was weakened by different positions'.[30]

Most of the participants saw 'the long row over British membership of the EEC as the start of the fundamental split . . . Jenkins . . . stuck to his long-held convictions in favour of entry . . . he . . . was progressively alienated from the other members of that government in turn, as each peeled away from the European cause, first Callaghan, then Wilson, finally even Healey and Crosland. For the first time in a generation the right was split.' Simultaneously, the persuasive voice of Tony Benn was heard in the wider party as he embarked on his influential period as party chairman. The

pro-Europeans' loss of influence in the Labour Party after 1971 was precipitate. Jenkins resigned the deputy leadership in 1972 . . . He lost at once both his place on Labour's National Executive and the post of Shadow Chancellor. With him into the wilderness, for a crucial period, went a number of others: Lever, Thomson, Owen and Taverne . . . As the party moved left in the debates which led up to the formulation of the 1973 programme, Jenkins and his allies seemed even more isolated.

After his disappointing performance in the 1976 leadership election and failure to obtain his desired post of Foreign Secretary in the Callaghan administration (which, ironically perhaps, was awarded to Crosland), Jenkins left the Labour Party to take up the presidency of the EEC. At Westminster, 'those of Jenkins's old persuasion clustered together for comfort in a cold climate in the Manifesto Group . . . The Jenkinsite chapter seemed over'.[31]

Under the pressure of events and its own internal divisions, the parliamentary Labour right offered little cohesive resistance to the Labour left within 'the formal structure of the Labour Party'.[32] The parliamentary Labour right was not a homogeneous, cohesive unit within the context of Labour and British politics of the 1970s, but a diverse coalition of ideological, policy and political perspectives, preferences and priorities. The underlying complexity and divisions of the parliamentary Labour right were particularly exposed by the dilemmas of a problematic economic and political context, as the adhesive and unifying ideological and political framework of Keynesian social democracy which, for the most part, had concealed the inherent diversity and divisions of the Labour right, gradually unravelled. As this diversity and divisions became increasingly explicit in the face of critical policy and political themes, cooperation and compromise proved difficult and presented a weak, divided front that undermined the unity and efficacy of the Labour right, which was reflected in issues of intra-party organisation and party management and leadership. The divisions of Labour's centre-right 'dominant coalition' became particularly apparent and problematic as simultaneous developments contributed to a shift in the intra-party balance of power after 1970. After the election defeat, 'which was a crucial turning point, both the left and the unions became more powerful . . . With the defeat of *In Place of Strife* and the successful assault on the Conservative Industrial Relations Act, the unions' political clout . . . increased substantially which made governing, especially for a Labour administration, more difficult.'[33] In these inauspicious party circumstances, and under pressure of the collapse of its intellectual and political framework and divisions 'from within', the Labour right imploded. It 'took quite a long while' and 'the shock of the formal split of the Labour right in the creation of the SDP, before the centre-right re-grouped and started looking for solidarity each with the other'. Those that were left 'either had to develop the hard-nosed cutting edge or drift, give up and surrender'.[34]

Notes

1 Marquand, Interview with the author, 16 January 2001.
2 K. Jefferys, *Anthony Crosland: A New Biography*, London, Richard Cohen Books, 1999, p. 167.
3 R. Desai, *Intellectuals and Socialism: 'Social Democrats' and the Labour Party*, London, Lawrence & Wishart, 1994, pp. 145–52, 162; P. Whitehead, *The Writing on the Wall: Britain in the Seventies*, London, Michael Joseph, 1985, pp. 339, 340–1.
4 See L. Minkin, *The Contentious Alliance: Trade Unions and the Labour Party*, Edinburgh, Edinburgh University Press, 1991, pp. 208–37.

5   See Jefferys, *Anthony Crosland*, pp. 119–21, 166–70; D. Marquand, *The Progressive Dilemma: From Lloyd George to Kinnock*, London, Heinemann, 1991, p. 169.

6   G. Radice, *Friends & Rivals: Crosland, Jenkins and Healey*, London, Little, Brown, 2002, pp. 3–5, 238–9, 329–34; W. Rodgers, Interview with the author, 18 February 2001; also see D. Healey, *Time of My Life*, London, Michael Joseph, 1989, p. 329; D. Healey, 'The death of a singularly civilised man: Lord Jenkins of Hillhead', *Financial Times*, 6 January 2003; R. Jenkins, *A Life at the Centre*, London, Macmillan, 1991, p. 217.

7   See G. Foote, *The Labour Party's Political Thought: A History*, third edition, Basingstoke, Macmillan, 1997, pp. 235–55.

8   C. A. R. Crosland, *A Social Democratic Britain*, London, Fabian Society, 1971; C. A. R. Crosland, *Socialism Now and Other Essays*, London, Jonathan Cape, 1974, pp. 34, 44.

9   Foote, *The Labour Party's Political Thought*, pp. 235–8.

10 *Ibid.*, pp. 238–9, 243, 251; D. Owen, *Face the Future*, Oxford, Oxford University Press, 1981, p. 147.

11 J. Gyford and S. Haseler, *Social Democracy: Beyond Revisionism*, London, Fabian Society, 1971; D. Taverne, *The Future of the Left: Lincoln and After*, London, Jonathan Cape, 1974, p. 147; also see Foote, *The Labour Party's Political Thought*, pp. 238–9, 249–51; Owen, *Face the Future*, pp. 5, 295.

12 Foote, *The Labour Party's Political Thought*, pp. 239–43; G. Rosen, 'John Mackintosh: His Achievements and Legacy', *Political Quarterly*, 70 (2), 1999, pp. 210–18.

13 See J. P. Mackintosh, 'Britain's Malaise: Political or Economic?', in D. Marquand (ed.), *John P. Mackintosh on Parliament and Social Democracy*, London, Longman, 1982, p. 203; J. P. Mackintosh, 'Is Labour Facing Catastrophe?', in Marquand (ed.), *John P. Mackintosh*, p. 167; J. P. Mackintosh, 'Taming the Barons', in Marquand (ed.), *John P. Mackintosh*, p. 115.

14 Foote, *The Labour Party's Political Thought*, pp. 243, 246.

15 The 'hard', authoritarian trade union right, epitomised by Callaghan and key lieutenants such as Houghton, Mellish and Merlyn Rees, were 'always tied to the trade unions whatever the situation' and attuned to the Labourist demands of key policy and political circumstances. The centrist, corporatist leadership position was often reinforced by the flexible, hard-nosed 'pragmatism' of those such as Healey, who lacked affiliation and commitment to particular groups, much to the chagrin of 'principled' Jenkinsite revisionists: see Foote, *The Labour Party's Political Thought*, p. 246; D. Healey, Interview with the author, 9 February 1999; Radice, *Friends & Rivals*, pp. 329–30; Rodgers, Interview with the author.

16 D. Marquand, Interview with the author, 16 January 2001; D. Taverne, Interview with the author, 18 January 2001.

17 See Marquand, *The Progressive Dilemma*, pp. 166–78; Rodgers, Interview with the author, 18 February 2001; Taverne, Interview with the author.

18 He had been subjected to the same accusation as Crosland of demonstrating 'the triumph of expediency over principle' by the Jenkinsites, not for his failure to support the Labour Europeans in the vote of October 1971, but for both his failure to resign and for accepting promotion from Wilson when Jenkins and others later resigned over Labour's referendum decision: Taverne, Interview with the author.

19 Marquand, Interview with the author; S. Williams, Interview with the author, 25 June 2002; also see Foote, *The Labour Party's Political Thought*, pp. 246–8, 325–6; S. Williams, *Politics is for People*, Harmondsworth, Penguin, 1981.

20 Foote, *The Labour Party's Political Thought*, pp. 252–5; also see P. Whitehead, *The Writing on the Wall: Britain in the Seventies*, London, Michael Joseph, 1985, pp. 339–46.

21 Taverne, Interview with the author.
22 See D. Taverne, *The Future of the Left: Lincoln and After*, London, Jonathan Cape, 1974; Whitehead, *The Writing on the Wall*, pp. 339–46.
23 Marquand, Interview with the author.
24 D. Lipsey, Interview with the author, 17 January 2001; Taverne, Interview with the author.
25 Marquand, Interview with the author; also S. Haseler, Interview with the author, 23 January 2001; Rodgers, Interview with the author; Williams, Interview with the author.
26 Marquand, Interview with the author.
27 *Ibid.*
28 Lipsey, Interview with the author; Rodgers, Interview with the author; Williams, Interview with the author.
29 Rodgers, Interview with the author.
30 Lipsey, Interview with the author.
31 Whitehead, *The Writing on the Wall*, pp. 339–41, 346.
32 Marquand, Interview with the author; J. Tomlinson, Interview with the author, 27 March 2001.
33 Radice, *Friends & Rivals*, pp. 329–30.
34 Tomlinson, Interview with the author; also see D. Hayter, *Fightback! Labour's traditional right in the 1970s and 1980s*, Manchester, Manchester University Press, 2005, pp. 8–16.

Bibliography

Manuscript collections

Unpublished private papers

Anthony Crosland Papers, British Library of Political and Economic Science, London
John P. Mackintosh Papers (Deposit 323), National Library of Scotland, Edinburgh
David Owen Papers (D 709), University of Liverpool
Reg Prentice Papers, British Library of Political and Economic Science, London
Neville Sandelson Papers, British Library of Political and Economic Science, London

Unpublished Labour Party papers

Labour Party, Labour Committee for Europe Minutes and Papers 1964–80 (LP/LCE),
    Labour History Archive, Manchester
Labour Party, Manifesto Group Papers (LP/MANIF), Labour History Archive, Manchester
Labour Party, National Executive Committee Minutes (LP/NEC/MINUTES), Labour
    History Archive, Manchester
Labour Party, Parliamentary Labour Party Minutes (LP/PLP), Labour History Archive,
    Manchester

Personal interviews

Leo Abse, 20 June 2001
George Cunningham, 21 November 2001
Stephen Haseler, 23 January 2001
Denis Healey, 9 February 1999
John Horam, 16 February 2001
Dick Leonard, 23 January 2001
David Lipsey, 17 January 2001
Tom McNally, 16 June 1998
David Marquand, 16 January 2001
Kenneth O. Morgan, 17 October 1997
Dick Newby, 12 December 2001
Bill Rodgers, 18 February 2001
Peter Shore, 3 March 1999

Dick Taverne, 18 January 2001
John Tomlinson, 27 March 2001
Phillip Whitehead, 20 January 2001
Alan Lee Williams, 17 January 2001
Shirley Williams, 25 June 2002

Labour Party publications

Labour Party, *Report of the Fifty-Fifth Annual Conference of the Labour Party*, London, Labour Party, 1956

Labour Party, *Report of the Fifty-Ninth Annual Conference of the Labour Party*, London, Labour Party, 1960

Labour Party, *Report of the Sixty-First Annual Conference of the Labour Party*, London: Labour Party, 1962

Labour Party, *Britain and the Common Market: Texts of speeches made at the 1962 Labour Party Conference by the Rt Hon. Hugh Gaitskell MP and the Rt Hon. George Brown MP together with the policy statement accepted by Conference*, London, Labour Party, 1962

Labour Party, *The New Britain*, London, Labour Party, 1964

Labour Party, *Now Britain's Strong – Let's Make it Great to Live In*, London, Labour Party, 1970

Labour Party, *Labour and the Common Market*, Report of a special conference of the Labour Party, Central Hall Westminster, 17 July 1971, London, Labour Party, 1971

Labour Party, *Report of the Seventy-Sixth Annual Conference of the Labour Party*, London, Labour Party, 1971

Labour Party, *Labour's Programme 1973*, London, Labour Party, 1973

Labour Party, *Labour's Programme: Campaign Document 1974*, London, Labour Party, 1974

Labour Party, *Let Us Work Together: Labour's Way Out of the Crisis*, London, Labour Party, 1974

Labour Party, *Labour and the Common Market*, Report of a special conference of the Labour Party, Sobell Sports Centre Islington London, 26 April 1975, London, Labour Party, 1975

Labour Party, *Labour's Programme 1976*, London, Labour Party, 1976

Labour Party, *Report of the Seventy-Sixth Annual Conference of the Labour Party*, London, Labour Party, 1977

Labour Party, *Democratic Socialist Aims and Values*, London, Labour Party, 1988

Official papers

In Place of Strife: A Policy for Industrial Relations, Cmnd 3888, London, HMSO, January 1969

The Official Report, House of Commons, 5th and 6th series

Newspapers and periodicals

Daily Telegraph
Dissent
Economist
Encounter

Financial Times
Forward
Guardian
Listener
New Statesman
The Observer
Socialist Commentary
Sunday Times
The Times
Tribune

Books, articles, essays and journalism

Abrams, M. and Rose, R., *Must Labour Lose?*, Harmondsworth, Penguin, 1960

Abse, L., *Private Member*, London, Macdonald, 1973

Addison, P., *The Road to 1945: British Politics and the Second World War*, London, Jonathan Cape, 1974

Albu, A. H., Prentice, R. and Bray, J., 'Lessons of the Labour Government', *Political Quarterly*, 41 (2), 1970, pp. 141–55

Arblaster, A., 'Anthony Crosland: Labour's Last "Revisionist"?', *Political Quarterly*, 48 (4), 1977, pp. 416–28

Artis, M. and Cobham, D. (eds), *Labour's Economic Policies 1974–79*, Manchester, Manchester University Press, 1991

Artis, M., Cobham, D. and Wickham-Jones, M., 'Social Democracy in Hard Times: The Economic Record of the Labour Government', *Twentieth Century British History*, 3 (1), 1992, pp. 32–58

Baker, D., Gamble, A. and Ludlam, S., 'Mapping Conservative Fault Lines: Problems of Typology', in P. Dunleavy and J. Stanyer (eds), *Contemporary Political Studies, Volume One*, Belfast, Political Studies Association, 1994, pp. 278–98

Bale, T., 'Managing the Party and the Trade Unions', in B. Brivati and T. Bale (eds), *New Labour in Power: Precedents and Prospects*, London, Routledge, 1997, pp. 159–78

Bale, T., 'Struggling out of the Straitjacket? Culture and Leadership in the British Labour Party', paper presented to the ECPR Workshop, 'Cultural Theory in Political Science: Comparisons and Applications', Bern, 27 February–4 March 1997

Bale, T., 'Towards a "Cultural Theory" of Parliamentary Party Groups', *Journal of Legislative Studies*, 3 (4), 1997, pp. 25–43

Bale, T., 'Broad Churches, Big Theory and One Small Example: Cultural Theory and Intra-party Politics', in M. Thompson, G. Grendstad and P. Selle (eds), *Cultural Theory as Political Science*, London, Routledge, 1999, pp. 77–89

Bale, T., *Sacred Cows and Common Sense: The Symbolic Statecraft and Political Culture of the British Labour Party*, Aldershot, Ashgate, 1999

Bale, T., 'The Logic of No Alternative? Political Scientists, Historians, and the Politics of Labour's Past', *The British Journal of Politics and International Relations*, 1 (2), 1999, pp. 192–204

Barnett, J., *Inside the Treasury*, London, Andre Deutsch, 1982

Baston, L., 'Roy Hattersley', in K. Jefferys (ed.), *Labour Forces: From Ernest Bevin to Gordon Brown*, London, I. B. Tauris, 2002, pp. 221–35

Bealey, F. (ed.), *The Social and Political Thought of the British Labour Party*, London, Weidenfeld & Nicolson, 1970

Beech, M., 'Analysing the Revisionist Tradition of Political Thought in the Labour Party: Eduard Bernstein to New Labour', paper presented to the Third Essex Graduate Conference in Political Theory, University of Essex, Department of Government, 17–18 May 2002

Beech, M., 'The Political Thought of David Owen: From Social Democrat to Neo-Liberal?', Working Paper No. 21, University of York, Department of Politics, 2005

Beech, M., *The Political Philosophy of New Labour*, London, I. B. Tauris, 2006

Beer, S. H., *Modern British Politics: A Study of Parties and Pressure Groups*, London, Faber & Faber, 1965

Bell, P., *The Labour Party in Opposition 1970–1974*, London, Routledge, 2004

Beller, D. C. and Belloni, F. P., 'Party and Faction: Modes of Political Competition', in F. P. Belloni and D. C. Beller (eds), *Faction Politics: Political Parties and Factionalism in Comparative Perspective*, Santa Barbara, CA and Oxford, ABC-Clio, 1978

Belloni, F. P. and Beller, D. C., 'The Study of Party Factions as Competitive Political Organisations', *Western Political Quarterly*, 29 (4), 1976, pp. 531–49

Benn, T., *Office Without Power: Diaries 1968–72*, London, Hutchinson, 1988

Benn, T., *Against the Tide: Diaries 1973–76*, London, Hutchinson, 1989

Berger, S., *The British Labour Party and the German Social Democrats 1900–1931*, Oxford, Oxford University Press, 1994

Berger, S., 'Labour in Comparative Perspective', in D. Tanner, P. Thane and N. Tiratsoo (eds), *Labour's First Century*, Cambridge, Cambridge University Press, 2000, pp. 309–40

Berrington, H., 'The Common Market and the British Parliamentary Parties, 1971: Tendencies, Issue Groups ... and Factionalism', paper presented to the ECPR Workshop, 'Factionalism in the Political Parties of Western Europe', Florence, 25–29 March 1980

Berrington, H., 'The Labour Left in Parliament: Maintenance, Erosion and Renewal', in D. Kavanagh (ed.), *The Politics of the Labour Party*, London, George Allen & Unwin, 1982, pp. 69–94

Bevir, M., *New Labour: A Critique*, Abingdon, Routledge, 2005

Black, L., 'Social Democracy as a Way of Life: Fellowship and the Socialist Union, 1951–9', *Twentieth Century British History*, 10 (4), 1999, pp. 499–539

Black, L., '"The Bitterest Enemies of Communism": Labour Revisionists, Atlanticism and the Cold War', *Contemporary British History*, 15 (3), 2001, pp. 26–62

Black, L., *The Political Culture of the Left in 'Affluent' Britain, 1951–1964: Old Labour, New Britain?*, Basingstoke, Palgrave, 2002

Blair, T., *Let Us Face the Future: The 1945 Anniversary Lecture*, London, Fabian Society, 1995

Blair, T., *New Britain: My Vision of a Young Country*, London, Harper Collins, 1996

Blair, T., 'Foreword', in G. Goodman (ed.), *The State of the Nation: The Political Legacy of Aneurin Bevan*, London, Gollancz, 1997, pp. 11–13

Blair, T., *The Third Way: New Politics for the New Century*, London, Fabian Society, 1998

Booker, C., *The Seventies: Portrait of a Decade*, Harmondsworth, Penguin, 1980

Bradley, I., *Breaking the Mould? The Birth and Prospects of the Social Democratic Party*, Oxford, Martin Robertson, 1981

Brand, J., 'Faction as its Own Reward: Groups in the British Parliament 1945 to 1986', *Parliamentary Affairs*, 42 (3), 1989, pp. 148–64

Brittan, S., *Left and Right: The Bogus Dilemma*, London, Secker & Warburg, 1968

Brittan, S., 'Further Thoughts on Left and Right', in S. Brittan, *Capitalism and the Permissive Society*, London, Macmillan, 1973, pp. 354–73

Brivati, B., 'Campaign for Democratic Socialism', *Contemporary Record*, 4 (1), pp. 11–12

Brivati, B., *The Campaign for Democratic Socialism 1960–1964*, unpublished Ph.D. Thesis, University of London, 1992

Brivati, B., 'Hugh Gaitskell and the EEC', *Socialist History*, 4, 1994, pp. 16–32

Brivati, B., 'Hugh Gaitskell: A Reassessment', paper presented to the Twentieth Century British History Seminar, Institute of Historical Research, London, n.d.

Brivati, B., 'Revisionists', *Socialist History*, 9, 1996, pp. 109–14

Brivati, B., *Hugh Gaitskell*, London, Richard Cohen, 1996

Brivati, B. and Cockett, R. (eds), *Anatomy of Decline: The Political Journalism of Peter Jenkins*, London, Cassell, 1995

Brivati, B. and Wincott, D. (eds), 'The Campaign for Democratic Socialism 1960–64', *Contemporary Record*, 7 (2), 1993, pp. 363–85

Brivati, B. and Wincott, D. (eds), 'The Evolution of Social Democracy in Britain', *Contemporary Record*, 7 (2), 1993, pp. 360–62

Brivati, B. and Wincott, D. (eds), 'The Labour Committee for Europe', *Contemporary Record*, 7 (2), 1993, pp. 386–416

Broad, R., *Labour's European Dilemmas: From Bevin to Blair*, Basingstoke, Palgrave, 2001

Broad, R. and Geiger, T. (eds), 'The 1975 British Referendum on Europe', *Contemporary British History*, 10 (3), 1996, pp. 82–105

Broad, R., Kandiah, M. D. and Staerck, G. (eds), 'Britain and Europe', Witness Seminar, Institute of Contemporary British History, 2002, available from: http://www.icbh.ac.uk/icbh/witness/brussels/brussels.pdf

Brooke, S., 'Evan Durbin: Reassessing a Labour "Revisionist"', *Twentieth Century British History*, 7 (1), 1996, pp. 27–52

Brown, G., *In My Way*, Harmondsworth, Penguin, 1972

Brown, G., 'Why Labour is still loyal to the poor', *The Guardian*, 2 August 1997

Brown, G., 'Equality – Then and Now', in D. Leonard (ed.), *Crosland and New Labour*, Basingstoke, Macmillan, 1999, pp. 35–48

Burk, K., 'Symposium: 1976 IMF Crisis', *Contemporary Record*, 3 (2), 1989, pp. 39–45

Burk, K., 'The Americans, the Germans and the British: The 1976 IMF Crisis', *Twentieth Century British History*, 5 (3), 1994, pp. 351–69

Burk, K. and Cairncross, A., *'Goodbye, Great Britain': The 1976 IMF Crisis*, London, Yale University Press, 1992

Burns, E., *Right Wing Labour: Its Theory & Practice*, London, Lawrence & Wishart, 1961

Butler, D. and Kavanagh, D., *The British General Election of February 1974*, London, Macmillan, 1974

Butler, D. and Kitzinger, U., *The 1975 Referendum*, London, Macmillan, 1976

Callaghan, James, *James Callaghan on the Common Market*, London, Labour Committee for Safeguards on the Common Market, 1971

Callaghan, James, *Time and Chance*, London, William Collins, 1987

Callaghan, John, 'The Left: The Ideology of the Labour Party', in L. Tivey and A. Wright (eds), *Party Ideology in Britain*, London, Routledge, 1989, pp. 23–48

Callaghan, John, *The Retreat of Social Democracy*, Manchester, Manchester University Press, 2000

Callaghan, John, 'Social Democracy in Transition', *Parliamentary Affairs*, 56 (1), 2003, pp. 125–40

Campbell, J., *Roy Jenkins: A Biography*, London, Weidenfeld & Nicolson, 1983

Carter, M., 'Tony Crosland', in G. Rosen (ed.), *Dictionary of Labour Biography*, London, Politico's, 2001, pp. 144–7

Carter, M., *T. H. Green and the Development of Ethical Socialism*, Exeter, Imprint Academic, 2003

Castle, B., *The Castle Diaries 1974–76*, London, Weidenfeld & Nicolson, 1980

Castle, B., *The Castle Diaries 1964–70*, London, Weidenfeld & Nicolson, 1984

Castle, B., *The Castle Diaries 1964–1976*, London, Macmillan, 1990

Castle, B., *Fighting All The Way*, London, Macmillan, 1994

Clark, T., 'The Limits of Social Democracy? Tax and Spend under Labour, 1974–79', Institute for Fiscal Studies, Working Paper 01/04, January 2001, available from http://www.ifs.org.uk/workingpapers/wp0104.pdf

Clarke, P., *Liberals and Social Democrats*, Cambridge, Cambridge University Press, 1978

Clarke, P., *A Question of Leadership: From Gladstone to Thatcher*, Harmondsworth, Penguin, 1992

Clarke, P., 'Wilson and the Historians', *Twentieth Century British History*, 4 (2), 1993, pp. 171–3

Clarke, P., 'The Keynesian Consensus and its Enemies: The Argument over Macroeconomic Policy since the Second World War', in D. Marquand and A. Seldon (eds), *The Ideas that Shaped Post-War Britain*, London, Fontana, 1996, pp. 67–87

Clements, R., 'Roy Jenkins: the politics of nostalgia', *Tribune*, 29 September 1972

Clift, B., 'New Labour's Third Way and European Social Democracy', in S. Ludlam and M. J. Smith (eds), *New Labour in Government*, Basingstoke, Macmillan, 2001, pp. 55–72

Coates, D., *The Labour Party and the Struggle for Socialism*, Cambridge, Cambridge University Press, 1975

Coates, D., *Labour in Power? A Study of the Labour Government 1974–1979*, London, Longman, 1980

Coates, D., 'Labour Governments: Old Constraints and New Parameters', *New Left Review*, 219 (September–October), 1996, pp. 62–77

Coates, K. (ed.), *What Went Wrong: Explaining the Fall of the Labour Government*, Nottingham, Spokesman, 1979

Coates, K., *The Social Democrats: Those Who Went and Those Who Stayed: The Forward March of Labour Halted?*, Nottingham, Spokesman, 1983

Cole, J., *As it Seemed to Me*, London, Weidenfeld & Nicolson, 1995

Commission on Social Justice, *Social Justice: Strategies for National Renewal*, London, Vintage, 1994

Coopey, R. and Woodward, N. (eds), *Britain in the 1970s: The Troubled Economy*, London, UCL Press, 1996

Coopey, R., Fielding, S. and Tiratsoo, N., 'Introduction: The Wilson Years', in R. Coopey, S. Fielding and N. Tiratsoo (eds), *The Wilson Governments 1964–1970*, London, Pinter, 1993, pp. 1–9

Crewe, I. and King, A., 'Loyalists and Defectors: The SDP Breakaway from the Parliamentary Labour Party 1981–2', in P. Jones (ed.), *Party, Parliament and Personality: Essays Presented to Hugh Berrington*, London, Routledge, 1995, pp. 61–83

Crewe, I. and King, A., *SDP: The Birth, Life and Death of the Social Democratic Party*, Oxford, Oxford University Press, 1995

Crosland, C. A. R., 'The Transition from Capitalism', in R. H. S. Crossman (ed.), *New Fabian Essays*, London, Turnstile Press, 1952, pp. 33–68

Crosland, C. A. R., *The Future of Socialism*, London, Jonathan Cape, 1956

Crosland, C. A. R., *Can Labour Win?*, London, Fabian Society, 1959

Crosland, C. A. R., 'New Moods, Old Problems: On Politics in the Welfare State', *Encounter*, 16 (2), 1961, pp. 3–6

Crosland, C. A. R., *The Conservative Enemy: A Program of Radical Reform for the 1960s*, London, Jonathan Cape, 1962

Crosland, C. A. R., *A Social Democratic Britain*, London, Fabian Society, 1971

Crosland, C. A. R., 'The Anti-growth Heresy', *New Statesman*, 8 January 1971

Crosland, C. A. R., *Socialism Now and Other Essays*, London, Jonathan Cape, 1974

Crosland, C. A. R., *Social Democracy in Europe*, London: Fabian Society, 1975

Crosland, C. A. R., 'Equality in Hard Times', *Socialist Commentary*, October 1976

Crosland, S., *Tony Crosland*, London, Jonathan Cape, 1982

Cyr, A., 'Cleavages in British Politics', in F. P. Belloni and D. C. Beller (eds), *Faction Politics: Political Parties and Factionalism in Comparative Perspective*, Santa Barbara, CA and Oxford, ABC-Clio, 1978

Dahrendorf, R., *Life Chances: Approaches to Social and Political Theory*, London, Weidenfeld & Nicolson, 1980

Daly, G., *The Crisis in the Labour Party 1974–81 and the Origins of the 1981 Schism*, unpublished Ph.D. Thesis, University of London, 1992

Daly, G., 'The Campaign for Labour Victory and the Origins of the SDP', *Contemporary Record*, 7 (2), 1993, pp. 282–305

Daniels, P. and Ritchie, E., '"The Poison'd Chalice": The European Issue in British Party Politics', in P. Jones (ed.), *Party, Parliament and Personality: Essays Presented to Hugh Berrington*, London, Routledge, 1995, pp. 84–98

Dell, E., *A Hard Pounding: Politics and Economic Crisis 1974–1976*, Oxford, Oxford University Press, 1991

Dell, E., *A Strange Eventful History: Democratic Socialism in Britain*, London, Harper Collins, 1999

Desai, R., *Intellectuals and Socialism: 'Social Democrats' and the Labour Party*, London, Lawrence & Wishart, 1994

Diamond, P., *New Labour's Old Roots: Revisionist Thinkers in Labour's History 1931–1997*, Exeter, Imprint Academic, 2004

Donoughue, B., *Prime Minister: The Conduct of Policy under Harold Wilson & James Callaghan*, London, Jonathan Cape, 1987

Douglas, R. M., 'No Friend of Democracy: The Socialist Vanguard Group 1941–50', *Contemporary British History*, 16 (4), 2002, pp. 51–86

Driver, S. and Martell, L., *New Labour: Politics after Thatcherism*, Cambridge, Polity Press, 1998

Driver, S. and Martell, L., 'From Old Labour to New Labour: A Comment on Rubinstein', *Politics*, 21 (1), 2001, pp. 47–50

Driver, S. and Martell, L., *Blair's Britain*, Cambridge, Polity Press, 2002

Driver, S. and Martell, L., *New Labour*, Cambridge, Polity Press, 2006

Drucker, H. M., *The Political Uses of Ideology*, London, Macmillan, 1974

Drucker, H. M., *Doctrine and Ethos in the Labour Party*, London, Allen & Unwin, 1979

Drucker, H. M., 'Changes in the Labour Party Leadership', *Parliamentary Affairs*, 34 (4), 1981, pp. 369–91

Dunleavy, P., 'The Political Parties', in P. Dunleavy, A. Gamble, I. Holiday and G. Peele (eds), *Developments in British Politics 4*, London, Macmillan, 1993, pp. 123–43

Durrant, S., 'Denis Healey: Silly Billy', *The Guardian*, 19 June 2000

Elliot, G., *Labourism and the English Genius: The Strange Death of Labour England?*, London, Verso, 1993

Ellison, N., *Egalitarian Thought and Labour Politics: Retreating Visions*, London, Routledge, 1994

Farrelly, P., 'John Golding', in G. Rosen (ed.), *Dictionary of Labour Biography*, London, Politico's, 2001, pp. 214–15

Favretto, I., '"Wilsonism" Reconsidered: Labour Party Revisionism 1952–64', *Contemporary British History*, 14 (4), 2000, pp. 54–80

Favretto, I., *The Long Search for a Third Way: The British Labour Party and the Italian Left since 1945*, Basingstoke, Palgrave Macmillan, 2003

Fielding, S., '"Labourism" and Locating the British Labour Party within the European Left', Working Papers in Contemporary History and Politics 11, European Studies Research Institute, University of Salford, 1996

Fielding, S., '"But westward, look, the land is bright!" Labour's revisionists and the imagining of America', in Holliwell, J. (ed.), *Anglo-American Relations in the Twentieth Century*, Basingstoke, Macmillan, 2000

Fielding, S., 'New Labour and the Past', in D. Tanner, P. Thane and N. Tiratsoo (eds), *Labour's First Century*, Cambridge, Cambridge University Press, 2000, pp. 367–92

Fielding, S., *The Labour Party: Continuity and Change in the Making of 'New' Labour*, Basingstoke, Palgrave, 2002

Fielding, S. and McHugh, D., 'The *Progressive Dilemma* and the Social Democratic Perspective', in J. Callaghan, S. Fielding and S. Ludlam (eds), *Interpreting the Labour Party: Approaches to Labour Politics and History*, Manchester, Manchester University Press, 2003, pp. 134–49

Foote, G., *The Labour Party's Political Thought: A History*, third edition, Basingstoke, Macmillan, 1997

Francis, M., 'Mr Gaitskell's Ganymede? Re-assessing Crosland's *The Future of Socialism*', *Contemporary British History*, 11 (2), 1997, pp. 50–64

Freeden, M., *Ideologies and Political Theory: A Conceptual Approach*, Oxford, Clarendon Press, 1996

Gaitskell, H., *Socialism and Nationalisation*, London, Fabian Society, 1956

George, S., *An Awkward Partner: Britain in the European Community*, Oxford, Oxford University Press, 1998

Giddens, A., *The Third Way: The Renewal of Social Democracy*, Cambridge, Polity Press, 1998

Goodhart, P., *Referendum*, London, Tom Stacey, 1971

Goodman, G., *Awkward Warrior: Frank Cousins, His Life and Times*, London, Davis Poynton, 1979

Goodman, G., 'The Soul of Socialism', in G. Goodman (ed.), *The State of the Nation: The Political Legacy of Aneurin Bevan*, London, Gollancz, 1997, pp. 15–35

Gould, B., *Socialism and Freedom*, Basingstoke, Macmillan, 1985

Gould, P., *The Unfinished Revolution: How the Modernisers Saved the Labour Party*, London, Little, Brown, 1998

Gourevitch, P., *Politics in Hard Times: Comparative Responses to International Economic Crises*, New York, Cornell University Press, 1986

Greenleaf, W. H., *The British Political Tradition: Volume Two: The Ideological Heritage*, London, Methuen, 1983

Gyford, J. and Haseler, S., *Social Democracy: Beyond Revisionism*, London, Fabian Society, 1971

Hall, P. A., 'Policy Paradigms, Social Learning, and the State: The Case of Economic Policymaking in Britain', *Comparative Politics*, 25 (April), 1993, pp. 275–96

Hames, T., 'At last it can be told: David Owen was Tony Blair's secret political father', *The Times*, 13 June 2005

Harmon, M., 'The 1976 UK-IMF Crisis: The Markets, the Americans, and the IMF', *Contemporary British History*, 11 (3), 1997, pp. 1–17

Harmon, M., *The British Labour Government and the 1976 IMF Crisis*, Basingstoke, Macmillan, 1997

Harrison, R., 'Labour Party History: Approaches and Interpretations', *Labour History Review*, 56 (1), 1991, pp. 8–12

Haseler, S., *The Gaitskellites: Revisionism in the British Labour Party 1951–64*, London, Macmillan, 1969

Haseler, S., *The Death of British Democracy*, London, Elek Books, 1976

Haseler, S., *The Tragedy of Labour*, Oxford, Blackwell, 1980

Hattersley, R., *Who Goes Home? Scenes from a Political Life*, London, Little, Brown, 1985

Hattersley, R., *Choose Freedom: The Future for Democratic Socialism*, London, Michael Joseph, 1987

Hattersley, R., *Fifty Years On: A Prejudiced History of Britain since the Second World War*, London, Abacus, 1997

Hattersley, R., *In Praise of Ideology*, Southampton, University of Southampton, 1997

Hattersley, R., 'Why I'm no longer loyal to Labour', *The Guardian*, 26 July 1997

Hattersley, R., 'Up and down the social ladder', *New Statesman*, 22 January 1999

Hattersley R., 'It's no longer my party', *The Observer*, 24 June 2001

Hattersley, R. 'Crosland died 25 years ago: But his definition of a good society is still the best I know', *The Guardian*, 18 February 2002

Hattersley, R., 'Barbara the brave – a woman to reckon with', *The Observer*, 5 May 2002

Hattersley, R., 'He would have made a great PM', *The Guardian*, 6 January 2003

Hattersley, R., 'The importance of loyalty to an idea is not just a matter of personal conscience. It is a requirement of genuine democracy', *New Statesman*, 11 July 2005

Hattersley, R., 'The enemy of liberty', *The Guardian*, 31 October 2005

Hattersley, R., 'Meritocracy is no substitute for equality', *New Statesman*, 6 February 2006

Hattersley, R., 'Is Equality Outdated?', *Political Quarterly*, 77 (1), 2006, pp. 3–11

Hay, C., 'Labour's Thatcherite Revisionism: Playing the "Politics of Catch-Up"', *Political Studies*, 42 (4), 1994, pp. 700–7

Hay, C., *The Political Economy of New Labour: Labouring Under False Pretences?*, Manchester, Manchester University Press, 1999

Hayter, D., *Fightback! Labour's Traditional Right in the 1970s and 1980s*, Manchester, Manchester University Press, 2005

Healey, D., 'Political Objections to British Entry into the Common Market', *The Observer*, 25 May 1961

Healey, D., *Time of My Life*, London, Michael Joseph, 1989

Healey, D., 'The death of a singularly civilised man', *Financial Times*, 6 January 2003

Heffer, E., *The Class Struggle in Parliament*, London, Gollancz, 1973

Heffernan, R., 'Accounting for New Labour: The Impact of Thatcherism 1979–1995', in I. Hampsher-Monk and J. Stanyer (eds), *Contemporary Political Studies 1996*, Exeter, Political Studies Association, 1996, pp. 1280–90

Heffernan, R., *New Labour and Thatcherism: Exploring Political Change*, Basingstoke, Macmillan, 1999

Heffernan, R., 'Leaders and Followers: The Politics of the Parliamentary Labour Party', in B. Brivati and R. Heffernan (eds), *The Labour Party: A Centenary History*, Basingstoke, Macmillan, 2000, pp. 246–67

Hickson, K., 'The 1976 IMF Crisis', paper presented to the PSA Labour Movements Group Annual Conference, Clifton Hill House, University of Bristol, 4–5 July 2002

Hickson, K., 'From Them that Hath: New Labour and the Question of Redistribution', Catalyst, September 2002, available from: http://www.catalystforum.org.uk/pubs/article5a.html

Hickson, K., 'The Postwar Consensus Revisited', *Political Quarterly*, 75 (2), 2004, pp. 142–54

Hickson, K., *The IMF Crisis of 1976 and British Politics*, London, I. B. Tauris, 2005

Hine, D., 'Factionalism in West European Parties: A Framework for Analysis', *Journal of West European Politics*, 5 (1), 1982, pp. 36–53

Holmes, M., *The Labour Government 1974–1979: Political Aims and Economic Reality*, London, Macmillan, 1985

Howard, A., 'Exciting Friend', *New Statesman*, 3 May 1999

Howard, A., 'It is savagely appropriate that the 25th anniversary of Crosland's death should mark the moment Labour renounces loyalty to him', *The Times*, 12 February 2002

Howell, D., *British Social Democracy: A Study in Development and Decay*, London, Croom Helm, 1976

Howell, D., 'Wilson and History: "1966 and All That"', *Twentieth Century British History*, 4 (2), 1993, pp. 174–87

Jackson, B., 'Socialism, Revisionism and Equality', paper presented to the 51st Annual Conference of the Political Studies Association, University of Manchester, 10–12 April 2001

Jackson, B., 'Equality or Nothing? The British Left's Theory of Social Justice, c. 1910–31', paper presented to the PSA Labour Movements Specialist Group Annual Conference, Clifton Hill House, Bristol, 4–5 July 2002

Janosik, E. G., *Constituency Labour Parties in Britain*, London, Pall Mall, 1968

Jay, D., 'The Real Choice', *New Statesman*, 25 May 1962

Jay, D., *Socialism in the New Society*, London, Longman, 1962

Jay, D., *The Truth About the Common Market*, London, Forward Britain Movement, 1962

Jay, D., *After the Common Market: A Better Alternative for Britain*, Harmondsworth, Penguin, 1968

Jay, D., *Beyond State Monopoly*, London, Fabian Society, 1969

Jay, D., *Change and Fortune: A Political Record*, London, Hutchinson, 1980

Jefferys, K., *The Labour Party since 1945*, Basingstoke, Macmillan, 1993

Jefferys, K., *Anthony Crosland: A New Biography*, London, Richard Cohen Books, 1999

Jefferys, K., 'The Old Right', in R. Plant, M. Beech and K. Hickson (eds), *The Struggle for Labour's Soul: Understanding Labour's Political Thought since 1945*, London, Routledge, 2004, pp. 68–85

Jenkins, M., *Bevanism: Labour's High Tide*, Nottingham, Spokesman, 1979

Jenkins, P., *The Battle of Downing Street*, London, Charles Knight & Co, 1970

Jenkins, P., 'The first priority', *The Guardian*, 23 December 1976

Jenkins, P., 'The Crumbling of the Old Order', in W. Kennet (ed.), *The Rebirth of Britain*, London, Weidenfeld & Nicolson, 1982, pp. 33–60

Jenkins, P., *Mrs. Thatcher's Revolution: The Ending of the Socialist Era*, London, Jonathan Cape, 1987

Jenkins, R., 'Equality', in R. H. S. Crossman (ed.), *New Fabian Essays*, London, Turnstile Press, 1952

Jenkins, R., *Pursuit of Progress: A Critical Analysis of the Achievement and Prospect of the Labour Party*, London, Heinemann, 1953

Jenkins, R., *The Labour Case*, Harmondsworth, Penguin, 1959

Jenkins, R., *What Matters Now*, London, Fontana, 1972

Jenkins, R., 'Home Thoughts from Abroad: The 1979 Dimbleby Lecture', in W. Kennet (ed.), *The Rebirth of Britain*, London, Weidenfeld & Nicolson, 1982, pp. 9–29

Jenkins, R., *European Diary 1977–81*, London, Harper Collins, 1989

Jenkins, R., *A Life at the Centre*, London, Macmillan, 1991

Jones, G., 'A left house built on sand', *Socialist Commentary*, November 1978

Jones, P., *America and the British Labour Party: The Special Relationship at Work*, London, I. B. Tauris, 1997

Jones, T., *Remaking the Labour Party: From Gaitskell to Blair*, London, Routledge, 1996

Jones, T., '"Taking Genesis out of the Bible": Hugh Gaitskell, Clause IV and the Socialist Myth', *Contemporary British History*, 11 (2), 1997, pp. 1–23

Joyce, P., *Realignment of the Left? A History of the Relationship between the Liberal Democrat and Labour Parties*, Basingstoke, Macmillan, 1999

Jupp, J., 'The British Social Democrats and the Crisis in the British Labour Party', *Politics*, 16 (2), 1981, pp. 253–60

Kavanagh, D., 'Introduction', in D. Kavanagh (ed.), *The Politics of the Labour Party*, London, Allen & Unwin, 1982, pp. 1–8

Kavanagh, D. and Morris, P., *Consensus Politics from Attlee to Thatcher*, Oxford, Blackwell, 1989

Kellner, P. and Hitchens, C., *Callaghan: The Road to Number Ten*, London, Cassell, 1976

Kerr, P., 'The Post-War Consensus: A Woozle that Wasn't?', in D. Marsh *et al.* (eds), *Post-war British Politics in Perspective*, Cambridge, Polity Press, 1999, pp. 66–86

Kinnock, N., 'New? We've always been new', *New Statesman*, 28 February 2000

Kitschelt, H., *The Transformation of European Social Democracy*, Cambridge, Cambridge University Press, 1994

Kitzinger, U., *The Challenge of the Common Market*, Oxford, Blackwell, 1961

Kitzinger, U., *Diplomacy and Persuasion: How Britain Joined the Common Market*, London, Thames & Hudson, 1973

Kogan, D. and Kogan, M., *The Battle for the Labour Party*, London, Kogan Page, 1982

Larkin, P., 'New Labour and Old Revisionism', *Renewal*, 8 (1), 2000, pp. 42–9

Larkin, P., *Revisionism & Modernisation in the Post-war British Labour Party*, unpublished D.Phil. Thesis, University of Sussex, 2000

Larkin, P., 'New Labour in Perspective: A Comment on Rubinstein', *Politics*, 21 (1), 2001, pp. 51–5

Laser, H., 'British Populism: The Labour Party and the Common Market Parliamentary Debate', *Political Science Quarterly*, 91 (2), 1976, pp. 259–77

Lawrence, J., 'Labour – The Myths it has Lived By', in D. Tanner, P. Thane and N. Tiratsoo (eds), *Labour's First Century*, Cambridge, Cambridge University Press, 2000, pp. 341–66

Leonard, D. (ed.), *Crosland and New Labour*, Basingstoke, Macmillan, 1999

Leonard, D., 'Would Crosland feel betrayed by Blair and Brown?', *The Observer*, 17 February 2002

Lipsey, D., 'Crosland's Socialism', in D. Lipsey and D. Leonard (eds), *The Socialist Agenda: Crosland's Legacy*, London, Jonathan Cape, 1981, pp. 21–43

Lipsey, D., 'Revisionists Revise', in D. Leonard (ed.), *Crosland and New Labour*, Basingstoke, Macmillan, 1999, pp. 13–17

Lipsey, D., 'Roy Jenkins', in K. Jefferys (ed.), *Labour Forces: From Ernest Bevin to Gordon Brown*, London, I. B. Tauris, 2002, pp. 103–17

Ludlam, S., 'The Gnomes of Washington: Four Myths of the 1976 IMF Crisis', *Political Studies*, 40 (4), 1992, pp. 713–27

Ludlam, S., 'New Labour: What's Published is What Counts', *The British Journal of Politics & International Relations*, 2 (2), 2000, pp. 264–76

Ludlam, S., 'Norms and Blocks: Trade Unions and the Labour Party since 1964', in B. Brivati and R. Heffernan (eds), *The Labour Party: A Centenary History*, Basingstoke, Macmillan, 2000, pp. 220–45

Ludlam, S., 'New Labour and the Unions: The End of the Contentious Alliance?', in S. Ludlam and M. J. Smith (eds), *New Labour in Government*, Basingstoke, Macmillan, 2001, pp. 111–29

Mackintosh, J. P., 'Anybody Still for Democracy? Troubled Reflections of a Westminster MP', *Encounter*, November 1972, pp. 19–27.

Mackintosh, J. P., 'The Problem of the Labour Party', *Political Quarterly*, 43 (1), 1972, pp. 2–19

Mackintosh, J. P., 'Socialism or Social Democracy? The Choice for the Labour Party', *Political Quarterly*, 43 (4), 1972, pp. 470–84.

Mackintosh, J. P., 'Do we want a referendum?', *The Listener*, 22 August 1974

Mackintosh, J. P., 'The Case against a Referendum', *Political Enquiry*, 46 (1), 1975, pp. 73–82

Mackintosh, J. P., 'The case for a realignment of the Left', *The Times*, 22 July 1977

Mackintosh, J. P., 'Has Social Democracy Failed in Britain', *Political Quarterly*, 49 (3), 1978, pp. 259–70

Mackintosh, J. P., 'The Battle for Entry', in D. Marquand (ed.), *John P. Mackintosh on Parliament and Social Democracy*, London, Longman, 1982 [1971], pp. 244–8

Mackintosh, J. P., 'Taming the Barons', in D. Marquand (ed.), *John P. Mackintosh on Parliament and Social Democracy*, London, Longman, 1982 [1974], pp. 112–35

Mackintosh, J. P., 'Is Labour Facing Catastrophe?', in D. Marquand (ed.), *John P. Mackintosh on Parliament and Social Democracy*, London, Longman, 1982 [1977], pp. 168–78

Mackintosh, J. P., 'Liberty and Equality: Getting the Balance Right', in D. Marquand (ed.), *John P. Mackintosh on Parliament and Social Democracy*, London, Longman, 1982 [1977–8], pp. 182–9

Mackintosh, J. P., 'Britain's Malaise: Political or Economic?', in D. Marquand (ed.), *John P. Mackintosh on Parliament and Social Democracy*, London, Longman, 1982 [1978], pp. 202–20

Mandelson, P. and Liddle, R., *The Blair Revolution: Can New Labour Deliver?*, London, Faber & Faber, 1996

Marquand, D., 'Myths about Ideology', *Encounter*, February 1996

Marquand, D., 'Europe', in B. Whitaker (ed.), *A Radical Future*, London, Jonathan Cape, 1967, pp. 21–35

Marquand, D., 'The Challenge to the Labour Party', *Political Quarterly*, 46, 1975

Marquand, D., 'Inquest on a Movement: Labour's Defeat and its Consequences', *Encounter*, July 1979, pp. 8–18

Marquand, D., 'Trying to Diagnose the British Disease', *Encounter*, December 1980

Marquand, D., 'Why Labour cannot be saved', *Spectator*, 27 September 1980

Marquand, D., 'Russet-Coated Captains: The Challenge of Social Democracy', Open Forum Papers, No. 5, London, Social Democratic Party, 1981

Marquand, D., 'Introduction', in D. Marquand (ed.), *John P. Mackintosh on Parliament and Social Democracy*, London, Longman, 1982, pp. 1–26

Marquand, D., *The Unprincipled Society: New Demands and Old Politics*, London, Jonathan Cape, 1988

Marquand, D., *The Progressive Dilemma: From Lloyd George to Kinnock*, London, Heinemann, 1991

Marquand, D., 'Moralists and Hedonists', in D. Marquand and A. Seldon (eds), *The Ideas that Shaped Post-War Britain*, London, Fontana, 1996, pp. 5–28

Marquand, D., *The New Reckoning: Capitalism, States and Citizens*, Cambridge, Polity Press, 1997

Marquand, D., *The Progressive Dilemma: From Lloyd George to Blair*, London, second revised edition, Orion/Phoenix, 1999

Marquand, D., 'History Today', *Fabian Review*, 112 (1), 2000, pp. 2–3

Marquand, D., Mackintosh, J. and Owen, D., 'Change Gear! Towards A Socialist Strategy', Special Supplement, *Socialist Commentary*, October 1967

Marquand, D. and Seldon, A., 'Introduction: Ideas and Policy', in D. Marquand and A. Seldon (eds), *The Ideas that Shaped Post-War Britain*, London, Fontana, 1996, pp. 1–4

Marris, R., 'The Unauthorised Programme', *New Statesman*, 8 September 1972

Mason, R., *Paying the Price*, London, Robert Hale, 1999

Mayhew, C., *Time to Explain: An Autobiography*, London, Hutchinson, 1987

McKee, V., *Right-wing Factionalism in the British Labour Party 1977–87*, unpublished M.Phil. Thesis, City of Birmingham Polytechnic (CNAA), 1988

McKee, V., 'Fragmentation on the Labour Right 1975–87', *Politics*, 11 (1), 1991, pp. 23–9

McKee, V., 'Scattered Brethren: British Social Democrats', *Social Studies Review*, 6 (5), 1991, pp. 170–4

McKibbin, R., 'Homage to Wilson and Callaghan', *London Review of Books*, 24 October 1991

Meredith, S., 'New Labour: "The Road Less Travelled"?', *Politics*, 23 (3), 2003, pp. 163–71

Meredith, S., 'Labour Party Revisionism and Public Expenditure: Divisions of Social Democratic Political Economy in the 1970s', *Labour History Review*, 70 (3), 2005, pp. 253–73

Meredith, S., 'Mr. Crosland's Nightmare? New Labour and Equality in Historical Perspective', *British Journal of Politics & International Relations*, 8 (2), 2006, pp. 238–55

Meredith, S., 'New Labour and Equality: A Response to Hickson', *British Journal of Politics & International Relations*, 9 (1), 2007, pp. 169–70.

Michie, A. and Hoggart, S., *The Pact: The Inside Story of the Lib-Lab Government, 1977–8*, London, Quartet Books, 1978

Miliband, R., *Parliamentary Socialism: A Study in the Politics of Labour*, London, Allen & Unwin, 1961

Minion, M., 'The Labour Party and Europe during the 1940s: the strange case of the Socialist Vanguard Group', South Bank European Papers, No. 4/98, European Institute, South Bank University, 1998

Minion, M., 'The Fabian Society and Europe during the 1940s: The Search for a "Socialist Foreign Policy"', *European History Quarterly*, 30 (2), 2000

Minion, M., 'Left, Right or European? Labour and Europe in the 1940s: The Case of the Socialist Vanguard Group', *European Review of History*, 7 (2), 2000, pp. 229–50

Minkin, L., *The Labour Party Conference: A Study in the Politics of Intra-Party Democracy*, London, Allen Lane, 1978

Minkin, L., *The Contentious Alliance: Trade Unions and the Labour Party*, Edinburgh, Edinburgh University Press, 1991

Mitchell, A., *The Case for Labour*, London, Longman, 1983

Morgan, K. O., *Callaghan: A Life*, Oxford, Oxford University Press, 1997

Morgan, K. O., 'Aneurin Bevan', in K. Jefferys (ed.), *Labour Forces: From Ernest Bevin to Gordon Brown*, London, I. B. Tauris, 2002, pp. 81–99

Mullard, M., *The Politics of Public Expenditure*, London, Croom Helm, 1987

Nairn, T., 'The Left Against Europe', *New Left Review*, 75 (September–October), 1972

Nairn, T., *The Left Against Europe?*, Harmondsworth, Penguin, 1973

Norton, P., *Dissension in the House of Commons: Intra-Party Dissent in the House of Commons Division Lobbies 1945–74*, London, Macmillan, 1975

Norton, P., *Dissension in the House of Commons 1974–1979*, Oxford, Clarendon Press, 1980

Nuttall, J., '"Psychological socialist": "militant moderate": Evan Durbin and the Politics of Synthesis', *Labour History Review*, 68 (2), 2003, pp. 235–52

Nuttall, J., 'Tony Crosland and the Many Falls and Rises of British Social Democracy', *Contemporary British History*, 18 (4), 2004, pp. 52–79

Oliver, M. J., 'From Anodyne Keynesianism to Delphic Monetarism: Economic Policy-making in Britain, 1960–79', *Twentieth Century British History*, 9 (1), 1998, pp. 139–50

Owen, D., *Face the Future*, Oxford, Oxford University Press, 1981

Owen, D., *Time to Declare*, London, Michael Joseph, 1991

Padgett, S. and Paterson, W. E., *A History of Social Democracy in Postwar Europe*, London, Longman, 1991

Paterson, W. E. and Thomas, A. H., 'Introduction', in W. E. Paterson and A. H. Thomas (eds), *The Future of Social Democracy: Problems and Prospects of Social Democratic Parties in Western Europe*, Oxford, Clarendon Press, 1986, pp. 1–18

Pearce, E., *Denis Healey: A Life in Our Times*, London, Little, Brown, 2002

Pimlott, B., *Labour and the Left in the 1930s*, Cambridge, Cambridge University Press, 1977

Pimlott, B., 'The Myth of Consensus', in L. M. Smith (ed.), *The Making of Britain: Echoes of Greatness*, London, Macmillan, 1988, pp. 129–41

Pimlott, B., *Harold Wilson*, London, Harper Collins, 1992

Pimlott, B., 'The Fall and Rise of Harold Wilson', in B. Pimlott, *Frustrate Their Knavish Tricks: Writings on Biography, History and Politics*, London, Harper Collins, 1995, pp. 31–6

Piper, R., 'Backbench Rebellion, Party Government and Consensus Politics: The Case of the Parliamentary Labour Party 1966–70', *Parliamentary Affairs*, 27, 1974, pp. 384–96

Plant, R., 'Is Labour Abandoning its Socialist Roots? The Case for the Defence', *Contemporary Record*, 3 (2), 1989, pp. 7–8

Plant, R., 'Social Democracy', in D. Marquand and A. Seldon (eds), *The Ideas that Shaped Post-war Britain*, London, Fontana, 1996, pp. 165–94

Plant, R., 'Crosland, Equality and New Labour', in D. Leonard (ed.), *Crosland and New Labour*, Basingstoke, Macmillan, 1999, pp. 19–34

Plant, R., Beech, M. and Hickson, K. (eds), *The Struggle for Labour's Soul: Understanding Labour's Political Thought since 1945*, London, Routledge, 2004

Ponting, C., *Breach of Promise: Labour in Power 1964–1970*, Harmondsworth, Penguin, 1990

Powell, M., 'Something Old, Something New, Something Borrowed, Something Blue: The Jackdaw Politics of New Labour', *Renewal*, 8 (4), 2000, pp. 21–31

Preston, P., 'Ambition impossible', *The Observer*, 8 September 2002

Przeworski, A., *Capitalism and Social Democracy*, Cambridge, Cambridge University Press, 1985

Radice, G., 'Revisionism Revisited', *Socialist Commentary*, May 1974, pp. 25–7

Radice, G., *The Industrial Democrats: Trade Unions in an Uncertain World*, London, Allen & Unwin, 1978

Radice, G., 'Labour and the Unions', in D. Lipsey and D. Leonard (eds), *The Socialist Agenda: Crosland's Legacy*, London, Jonathan Cape, 1981, pp. 117–31

Radice, G., 'The Case for Revisionism', *Political Quarterly*, 59 (4), 1988, pp. 404–15

Radice, G., *Labour's Path to Power: The New Revisionism*, Basingstoke, Macmillan, 1989

Radice, G., *Offshore: Britain & the European Idea*, London, I. B. Tauris, 1992

Radice, G., *Friends & Rivals: Crosland, Jenkins and Healey*, London, Little, Brown, 2002

Robbins, L. J., *The Reluctant Party: Labour and the EEC 1961–75*, Ormskirk, G. W. & A. Hesketh, 1979

Rodgers, W., 'Socialism Without Abundance', *Socialist Commentary*, July–August 1977

Rodgers, W., *The Politics of Change*, London, Secker & Warburg, 1982

Rodgers, W., *Fourth Among Equals*, London, Politico's, 2000

Rose, R. 'Parties, Factions and Tendencies in Britain', *Political Studies*, 12 (1), 1964, pp. 33–46

Rosen, G., 'John Mackintosh: His Achievements and Legacy', *Political Quarterly*, 70 (2), 1999, pp. 210–18

Rubinstein, D., 'A New Look at New Labour', *Politics*, 20 (3), 2000, pp. 161–7

Runciman, W. G., *Where is the Right of the Left?*, London: The Tawney Society, 1983

Ryan, J. E., *The British Social Democrats: A Case Study of Factionalism in Left-of-Center Parties 1964–1981*, unpublished Ph.D. Thesis, Georgetown University, Washington, DC, 1987

Samuel, R. and Stedman Jones, G., 'The Labour Party and Social Democracy', in R. Samuel and G. Stedman Jones (eds), *Culture, Ideology and Politics: Essays for Eric Hobsbawm*, London, Routledge & Kegan Paul, 1982, pp. 320–9

Seldon, A. and Hickson, K. (eds), *New Labour, Old Labour: The Wilson and Callaghan Governments, 1974–79*, London, Routledge, 2004

Seyd, P., *Factionalism within the Labour Party: A Case Study of the Campaign for Democratic Socialism*, unpublished M.Phil. Thesis, University of Southampton, 1968

Seyd, P., 'Factionalism within the Labour and Conservative Parties: Real or Unreal?', paper presented to the ECPR Workshop, 'Factionalism in the Political Parties of Western Europe', Florence, 25–29 March 1980

Seyd, P., *The Rise and Fall of the Labour Left*, Basingstoke, Macmillan, 1987

Shaw, E., 'From Old Labour to New Labour', *Renewal*, 4 (3), 1996, pp. 51–9

Shaw, E., *The Labour Party since 1945*, Oxford, Blackwell, 1996

Skidelsky, R., 'The Decline of Keynesian Economics', in C. Crouch (ed.), *State and Economy in Contemporary Capitalism*, London, Croom Helm, 1979

Smith, M. J., 'A Return to Revisionism? The Labour Party's Policy Review', in M. J. Smith and J. Spear (eds), *The Changing Labour Party*, London, Routledge, 1992, pp. 13–28

Smith, M. J., 'Understanding the "Politics of Catch-Up": The Modernisation of the Labour Party', *Political Studies*, 42 (4), 1994, pp. 708–15

Socialist Union, *Socialism: A New Statement of Principles*, London, Lincolns-Prager, 1952

Socialist Union, *Twentieth Century Socialism*, Harmondsworth, Penguin, 1956

Stephenson, H., *Claret and Chips: The Rise of the SDP*, London, Michael Joseph, 1982

Sykes, P. L., *Losing from the Inside: The Cost of Conflict in the British Social Democratic Party*, New Brunswick, NJ, Transaction Publishers, 1990

Tanner, D., *Political Change and the Labour Party 1900–1918*, Cambridge, Cambridge University Press, 1990

Taverne, D., *The Future of the Left: Lincoln and After*, London, Jonathan Cape, 1974

Taylor, R., *The Trade Union Question in British Politics: Government and Unions since 1945*, Oxford, Blackwell, 1993

Taylor, R., 'Out of the Bowels of the Movement: The Trade Unions and the Origins of the Labour Party 1900–18', in B. Brivati and R. Heffernan (eds), *The Labour Party: A Centenary History*, Basingstoke, Macmillan, 2000, pp. 8–49

Taylor, R., *The TUC: From the General Strike to New Unionism*, Basingstoke, Palgrave, 2000

Thompson, M., Ellis, R. and Wildavsky, A., *Cultural Theory*, Boulder, CO, Westview Press, 1990

Thompson, N., *Political Economy and the Labour Party*, London, UCL Press, 1995

Thompson, W., *The Long Death of British Labourism: Interpreting a Political Culture*, London, Pluto Press, 1983

Tivey, L., 'Introduction: Left, Right, and Centre', in L. Tivey and A. Wright (eds), *Party Ideology in Britain*, London, Routledge, 1989, pp. 1–22

Toye, R., '"The Smallest Party in History"? New Labour in Historical Perspective', *Labour History Review*, 69 (1), 2004, pp. 83–103

Tracy, N., *The Origins of the Social Democratic Party*, London, Croom Helm, 1983

Tyler, R., '"Victims of our History"? Barbara Castle and *In Place of Strife*', *Contemporary British History*, 20 (3), 2006, pp. 461–76

Warde, A., *Consensus and Beyond: The Development of Labour Party Strategy since the Second World War*, Manchester, Manchester University Press, 1982

Wertheimer, E., *Portrait of the Labour Party*, New York, Putnam, 1929

White, M., 'Gang leader who paved way for Blair', *The Guardian*, 5 January 2003

Whitehead, P., *The Writing on the Wall: Britain in the Seventies*, London, Michael Joseph, 1985

Whitehead, P., 'The Labour Governments, 1974–1979', in P. Hennessy and A. Seldon (eds), *Ruling Performance: British Governments from Attlee to Thatcher*, Oxford, Blackwell, 1987, pp. 241–73

Wickham-Jones, M., 'Recasting Social Democracy: A Comment on Hay and Smith', *Political Studies*, 43 (4), 1995, pp. 698–702

Wickham-Jones, M., *Economic Strategy and the Labour Party: Politics and Policy-Making, 1970–83*, London, Macmillan, 1996

Wicks, R., 'Revisionism in the 1950s: The Ideas of Anthony Crosland', in C. Navari (ed.), *British Politics and the Spirit of the Age*, Keele, Keele University Press, 1996, pp. 199–217

Wicks, R., 'The Case for the Defence: The Labour Party, Political Ideas and Nuclear Disarmament in the 1980s', in I. Hampsher-Monk and J. Stanyer (eds), *Contemporary Political Studies 1996: Volume II*, Belfast, Political Studies Association, 1996, pp. 838–44

Wildavsky, A., 'Choosing Preferences by Constructing Institutions: A Cultural Theory of Preference Formation', *American Political Science Review*, 81 (1), 1987, pp. 3–21

Williams, G. L. and Williams, A. L., *Labour's Decline and the Social Democrats' Fall*, London, Macmillan, 1989

Williams, P., *Hugh Gaitskell*, London, Jonathan Cape, 1979

Williams, P., *Hugh Gaitskell*, revised and abridged edition, Oxford, Oxford University Press, 1982

Williams, S., *Politics is for People*, Harmondsworth, Penguin, 1981

Williams, S., 'The New Authoritarianism', *Political Quarterly*, 60 (1), 1989

Wood, D. M. and Jacoby, W. G., 'Intraparty Cleavage in the British House of Commons: Evidence from the 1974–1979 Parliament', *American Journal of Political Science*, 28 (1), 1984, pp. 203–23

Wright, T., *Socialisms Old and New*, London, Routledge, 1996

Young, H., *This Blessed Plot: Britain and Europe from Churchill to Blair*, Basingstoke, Macmillan, 1988

Young, J. W., 'Foreign, Defence and European Affairs', in B. Brivati and T. Bale (eds), *New Labour in Power: Precedents and Prospects*, London Routledge, 1997, pp. 137–58

Young, J. W., *Britain and European Unity 1945–1999*, Basingstoke, Palgrave, 2000

Young, J. W., 'Introduction', in R. Broad, M. D. Kandiah and G. Staerck (eds), 'Britain and Europe', Witness Seminar, Institute of Contemporary British History, 2002, pp. 15–20, available from: http://www.icbh.ac.uk/icbh/witness/brussels/brussels.pdf

Zentner, P., *Social Democracy in Britain: Must Labour Lose?*, London, John Martin, 1982

Ziegler, P., *Wilson: The Authorised Life*, London, Weidenfeld & Nicolson, 1993

Index

1963 Club 49, 81

Alternative Economic Strategy (AES) 7
Amalgamated Union of Engineering
    Workers (AUEW) 119
anti-Marketeers 93

Benn, Tony 9, 11, 17, 48, 78–80, 88, 90,
    93, 142, 145, 175, 179
Bevan, Anuerin 33
    Bevanism 72
    Bevanite group 48
Bill of Rights 123
Blair, Tony 159–60
Booth, Albert 11
Bowden, Bert 78–9
Bradley, Tom 49, 111
Brown, George 32, 36, 49, 74, 77–8, 82, 93

Callaghan, James 6, 8–10, 14, 17, 32, 34,
    46, 52–3, 61, 74, 77–80, 82, 85, 87,
    88–9, 93, 105–6, 108–12, 114–15,
    118–19, 122, 126, 145, 174, 180
    anti-European speeches 83
    Callaghanite 111–12, 117
    'Keeper of the Cloth Cap' 126
Callaghan Government 126, 165, 181
Campaign for Democratic Socialism
    (CDS) 12, 44, 49–51, 60–1, 64, 72,
    75, 176, 179
Campaign for Labour Party Democracy
    (CLPD) 11, 26, 46
Campaign for Labour Victory (CLV) 12

Campaign for Nuclear Disarmament
    (CND) 110
case studies 13
    Europe and the Common Market
    debate 14
    industrial relations and trade union
    reform 15
    public expenditure 16
Castle, Barbara 15, 78–9, 106–7, 109,
    110–12, 114, 149
Clause IV 94, 111, 177
Clay Cross councillors 121
Common Agricultural Policy (CAP) 79, 93
Common Market 4, 6, 16, 32, 34, 45, 49,
    51–3, 71–3, 75–7, 109, 113, 179
    Common Market parliamentary vote
    (October 1971) 85
    Common Market referendum (1975)
    34, 91
    Labour Party Common Market special
    conference (1971) 82
    Wilson application (1967) 78
Commonwealth 72–3, 77–8, 145
Confederation of British Industry (CBI)
    122, 177
Conservative Government (1970–74) 45,
    71
    Industrial Relations Act 119, 121,
    181
    Industrial Relations Bill 115
Conservative Housing Finance Act 121
Conservative monetarist policies 163
Conservative Party 43, 53, 57, 140, 146

Constituency Labour Parties (CLPs) 11, 56
corporatism 126
Court of Industrial Relations (CIR) 107,
    110, 114
Crosland, Anthony 3, 5, 7–8, 10–11, 14,
    16–18, 27–9, 31–2, 34, 36, 48, 50,
    53–4, 58–9, 78–81, 83–5, 87, 90,
    93–4, 103, 105, 108, 110–13, 117,
    119, 121–2, 127, 138, 140, 142–3,
    145–9, 151, 165, 168, 174, 176–80
    'Croslandism' 13, 140, 150, 162, 165,
        167
    crisis of 138
    Croslandite 11, 32, 48, 113, 143, 165
    Croslandite revisionism 139–41, 147,
        150–1, 166
    The Future of Socialism (1956) 13,
        27, 31
    political economy 18
    'post-Croslandite' social democracy 5
Crossman, Richard 36, 78, 108, 112
Cousins, Frank 126

Deakin, Arthur 179
'declinism' thesis 137
De Gaulle, Charles 78–9
    veto 78, 80
democratic socialism 11, 58, 141
devaluation 17
Diamond, Jack 77
Dock Work Regulation Bill 124
Donovan Commission 106
    Report of 108–10
Douglas-Mann, Bruce 123, 139
Durbin, Evan 30–1, 33, 151

Ennals, David 17, 145
European Accession Bill 14
European Commission 10, 13, 50, 103
European divisions 71, 74
European Economic Community (EEC)
    10, 14, 33, 55, 59, 62, 71–8, 141–2,
    151, 180–1
European Free Trade Association (EFTA)
    73, 75
European integration 71
    Labour divisions in opposition 80
    the Labour Party and 14, 72
    Wilson application (1967) 78

European social democracy 4
Exchange Rate Mechanism (ERM) 93

Fabian Society 142
    Fabiansim 35–6
factionalism 42, 45, 47
Feather, Vic 88
Flanders, Alan 127
Foot, Michael 9–11, 26, 46, 81, 87, 93,
    119, 121–2, 124, 180

Gaitskell, Hugh 14, 17, 28, 36, 52, 55, 74,
    79, 83, 93, 103, 111, 127, 137, 140,
    159, 179
    Gaitskell-Crosland philosophy 140
    Gaitskellite 33, 48–9, 53, 86, 92, 94,
        113, 148–9, 166
    Gaitskellite CDS 46
    Gaitskellite revisionism 2, 4, 26, 28, 63,
        72, 81, 112, 120, 126–7, 162, 174
Golding, John 34
Gordon-Walker, Patrick 17, 33, 77–9, 86,
    109, 112
Gould, Bryan 31, 67
Gunter, Ray 15, 77, 79

Harris, John (Lord) 50, 57, 123
Hattersley, Roy 10, 17–18, 29–31, 34, 49,
    62, 86–9, 111–12, 123, 139, 143,
    145, 148–50, 166, 175, 178
Hayter, Dianne 2, 3
Healey, Denis 3, 6, 9–11, 14, 17, 26–7, 34,
    36, 46, 53, 74, 78–9, 80–1, 83, 85–6,
    89, 95, 105, 109, 111, 117, 119, 127,
    145, 149, 180
Heath, Edward 80, 92
Heath Government (1970–74) 6, 14, 33–4,
    80, 82–5, 88
    Industrial Relations Act 16, 104–5,
        113
Hinden, Rita 31
Horan, John 55, 57, 61–2
Houghton, Douglas 77–8, 86, 110–11
Hughes, Cledwyn 10, 12, 78–9, 92

Industrial relations policy 4, 103
    incomes policy 139
    inflation control 5
In Place of Strife 15–16, 82, 106, 181

International Monetary Fund (IMF)
    Cabinet debates 17, 144–5, 148
    IMF crisis (1976) 6, 17, 30, 143–4, 146,
        148
    IMF loan 17

Jay, Douglas 73–6, 78–9, 92–4, 164, 174
Jay, Peter 17
Jenkins, Peter 60
Jenkins, Roy 3, 8, 14, 16–17, 27–8, 34, 36,
        46, 48–9, 51, 53–4, 57, 63, 67, 71–2,
        74–5, 77, 78–9, 81, 84–5, 87, 88–91,
        92, 94, 105, 108–15, 120–3, 142,
        144, 174, 176, 180
    President of the European Commission
        93
    What Matters Now 52, 142
Jenkinsites 8–10, 13–14, 16, 30, 33, 42, 47,
        49–51, 55, 57, 63, 72, 81, 83, 87–8,
        94, 109, 111, 113, 142, 151, 174,
        178, 181
    ideology 112
    perspective 110
    strand 117
Jones, Jack 82, 118–20, 122–4

Kauffman, Gerald 34, 62
Keynesianism 7, 140, 173, 177
Keynesian social democracy 1–2, 7, 18,
        104, 162, 174, 180–1
Keynesian socialism 31–2, 35

Labour Government (1974–79) 5
    Labour leadership contest (1976) 8, 27
Labour left 1–2, 11, 45, 47, 163, 173, 176,
        180
Labour movement 105, 128
Labour Party revisionism 3–4, 7–9, 14,
        16–17, 19, 30, 37, 53, 74, 149–51,
        173, 176
Labour Party special conference on
        Europe (1971) 82
Labour Party-TUC Liaison Committee 55,
        57, 104, 118
Labour Party-TUC 'social contract' 6,
        117–20
Labour Solidarity 44
Labour's Programme 1973 46
Labour's Programme 1976 124

Leonard, Dick 139
Lester, Anthony 123
Lever, Harold 17, 52, 86, 145, 149
Lipsey, David 31, 147

Mabon, Dicken 50, 55, 67, 89
MacDonald, Ramsay 92, 168
Mackintosh, John 13, 46, 57, 67, 82, 86,
        111–12, 115, 124, 138–40, 142, 150,
        166, 167, 177–9
Maclennan, Robert 50, 86, 112
Magee, Brian 57
Manifesto Group 8, 12, 15, 26, 42–5,
        47, 55–63, 124, 150, 162–4, 175,
        181
    *What We Must Do: A Democratic
        Socialist Approach to Britain's Crisis*
        (1977) 57–8
    *The Wrong Approach: An Exposition of
        Conservative Policies* (1978) 61
Marquand, David 13, 48–50, 55, 57, 62,
        86, 93, 109, 112, 138–9, 142, 147,
        150, 166, 178
Marsh, Dick 15, 78, 108
Mason, Roy 77, 93
Mayhew, Christopher, 109
Mellish, Bob 88, 168
Mikardo, Ian 12, 55
Miners strike (1972) 114–15
Minkin, Lewis 104–5, 137
Mitchell, Austin 31, 34
Monnet, Jean 74
'Morrisonian consolidators' 18, 26, 34
Mulley, Fred 34, 85

National Executive Committee (NEC)
        4–5, 11–12, 15, 44, 52–3, 82,
        109–10, 124, 128, 180
    NEC Home Policy Committee 118,
        123–4
National Industrial Relations Court
        114
National Union of Journalists (NUJ) 120,
        122
'New' Labour 1, 3, 4, 18, 138, 159–60
    perspectives of 1, 159–60
New Liberalism 34, 36
North Atlantic Treaty Association
        (NATO) 76

oil crisis (1973) 7
'Old' Labour 1, 19, 160–1, 164–5
Owen, David 49–50, 85–6, 89–90, 94, 112,
    138, 142, 165–6, 178

Parliamentary Labour Party (PLP) 2,
    10–11, 15, 19, 26–7, 42, 44–5, 47,
    49, 50–7, 59, 61–3, 73, 77, 85–6,
    106–7, 109–10, 112, 121, 125
post-war consensus 6,-8, 13, 103
Prentice, Reginald 11
pro-Marketeers 77
public expenditure 137, 143, 162

Radice, Giles 3, 31, 37, 50, 55, 57, 138,
    141, 150
Rawls, John 29
Rees, Merlyn 93, 111
revisionist social democracy 5, 11, 13, 27,
    137, 139, 162, 173
    divisions of 141, 176, 179
Rodgers, Bill 29–30, 49–51, 85–6, 89, 93,
    112, 138, 144–6, 148, 164, 174
Roper, John 57

Scanlon, Hugh 82, 118–19, 122–3
Shadow Cabinet 52–3, 85, 89, 91
Shore, Peter 17, 36, 73, 81, 91, 93, 145
Short, Ted 90
'Shrewsbury Two' 121
Smith, John 10, 62
'social contract' 117
Social Democratic Alliance (SDA) 12
Social Democratic Party (SDP) 2–4,
    14–15, 18, 26, 29, 32, 37, 46–7, 51,
    71, 90–1, 95, 103–4, 123, 127–9,
    162, 165–7, 173–4, 181
social democratic political economy 4
social democratic theory 28
Social Democrats 90, 103–4, 125–6, 128,
    177–8
Socialist Commentary 12, 13, 31

'social reformism' 35
Steel, David 92
Stewart, Michael 77, 79, 86

Taverne, Dick 11, 49, 86, 89, 93–4, 109,
    112, 116
'third way' 4, 159
Thomson, George 49, 52, 72, 78, 82, 86,
    89, 91, 111, 149
Tomlinson, John 139
Trade Union Congress (TUC) 34, 106–9,
    111, 114, 121–2, 124–5, 177
Trade Union and Labour Relations Bill
    122
'trade union question' 103, 115, 120,
    123
Transport and General Workers Union
    (TGWU) 119
Treaty of Rome 72
Tribune Group 9–11, 26, 42–3, 50, 54–7,
    61–3, 124

Varley, Eric 34

Walden, Brian 13, 46, 124
Walker, Peter 92
Wellbeloved, James 85
Wembley special conference (1981) 128
Whitehead, Philip 37
Williams, Shirley 11, 17, 86, 91–2, 94, 120,
    123–4, 145, 149, 178
Wilson, Harold 17, 33, 45, 48, 50–2, 71,
    74, 77–9, 82–5, 88, 91, 106, 109–12,
    119, 122, 168, 178–80
    resignation of 8
    Wilson-Callaghan governments 93,
    104, 125, 147, 177
    Wilson governments (1964–70) 47, 52,
    72, 78–9, 180
'Wilsonism' 35, 112
'Winter of Discontent' 6, 119
Wrigglesworth, Ian 123